THE EUROPEAN ECONOMY
IN PERSPECTIVE

Edward Nevin (1925–1992) at the Ministry of Finance, Jamaica, 1958.

THE EUROPEAN ECONOMY IN PERSPECTIVE

Essays in Honour of Edward Nevin

Edited by
JEFFERY I. ROUND

CARDIFF
UNIVERSITY OF WALES PRESS
1994

© The Contributors, 1994

All rights reserved. No part of this book may be reproduced, stored in a retrieval system, or transmitted, in any form or by any means, electronic, mechanical, photocopying, recording or otherwise, without clearance from the University of Wales Press, 6 Gwennyth Street, Cardiff CF2 4YD.

British Library Cataloguing-in-Publication Data

A catalogue record for this book is available from the British Library.

ISBN 0−7083−1240−3

Typeset in England by Action Typesetting Limited, Gloucester
Printed in Wales by Dinefwr Press, Llandybïe

Contents

List of Contributors	vii
Edward Nevin ESMOND CLEARY	1
Introduction JEFFERY I. ROUND	7

I MONEY AND FINANCE

1. Counter-inflationary policy in the framework of the EMS
    M. J. ARTIS 15
2. Consumer credit in the EC 33
    GEORGE CLAYTON

II STRUCTURE

3. The structure of the European economy: a SAM perspective
    JEFFERY I. ROUND 59
4. Building Europe 85
    JOHN WILLIAMS

III SECTORS

5. The relevance of macroeconomics to agricultural problems
    G. H. PETERS 113
6. The Common Transport Policy and its impact on peripherality in the European Community 135
    J. HUGH REES

IV REGIONS

7 Labour-market flexibility in western Europe
    DAVID BLACKABY and ROBIN BLADEN-HOVELL   159

8 The impact of the European Community on regional
   policies in Wales
   D. ROY THOMAS   185

9 Agriculture and the rural economy of Wales
   G. O. HUGHES, D. I. BATEMAN and P. MIDMORE   205

V INTERNATIONAL PERSPECTIVES

10 VERs: theory and estimation with reference to
   EC imports from Japan
   ALI M. EL-AGRAA   225

11 The European Investment Bank and African
   development finance companies
   MICHAEL NEVIN   245

12 Capital funds in reforming socialist economies
   ALAN R. ROE   267

VI POLITICAL ECONOMY

13 European integration: a political and institutional
   process
   MICHAEL WATSON   297

14 An American economist in Paris, 1919
   CHARLES P. BLITCH   319

Publications by Professor Edward Nevin   337

Index   343

List of contributors

MICHAEL ARTIS

Professor of Economics, University of Manchester

Michael Artis was formerly Professor of Applied Economics at University College of Swansea and before that he was editor of the National Institute's *Economic Review*. He is a Fellow of the British Academy, a research fellow of the Centre for Economic Policy Research and an associate editor of the *Economic Journal*. He has written extensively in monetary and macroeconomics. His *Money in Britain*, co-authored with Professor Mervyn Lewis, is a leading text in monetary economics.

DAVID BATEMAN

Professor of Agricultural Economics, University College of Wales, Aberystwyth

Professor Bateman's research interests are the economics of rural land use with particular reference to the environment, the rural economy, and the role of agriculture. His recent publications include a study for the ESRC, undertaken with colleagues, of pluri-activity and the rural economy in Wales. Profesor Bateman is a graduate of the University of Liverpool, a former President of the Agricultural Economics Society and a Fellow of the Royal Agricultural Societies.

DAVID BLACKABY

Senior Lecturer in Economics, University College of Swansea

David Blackaby is a graduate of the University College of Swansea, who returned there to a lectureship after completing his postgraduate studies at the University of Manchester. His research interests are mainly in the areas of labour and regional economics and he is currently the convenor of the Labour Economics Study Group in the UK.

Robin Bladen-Hovell

Senior Lecturer in Economics, University of Manchester

Robin Bladen-Hovell is a graduate of the University College of Swansea. After completing postgraduate studies at Manchester he joined the staff as a lecturer. He is currently an associate editor of *The Manchester School*. His main areas of research interest are macroeconomics, international monetary economics, and labour economics.

Charles P. Blitch

Emeritus Professor of Economics, Old Dominion University, Virginia, USA

Charles Blitch received his doctorate from the University of North Carolina at Chapel Hill. For twenty-five years he was Professor of Economics at Old Dominion University. He spent one year as a visiting professor at the University College of Swansea. He is an authority on the American economist Allyn A. Young and has published articles in *History of Political Economy* and *Journal of Post-Keynesian Economics* relating to Young's contributions.

George Clayton

Emeritus Professor of Applied Economics, University of Sheffield

Before becoming Professor of Applied Economics at Sheffield, George Clayton was Professor of Economics at the University College of Wales, Aberystwyth. He served as a member of the Crowther Committee on Consumer Credit and the Scott Committee on Property Bonds and Equity-linked Insurance. He has also undertaken various missions for the Overseas Development Administration, is a past chairman of the Association of University Teachers of Economics, and is a former member of the Council of the Royal Economic Society. He has authored and contributed to ten books, including *Insurance Company Investment* and *British Insurance* and has written over sixty articles.

Esmond Cleary

Formerly Senior Lecturer in Economics, University College of Swansea

Esmond Cleary was a long-time colleague of Edward Nevin who shared his interests both in financial institutions, publishing *The Building Societies Movement* and *Building Societies in Ireland*, and in regional problems, writing (with R. E. Thomas) *The Economic Consequences of the Severn Bridge*.

ALI M. EL-AGRAA Professor of International Economics and European/American Economies, Fukuoka University, Japan

Ali El-Agraa commenced his career as senior scholar and lecturer in economics at the University of Khartoum. He then became a senior lecturer at the University of Leeds and a visiting professor of international economics at the International University of Japan. He has authored, co-authored and edited eleven books, including *The Economics of the European Community* (now in its fourth edition); *Britain within the European Community*; *The Theory and Measurement of International Economic Integration*; and most recently, *Public and International Economics*.

GARTH HUGHES

Lecturer in Agricultural Economics, University College of Wales, Aberystwyth

Garth Hughes is a graduate of the University of Wales, initially in Geography, but then in Economics when Edward Nevin was Professor of Economics at Aberystwyth. The topics covered by his publications and consultancies include a methodology for regional accounts for Welsh agriculture, the reform of the Common Agricultural Policy, structural change in the rural economy, and the evaluation of environmentally sensitive areas policy. His current research is on environmental conservation in the less favoured areas of the United Kingdom.

PETER MIDMORE

Lecturer in Agricultural Economics, University College of Wales, Aberystwyth

Peter Midmore's interests are in Welsh agriculture and its relationship to the natural environment. These interests, together with attempts to model the processes which link agriculture with overall economic activity, have led to a series of publications, including, most recently *Input-Output Models and the Agricultural*

Sector, an edited collection of papers. His current research interests are in organic farming, human ecology and rural economics.

MICHAEL NEVIN

Senior Consultant, Touche Ross, London

After graduating in PPE from Oxford Michael Nevin began his career working as an economist for the Government of St Lucia, West Indies. During the 1980s he worked as a loan officer with the European Investment Bank in Luxembourg, responsible for the Bank's lending operations in a number of states in central and southern Africa under the terms of the Lomé Convention. His publications include a book, *The Age of Illusions: the Political Economy of Britian, 1968–1982*, and a number of papers and articles published in academic journals.

GEORGE H. PETERS

Research Professor in Agricultural Economics, International Development Centre, Queen Elizabeth House, University of Oxford

After graduating from Aberystwyth and before spending a year at King's College, Cambridge, G. H. Peters helped Edward Nevin to compile the first set of Welsh social accounts. Following national service he became research assistant to Colin Clark at the Oxford Agricultural Economics Institute before his appointment to a lectureship. From 1970 he was Brunner Professor of Economic Science at Liverpool returning to Oxford in 1980. A past President of the Agricultural Economics Society, he is now editor of *Proceedings for the International Association of Agricultural Economists*. Publications include *Cost-Benefit Analysis and Public Expenditure*; *Private and Public Finance*; *Agriculture: A Review of United Kingdom Statistical Sources*; and (with B. F. Stanton) *Sustainable Agricultural Development – The Role of International Cooperation*.

J. HUGH REES

Head of Unit for Railways, Combined Transport and Waterways, Directorate General for Transport, Commission of the European Union, Brussels

Hugh Rees is a graduate in Economics from the University College of Wales, Aberystwyth, and commenced his career as a research officer in the Economic and Social Research Unit under the direction of Edward Nevin. He subsequently worked for the Government Economic Service in the Ministry of Transport, the European Council of Ministers of Transport (Paris), and the UK Atomic Energy Authority, before embarking on his career in the EEC.

ALAN R. ROE

Senior Lecturer in Economics, University of Warwick

Alan Roe was Chairman of the Department of Economics, 1983–6, and was subsequently the founding Director of the Warwick Research Institute. Prior to this he was a senior economist at the World Bank and a research fellow at the universities of Wales (Aberystwyth), Dar-Es-Salaam, and Cambridge. He has published numerous papers, monographs and books, including *The Financial Interdependence of the Economy*; (with Graham Pyatt and others) *Social Accounting for Development Planning*; and *Adjustment and Equity in Ghana*.

JEFFERY I. ROUND

Reader in Economics, University of Warwick

After commencing his career at Aberystwyth, first as a junior research officer assisting Edward Nevin and then as an assistant lecturer in economics, he was awarded a Harkness Fellowship at Havard University. He joined Warwick in 1970 although he has also been a visiting associate professor at Princeton and a consultant at the World Bank. He has published articles in academic journals on regional economics, social accounting, and economic modelling and statistics. His publications include (with Graham Pyatt) *Social Accounting Matrices: A Basis for Planning*.

ROY THOMAS

Senior Lecturer in Economics, Cardiff Business School, University of Wales College of Cardiff

Roy Thomas has published a number of papers on regional policy, especially relating to Wales, the United Kingdom and Europe. He also contributed a chapter on regional policy (with C. J. Mckenna) in *The Welsh Economy* (edited by K. D. George and L. Mainwaring), published by the University of Wales Press (1988). During his career, Roy Thomas has acted as a consultant to the Welsh Office and the

Commonwealth Secretariat, and has been a specialist adviser to the Select Committee on Welsh Affairs.

MICHAEL WATSON

Senior Lecturer in International Politics, University College of Wales, Aberystwyth

After graduating from Oxford in PPE, Michael Watson worked for the Economist Intelligence Unit before joining the Economic and Social Research Unit in Aberystwyth in 1964. He later became a lecturer in politics and has been Dean of the Faculty and Chair of European Studies. He co-directed an international project leading to the publication of *Planning, Politics and Public Policy*, and is also editor of *Contemporary Minority Nationalism*. He is a consultant to the Church in Wales's International and European Affairs Committee.

JOHN WILLIAMS

Profesor of Economic History, University College of Wales, Aberystwyth

Now in his last year before retirement, John Williams has been at Aberystwyth for most of his academic career. He has published extensively on Welsh economic and social history, including (with J. H. Morris) *The South Wales Coal Industry* and *Welsh Historical Statistics*, and also on the British economy, notably, *Britain and the World Economy, 1919–1970*. Amongst other recent publications he has written (with T. Cutler and K. Williams) *1992 – The Struggle for Europe* which has prompted his contribution to the present volume.

Edward Nevin MA (Wales), Ph.D.(Cantab)

ESMOND CLEARY

Edward Thomas (Ted) Nevin was born in February 1925 in Pembroke Dock, the second son of William Thomas and Mary Helen Nevin. He was also educated in Pembroke Dock, leaving the county school in 1941 to work for the Ministry of Aircraft Production. Ted Nevin joined the Royal Electrical and Mechanical Engineers in 1943, serving in the United Kingdom and subsequently with the 21st Army Group in France and Germany. He started his undergraduate studies at the University College of Wales in Aberystwyth in October 1946. At that time students typically pursued a two-subject pass degree before taking a further year of study for an honours classication. Ted Nevin graduated (under temporary wartime regulations) in June 1948 in law and economics and was awarded first class honours in economics in June 1949. The following year, while a temporary assistant lecturer at Aberystwyth, he began his research into British monetary policy and this resulted in an MA for his thesis on 'The market in gilt-edged securities, 1939–1949'.

In 1950, he was awarded a Houblon-Norman Fellowship to pursue a doctorate at Corpus Christi College, Cambridge. At Cambridge he noted particular intellectual debts to R. F. Henderson, R. F. Kahn, Sir Dennis Robertson and H. G. Johnson. This was a stimulating period in his career. By this time, Ted and his wife Elizabeth already had the first of their six children and this added to the imperative to complete his thesis within the two years of his scholarship. Elizabeth, to whom he was devoted, was to provide the stability and bedrock of support for Ted and their family until her death in 1983. He gained his Ph.D. in 1952 and the results of his research were published in two books: *The Problem of the National Debt* (1954) and *The Mechanism of Cheap Money* (1955). Both books were widely and favourably reviewed. It was characteristic of the boldness of his approach that he should even attempt to make a name in so well-populated an area as recent monetary policy. That he should succeed is a vindication of his confidence in his own ability.

From Cambridge, Ted Nevin returned to Aberystwyth where he was appointed to a lectureship in 1952. By this time Arthur Beacham had been appointed to the chair and, with his encouragement, it was with Aberystwyth as his base that Ted Nevin made a series of sorties into other economic milieux. From July 1953 he spent a year with the OECD in Paris. In October 1957 he moved for eighteen months to head the external finance division of Jamaica's Ministry of Finance in the critical period leading up to the island's independence from Britain. Here he had more practical experience of capital markets; soon after arrival he was in New York supervising the raising of a loan stock issue. It was his work in Jamaica that led to *Capital Funds in Underdeveloped Countries* (1961). From April 1961 he was, for two and a half years, a senior research officer at the Economic Research Institute in Dublin. These moves are reflected in his bibliography and they were certainly fruitful years in terms of his research. In 1956 he published the first ever attempt to create a set of economic accounts for Wales (1948–52), extended to 1956 a year later. It was at this time that Ted first became interested in communicating outside of academia. On the basis of his accumulating knowledge of the economic statistics of Wales, he contributed regular commentaries on the state of the Welsh economy for the *Western Mail* throughout the 1960s and 1970s.

The first edition of a very successful introductory textbook, *A Textbook of Economic Analysis*, appeared in 1958. This showed astute judgement in product differentiation: the text was aimed at the rapidly growing population of 'A' level economics candidates. Since most first-year economics undergraduates were still newcomers to the subject, the textbook also gained a sizeable share of that more crowded market. There were altogether five editions for the UK and the United States, the fifth edition being published in 1981, as well as two Irish editions and one in Tamil. The book was ideal for the audience for which it was written. It was clear, not overly technical and conveyed Ted's own enthusiasm and interest. An accompanying workbook appeared in 1966.

At Dublin, Ted Nevin was concerned with the structure of the Irish economy, and monetary economics became less prominent in his publications. On his return to Aberystwyth to a chair in 1963, structural problems of the Welsh economy became an important theme in his work. When the Welsh Economic Council was created in 1965 (in the expansionary days of the Department of Economic Affairs), Ted Nevin was one of its original members. A monograph on *The Structure of the Welsh Economy* (with A. R. Roe and J. I. Round) provided a firm factual base on which to speak and write. However, he felt that the Council was not sufficiently forceful, innovative and independent in its advice to the government, and he resigned from the Council in 1967.

In October 1968 he moved to a chair at the University College of Swansea where he was also head of department until his retirement in 1985; but he continued to lecture there until 1991. He was appointed professor emeritus in 1992. Regional economics and monetary policy were continuing areas of his academic interests: a major study of *The London Clearing Banks* (with E. W. Davis) appeared in 1970. However, Swansea's substantial commitment to engineering and metallurgy had its effect, broadening Ted's interests still further. There followed a number of papers and conference contributions on the economics of tribology and corrosion. His lectures to engineering students resulted in another textbook, *An Introduction to Microeconomics* (1973), which ran to a second edition.

As head of department, Ted Nevin showed himself to be a swift and efficient administrator. In times of increased democracy in departments, no one could complain that they had no opportunity to state their view. Nevertheless, while other voices could be influential, decisions finally rested with the head! Ted was also a willing and respected member of the various university committees that fell to his lot.

In 1974 Ted Nevin extended his public duties in a quite new direction. He took on a research project for the Police Federation which resulted in a report, *The Pay of Policemen*, in 1975. At this time police pay was the subject of annual acrimony which increased as the 1970s progressed. There was falling morale, increased turnover and a movement to give the Police Federation a right to strike. In 1976 Ted Nevin became economic advisor to the Federation and was to play an important part in resolving these problems. A committee of inquiry was set up in August 1977 under Lord Justice Edmund Davies, originally only to examine the machinery for negotiating police pay and the constitutions of the police staff associations. Four months later there was a decisive change, with the terms of reference extended to include the establishment of a proper basis for police pay. Its report in 1978 made provision for triennial earnings reviews and tied police pay to the index of average earnings. Ted Nevin continued as an advisor until the new system was well in place and the first review completed.

Ted Nevin did not start his work with the Police Federation as a newcomer to industrial disputes. For some years he had been involved as an independent member of the wages councils for the shirt-making, milk distribution and cutlery trades; latterly as deputy chairman of the first two councils. He was already an experienced arbitrator having, over the years, conducted many cases for the Arbitration and Conciliation Service. His sharp and incisive mind, and his ability to argue logically, were great assets in the arbitration process.

Alongside his academic career and his work on public bodies Ted Nevin also enjoyed an active broadcasting career. People would say that he had a good broadcasting voice, but his appeal was far more than that. In common with his skills as a teacher Ted knew how to communicate quite complex arguments clearly and simply, often with humour and always with interest. He contributed to many programmes on Welsh and national radio and television, including 'Good morning Wales', 'Meet for lunch' and 'Tea junction', as well as contributing many articles in the press. In 1985 he retired from his chair at Swansea continuing to live in Mumbles with his second wife Pat who brought renewed happiness to his life.

Ted Nevin was an early critical supporter of British entry into the European Economic Community and wrote a number of papers on the community's problems. This strand of his interest and research culminated in the publication in 1990 of *The Economics of Europe*.

In addition to his academic and broadcasting work Ted Nevin held a number of professional positions. He was a Royal Economic Society council member and also served on the editorial advisory board of its journal. He served terms as president of the economics section of the British Association; and chairman of the Association of University Teachers of Economics. He lectured widely on the university circuit as well as to a variety of outside audiences such as the Civil Service College and engineering and management institutions. He was a frequent visitor to the United States as visiting professor, fellow and conference speaker. A good example of his power as a lecturer was his address to the Economics Association on the subject of the distribution of income, which was subsequently published. In the light of the so-called 'Cambridge Mass. – Cambridge England' controversy he expounded this complex subject with a firm theoretical structure and with sharply relevant examples to sustain interest.

Throughout his career, Ted Nevin successfully spanned the bridge between economic theory and application. The formulation of his ideas was founded on a mastery of economic principles, tested against a comprehensive study of the historical evidence relevant to the issues being examined. This combination of theoretical rigour supported by detailed empirical analysis marked his early work on monetary economics, his research into the economic implications of the European Community, and his diagnoses and prescriptions for the Welsh economy, on which he remained the leading post-war authority until his death in 1992.

Much of his work has stood the test of time, and many of the predictions he made in the 1960s and 1970s about the likely evolution of the Welsh and European economies, and of particular industries such as coal, have come to pass during the 1980s and 1990s. He leaves those whose professional lives he touched a legacy of respect for the importance of ideas, together with a healthy scepticism for received orthodoxies and an underlying belief in the power of reason to resolve human problems.

Introduction

JEFFERY I. ROUND

This volume has been prepared as a tribute to Professor Edward Nevin to acknowledge his many contributions to economics and his interests in the European and Welsh economies in particular. It is a reflection of Ted Nevin's breadth of scholarship and the spread of his influence in the economics profession that all of the contributors had a close association with him at some stage of their careers either as students, colleagues, collaborators on joint work – or, indeed, as a son! There are many others who could and would have contributed to this volume, were it not for our need to be selective, either to adhere to our chosen theme or owing to limitations of space. However, the result is that there is a strong representation of contributors who worked with Ted Nevin during his period of tenure of chairs at Aberystwyth and Swansea. My own association began as a junior research officer in the Economic and Social Research Unit at Aberystwyth in the mid 1960s. The unit then occupied the whole of 'Penroc', opposite the pier on the sea front, and it is significant that five of the contributors were members of that unit at one time or another, all working on very different projects but all pursuing research under Ted Nevin's supervision.

The breadth, importance and style of Ted Nevin's own contributions is hopefully reflected in the diverse and wide-ranging set of essays included in this volume. While the underlying theme is the European economy, there is no pretence that it is either a comprehensive or an exhaustive treatise. That objective has been pursued by many others and, most notably, by Ted Nevin in his final book (Nevin 1990). Instead, the volume is a collection of in-depth papers on topics in which the authors have recognized expertise. However they do fall into a pattern and for that reason they are grouped into six sections representing different perspectives of the European economy: Money and Finance, Structure, Sectors, Regions, International Perspectives, and Political Economy. No doubt purists could argue about the choice of taxonomy and how the papers have been organized and allocated. Some of the papers could easily be grouped in other ways but there is another reason underlying the choice I have adopted and this provides the basis for introducing the papers included.

Part I deals with aspects of Money and Finance. UK monetary theory and policy was the first area to be researched by Ted Nevin (Nevin 1955) and it is therefore appropriate to commence the volume with two papers on this general theme. It is also appropriate that the two authors, George Clayton and Michael Artis, were the occupants of chairs of economics (at Aberystwyth and Swansea respectively) at the same time as Ted Nevin occupied his chair in subsequent periods at the two Welsh colleges. The two papers deal with very different topics. In the opening piece, Michael Artis considers the Walters 'critique' of the counter-inflationary properties of the EMS. He presents a formal treatment of the critique and consults the empirical evidence which, although yielding little general support for it, does suggest that additional policy instruments may be needed to rely on the EMS in combating inflation. From a practical policy standpoint, the breakdown of the ERM in August 1992 adds a poignant dimension to this essentially theoretical paper. By way of complete contrast, George Clayton examines consumer credit in the EC. Following an exposition of theory and motives underlying consumer credit, he considers the institutional differences between EC member states in their provision of credit. He also considers some of the changes and developments in this area arising from the creation of the EC single market.

The structural features of the EC are the subject of Part II. My own paper focuses on an examination of the appropriate statistical framework for organizing macroeconomic data in the EC. This is a derivative and extension of Ted Nevin's own work on regional accounting and the social accounts of the Welsh economy (Nevin, Roe and Round 1966). The paper introduces the concept of a European social accounting matrix (SAM) and shows how available data for individual member states can be integrated to measure the interdependence between economies as well as depicting the degree of distribution and redistribution both between and within economies in an EC context. The next paper, by John Williams, sets out a radical perspective on the appropriate way to build Europe. He is severely critical of the way in which the European Commission introduced the economic case for the 1992 single market and goes as far as to speculate that persistent economic inequalities within the EC may endanger future European unity. As with some other papers in the volume the difficulties encountered in ratifying the Maastricht Treaty in Denmark and the UK, and the (at least temporary) withdrawal of some European currencies from the ERM in mid-1992, affect the velocity of the argument, although not necessarily the direction, and John Williams's cogent reasoning provides the basis of an alternative strategy based on his radical and essentially federalist stance.

Part III brings together two papers relating to particular sectors of the EC economy. George Peters writes about the relevance of macroeconomics to agricultural problems, that is, the effects of macroeconomic policies on agriculture as well as the effects of agricultural policies on the economy at large. Although the origins of this fresh look at an old theme are identifiable with some recent work in the United States, George Peters considers this in the EC context with all the attendant budgetary costs of the CAP and exchange rate issues. Next, EC transport policy and its impact on the peripheral regions is dealt with by Hugh Rees. Deriving his material from an intimate first-hand knowledge of EC transport, he describes current policy in each of the major transport sectors: road, rail, inland waterways, air, and maritime services, as well as providing a cursory look at transport infrastructure more generally. Hugh Rees then questions whether transport policy is compatible with EC competition policy. In particular, he refers to the complex interrelationship between transport and regional policy, and argues that some intervention (and even a degree of pragmatism) should be maintained in implementing the common transport policy. This paper leads naturally into Part IV of the volume.

Three papers in Part IV are explicitly concerned with regional issues in an EC context. The first paper, by David Blackaby and Robin Bladen-Hovell, is to do with labour markets within the regions of Europe. They review the evidence on the apparent inflexibility in western European labour markets since the 1970s. They observe a wide regional diversity in unemployment rates (a measure of 'inflexibility'), with the highest rates being experienced in the peripheral regions of Europe. Indeed they argue that European integration may have exacerbated unemployment disparities within the EC relative to other OECD countries and, as in the case of the paper by Rees, they point to a need for more interventionist regional policy to reduce these disparities. Next, Roy Thomas carries out a comprehensive review of the changes in UK and EC regional policies over the past twenty years, referring especially to their effects on the Welsh economy. Even before the introduction of the 1988 structural reforms (the 'Delors package') which brought in new EC regional policies, UK regional policy, administered by the central government, was in sharp decline. Roy Thomas argues that while the post 1988 reform outcome is uncertain (and complex) it does appear that Wales is probably now a net contributor to structural funds and is likely to remain so for the forseeable future. The final paper in this section, by Garth Hughes, David Bateman and Peter Midmore, takes a more micro perspective by considering the effect of agriculture (and of changes in agricultural policy in particular) on the rural economy of Wales. They first debate how to measure the size and contribution of agriculture to the Welsh economy (and to rural Wales especially), the essence of their argument being to underline the importance of the multiplier which, as referred to earlier, was at the heart of Ted Nevin's own work on the Welsh economy in the 1960s. Their main concern, however, is to identify the potential consequences of particular changes in agricultural policy on rural Wales and again argue for some new regional policies to help mitigate the adverse effects these changes have generated.

Part V brings together three papers which, from the European standpoint, are all outward-looking and therefore assume an 'international' perspective. The first paper, by Ali M. El-Agraa, considers the costs of implementing 'voluntary export restraints' in the particular context of the import of cars by the EC from Japan. Although the theoretical exposition is confined to a partial equilibrium analysis he is able to show, under certain assumptions, some of the likely welfare effects of VERs in a broad EC context and the possible effects on the pattern of EC trade. The available empirical evidence confirms the welfare loss for the EC as a whole and, furthermore, the UK would seem to suffer the brunt of these costs among EC member states. The next two papers in this section relate directly to Ted Nevin's study thirty years ago of the role of capital funds in the development process (Nevin 1961). Michael

Nevin reviews the operations of the European Investment Bank in channelling capital funds to the ACP states through the African development finance companies under the Lomé conventions. He sets out the evidence and the experiences in helping to mobilize long-term capital to countries in the ACP region. It is especially interesting to note that the evidence is strongly supportive of the central thesis in Ted Nevin's own study; external capital inflow is insufficient to meet development needs, and therefore local sources of finance remain crucial to the process. Alan Roe takes up the same theme but applies it in a very different context. He has written a 'sequel' to Ted Nevin's study, focusing on the financial reforms required in the former socialist economies of eastern Europe, instead of those in the developing countries. There are huge differences and contrasts between the two situations, of course, but there are similarities too, and Alan Roe successfully adopts the same analytical framework used by Ted Nevin to identify the principal requirements of financial sector development in these reforming economies.

The final section, Part VI, contains two papers that focus on two different aspects of the political economy of Europe. Michael Watson provides a 'political economy' perspective on European integration. He contrasts two stereotypical positions, the liberal (free market) and the collectivist standpoints, the latter typified by some of the work of John Williams, who authors the fourth paper in this volume. Obviously, while political history and influence within the member states are important in understanding the integration process in Europe, Watson argues that to pose a choice between the liberal and collectivist conceptions is too simplistic. He draws attention to the importance and policy implications of the role played by Christian democracy in the political motivation behind EC integration, significant also in view of its contribution to communism's collapse in eastern Europe. The final paper in the volume is an insightful essay by Charles Blitch on the role played by the American economist Allyn A. Young in helping to formulate the Treaty of Versailles (1919). Young was essentially J. M. Keynes's counterpart heading the team of technical advisors who accompanied the US delegation to the Paris peace conference, although his contribution is not generally recognized. Indeed, Charles Blitch documents not only Young's disappointment with the failure of the United States to ratify the treaty but also his misgivings about Keynes's unflattering portrayal of President Wilson, which he felt strengthened reaction against Wilson. This is an intriguing insight into a profoundly important episode of European political and economic history.

One of our aims has been ensure that the papers in this volume are as up to date as possible at the time of going to press. Inevitably, however, there are instances where either the turn of events or the pace of change has been such that further revisions could have been made. For instance, on 1 November 1993, The Maastricht Treaty was formally ratified and the European Community (EC) became the European Union (EU). But no attempt has been made to change the many references to the EC in the text or to introduce any other associated changes of terminology and organization.

In some sense Professor Nevin began and ended his career with an involvement in the European economy. He took a position in the Organization for Economic Co-operation and Development in Paris soon after completing his doctorate at Cambridge, and his book *The Economics of Europe* (Nevin 1990) was a product of the lecture course he enjoyed teaching most in the final years of his academic career at Swansea. It is a great sadness to all those involved in the preparation of this volume that it was not completed before his untimely death in September 1992. Nevertheless our hope is that, as well as being a coherent volume of writings in its own right, it will stand as a lasting tribute to a Welsh scholar who was a fine communicator and teacher as well as providing immense inspiration to so many people throughout his life.

References

Nevin, Edward (1955). *Mechanism of Cheap Money: A Study of British Monetary Policy, 1931–1939* (Cardiff, University of Wales Press, 1955).

Nevin, Edward (1961). *Capital Funds in Underdeveloped Countries* (London and New York, Macmillan, 1961).

Nevin, Edward (1990). *The Economics of Europe* (London, Macmillan, 1990).

Nevin, Edward, Roe, A. R. and Round, J. I. (1966). *The Structure of the Welsh Economy* (Cardiff, University of Wales Press, 1966).

I MONEY AND FINANCE

1
Counter-inflationary policy in the framework of the EMS

M. J. ARTIS

1. Introduction

The literature on the 'optimal currency peg' offers a number of arguments for the formation of exchange rate unions (see for example Edison and Melvin 1990); prominent criteria include those pertaining to the direction of trade. If most of the trade of the economy of x is with that of y, and if x's economy is very open, the government of x would be well advised to consider pegging to y's currency. The basic reasoning is that in the circumstances outlined, manipulation of the nominal exchange rate between x's and y's currencies is unlikely to afford any significant lasting alteration in the real terms of trade between the two countries. Meanwhile there is a presumption that fixity of the exchange rate carries with it some advantages in terms of transaction-cost reduction and the reduction of uncertainty about the future value of that exchange rate, both leading to improved resource allocation. (These benefits are strengthened in the case in which a single common currency, replacing the individual x and y currencies, is projected.)

If y is 'big' relative to x, an exchange rate union between the two will lead to x's monetary policy being dependent on that of y. Inflation in x will tend towards that in y, provided that trade is relatively free, and nominal interest rates in x will tend towards those set by y, up to a margin, in the absence of frictions in the movement of capital, which reflects the market's belief in the residual probability of an exchange rate realignment. (Again, the limit of these arguments is represented by the case of a common currency, when nominal interest rates would be the same in both countries after allowing for risk exclusive of the now zero risk of exchange rate alteration.)

If the inflation record of y is attractively low, an exchange rate union with y might represent a bonus for x. The commitment to the exchange rate peg reinforces the commitment that the government of x might otherwise be prepared to undertake. The 'reputational policy' literature (e.g. Barro and Gordon 1983a and 1983b) suggests that this will directly lower the equilibrium inflation rate in x, representing a costless counter-inflationary gain.

The case for the United Kingdom's membership of the exchange rate mechanism (ERM) of the European Monetary System (EMS) was made on grounds such as these. The 'standard account' of how the ERM operates has put Germany in the role of country y, with other adherents playing the role of x.[1]

A good deal of ink has been spilt in attempts to show how this mechanism worked in practice, and in efforts to capture the value of the counter-inflationary bonus provided by the EMS framework (e.g. Giavazzi and Giovannini 1988, Collins 1988, Kremers 1990, Dornbusch 1991). Not all of these evaluations have been favourable.

One qualification to the expectation that the EMS should provide an effective counter-inflationary framework was provided by Sir Alan Walters in his 'critique' (Walters 1986). It is with aspects of this critique that the present paper is concerned.

In what follows, we first rehearse the critique informally and consider its policy implications. In section three, we expose a formal representation of it. The critique was supposed to apply in the conditions of the realignment-free period of the EMS (the 'new EMS') from 1987 to 1992 (before the near-collapse of the system in September 1992); but a straightforward piece of formal reasoning shows that it has a clear application to the conditions of earlier years – the 'old EMS' – also. In section four, we go on to examine the empirical evidence. This evidence gives little support to the Walters critique, and suggests that the counter-inflationary achievements of the EMS countries have not been frustrated by the operation of the critique. However, the critique has weight in certain conditions, and in section five we consider what policy responses are called for in such situations. Section six presents a summary and some conclusions.

2. The Walters critique

In Walters (1986), the EMS is treated as a system of fixed exchange rates. In such a system, without capital controls, the uncovered interest parity (UIP) theorem indicates that nominal rates of interest must be the same everywhere. UIP states that the interest rate in country x will be the same as that in country y plus a margin to allow for the expected rate of depreciation of country x's currency in terms of country y's. Since, by hypothesis, the expected rate of depreciation is zero, nominal interest rates must converge. The point of the Walters critique, however, is that real rates of interest will be forced apart by such a convergence. While goods market integration remains imperfect, inflation rates may be different in the different countries. But this means that the countries with the highest inflation rates are those with the lowest real rates of interest − a perverse ranking.[2]

Giavazzi and Spaventa (1990) noted a similar phenomenon, which they termed 'excess credibility'. They noted that there had been no exchange rate realignments in the EMS since 1987. This lent weight to the idea that the existing parities were highly credible. However, as disparities in inflation rates persisted, countries setting high interest rates to beat domestic inflation would find their currencies driven to the top of their fluctuation bands vis-à-vis other currencies. The real interest-rate perversity noted by Walters could occur. The contemporary and subsequent behaviour of the currencies of two high-inflation countries, Italy and Spain (especially the latter) appeared to confirm this concern.

Various responses to the revelation of the Walters critique are possible. One, which might seem implied in the description 'excess credibility' offered by Giavazzi and Spaventa (1990), is that the phenomenon is purely transitory. Miller and Sutherland (1991) take this view. To maintain the exchange rate peg will require that inflation rates must ultimately converge,[3] so the belief that exchange rates will not be changed cannot survive non-convergence for very long. While it does so, the market is obviously suffering from excessive credulity. This position is surely correct; indeed, *part* of the explanation of the 1992 crash is that it represented a correction of the cumulative misalignment of real exchange rates resulting from the earlier period of exchange rate variability. However, this is only a part of the explanation. It does appear that the calendar time equivalent of the 'transitory' period during which the Walters critique applies can be embarrassingly long for policy-makers. Suppose then that − as seems reasonable − the phenomenon identified in the Walters critique is a serious one. What then?

The force of the critique is that counter-inflationary stabilization can be frustrated by the credibility of the EMS itself. However, it might be argued that if other policy instruments are available, the compromise of one (the nominal rate of interest) need not impair the counter-inflationary stabilization process; some other policy tools – fiscal or incomes policy, say – may be used. This is a point we examine more formally below. If it is not possible to invoke alternative policy instruments, the problem would be more serious, for the only remedies available go against the grain of the development of the EMS. Thus one remedy is to prick the bubble of excess credibility by engineering a realignment. Another is for the high-inflation countries to deploy 'outward-facing' capital controls to prevent the inflow of capital from forcing the authorities' hand on interest rates.

3. Interest rates and disinflation

The disinflation process envisioned in the Walters critique turns entirely on the real rate of interest. As Giavazzi and Spaventa (1990) point out, this neglects the role of competitiveness; it also leaves out other policies.

A specification of the inflation process which includes both these additional factors and allows for inertia in the inflation process could be written, with all variables except proportions in log form, as follows:

$$\dot{z} = \delta D \tag{1}$$

$$D = y - \bar{y} \tag{2}$$

$$y = \alpha_0 - \alpha_1 \rho - \alpha_2 R - \alpha_3 X \tag{3}$$

where $\alpha_1, \alpha_2, \alpha_3 > 0$.

This says that excess demand (D) causes inflation (z) to accelerate. In the absence of excess demand, inflation will simply proceed at its core (inertial) rate. Excess demand is defined in equation (2), where the equilibrium ('natural') level of output ($\bar{y}$) is exogenously determined, whilst the demand for output depends negatively on the real interest rate, ρ, on the real exchange rate, R, and on a suitably defined measure of other policies.[4]

Taking into account Germany's dominant role as the anchor

country, the real exchange rate can be measured with respect to Germany; if the nominal exchange rate vis-à-vis Germany is quasi-fixed, as it was in the 'new EMS', then the real exchange rate will evolve as:

$$R = z - z_g \qquad (4)$$

where z_g is German inflation. The real interest rate is simply defined as:

$$\rho = i - z \qquad (5)$$

where i is the nominal rate of interest.

The system can be illustrated in a phase diagram, as in Figure 1. Inflation is measured along the vertical axis and the real exchange rate along the horizontal. 'Excess credibility' is assumed, so the nominal interest rate is taken as fixed (presumably at the German level), along with the nominal exchange rate. Then the horizontal line at $z = z_g$ is also a line along which the real exchange rate and competitiveness are unchanging. Above this line z exceeds z_g and the real exchange rate (competitiveness) is appreciating (falling). Below the line, the real exchange rate is depreciating and competitiveness is increasing. The point E is chosen to represent the equilibrium value of the real exchange rate. Through this point is drawn the schedule to equation (1) for $\dot{z} = 0$: it is the locus of combinations of the real interest rate and real exchange rate at which excess demand (for given X) is zero and inflation proceeds at the core rate. As the nominal rate of interest is fixed, the real rate of interest falls along the $\dot{z} = 0$ schedule moving from left to right, but the effect of this on inflation is countered by the higher real exchange rate. Points above the schedule are 'inflationary', whilst points below it are 'deflationary'. The 'perversity' of real interest rates, that they fall with higher inflation, is dampened by the loss of competitiveness which occurs with higher inflation. An economy which starts, say, at point A may find that its inflation eventually starts to be checked by its loss of competitiveness. If, in fact, the loss of competitiveness begins to drive down inflation, the real interest rate will rise, reinforcing the disinflation. In order to wind up with German inflation and the equilibrium real rate of exchange at E, inflation will have to fall below German levels for a period. When this happens, competitiveness will start to rise

20 *Counter-inflationary policy and the EMS*

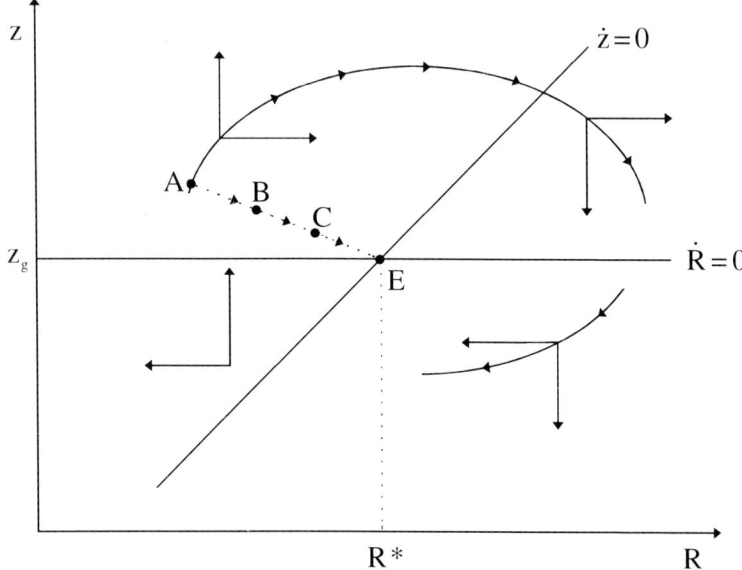

Figure 1. Inflation and competitiveness with constant nominal interest rates

and real interest rates will be quite low. But formal examination (Appendix 1) shows that, far from convergence on E being guaranteed, the system is in fact unstable.

Equation (1), however, embodies the possibility of using other policies (X) to combat inflation. These could be tuned to the current state of inflation so that, at a point like A in Figure 1, there is a downward pressure on demand and inflation, thus forcing adjustment to proceed along a path like A→B→C to E. It seems, indeed, that in the past, such additional counter-inflationary policies must have been heavily involved. To see this, consider the position in the 'old EMS' when countries used capital controls and there was a limited degree of exchange-rate flexibility in that these countries resorted to exchange-rate realignments from time to time. The realignment 'rule' of the 'old EMS' was to 'under-index' inflation, adjusting exchange rates by less than purchasing power parity (PPP) (Padoa-Schioppa 1985). This was consciously done to penalize wage and price setters and the governments of inflationary countries. The implication would be that the exchange rate would move by a fraction of the amount suggested by relative inflation. Hence, assuming that speculators were aware of the rule, and invoking uncovered interest parity again, the interest rate in the non-German country could be written as:

$$i = i_g + \Phi(z - z_g) \qquad 0 < \Phi < 1 \quad (6)$$

Writing $\gamma = (1 - \Phi)$ and subtracting z from both sides of (6), we can easily obtain:

$$\rho = \rho_g - \gamma(z - z_g) \qquad (7)$$

Thus the real rate of interest in the non-German country would fall below that in Germany by a margin that increases with the inflation differential between the two countries, for a given under-indexing realignment rule (i.e. for given Φ).

Finally, capital controls generally seem to have driven a wedge between on-shore (domestic) interest rates and off-shore (Euro) rates. (See the collection of articles in the *European Economy*, May 1988, which deal with this issue.) Whilst equation (7) would hold for the off-shore rates, capital controls would reduce on-shore rates in country i below this level. Since these controls were used in the high-inflation countries, and not in Germany, it would appear *a fortiori* that in the 'old EMS', real interest rates in the higher-inflation countries would lie below those prevailing in low-inflation countries. If this were so, and inflation nevertheless eventually converged over time on German levels, it would appear that other policy instruments than nominal interest rates must have been used. We now turn to consider some empirical evidence.

4. The empirical evidence

Figure 2 shows real interest rates, inflation and exchange-rate change (appreciation) for six members of the ERM, excluding (for data reasons) the Republic of Ireland. The variables have been constructed as twelve-month forward rates, i.e. on an assumption of perfect foresight and for annual horizons (so that in January 1978, for example, the value of retail price inflation shown is computed as the actual inflation in retail prices over the ensuing twelve months). The availability of comparable interest-rate data leaves something to be desired, but the intention of the transformations described in Appendix 2 is to generate annual interest rates, so

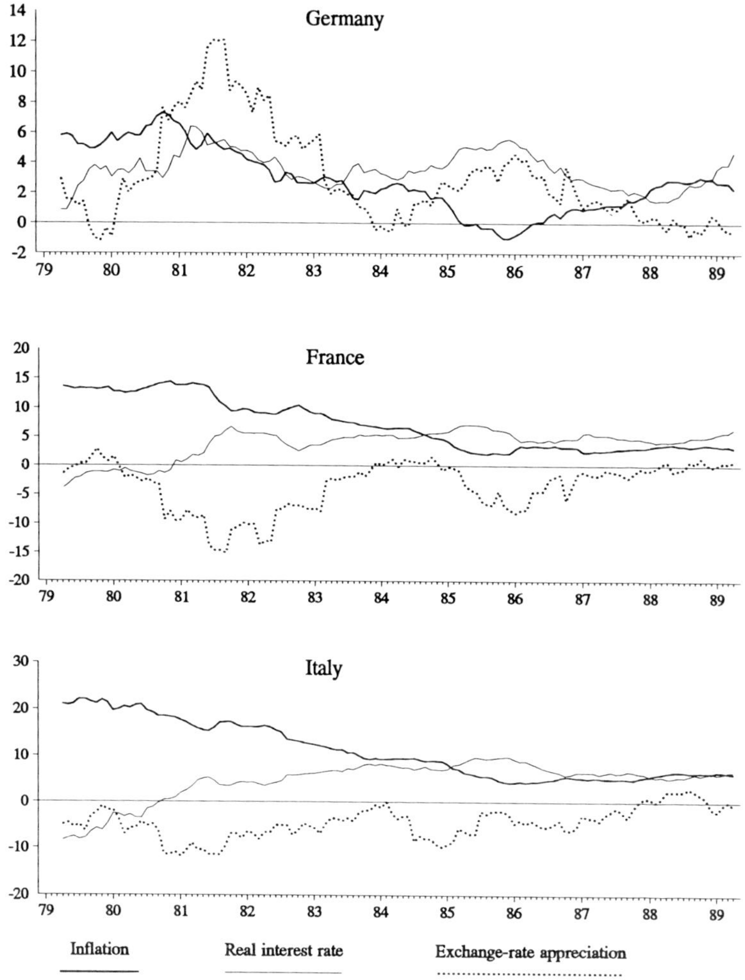

Figure 2A. Inflation, the real interest rate and exchange-rate appreciation (twelve-month forward rates)

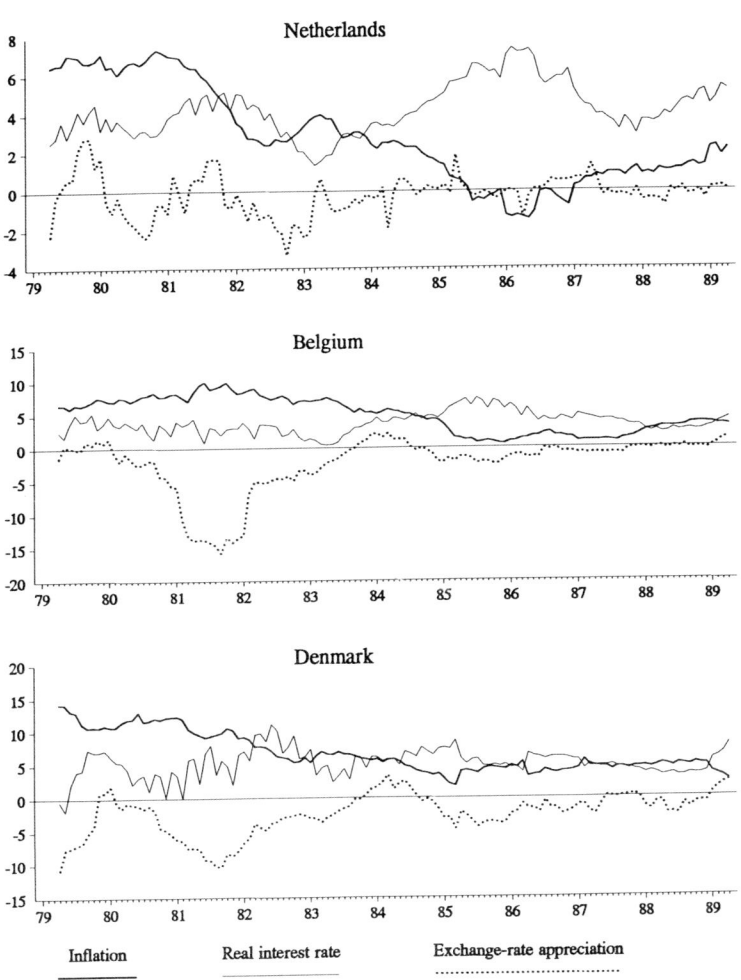

Figure 2B. Inflation, the real interest rate and exchange-rate appreciation (twelve-month forward notes)

Table 1: Correlation coefficient of real interest rate and inflation

Country:	79:4 v 82:12	83:1 v 89:4	79:4 v 83:12	84:1 v 89:4	79:4 v 84:12	85:1 v 89:4
Germany	−.061	−.729	.132	−.723	.161	−.759
France	−.822	−.366	−.827	−.244	−.827	−.619
Italy	−.949	−.074	−.931	−.053	−.924	−.341
Netherlands	−.131	−.887	.198	−.797	.059	−.753
Belgium	−.365	−.664	−.140	−.405	−.431	−.672
Denmark	−.756	−.575	−.549	−.665	−.550	−.914
Overall	−.602	.221	−.502	.294	−.482	.192

Note 1. Interest rate: money market rate

Table 2: Kendall's rank correlation τ and partial correlation

	79:4 v 82:12	83:1 v 89:4	79:4 v 83:12	84:1 v 89:4	79:4 v 84:12	85:1 v 89:4	79:4 v 85:12	86:1 v 89:4	79:4 v 89:4
Group 6									
RIR & RPI	−0.60+	0.73*	−0.60+	0.73*	−0.47	0.47	−0.20	0.33	0.33
RIR & EXC	0.73*	−0.73*	0.60+	−0.73*	0.60+	−0.73*	0.33	−0.60	−0.46
RPI & EXC	−0.87**	−0.73*	−0.87**	−0.73*	−0.87**	−0.73*	−0.87**	−0.73*	−0.87**
RIR & RPI/EXC	0.10	0.42	−0.20	0.42	0.13	−0.13	0.19	−0.20	−0.16
Group 5									
RIR & RPI	−1.00**	0.60	−1.00**	0.60	−0.80*	0.60	−0.40	0.40	0.40
RIR & EXC	1.00**	−0.80*	1.00**	−0.80*	0.80*	−0.80*	0.40	−0.60	−0.60
RPI & EXC	−1.00**	−0.80*	−1.00**	−0.80*	−1.00**	−0.80*	−1.00**	−0.80*	−0.80*
RIR & RPI/EXC	−	−0.11	−	−0.11	−	−0.11	−	−0.17	−0.17

Note 1. RIR: Real interest rate; RPI: Retail prices index; EXC: Exchange rate
Note 2. ** indicates the rejection of null hypothesis at 1% level; * at 5% level; + at 10% level (one-sided test)
H_0: zero correlation
H_1: negative correlation or positive correlation depending on the value of τ
Note 3. RIR & RPI/EXC: partial correlation between RIR & RPI keeping EXC fixed
Note 4. No test available for the significance of partial correlation τ
Note 5. Group 5: without Denmark

that the resultant real interest-rate series obtained by subtracting inflation is a proxy for the annual expected real rate.

Figure 2 and the simple correlation coefficients displayed in Table 1 indicate that over time there was a predominantly negative correlation between inflation and the real rate of interest in the EMS period as a whole. This negative correlation is particularly large for the first part of the EMS period in the case of France and Italy, on any of the three sample separations given in the table. For Germany and the Netherlands, the negative correlation is stronger in the second half of the period, whilst for Belgium and Denmark the strength of the negative correlation is rather more evenly distributed between periods.

What relationship should be expected over time between real interest rates and inflation is not clear *a priori*. Two-way causation is an obvious problem. On the one hand, the policy reaction to high inflation might be to raise interest rates (positive correlation); on the other hand, low real rates might lead to inflation (negative correlation). The menu of policy instruments available to the authorities changes over time, and even for a given menu the appropriate mix, guided by political and technical considerations, will certainly change. We can really only conclude that through the particular slice of time examined here there happens to have been, for these particular countries, a negative correlation between the expected real rate of interest and expected inflation.

However, we might hope to find that cross-country relationships would be purged of some of the business-cycle features that plague the time series. In any case, the Walters critique is naturally directed at the country cross-section. The burden of the argument, to recall, is that nominal interest rates are forced into greater conformity across countries than inflation; this produces the expectation of an inverse correlation across countries between inflation and real rates of interest.

In the top row of Table 2, we show rank correlations across countries of inflation and real interest rates. These measures are a response to the question, 'Is the ranking of countries by inflation rates similar to, unrelated or inverse to their ranking by real interest rates?'. The rank correlations are conducted for period averages. In the remaining rows of the table, rank correlations are reported for real interest rates and exchange-rate change (appreciation), and for inflation and exchange-rate change. In the last row the partial rank correlation of the real interest rate and inflation is shown, conditioned on exchange-rate change. Results are reported for the full group of six countries and also for a subset of five excluding Denmark. The latter exclusion was guided by doubts about the comparability of some Danish data; but the results are qualitatively the same whether Denmark is included or excluded, although they are rather more dramatic in the latter case.

The striking result is that the rank correlations of real interest rates and inflation are predominantly negative in the first sub-period and positive in the second, whichever one of the four sample separations is chosen. The inverse correlation in the first sub-period weakens as the sample separation point is extended beyond the end of 1984. This is the reverse of what we would have expected on the basis of the Walters critique, although we were able to demonstrate in section three that the conditions of the 'old EMS' could have been expected to produce the negative correlations we observe.

In addition to this fundamental point, the data also show that the correlation between inflation and exchange-rate change (measured as appreciation) has weakened only very slightly over the sub-periods and that rank correlations between real interest rates and exchange-rate appreciation have changed in sign from positive to negative over the period. In view of the continuing correlation between exchange-rate change and inflation it is not too surprising to find that when the rank correlation for inflation is conditioned on the change in the exchange rate, as in the partial correlation measures reported, it virtually disappears.

A strong Walters effect is, therefore, not vindicated by these results. We do not find positive rank correlations of inflation and real interest rates under the 'old EMS' giving way to inverse (negative) correlations in the later, 'new' EMS. In fact, we find the opposite. Nevertheless, the phenomenon identified by Walters is a real problem, as we now go on to discuss.

5. Taking the critique seriously

The fact that the rank correlations do not bear out the predictions of the Walters critique as we described them earlier does not mean that Walters' point is unimportant.

First of all, it only takes one high-inflation country in the system to be invested with excess credibility for a systemic problem to arise. Spain is an example of such a case. For the larger part of the UK's period of membership of the ERM (from October 1990 to September 1992) the peseta was the strongest currency in the system. Spain's desire to maintain high interest rates to bear down on inflation kept the peseta strong. As the basis of the ERM is the system of bilateral exchange-rate bands, it was

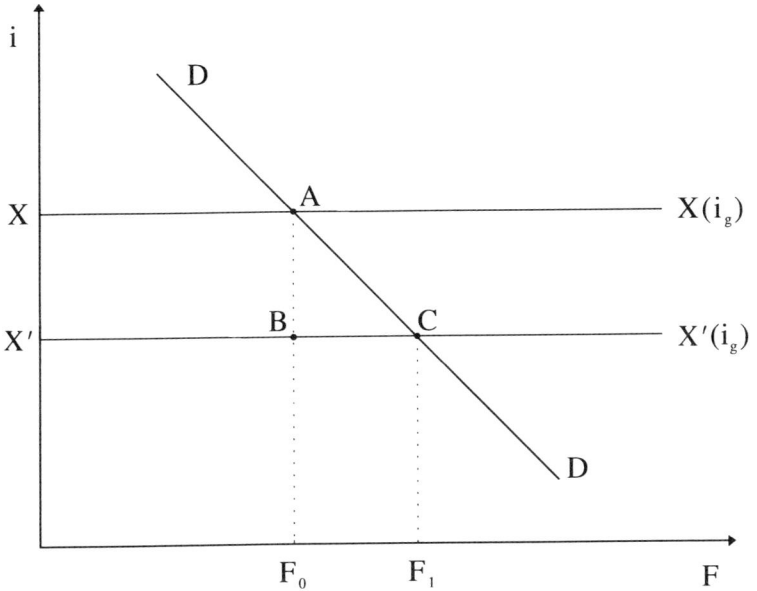

Figure 3. Excess credibility: a missing policy instrument?

Spanish strength which, for the UK, was the proximate check on a more relaxed domestic monetary stance.

The second point that should be made is this: although on the evidence of the rank correlations, the real rate perversity of the Walters critique seems to have prevailed quite generally in the 'old EMS', it was in this period that the counter-inflationary potential of the EMS as a framework was realized. This suggests that other policies were used to combat inflation, as indeed they were – most noticeably, the de-indexing of wages; but over time, reliance on these other policies has waned (de-indexing, after all, can only occur once). A Walters effect is more difficult to deal with if, as in the UK, the menu of policy instruments has been effectively reduced to one – control of 'the' short-term interest rate. A solution is to resuscitate or create afresh some additional policy instrument, say, fiscal policy. In Figure 3, we draw a companion diagram to the earlier Figure 1 for the short run. Along the horizontal axis, we plot an index of fiscal policy; along the vertical axis, the nominal rate of interest. For fixed exchange rates, and a given level of core inflation, the schedule *DD* is a zero excess demand line, sloping down from left to right indicating the trade-off between the nominal interest rate and fiscal policy as demand controllers. Points below the line represent positive excess demand, points above a deficiency in demand. The schedule XX passing through A is drawn for a given level of German interest rates and a given level of credibility of the exchange-rate peg. An attack of excess credibility would drive the XX schedule down to, say, $X'X'$. If fiscal instruments are rigid, F remains at F_0 and the economy moves from A to B. B is a point of excess demand at which inflation is liable to accelerate. A remedy is clearly to tighten fiscal policy; point C, with F_I, would be no more inflationary than A. In the absence of any exchange rate commitment, XX is irrelevant and the nominal rate can be freely used – should the DD schedule shift – to accommodate any fiscal rigidity. In effect, what the figure illustrates is simply the Tinbergen 'counting rule', according to which there should be at least as many independent policy instruments as there are objectives. If the nominal rate of interest is lost as an instrument to control inflation, then another instrument should be brought into use.

6. Conclusions

The success of the EMS in the 1980s raised its credibility. But financial market integration ran ahead of goods market integration. This raised the possibility that whilst inflation rates remained divergent, nominal interest rates would be forced to converge. Walters (1986) argued that this would produce a perverse, negative association between real interest rates and inflation – with undesirable implications for counter-inflationary policy. Giavazzi and Spaventa (1990) also pointed to some difficulties arising in the conditions of the 'new EMS'. In this paper we have given these propositions a formal expression and then consulted the empirical evidence. The latter does not point to a general perversity of the kind suggested by Walters, but shows that in fact such a negative relationship held good in the early years of the EMS, rather than in the latter years. However it is clear from the experience with respect to the more recent membership of Spain, at least up to the corrective devaluations of 1992, that the Walters problem is not negligible.

The policy conclusion suggested both by analysis and from what we know of the policy effort undertaken in the first half of the 1980s is that an additional policy instrument may be needed, perhaps in the form of a resuscitation of active fiscal policy where appropriate.

Acknowledgements

The work reported in this paper was supported by the Leverhulme Foundation under a grant administered through the Centre for Economic Policy Research. Wenda Zhang rendered expert research assistance. Robin Bladen-Hovell, Derek Leslie and David Vines commented freely on earlier drafts (to some avail). All these are gratefully acknowledged without implication.

Notes

1. Indicatively, when British officials announced the decision to participate in the ERM it was the central rate for the DM/£ exchange rate which was stressed – much to the annoyance of Commission officials, who would have preferred the decision to be cast in terms of the ECU/£ rate.
2. This perversity clearly arises when the real rate of interest is defined using the *current* inflation rate. However, *if* the exchange-rate peg is to be maintained, PPP considerations suggest that over some *long horizons* inflation in the currently high-inflation country must fall *below* that in Germany so that price *levels* may ulitmately converge. So, for these long horizons, the expected real interest rate in the high-inflation country will be higher, not lower, than that in Germany.
3. In the intervening period, the erstwhile high-inflation country will need to inflate less quickly than the low-inflation leader to restore lost competitiveness.
4. The natural interpretation of X in this specification is that it represents fiscal policy. Other policies (e.g. incomes policies) could readily be imagined to impact on the inflation process other than through the excess demand term in (3).

References

Barro, R. J. and Gordon, D. (1983a) 'A positive theory of monetary policy in a natural rate model', *Journal of Political Economy*, 91 (August 1983).

Barro, R. J. and Gordon, D. (1983b). 'Rules, discretion and reputation in a model of monetary policy', *Journal of Monetary Economics* (July 1983).

Beavis, B. and Dobbs, I. (1990). *Optimization and Stability Theory for Economic Analysis* (Cambridge University Press, 1990).

Collins, S. (1988). 'Inflation and the European monetary system', in F. Giavazzi, S. Micossi, and M. H. Miller (eds.), *The European Monetary System* (Cambridge University Press, 1988).

Dornbusch, R. (1991). 'Problems of European monetary integration', in A. Giovannini and C. Mayer (eds.), *European Financial Integration* (Cambridge University Press, 1991).

Edison, H. J. and Melvin, M. (1990). 'The determinants and implications of the choice of an exchange rate system', in W. S. Haraf and T. D. Willett (eds.), *Monetary Policy for a Volatile Global Economy* (AEI Press, 1990).

Giavazzi, F. and Giovannini, A. (1988). 'The role of the exchange rate regime in disinflation: empirical evidence on the European Monetary System', in F. Giavazzi, S. Micossi and M. H. Miller (eds.), *The European Monetary System* (Cambridge University Press, 1988).

Giavazzi, F. and Spaventa, L. (1990). 'The 'new' EMS' in P. de Grauwe and L. Papademos, *The European Monetary System in the 1990s* (London, Longman, 1990).

Kremers, J. J. M. (1990). 'Gaining policy credibility for a disinflation', *IMF Staff Papers*, 37 (March 1990), 116–145.

Miller, M. H. and Sutherland, A. (1991). 'The "Walters Critique" of the EMS – a case of inconsistent expectations', *The Manchester School Supplement*, (June 1991).

Padoa-Schioppa, T. (1985). 'Policy cooperation and the EMS experience', in W. E. Buiter and R. C. Marston, *International Economic Policy Coordination* (Cambridge University Press, 1985).

Walters, A. A. (1986). *Britain's Economic Renaissance* (Oxford University Press, 1986).

Appendix 1

In this appendix we augment the system set out in section three of the text and show how stability can be achieved by using exchange controls to break UIP.

The system set out in the text is repeated below as equations (1) to (5). The nominal exchange rate is fixed. Equation (6), however, sets out an equation for the nominal interest which permits deviations from the German rate, according to the value assumed by β.

$$\dot{z} = \delta D \quad \text{(Equation 1)}$$
$$D = y - \bar{y} \quad \text{(Equation 2)}$$
$$y = \alpha_0 - \alpha_1 \rho - \alpha_2 R - \alpha_3 X \quad \text{(Equation 3)}$$
$$\dot{R} = z - z_g \quad \text{(Equation 4)}$$
$$\rho = i - z \quad \text{(Equation 5)}$$
$$i = i_g + \beta(z - z_g) \quad \text{(Equation 6)}$$

In the text it is assumed that the nominal interest rate is compelled to converge on i_g, the German interest rate. In (6) this is the special case when $\beta = 0$. In the conditions described, either 'inconsistent' expectations or outward-facing capital controls could make for positive values of β. The special case $\beta = 1$ makes the real interest rate the same as in Germany, whilst with $\beta > 1$, the real interest rate rises with the inflation differential against Germany.

The system described by (1) to (6) has the solution in matrix form shown below:

$$\begin{bmatrix} \dot{z} \\ \dot{R} \end{bmatrix} = \begin{bmatrix} \delta\alpha_1(1-\beta) & -\delta\alpha_2 \\ 1 & 0 \end{bmatrix} \begin{bmatrix} z \\ R \end{bmatrix} + \begin{bmatrix} B \\ -z_g \end{bmatrix}$$

where $B = \delta[\alpha_0 - \alpha_1 i_g + \alpha_1 \beta z_{1g} - \bar{y} - \alpha_3 X]$.

The determinant and trace of the square matrix determine stability (Beavis and Dobbs. 1990); denoting the matrix as A, the values of these are:

If $\beta = 0$ $A > 0$ tr $A > 0$ unstable

       $\beta = 1$ $A > 0$ tr $A > 0$ unstable

       $\beta > 1$ $A > 0$ tr $A < 0$ stable

Thus only when the real interest rate rises with inflation is the system stable, and the set-up illustrated in the text (where $\beta = 0$) is unstable.

Appendix 2

The data used in the construction of Tables 1 and 2 and Figure 2 are drawn from the IMF *International Financial Statistics* (IFS) data tape.

Inflation rates are measured, monthly, as
$p_t = [(p_{t+12} - p_t) * 100/p_t]$, where p is the retail price index.

Exchange rate appreciation is measured, monthly, as
$e_t = [(e_{t+12} - e_t) * 100/e_t]$, where e is the national currency/DM exchange rate. For Germany, the exchange rate was measured as an effective rate, in DM, with weights derived from a renormalization of the ECU weights prevailing at December 1988 for the French franc, Italian lira, Belgian franc, Dutch guilder and Danish kronor.

One year interest rates are estimated, monthly, as
$R_t = (r_t * r_{t+3} * r_{t+6} * r_{t+9})^{1/4}$, where r_t, r_{t+3}, etc. are in principle three-month rates (proxied by the money market rates given in IFS).

Real interest rates are estimated as $R_t - p_t$.

2
Consumer credit in the EC

GEORGE CLAYTON

1. Introduction

I have various objectives in mind in writing this contribution in honour of my friend and former colleague, Professor Edward Nevin. Firstly, I wish to examine the basic structural features of a developed financial system and to consider the process of financial intermediation whereby consumer credit is provided. Secondly, I wish to examine the motives for using consumer credit. Thirdly, I wish to examine some theoretical aspects. Fourthly, I wish to consider the structural differences in the institutional framework whereby consumer credit is provided in each member country of the EC. Finally, I wish to review some of the changes which have occurred in the consumer credit market during the retail banking revolution and hazard some guesses about future developments following the creation of a single market in 1992.

2. Basic structural features of developed financial systems

The financial system of a developed country consists of a set of financial markets, which have complex interrelationships and links with each other and exhibit many diverse features. However, there are certain basic characteristics which are common to them all and, I believe, worth emphasizing.

First, all member countries have a short-term market, where money is lent for as short a period as a day or overnight. There are considerable differences in the characteristics of this market. For example, the United Kingdom has the very distinctive feature of discount houses which fulfil a unique role in the discount and bill markets. Nevertheless, whatever its particular characteristics, there exists in each country a market in very short-term money which provides one of the first indicators of financial stress or financial ease. Secondly, all advanced countries possess a medium-term market, which may be defined in various ways, but is usually described as a market in loans for anything from three months to nine months or twelve months; this is usually the prerogative of the commercial banking system. It certainly is in the UK. The emphasis on short-term financing by the commercial banks is a distinguishing feature of the British financial system, for the major difference between the UK and many other EC members is that by tradition the latter have tended to make loans of medium-and long-term duration.

Thirdly, all countries possess a market for long-period capital, which in the UK is called the new issue market and specializes in the issue of new bonds and new equity stock for the creation of new long-lasting assets. Fourthly, closely allied to this market, there is a market in second-hand securities − second-hand bonds and second-hand ordinary shares − variously termed as the Stock Exchange or the Bourse. Finally, and this is where the finance houses come in and also where the greatest diversity occurs, there exists a cluster of specialized financial institutions which act as links between savers and borrowers who are both general and specialized. Into this area come insurance companies, pension funds, investment trusts, finance houses, savings banks and so forth. The generic term for these institutions is financial intermediaries, thus emphasizing this link between savers and borrowers. It is a recognized feature of developed countries that the degree of this financial intermediation has been steadily increasing during the second half of this century. It is interesting to note that it appears to have reached its peak in the United States and now there is a tendency for a certain amount of disintermediation or decline in the degree of financial intermediation. But for the time being I would say that it is characteristic of all EC members that the degree of financial intermediation is increasing.

What lies behind this growth of financial intermediation? The principal function of any capital market is to accumulate the funds of the surplus spending units, which we can define as any unit whose expected income is in excess of expected expenditure, and to distribute those surplus funds to deficit units and to facilitate the change in ownership of the financial claims which the process invariably creates. Transfer of funds to deficit spending units, defined as those whose expected expenditure exceeds expected income, can be effected in two ways. In the first instance, it can be effected directly, as when ultimate lenders purchase the financial claims of ultimate borrowers (usually described as primary securities), in which case the role of the capital market institution is essentially that of a broker bringing the two parties together. Alternatively, it can be effected indirectly, as when ultimate lenders purchase the indirect debt or secondary securities of financial intermediaries which in turn purchase the direct claims of ultimate borrowers and also, in a complicated chain, the indirect claims (or secondary securities) of other financial intermediaries. Growth of financial intermediation in this sense will depend on whether they transfer funds from savers to investors more efficiently than by a mechanism of direct exchange. The source of efficiency in this function arises primarily from the economies of scale in obtaining information on borrowers and from other market expertise, which reduces transaction costs and information costs in general.

A second reason for the development of an intermediary system arises from changes in personal savings habits. The institutionalization of savings, which is a common feature of all EC countries, makes it attractive to save on a regular basis by the sheer convenience and ease of doing so. A third reason for intermediation is the attraction of being able to lower interest rates by altering the terms on which primary securities are held. This does not require an increase in the total volume of savings; simply the mere existence of intermediaries whose demand functions for primary securities have more favourable parameters than those of the non-financial sector. At given interest rates, financial intermediaries are more willing to hold primary securities than householders or consumers in general.

A fourth reason for the growth and development of financial intermediaries is product differentiation in the form of a new range of indirect financial claims which intermediation produces – these claims vary in risk, net monetary yield, transferability, ease of acquisition and storage and division of income between capital gain and interest. Intermediation also facilitates the introduction of new direct claims – an outstanding example in the UK was the issue of property bonds and equity-linked life assurance in the 1950s and 1960s.

Thus financial intermediaries are an aid to the efficient allocation of resources and their growth should be encouraged and fostered. Improvements in their efficiency and the development of new financial intermediaries are analogous to productivity improvement and innovation in industry. It would appear that the *secular* growth of financial intermediaries in general, and of particular financial intermediaries, may be explained by a variety of factors including, (a) the advantages of financial intermediaries' economies of scale over direct financing, and (b) innovation, both in the creation of new indirect claims and new forms of credit, and in technique of operation. We would normally expect the relative long-term growth of given financial intermediaries to be explicable in terms of these factors.

3. Definitions of consumer credit

The broad definition of consumer credit which I employ in this chapter embraces firstly money that is lent and borrowed as money, without being tied to the purchase of specific goods and services. This is usually termed *lender credit*. Secondly, and by way of contrast, there is another form of credit, named *vendor credit*, which covers transactions that are not legally loans, but contracts for the sale or hire of goods, such as hire-purchase and credit sale agreements and many others.

Another distinction is between secured and unsecured credit. A great deal of both lender and vendor credit is secured, in the sense that the debtor executes a document giving the creditor certain rights over his (the borrower's) property in the event of default in payment. Much lender and vendor credit, however, in the UK at least, is unsecured.

A further significant distinction arises from the period for which the credit is given. For this purpose it is convenient to adopt the following threefold classification:

(i) short-term credit of three months' duration or less;
(ii) medium-term or intermediate-term credit, defined as being of more than three but not more than sixty months' duration;
(iii) long-term credit, which is normally of more than five years' duration and may extend over a period of twenty years or more.

In the field of short-term credit there have been important innovations in recent years, such as the budget and revolving accounts offered by retailers and public utilities, but I propose to exclude these from consideration on practical grounds, because in most countries it is extremely difficult to obtain comparable data. Long-term credit in the consumer field is mainly concerned with first mortgage loans for the purchase of houses. In most EC countries, housing finance is the subject of complex legislation of quite a distinct form from that which governs the provision of all other forms of consumer credit. Again on practical grounds I propose to exclude it from consideration, while at the same recognizing that mortgage finance can be a potent way of enabling consumers to release part of the equity stake in their homes and spend it on general consumption.

This leaves us with medium-term credit as our major area of interest. This covers all the main categories of what are usually known as consumer credit – namely, hire purchase, conditional sale, credit sale, check trading and cash loans for consumer purposes.

Within this category of medium-term consumer credit a distinction may he made between instalment credit and non-instalment credit. Many loans are, in the event, repaid by instalments, since the debtor finds himself unable to find the full sum at once and the creditor is willing to accept it in several instalments. The term 'instalment credit', however, should be restricted to transactions where repayment by instalments was foreseen from the start and where there is, accordingly, a contract regulating their frequency and amount. Since we have already decided to exclude account credit, it is a matter of practical convenience to define an instalment credit transaction as one envisaging from the outset that repayment will be made by three or more instalments, not counting any initial deposit.

The earliest evidence of instalment credit comes from France and the United States in the sale of furniture to the relatively affluent members of society. It seems probable that it came into use in the United Kingdom in the early nineteenth century and it was soon adapted to the supply of goods for the middle and working classes. In Victorian times, instalment credit seems to have been largely confined to financing the purchase of furniture, pianos and sewing machines, most of it being financed by the manufacturer or dealer. Indeed, it was not until the 1920s, certainly in the United Kingdom, that the specialized finance houses became heavily involved in the provision of instalment credit for goods such as cars, radios and vacuum cleaners. Many of the finance houses in the UK started, of course, by financing the purchase of rolling stock on the railways – hence a company trading as the Wagon Finance Company – and that was typical of a significant number of those that were to become the largest finance houses. In the case of the dearer items which were financed by instalment credit it is obvious that, if the finance houses had not deployed this device which enabled payment to be spread over two or three years, the boom in the various consumer goods industries, which occurred in the inter-war period – not a particularly favourable period – might well have been delayed by several decades, and in the case of most EC countries would perhaps not have occurred until the 1950s and the 1960s. As it happened, the mass consumption of consumer durables was made feasible as early as it was by the availability of instalment credit. It is a classic example of innovation in financial intermediation, which has been of immense value to consumers in all the countries with which we are concerned.

4. Motives for using consumer credit

The motives which prompt an individual to use consumer credit in all its forms are various. Firstly, it enables him or her to achieve great practical convenience in paying for the purchase of goods and services. Secondly, it enables him or her to bridge the gap between income and expenditure in the interval between the receipt of income, be it a week, a month or longer. These two motives may be disposed of quickly. One of the most obvious means of satisfying them is by the use of account credit, but we have decided for practical reasons to omit this from consideration. Credit cards, which are a comparatively recent development in Europe, perform a similarly useful function. The individual derives several advantages from their use by reducing both the amount of cash which he or she needs to carry in his or her pocket and exposure to the risk of theft or loss, and by diminishing the inconvenience of running out of cash, which is of as much concern to the wealthy as to the poor. It follows that it is perfectly rational for a rich man to use consumer credit in this particular form.

The third motive for using consumer credit – in order to

purchase goods and services in excess of income over a period longer than the interval between income payments – is satisfied in a variety of ways, such as by budget and other revolving credit accounts, check trading and mail order. In this case consumer credit confers a benefit on the user, providing that the amount of satisfaction derived from the current use of the loan proceeds is greater than the loss of satisfaction involved in using future income to repay the loan. In a period of rising prices and incomes this motive is considerably strengthened.

A fourth and obvious motive which impels an individual to use consumer credit is the desire to purchase real and financial assets of greater value than his or her accumulated savings. It enables him or her to add to his or her supply of capital equipment in the form of houses, furniture, motor cars, refrigerators, washing machines, freezers, and so on. Although by convention only houses among such goods are treated as capital in the United Kingdom National Income Accounts, conceptually all the others are just as much consumer capital, in that they render a stream of services and yield satisfaction to their owners over a period – admittedly in most cases a shorter one than for a house. A washing machine is just as much a capital good as the commercial laundry's equipment for which it is a partial substitute. Borrowing for the purpose of installing capital equipment in a house is, in principle, no less justifiable than borrowing for the purchase of the house itself.

The use of consumer credit for this purpose confers various benefits on the borrower. Firstly, it enables individuals to enjoy the services of consumer durable goods sooner than they otherwise would and, in a period of inflation, offers them a real prospect of acquiring them more cheaply. Consumers in general are able to obtain a more satisfying 'basket' of goods and services with the same income. Thus consumer credit may be said to enhance consumer satisfaction. Secondly, the consumer may use credit to substitute cheaper 'inside' services. For example, he or she may buy a washing machine as a replacement for the services of a commercial laundry. Thirdly, consumer credit used for the purchase of physical assets may confer benefits even on consumers who have adequate financial resources. The cost of that credit may be less, in their opinion, than the loss of income and security involved in disturbing and liquidating their asset structure.

To sum up, consumer credit offers certain advantages to the individual which include both monetary and non-monetary returns. Thus it can be argued that consumer credit contributes to a better allocation of resources by increasing both consumer satisfaction and economic efficiency. Ideally, a rational consumer should increase his or her use of consumer credit up to the point where the additional satisfaction from the goods and services thus acquired is equal to the additional cost of credit incurred in purchasing them within the constraints imposed upon him or her by income and net worth. Given the considerable benefits which consumer credit confers upon the individual, it is possible to use too little as well as too much.

5. Criticisms of consumer credit

Critics of consumer credit usually have recourse to the following arguments about its undesirable effects. Firstly, by enabling consumers to increase their expenditure it is said to contribute to the pressure on the nation's resources and to make the problem of inflation more intractable. In an open economy like the UK, this produces unwelcome side-effects on the balance of payments. Secondly, consumer credit is said to encourage consumption at the expense of savings and hence to reduce the potential flow of funds for capital formation, thus inhibiting the rate of economic growth. Thirdly, it fosters the demand for consumer-durable goods and increases the instability of the industries producing these goods. Fourthly, it increases the instability of the whole economy, because there is a risk that the weight of debt might become so burdensome that all net borrowing would cease and a sharp decline in consumer demand occur.

Let us take the first criticism about the inflationary impact of consumer credit. A considerable number of the people who gave evidence to the Radcliffe Committee on the Working of the Monetary System[1] including Dr R. F. Henderson, were in no doubt that 'the growth of hire purchase is inflationary'. Since hire purchase is provided by banks and other financial intermediaries, the problem boils down to the question of whether all credit thus provided is inflationary. As I have demonstrated elsewhere (Clayton 1962), both commercial banks and non-bank financial intermediaries can add to the net supply of loanable funds and thereby increase effective demand, although they do it by different processes. Whether an extension of credit actually does increase effective demand depends on the source of the funds out of which it is financed. Thus an increase in consumer credit, like any other form of credit, may or may not be inflationary. However, if we are to understand the aggregate impact of consumer credit, we must not concentrate exclusively on new extensions of credit to new borrowers. We also must consider the effects of past commitments. This is most obvious in the case of hire purchase. Whether at any time hire purchase is having an inflationary or deflationary impact depends upon the relationship between new extensions and repayments or, in other words, on the movement of total hire purchase debt outstanding. If those who are repaying debt have to save compulsorily in order to pay their instalments, this will offset the potential inflationary effects of the spending of new borrowers. Therefore, it might be concluded that when total debt outstanding is growing, hire purchase is having an inflationary impact, but when total debt is falling, it is exerting a deflationary effect. But this is too simple a view, for it implicitly assumes that all extensions of new credit are inflationary and all repayments are deflationary. In fact, there are no *a priori* grounds for concluding that a given change in total hire-purchase debt outstanding is unambiguously inflationary or deflationary.[2] Moreover, in considering the full implications for the economy we should take into account indirect effects such as, for example, increased expenditure on petrol and oil as a result of the acquisition of motor cars through instalment credit. However, whatever the range of theoretical outcomes, there is a fair presumption that additional consumer credit financed by the banks or other financial intermediaries is potentially inflationary, especially when the multiplier effects are taken into account.

The second criticism of consumer credit, and of instalment credit in particular, is that it has adverse effects on personal-sector savings. This has provoked a similar degree of controversy. For example, Dr F. R. Oliver concludes that 'in spite of the inducement to save provided by the need to repay instalments, hire purchase has, on balance, the effect of promoting dissaving' (Oliver 1961, 70). A crucial factor is the extent to which consumer credit is used to acquire durable consumer goods of a kind that can legitimately be treated as capital goods.[3] Strictly speaking, only the depreciation and obsolescence over time of such goods actually constitute consumption. For example, if instalment payments were extended over the life of a consumer asset, the initial outlays would be capital expenditure and the instalment payments of interest and principal would be the consumption expenditures. If we consider consumer-durable expenditure in this light, we are justified in concluding that consumer credit facilitates the growth of consumers' capital stock and that that growth compensates for the reduced accumulation of producers' capital stock which the diversion of savings to the acquisition of consumer durables may necessitate. Certainly, we have no reason to reach the dogmatic conclusion that the growth and development of consumer credit is likely to reduce the rate of accumulation of the nation's capital stock or, alternatively, its rate of savings. On the contrary, since instalment credit payments more often than not are completed before the termination of the life of the asset which they have financed, it is a tenable proposition that this disciplined form of saving may increase the rate of saving and the rate of capital accumulation.

The third major criticism of consumer credit is that it is a source of instability in the economy because it diverts consumers' expenditure away from industries producing non-durable goods and services, which are by their nature relatively stable and towards industries producing durable goods, which are inherently less stable. It is clear that in theory anything that increases the proportion of the total national expenditure spent on durable goods will tend to increase the instability of the whole economy. But the particular criticism of consumer credit is that its availability, by multiplying (for a time) the potential purchasing power of the public, may still further increase the tendency of the demand for durable goods to fluctuate over time, rising rapidly when the public (for whatever reason) decides it wants to buy them and borrow money for the purpose, and falling again when the repayments have to be made. This is hardly contestable but there is a danger of losing sight of the scale of the problem. For example, a US study concluded that, although movements in instalment credit are a destabilizing factor, they have not been a major source of changes in general business conditions and have been markedly less important than swings in business inventory accumulation during reversals of economic activity.

Finally, we must consider another issue. Some writers[4] who attribute instability in business activity to the malfunctioning of instalment credit typically employ what may be called, for the lack of a better term, the 'burden' theory of business fluctuations. According to this theory, business depression has its cause in the over-expansion of credit which inevitably occurs in a boom. When the consumers have finally burdened themselves to the limit with debts and repayments, further credit expansion must cease and this is considered enough to trigger off a slump in durable goods industries and eventually in the economy as a whole.

The presumption that the growth of consumer instalment credit tends to exceed indefinitely that of incomes has been criticized by Alain Enthoven (1957). He developed a life-cycle model of debt generation in which instalment credit financing occurs once in the life-cycle of an individual — when he or she first gets married. There is thus a steady supply of new borrowers to replenish that of previous borrowers. While some consumers may indeed be overburdening themselves at certain times, the fact that debt grows relatively faster than income is not *prima facie* evidence that they are doing so. His model shows that it may be incorrect to infer, from the fact that outstanding consumer debt in the US grew more than four times as much as income in 1955, that the weight of debt would soon become so burdensome as to stop all net borrowings. Furthermore, the model reveals that a falling relative rate of increase in outstanding debt is compatible with an increasing absolute rate of increase. Now since the stimulating and depressing effects of consumer instalment credit presumably depend on the absolute rate of increase, a falling relative rate is not inconsistent, therefore, with a continued expansion of national income.

This theoretical analysis of the impact of consumer credit on the economy suggests that many of the criticisms have been exaggerated. On balance, the use of credit to finance consumer expenditure does not appear to pose any greater threat to the economy's stability than its use for other forms of expenditure.

6. Consumer credit provision in the EC

At the beginning of the 1970s the personal sector did not figure prominently in the activities of most countries' financial sectors.

Lending to the personal sector was limited, because there was an unwillingness on the part of borrowers to approach lenders for financing the purchase of consumer durables. This rather negative attitude was reinforced by the actions of the monetary authorities, who almost universally placed direct restrictions on consumer credit. These took the form of either general quantitative restrictions on domestic credit expansion, or of specific controls on personal lending, or both. The only major exception was Germany which chose to leave personal borrowing almost completely unfettered.

In general, official attempts to curb consumer credit other than for house purchase were in tune with the prevailing mores of the time. Borrowing for house purchase was widely encouraged, while incurring debt in order to install capital equipment in the house was not so easily accepted as prudent financial behaviour. Some religious bodies went as far as coupling hire purchase with gambling as certain roads to financial disaster for low-income families. This attitude ignored the fact that for many such families the borderline between success and disaster is extremely narrow and to be as little as five pounds on the wrong side may have serious consequences. The temptations for households working on extremely narrow budget margins to dip into the sums set aside for purchases of clothing, bedding and other furnishings is such that the compelling necessity to balance the weekly budget may render it virtually impossible to make such important purchases in the absence of the commitment to pay a certain given sum to the representative of a lending institution.

By 1970 there had been a transformation in the perception of the value of consumer credit both by borrowers and lenders. Clearly, an important factor in fostering the willingness of consumers to borrow was the prolonged economic boom in western Europe from 1948 to 1970, which saw a dramatic rise in standards of living and an equally dramatic increase in security of employment. Other significant factors include the drift from the rural areas to urban centres, where the social taboos on debt operate with relatively less force, and a decline in the influence of organized religion. Whatever the reasons, consumers in Europe have become aware that borrowing may legitimately be used not only as a way of coping with financial misfortune but also as a method of anticipating future economic improvement. The increasing prosperity of the personal sector triggered off, among other things, a rapid growth in retail banking during the 1970s and 1980s, as the banks recognized the growing importance of the personal sector as a major source of funds, and also that of its burgeoning demand for credit for the purchase of consumer durables and for housing purposes. The financial institutions became increasingly aware of the opportunities arising from offering financial intermediation exclusively for the personal sector by borrowing from surplus units and lending to deficit units, and frequently providing deposit and loan facilities to the same customers.

Paradoxically, this consumer confidence survived the return of unemployment as a major economic problem in the early 1980s, evidenced by the fact that in most EC countries there was barely a perceptible pause in the rate of growth of the personal sector's indebtedness. The explanation may lie in the phenomenon which manifested itself during the UK credit boom from 1988−90, when the 90 per cent of the population who were enjoying stable employment willingly increased their financial assets and liabilities to such an extent that decisions by the unemployed 10 per cent to reduce their indebtedness and liquidate their assets were completely swamped.

Not surprisingly, the buoyancy of the consumer credit market has led to important changes in its operation. In most EC member states there has been a significant expansion in borrowing through overdrafts, personal loans and the use of credit cards.

A variety of financial institutions, retail outlets, public utilities and specialist suppliers issue credit cards at variable rates of interest. Retailers provide credit in a variety of ways including what is called account credit (settled monthly) which for practical reasons we have excluded from consideration earlier, along with revolving budget-account cards. Our interest here lies in the issue of option-account cards, which offer customers the option of paying the outstanding amount in full or taking advantage of the extended credit facility for the balance on rather expensive items. The major credit institution cards (predominantly bank cards) are of the option-account variety and most have the competitive advantage that they enable holders to make purchases at shops, restaurants etc. anywhere in the world. A recent step in the evolution of this type of credit facility has been the provision of premium credit cards, which offer the holder additional services such as travel insurance and access to overdraft facilities.

Throughout the EC the individual consumer credit markets have many common characteristics but there are examples of marked disparities. Common features include the large number of credit-granting entities which play a role in the different markets, and the speed with which the volume of consumer credit has grown in the past decade. Significant disparities are to be found in the relative importance of the various forms of consumer credit and in the extent to which the market is segmented. Custom and practice in all countries has been for commercial banks to be major players in the market, followed by finance companies, retailers and money lenders. The commercial banks are increasingly aware that, given the costs of providing an efficient payments and delivery system, consumer deposits will still rank as being a cheaper source of funds than 'bought in' funds from the money markets, and that to retain them they have to be on their toes. However, there are important disparities in the methods of providing consumer credit. Instalment lending has traditionally been the preferred vehicle in France, West Germany and Spain, whereas overdraft facilities are most widely used in the United Kingdom where they originated. However the situation is changing. Recently, British commercial banks have tended to place less emphasis on the overdraft system and have attempted to encourage their customers to use more expensive fixed-term loans. They have also adopted the policy of differential charging by imposing additional penalty charges for unauthorized overdrafts. At the same time commercial banks in Germany, the Netherlands and France have begun to provide customers with generous overdraft facilities on chequeing accounts into which their salaries are paid. In Germany, for instance, all types of universal bank pursue the practice of granting overdrafts of up to two or three times their depositors' net monthly salaries; in the Netherlands, the custom of the bank is to allow customers to overdraw any time up to the limit of one month's salary; while French banks, similarly, are willing to make agreements about overdraft limits related to the customer's net monthly salary.

A major difference between the various consumer credit markets concerns the relative importance of credit-card lending. Access and Visa dominate the UK bank-issued credit-card market, whereas the rest of Europe can be split into countries like France, Italy and Spain where Visa is the major card and countries where Eurocheques serve as the domestic chequeing system like Belgium, Germany, the Netherlands and Luxembourg. In the latter group, Visa has been virtually boycotted and the Master Card-linked Eurocard has been promoted in the travel and entertainment segment of the market. In Germany, in particular, banks have sought to make Eurocheque cards look more like credit cards.

Retail cards account for the bulk of plastic cards in circulation in European markets. Their competitive position vis-à-vis bank credit cards has been strengthened by their provision of cash withdrawal facilities through ATM (automated teller machines) networks. This has major implications for European banks because, if they lose control of the payments system, they are in danger of losing the deposits that go with it and will find it difficult to hold on to a dominant share of payments provision.

Another distinction arises from the relative importance of finance companies in credit markets. In most EC countries, there are few independent consumer finance companies and, where they do exist, they tend to be overshadowed by the largest companies, which are subsidiaries of the main banking groups. In the Netherlands, for example, there have been some dramatic changes during the last thirty years. Whereas in 1960 hire-purchase and instalment credit granted by finance companies accounted for over 80 per cent of total consumer credit, they now account for less than 10 per cent; the other 90 per cent is divided equally between overdrafts on wage and salary accounts and personal loans.

In all the EC countries consumer credit tends to be markedly more expensive than mortgages. Overdrafts are the cheapest form of consumer credit but their availability is limited to higher income groups. Personal loans by the commercial banks in all countries are the next cheapest form of credit, the charges on average being two or three percentage points above the overdraft rate. A common feature of all markets is that the forms of credit most frequently used by the lower income groups – hire purchase, retailers' credit and credit-card lending – are considerably more expensive than the personal loans preferred by the more affluent. Hire purchase, which is predominantly granted by finance companies, is more costly because they pay high commission to their agents and typically have higher bad-debt ratios. Because of its convenience, many borrowers accept credit at the point of sale, even though they are aware of the high interest cost.

A recent study by Cecchini (1988) has predicted that substantial economic gains may he expected from the real integration of the European financial services market. An order of magnitude of ECU 22billion is his estimate for the gains forecast for eight EC countries as a result of the integration of the three main areas of financial service activity: banking and credit, insurance, brokerage and securities. The core element of this calculation was the analysis of the present price differentials between the eight markets – France, Germany, Italy, Spain, the UK and the Benelux countries – for a representative basket of financial services (consumer credit, mortgages etc.) and of their price developments under the competitive pressures of integration. Divergences of as much as 50 per cent were detected – these were particularly apparent in the case of home loans and consumer credit.

Of considerable significance for the consumer credit markets in the EC countries has been the movement towards financial deregulation, which has had the obvious effect of intensifying competition and increasing the pace of financial innovation. In the past the consumer credit markets' exposure to competition was blunted, to say the least. There were two reasons for this. Firstly, consumers display a considerable amount of inertia in their buying habits and, even if they are aware of differences in the cost of credit, prefer the convenience of dealing with familiar suppliers. Herein lies the explanation of the popularity of credit at the point of sale, despite the high cost. Secondly, many consumers, through a failure to shop around, are simply unaware of existing variations in the cost and availability of various forms of credit. Recent developments in the degree of competition have reduced the extent of this inertia and ignorance.

One final aspect which should be mentioned is the likely effect of the European Commission directives which are intended to promote the harmonization of the legislative and regulatory provisions of the member states. The Commission is entering a veritable minefield of differing administrative and legal practices. In so far as the objective is to optimize information and disclosures there is little room for controversy. However, when it comes to social goals such as the prevention of over-indebtedness, there is much greater scope for difference of opinion. For example, the new Consumer Credit Act in the Netherlands, which came into force at the beginning of 1992, is committed to employing an interest-rate ceiling as a key instrument in the prevention of over-indebtedness. The philosophy underlying this is that there is always an economic balance between risk and price. By controlling the credit price, the authorities restrict risk, because the strategy prevents consumers with relatively low credit-worthiness from gaining access to consumer credit at very high prices. It is difficult to believe that such an approach will gain much favour with the 'market forces' brigade in other member states.

It is believed at the moment that the best way to achieve market integration is via harmonization through EC directives. This causes increasing difficulties, which is the reason why 'Brussels' is opting for the instrument of mutual recognition which implies that member countries accept each other's regulations as equivalent. Unfortunately, mutual recognition may well cause a tendency to accept the lowest level of market regulation. For it implies that foreign suppliers of credit must be allowed access to a member state's market, if these suppliers comply with regulations in their home market. Under circumstances in which the home country regulations are less restrictive than in the host country, suppliers in the latter may well find themselves at a competitive disadvantage, with the result that they demand a loosening of their domestic market restrictions. Ultimately, the level playing field which emerges may be the lowest level of market regulation in the Community. This could constitute a setback for the interests of users of consumer credit in all member states.

Notes

1. See Radcliffe Committee (1959), 'Memoranda of Evidence', Vol.3, 125.
2. I discuss the theoretical arguments at some length in *Report of the Committee on Consumer Credit* (1971), 124–5.
3. See Runcie (1969), 107 and *passim*.
4. See Harris (1956), 358.

References

Cecchini, A. (1988) *The Economics of 1992* (European Commission, 1988).

Clayton, G. (1962). 'British financial intermediaries in theory and practice', *Economic Journal*, LXII (December 1962), 869–86.

Crowther Committee (1971) *Report of the Committee on Consumer Credit*, Cmnd 4596 (London HMSO, 1971), 124–131.

Enthoven, A. (1957). 'The growth of instalment credit and the future of prosperity', *American Economic Review*, XLVII (1957), 913–29.

Harris, S. E. (1956) 'The economics of Eisenhower: a symposium', *Review of Economics and Statistics*, XXXVIII (1956).

Oliver, F. R. (1959). *The Control of Hire Purchase* (London, Allen and Unwin, 1961).

Radcliffe Committee (1959). *The Report on the Working of the Monetary System*, Cmnd 827 (London, HMSO, 1959).

Runcie, N. (1969). *The Economics of Instalment Credit* (London, University of London Press, 1969).

Statistical appendix

Table 1: Consumer credit in the Netherlands, outstanding year-end 1986 and year-end 1990

Type of institution	1986 NLG/bn	%	1990 NLG/bn	%
Municipal credit banks	0.6	5.0	0.8	5.1
Finance companies	6.4	52.9	8.6	55.5
Banks	5.2	41.6	6.1	39.3
Various social institutions	0.02	0.5	0.01	0.1
TOTAL	12.1	100.0	15.5	100.0

Type of credit	1986 NLG/bn	%	1990 NLG/bn	%
Loans with or without collateral	5.5	45.8	6.4	41.5
Overdrafts on current account	5.6	45.9	7.3	47.4
Instalment & hire-purchase credit	0.9	8.3	1.7	10.1
TOTAL	12.0	100.0	15.4	100.0

Source: Netherlands Central Bank

Table 2: Consumer credit in Italy, outstanding year-end 1986 and year-end 1990

Type of institution	1986 Lire/bn	%	1990 Lire/bn	%
Finance companies	5.9	46.4	13.1	39.3
Banks	6.8	53.6	20.2	60.7
TOTAL	12.7	100.0	33.3	100.0

Source: Banca d'Italia

Table 3: Consumer credit in Eire, outstanding year-end 1986 and year-end 1990

Type of institution	1986 IR£/m	%	1990 IR£/m	%
Associated banks	747.5	47.3	1,546.7	53.2
Non-associated banks	260.7	16.4	346.4	11.9
Credit unions	300.1	18.9	484.8	16.7
Trustee savings banks	59.1	3.8	115.5	3.9
Hire-purchase finance cost	73.6	4.6	184.0	6.3
Trading firms	36.8	2.3	27.6	0.9
State-sponsored bodies	22.3	1.4	40.4	1.3
Credit-card companies	79.6	5.3	163.5	5.8
TOTAL	1,580.1	100.0	2,908.9	100.0

Source: Central Bank of Ireland

Table 4: Consumer credit in Greece, outstanding year-end 1986 and year-end 1990

Type of institution	1986 Drachma/m	%	1990 Drachma/m	%
Banks	7.5	60.0	42.8	66.2
Consumer credit institutions	5.0	40.0	21.8	33.8
TOTAL	12.5	100.0	64.6	100.0

NOTE: The credit institutions are all bank subsidiaries. Normally, their lending is subsumed under consumer credit loans by the banks; the figures here are an unofficial estimate.

Source: Bank of Greece

Table 5: Danish commercial bank lending, outstanding year-end 1986 and year-end 1990

Type of credit	1986 Kr bn	%	1990 Kr bn	%
Business lending	153.4	56.0	222.3	63.5
Consumer lending	120.5	44.0	127.6	36.5
TOTAL	273.9	100.0	349.9	100.0

NOTE: Danish monetary statistics do not distinguish between different types of consumer loan. Consumer lending, therefore, embraces all forms of personal lending including housing finance.

Source: Danmarks Nationalbank

Table 6: Personal lending including housing in Germany, outstanding by universal banks year-end 1986 and year-end 1990

Type of loan	1986 Dm bn	%	1990 Dm bn	%
Consumer lending	164.7	27.8	254.3	33.2
House lending	427.1	70.2	510.9	66.8
TOTAL	591.8	100.0	765.2	100.0

NOTE: Up to November 1986 the Deutsche Bundesbank had listed what are known as instalment-sales financing institutions, the core business of which is consumer credit, as a separate category of bank, but since then no such distinction has been made.

Source: Deutsche Bundesbank

Table 7: Consumer credit extended by UK financial institutions, outstanding year-ending 1986 and year-end 1990

Comercial banks	1986 £ m	%	1990 £ m	%
Commercial banks	23,031	45.0	41,683	45.0
Finance houses	10,276	20.2	17,274	18.7
Bank credit cards	12,916	25.3	27,633	27.7
Retailers	4,865	9.5	4,750	8.6
TOTAL	51,088	100.0	92,577	100.0

Source: Annual Abstract of Statistics

Table 8a: Types of consumer lending in Belgium, outstanding at various dates

Type of Credit	1980 BEF/bn	%	1986 BEF/bn	%	1990 BEF/bn	%
Instalment finance contracts	74.7	42.5	111.7	46.8	182.3	46.8
Personal loans	95.5	54.3	112.5	47.1	180.2	46.2
Credit-card lending	5.6	3.2	14.6	6.1	27.0	7.0
TOTAL	175.8	100.0	238.8	100.0	389.5	100.0

Source: Belgian National Institute for Statistics

Table 8b: Sources of consumer lending in Belgium 1980 and 1990

Type of institution	1980 BEF/bn	%	1990 BEF/bn	%
Banks	99.2	56.4	213.6	54.8
Other financial institutions	66.2	37.6	161.4	41.4
Other (retailers, etc)	10.4	6.0	14.5	3.8
TOTAL	175.8	100.0	389.6	100.0

Source: Banque de Belgique

Table 9: Total consumer credit outstanding in France, year-end 1986 and year-end 1990

Type of institution	1986 FF/m	%	1990 FF/m	%
Banks	1,569,678	47.0	2,509,050	49.3
Co-operative banks	689,323	21.0	1,125,842	22.1
Savings banks	143,190	4.3	240,445	4.7
Municipal banks	8,514	0.2	13,569	0.27
Finance companies	352,431	10.5	369,875	7.7
Specialized financial institutions	571,835	18.0	804,702	17.0
TOTAL	3,334,971	100.0	5,090,506	100.0

Source: Banque de France

Table 10: Plastic cards in Europe, thousands at year-end 1986

Card		UK	France	Germany	Italy	Netherlands
Visa	Barclaycard	8,488	Carte Blue	100	1,200	30
	Trustcard	2,540	8,600			
	Other	1,092				
MasterCard	Access	9,850	–	–	–	–
Eurocard		–	6,200	470	600	125
American Express		950	410	470	280	130
Diners Club		280	170	250	180	70
Retailers' cards		15,000	5,000	700*	600*	150
TOTAL		38,200	20,380	2,000	2,860	505

*Rough estimates

Source: E. P. M. Gardener, and P. Molyneux, Changes in Western European Banking, (London: Routledge).

Table 11: Percentage differences in prices of standard financial products compared with the average of the four lowest national prices

Name of standard service	Description of standard service	Bel.	Ger.	Sp.	Fr.	It.	Lux.	NL	UK
Banking services									
1 Consumer credit	Annual cost of consumer loan of 500 ECU. Excess interest rate over money market rates.	−41	136	39	na	121	−21	31	121
2 Credit cards	Annual cost assuming 500 ECU debit. Excess interest rate over money market rates.	79	60	26	−30	89	−12	43	16
3 Mortages	Annual cost of home loan of 25,000 ECU. Excess interest rate over money market rates.	31	57	118	78	−4	na	−6	−20
4 Letters of credit	Cost of letter of credit of 50,000 ECU for three months.	22	−10	59	−7	9	27	17	8
5 Foreign exchange drafts	Cost to a large commercial client of purchasing a commercial draft for 30,000 ECU.	6	31	196	56	23	33	−146	16
6 Travellers cheques	Cost for a private consumer of purchasing 100 ECU worth of travellers cheques.	35	−7	30	39	22	−7	33	−7
7 Commercial loans	Annual cost (including commissions and charges) to a medium-sized firm of a commercial loan of 250,000 ECU.	−5	6	19	−7	9	6	43	46

Table 11 continued

Name of standard service	Description of standard service	Bel.	Ger.	Sp.	Fr.	It.	Lux.	NL	UK
Insurance services									
1 Life insurance	Average annual cost of term (life) insurance.	78	5	37	33	83	66	−9	−30
2 Home insurance	Annual cost of fire and theft cover for house valued at 70,000 ECU with 28,000 ECU contents.	−16	3	−4	39	81	57	17	90
3 Motor insurance	Annual cost of comprehensive insurance, 1.6 litre car, driver 10 years experience, no-claims bonus.	30	15	100	9	148	77	−7	−17
4 Commercial fire and theft	Annual cover for premises valued at 387,344 ECU.	−9	43	24	153	245	−15	−1	27
5 Public liability	Annual premium for engineering company with 20 employees and annual turnover of 1.29 million	13	47	60	117	77	9	−16	−7
Brokerage services									
1 Private equity transactions	Commission costs of cash bargain of 1440 ECU.	36	7	65	−13	−3	7	114	123
2 Private gilts transactions	Commission costs of cash bargain of 14,000 ECU.	14	90	217	21	−63	27	161	36
3 Institutional equity transactions	Commission costs of cash bargain of 288,000 ECU.	26	69	153	−5	.47	68	26	−47
4 Institutional gilt transactions	Commission costs of cash bargain of 7.2 million ECU.	284	−4	60	57	92	−36	21	na

NOTE: The figures show the extent to which financial product prices, in each country, are above a low reference level. Each of these price differences implies a theoretical potential price fall from existing price levels to the low reference level.

Source: Cecchini (1988)

II STRUCTURE

3
The structure of the European economy: a SAM perspective

JEFFERY I. ROUND

1. Introduction

In the 1960s and 1970s, often regarded as the heyday of regional economic analysis, regions were generally considered as being geographical subdivisions of a national economy. Regional analysis often took the form of applying 'standard' macroeconomic analysis to the regions as if they were 'mini-nations' (Richardson 1978) without an explicit recognition of any spatial interactions within or between parts of the regional system. In the case of the UK regions this approach probably had (and still has) a special relevance for Wales, Scotland and Northern Ireland but the political, economic and social identities of the other standard planning regions of the UK have always been far less clear-cut. The standard macroeconomic analysis twenty-five years ago was essentially Keynesian, and many regional applications involved establishing variants of the Keynesian multiplier suitably modified to allow for the additional openness of regional economies, as well as interdependence between regions, and the dependence of the regions on the 'centre'.

Even in the earliest stages it was recognized that a proper empirical implementation of this analysis required the construction of a set of regional social accounts, in much the same way that national accounts underpinned Keynesian economics. The estimates derived for the Welsh economy by Nevin and his associates (1956 and 1957) were among the first ever produced for any region of the UK. This was a pioneering effort not only in terms of its attempt to measure and track the performance of a UK region but also in the advancement of regional accounting methodology. The work gave rise to the estimation of inter-regional input-output accounts for Wales and the rest of the UK and the construction of an associated input-output model (Nevin, Roe and Round 1966), one of the main purposes of which was to examine the implications for Wales of the subsequently ill-fated UK national plan.

The present paper is firmly rooted in the tradition of constructing social accounts at the regional level. However, the aim here is to focus on the European Community as an example of a supranational regional system and to try to establish an information base that is appropriate to analysis and economic policy modelling within an EC context. Moreover, the emphasis is on the 'meso' economy so as to bring into the frame the way in which policies affect income distribution and production structure. This requires information and analysis at a sectoral and/or micro-level (Hanson and Robinson 1991) to be reconciled with that for the macro-level.

Some parallels will be drawn with Nevin's work three decades ago on the Welsh economy as well as introducing some of the more recent developments in social accounting practice based on social accounting matrices (SAMs).

2. Accounts, markets and models

At first sight the economies in question are poles apart and the relevance of the earlier work on Wales to a study of the EC would seem tenuous at best. However, the Welsh social accounts and regional model recognized (and relied on) the close integration of the Welsh economy with that of the rest of the UK. For example, the estimates for Wales could not have been developed without an implicit assumption that there existed a single UK market in goods and services, and that prices were broadly uniform across all regions of the UK. Likewise, the possible emergence of a more integrated and even a 'federal' Europe, raises serious questions about the kind of regional economy that is being envisaged here. In essence, the accounts need to reflect whether markets are integrated or segmented.

On the one hand, there are certain respects (such as the 1992 programme and the completion of the internal market) in which the EC could be considered to be a single economy, albeit with important regional diversity. In principle the chosen regional delineations could cut across national boundaries, but for most practical purposes member states are likely to be included at least as one level of the regional hierarchy. On the other hand, the EC could be looked upon as a supranational region comprising interdependent national economies each with its own internal market for goods, services and resources of various kinds but having some reliance on the 'centre', in this case the Community institutions. Either way the EC can be seen to have regional features which need to be highlighted in a macroeconomic information system, although which viewpoint is chosen does have implications for the way in which economy-wide models are developed and the social accounts are structured. In many instances these choices are to do with the appropriate levels of aggregation so it makes sense to start at least from a base disaggregated by member state.

Although this paper is not concerned with modelling *per se*, a discussion of macroeconomic accounting systems cannot be divorced from any mention of economic models or other analytical uses to which the accounts may be put. One should note therefore that most social accounting systems to date are inherently production-oriented, with estimates of the main aggregates being based on reconciliations of detailed commodity balances between producers and users. Indeed the 1968 United Nations *System of National Accounts* (United Nations 1968) was underpinned by input-output accounts and an associated input-output model. In parallel with this and with Nevin's earlier work on the Welsh accounts and input-output model, it may be of interest to note that the input-output literature provides some antecedents to both the regional modelling issues and the alternative regional accounting systems that are possible. For example, the Leontief–Strout gravity model and the Isard pure interregional model are polar cases in terms of the way regional commodity markets are represented (Hewings and Jensen 1989). In the Leontief–Strout model commodities are traded in a single (national) market (referred to as a commodity pool) whereas in the Isard model separate (regional) markets are assumed for each commodity with separate accounts being constructed accordingly. Furthermore it is interesting to note that the Leontief 'balanced' regional model, subsequently developed by Tinbergen, in which local, regional and national markets are distinguished is, in this particular sense, intermediate to the other two. Clearly this gives an important clue about how much disaggregation of commodity accounts may be desirable at a regional and national level.

More recently, multisectoral modelling capability has been

62 The European economy: a SAM perspective

extended towards the implementation of computable general equilibrium (CGE) models, where markets in different factors of production and assets are distinguished as well as markets in commodities. Also other facets of the circular flow of income and expenditure are introduced in addition to the supply and demand of commodities. In fact, input-output models can be considered as a special case of CGE models. The implications of this for data needs in general and for the social accounts in particular are profound and one of the underlying aims here is to generate an EC-level social accounting framework that is sufficiently flexible to support CGE modelling as well as more aggregative macroeconometric modelling and analysis. It is against this background that a viable framework is now posited and considered.

3. SAMs and the ESA

The national accounts for each of the member states of the EC are compiled by individual national statistical offices, and are assembled and published by Eurostat in accordance with the *European System of Integrated Economic Accounts* (ESA) (Eurostat 1979). There are a few technical differences between the ESA conventions and those adopted by individual member states, and indeed between the ESA and the widely used United Nations System of National Accounts (SNA). A major similarity between them, however, is that all these systems usually represent the basic macro balances in the form of 'T' accounts, where all transactions and transfers between accounts are shown in a conventional balance-sheet format. An alternative to the 'T' accounts is to present the transactions in a social accounting matrix (SAM) format, a system pioneered by Stone (Cambridge 1962) and developed subsequently by Pyatt and Thorbecke (1976) and others as an information base for computable general equilibrium modelling.

Much has been written on SAMs, their features and properties, and on the kinds of model which can be based on them (Pyatt and Round 1985; Pyatt 1988). It may therefore be sufficient to say that a SAM is essentially a square matrix whose rows and columns correspond to the incomings and outgoings of the accounts of an economy and whose cells record the transactions between them. Hence the accounting conventions are similar to an input-output table, except that the accounts are not confined to production sectors, nor are the models based on SAMs necessarily restricted to fixed-price, fixed-coefficient input-output models. Indeed a principal motivation for compiling SAMs is to be able to integrate information on many kinds of transactions between economic agents to help in representing the accounts of society as a whole and ultimately in understanding how an economy works. SAMs tend to focus on the generation of income through factor markets, and the distribution, redistribution and use of this income amongst institutions, especially households. These are the empirical representations of the link between production structure and income distribution which make SAMs such an effective accounting system for meso-level analysis.

A simple macro-SAM for the United Kingdom in 1990 is illustrated in Table 1. In fact this is simply a rearrangement of the aggregate ESA national accounts (Eurostat 1992) in matrix format. It shows none of the structural or distributive features of the UK economy and is therefore far removed from the main reasons for compiling SAMs as described above. Furthermore the five accounts are fewer than the seven basic accounts distinguished in the ESA. However, the table does serve to illustrate the overall structure of a SAM without oversimplifying it or eliminating anything essential. It contains two panels: Table 1a defines the cell entries schematically, while Table 1b shows estimates for 1990 derived from the most recent set of published Eurostat accounts. To facilitate a comparison with the ESA accounts particular ESA aggregates are shown in parentheses in Table 1a.

The SAM can be read as follows. Income generated from domestic production (column 1) is paid to factors of production (N1) (row 2). This income is subsequently paid (column 2) to domestic institutions (N3) (row 3) according to their ownership and supply of these factors' services, after allowing for the receipt of income from abroad, less income paid abroad. Traditionally, in most SAMs the accounts receiving income generated are referred to as factor accounts so as to relate directly to the different types of factor of production and hence to separate markets for these factors. Table 1 includes a single aggregate factor account which is referred to as an 'income generation' account in accordance with the ESA. In fact in the ESA a distinction is drawn between the generation, distribution, and use of income, whereas in Table

Table 1a: Macro-SAM: schematic form

	Production	Income generation	Institutions	Combined capital	Rest of world	Total
Production			Current expenditure (P3A)	Investment (P41+P42)	Exports (P50+P33)	t_1
Income generation	GDP at market places (N1)				Resources from abroad	t_1
Institutions (current)		Gross national disposable income (N3)				t_3
Combined capital			Gross national savings (N4)		Capital transfers from abroad	t_4
Rest of world (current)	Imports (P60+P32)	Uses paid abroad		Current balance of payments surplus (N7)		t_5
Total	t_1	t_2	t_3	t_4	t_5	

Table 1b: Macro-SAM: UK 1990 (£ billion)

	Production	Income generation	Institutions	Combined capital	Rest of world	Total
Production			457.1	104.5	134.9	696.5
Income generation	548.5				11.2	559.7
Institutions (current)		542.1				542.1
Combined capital			85.0			85.0
Rest of world (current)	148.0	17.6		−19.5		146.1
Total	696.5	559.7	542.1	85.0	146.1	

1 the income 'generation' and 'distribution' accounts are consolidated. Also, the 'use of income' account is referred to here as the 'institutions current' account. The terminology is not especially important but a clear reference to 'institutions' does help later to focus on distributional issues.

A feature of the ESA system is that each account is linked with the next account in the sequence by a residual entry. In the macro-SAM this is easily demonstrated by the appearance of a series of entries falling immediately below the leading diagonal. Thus GDP at market prices (N1) is the residual item in the production account and this is shown as a receipt (a resource) in the income generation account. The residuals are labelled N1, N2 (which is subsumed for our purposes within N3), N3, etc., and they constitute the key national accounts aggregates in the macroeconomic balance sheet. The circular flow is completed by virtue of the fact that the residual for the combined capital account is 'net borrowing of the nation' (N5) which is equivalent to the current account surplus on the balance of payments (N7) after making allowance for the balancing item in the financial account (N6).

Finally note one further simplification built into the macro-SAM. Gross national disposable income is shown as the main 'national' aggregate in preference to either national income or GNP. However with a simple reorganization of the entries, one could resurrect the latter aggregates and this would create little difficulty either in principle or in practice. For example, 'resources from abroad' and 'uses paid abroad' each could be subdivided into factor and non-factor (that is, current transfer) receipts, the factor income being credited to (or debited from) the factor accounts and income transfers directly attributed to the current account of institutions. Clearly there would be no effect on the overall balance of the accounting system nor on the accounts for production, combined capital, or the rest of the world. Hence although the macro-SAM has been constructed to be consistent with the ESA aggregates, several alternative arrangements are possible. Table 1b shows that in 1990 UK gross domestic product (market prices) was £548.5 billion; gross national disposable income was £542.1 billion; gross national savings were £85.0 billion; and the current account balance of payments deficit was £19.5 billion. These figures differ slightly from the most recent Blue Book estimates because of revisions, as well as re-estimation by Eurostat to accord with ESA conventions.

4. Integrated accounts for the European Community

In order to assemble the social accounts of any regional economy, or a regional system of economies, several conceptual and practical obstacles have to be overcome. Earlier work on the social accounts of the Welsh economy showed, on the one hand, what can be achieved in a subnational situation where customs data are nonexistent and regional (i.e. Welsh) activities are sometimes hard to distinguish from national (i.e. UK) activities. On the other hand, one might expect the accounting problems associated with a supranational region consisting of twelve member states to be relatively few and much simpler to deal with. However, not all of these problems are conceptually straightforward, nor have they yet been resolved.

The national accounts for the member states of the EC are harmonized by Eurostat prior to publication. Clearly, the fact that we are dealing with a system of national economies does eliminate many of the problems faced at the subnational level and, not least, those which are a direct result of the lack of border checks or controls. However, on completion of the European single market some of these problems now appear in the context of the EC region. For example, customs declarations for goods traded between EC member states are being abolished and a new system (INTRASTAT) has had to be developed which links the collection of trade statistics to VAT returns. Also, in spite of the harmonization efforts of Eurostat, the published data (Eurostat 1992) reveal many gaps in several of the series for individual countries as well as some inconsistencies in deriving estimates and the treatment of accounts between countries.

These data problems are not confined to the smaller, poorer or newer members of the Community. For example, major difficulties relating to the measurement of the underground economy have led to a revision of the national accounts for Italy from 1980 onwards, and revised estimates have only recently been included in the latest Eurostat publications. Even the accounts for the Federal Republic of Germany, France and the United Kingdom reveal some missing (and inconsistent) series, and the reunification of Germany in 1990 has some statistical ramifications. But these problems are relatively minor in comparison with the scale of the incompleteness of the accounts for Portugal, Spain, Luxembourg and Ireland. Also, inconsistencies of treatment can markedly affect comparisons between countries. One area where this could be significant is in the definition of the household sector. In the ESA a distinction is made between private non-profit institutions serving households (S70) and households *per se* (S80). However only in the accounts for France, Denmark and Portugal is this distinction maintained in practice. Similarly in the accounts for West Germany and the Netherlands the sector comprising corporate and quasi-corporate enterprises (S10) also includes sole proprietorships, that is, the element of production activity which, in other countries' accounts, is included in the household sector (S80). Therefore the harmonization is still far from complete and care has to be exercised both in making comparisons and in aggregating estimates and accounts across member states.

The virtues of using a matrix approach to integrate the accounts of a system of interdependent economies was first explored by Stone (1961). He set out the 'building blocks' which underpin a regional SAM framework and his system has already been used as the basis for considering the formal structure of a SAM for Europe (Round 1991). In theory several alternative arrangements are possible but the availability of data means that the practical possibilities are strictly limited. The main difficulty faced is to be able to depict empirically the bilateral interactions between all pairs of member states. Some information does exist and, most importantly, on bilateral commodity trade but there appears to be little or no information on a bilateral basis to do with current or capital transfers. However, even in the case of commodity trade it would need to be established to what extent trade through intermediaries (that is, entrepôt trade, the so-called 'Rotterdam–Antwerp' effect) has already been eliminated. Indeed, the problem of entrepôts is not confined to commodities and it is likely to be at least as severe in relation to transfers of income and financial assets, even if data on bilateral transfers were available on a country-by-country basis. To circumvent these problems and yet still obtain a viable integrated system of accounts the individual SAMs for member states can

Table 2: A schematic form of a European SAM

	B	DK	D	GR	E	F	IRL	I	L	NL	P	UK	Member states	EC instns.	Other countries	Total
Belgium B	S_{11}												S_{1M}	S_{11}	S_{1O}	Y_1
Denmark DK		S_{22}											S_{2M}	S_{21}	S_{2O}	Y_1
Germany D			S_{33}										S_{3M}	S_{31}	S_{3O}	Y_3
Greece GR				S_{44}									S_{4M}	S_{41}	S_{4O}	Y_4
Spain E					S_{55}								S_{5M}	S_{51}	S_{5O}	Y_5
France F						S_{66}							S_{6M}	S_{61}	S_{6O}	Y_6
Ireland IRL							S_{77}						S_{7M}	S_{71}	S_{7O}	Y_7
Italy I								S_{88}					S_{8M}	S_{81}	S_{8O}	Y_8
Luxembourg L									S_{99}				S_{9M}	S_{91}	S_{9O}	Y_9
Netherlands NL										$S_{10\,10}$			S_{10M}	S_{101}	S_{10O}	Y_{10}
Portugal P											$S_{11\,11}$		S_{11M}	S_{111}	S_{11O}	Y_{11}
United Kingdom UK												$S_{12\,12}$	S_{12M}	S_{121}	S_{12O}	Y_{12}
Member states EC	S_{M1}	S_{M2}	S_{M3}	S_{M4}	S_{M5}	S_{M6}	S_{M7}	S_{M8}	S_{M9}	S_{M10}	S_{M11}	S_{M12}				
EC institutions	S_{I1}	S_{I2}	S_{I3}	S_{I4}	S_{I5}	S_{I6}	S_{I7}	S_{I8}	S_{I9}	S_{I10}	S_{I11}	S_{I12}				
Other countries	S_{O1}	S_{O2}	S_{O3}	S_{O4}	S_{O5}	S_{O6}	S_{O7}	S_{O8}	S_{O9}	S_{O10}	S_{O11}	S_{O12}				
Total	Y_1	Y_2	Y_3	Y_4	Y_5	Y_6	Y_7	Y_8	Y_9	Y_{10}	Y_{11}	Y_{12}				

be assembled as shown in Table 2. This requires some further explanation.

In common with any SAM, Table 2 depicts a square matrix with direct correspondence between rows and columns. The first twelve rows and columns represent the domestic accounts for each of the twelve member states of the EC. This means, in effect, that each one of the rows and columns is a block representation of the first four rows and columns of Table 1, one for each of the member states listed. The penultimate three rows and columns in Table 2 relate to the external transactions. As will shortly be seen these accounts are a subdivision (a disaggregation) of the 'rest of the world' account shown in Table 1 into three components: intra-EC transactions, European institutions, and extra-EC transactions. The final row and column contain the matching account totals. Therefore the structure of Table 2 can be seen to be particularly simple and it forms a useful basis for organizing the social accounts of Europe (Round 1991).

Table 3 shows a set of macro-SAM modules which have been assembled from the latest available statistics from Eurostat (1992). They are illustrative of the components of Table 2. Several points should be noted, however. Firstly, the external accounts are shown in consolidated form, so there is no disaggregation of the external account into separate extra-EC, intra-EC or EC institution accounts. Secondly, the transactions for each member state have been converted into ECUs at the prevailing 1990 exchange rates although other currency units (for example, purchasing power parities) would also preserve overall accounting balance. Thirdly, even at this level of aggregation, Table 3 provides a useful summary of the main comparative (and structural) features of the European member states. It clearly shows, for example, that 79 per cent of EC12 GDP in 1990 originated in four member states. It also shows the relative contributions of all member states to aggregate savings, current and capital expenditure, and so on. Finally, it should be noted that the external accounts for each member state are completed by entries showing net current transfers from, and net capital transfers to, the rest of the world. These entries are shown net so as to avoid too much complication even though more detail is available from published sources.

The key to integrating accounts across EC member states is really contained in the external transactions accounts. The intra-EC and

Table 3: Macro SAM modules for European member states 1990 (ECUbn)

Belgium (B)

	Production	Income generation	Institutions (current)	Capital	Rest of world	Total
Production			115.6	31.2	112.8	259.6
Income generation	151.7					151.7
Institutions (current)		148.7				148.7
Capital			33.1		−0.4	32.7
Rest of world	107.9	3.0		1.5		112.4
Total	259.6	151.7	148.7	32.7	112.4	

Denmark (DK)

	Production	Income generation	Institutions (current)	Capital	Rest of world	Total
Production			78.7	17.9	35.7	132.3
Income generation	101.8					101.8
Institutions (current)		97.1				97.1
Capital			18.3		0.1	18.4
Rest of world	30.5	4.7		0.5		35.7
Total	132.3	101.8	97.1	18.4	35.8	

Federal Republic of Germany (D)

	Production	Income generation	Institutions (current)	Capital	Rest of world	Total
Production			849.3	257.8	370.7	1477.8
Income generation	1171.7					1171.7
Institutions (current)		1143.9				1143.9
Capital			294.9		−2.9	292.0
Rest of world	305.8	27.8		34.2		367.8
Total	1477.5	1171.7	1144.2	292.0	367.8	

Table 3 (continued)

Greece (GR)

	Production	Income generation	Institutions (current)	Capital	Rest of world	Total
Production			48.6	10.4	11.3	70.3
Income generation	52.0					52.0
Institutions (current)		54.5				54.5
Capital			5.9		0.7	6.6
Rest of world	17.1	−2.5		−2.5		12.1
Total	69.1	52.0	54.5	7.9	12.0	

Spain (E)

	Production	Income generation	Institutions (current)	Capital	Rest of world	Total
Production			300.5	99.8	66.2	466.5
Income generation	387.2					387.2
Institutions (current)		386.0				386.0
Capital			85.5		1.1	86.6
Rest of world	79.3	1.2		−13.2		67.3
Total	466.5	387.2	386.0	86.6	67.3	

France (F)

	Production	Income generation	Institutions (current)	Capital	Rest of world	Total
Production			735.4	203.3	212.3	1151.0
Income generation	938.4					938.4
Institutions (current)		932.6				932.6
Capital			197.3		−3.5	193.8
Rest of world	212.7	5.8		−9.5		209.0
Total	1151.1	938.4	932.7	193.8	208.8	

Ireland (IRL)

Table 3 (continued)

	Production	Income generation	Institutions (current)	Capital	Rest of world	Total
Production			23.8	7.0	20.8	51.6
Income generation	33.5					33.5
Institutions (current)		31.6				31.6
Capital			7.8		0.3	8.1
Rest of world	18.0	1.9		1.1		21.0
Total	51.5	33.5	31.6	8.1	21.1	

Italy (I)

	Production	Income generation	Institutions (current)	Capital	Rest of world	Total
Production			679.8	178.6	180.3	1038.7
Income generation	858.6					858.6
Institutions (current)		845.4				845.4
Capital			165.6		0.9	166.5
Rest of world	180.2	13.2		−12.4		181.0
Total	1038.2	858.6	845.4	166.2	181.2	

Luxembourg (L)

	Production	Income generation	Institutions (current)	Capital	Rest of world	Total
Production			5.1	1.9	6.8	13.8
Income generation	6.9					6.9
Institutions (current)		9.2				9.2
Capital			4.2			4.2
Rest of world	6.8	−2.3		2.3		6.8
Total	13.7	6.9	9.3	4.2	6.8	

Table 3 (continued)

The Netherlands (NL)

	Production	Income generation	Institutions (current)	Capital	Rest of world	Total
Production			162.0	46.7	124.5	333.2
Income generation	219.8					219.8
Institutions (current)		217.5				217.5
Capital			55.8		−0.5	55.3
Rest of world	113.4	2.3		7.9		123.6
Total	333.2	219.8	217.8	54.6	124.0	

Portugal (P)

	Production	Income generation	Institutions (current)	Capital	Rest of world	Total
Production			37.5	13.7	17.1	68.3
Income generation	47.0					47.0
Institutions (current)		50.0				50.0
Capital			12.5		0.6	13.1
Rest of world	21.3	−3.0		−0.5		17.8
Total	68.3	47.0	50.0	13.2	17.7	

United Kingdom (UK)

	Production	Income generation	Institutions (current)	Capital	Rest of world	Total
Production			640.3	146.4	189.0	975.7
Income generation	768.3					768.3
Institutions (current)		759.4				759.4
Capital			119.1			119.1
Rest of world	207.3	8.9		−27.3		188.9
Total	975.6	768.3	759.4	119.1	189.0	

Notes: 1. Row and column sum discrepancies are due to rounding errors.
2. Aggregates are converted at 1990 ECU exchange rates.

Source: Eurostat (1992)

extra-EC components are fairly self-explanatory. In view of the difficulty in identifying bilateral transactions between member states, the intra-EC account (S91) simply fulfils the role of receiving and disbursing payments between them multilaterally. Similarly the extra-EC account (S93) relates to the rest of the world as seen from the standpoint of the whole of the EC, that is, it includes third countries and (non-EC) international organizations. The final external transactions account relates to payments to and from the institutions of the EC (S92). These institutions operate part of the EC redistributive mechanism and have to be separately identified in much the same way, in fact, as Nevin treated the central government account as an extra 'region' in his regional accounting scheme for Wales and the UK (Nevin 1955; also Stone 1961).

A further illustration of one of the components of Table 2 is provided by Table 4, which shows a more detailed example of the UK module. The estimates shown are derived solely from information published in Eurostat (1992). Although the ESA accounts are not fully articulated it is possible to trace the origin and destination of transactions from the information provided. It can be seen that the estimates are consistent with the UK aggregates shown in Table 1 although there are some additional features and some minor rearrangement, not least that there is now more detail provided in the domestic accounts. But before turning to the domestic accounts in the next section, let us consider further the external transactions (rest of the world) accounts. Three external transactions accounts are distinguished in accordance with the accounting structure shown in Table 2. So, for example, UK exports of commodities to other EC member states in 1990 amounted to £65.5 billion, to third countries they were £69.4 billion, plus a relatively small amount to EC institutions. A closer investigation into the EC balance of payments statistics reveals that commodity exports to EC institutions consist almost entirely of trade in services. Other elements of the external transactions account, including the overall balance can be disaggregated in a similar fashion. In 1990 the UK current account was in deficit on all three accounts, the largest deficit being with other member states of the EC.

Clearly, an advantage of the arrangement in Table 2 is that individual accounts can easily be aggregated across member states if markets are fully integrated, that is, if single markets are reckoned to exist in a particular good or resource. However, leaving aside further discussion of the domestic accounts until the next section, it should be noted that this representation of the integrated accounts for the EC region is not yet formally complete. Two points should be noted in conclusion. The first is to do with the balance of the external accounts and the second is a more far-reaching issue relating to the treatment of transport costs in the system.

If, for the present, we ignore all costs of transferring goods and resources between member states, then the first point is that, by definition, all intra-EC current account balances must net to zero. However, some of the EC budget receipts from member states are absorbed by administrative costs or are used for development aid, so in fact a transfer should be shown from the EC institutions account to the extra-EC account to achieve an overall balance. The second point is more complex. In order to properly accommodate transport and transfer costs and preserve accounting balance in the whole system a further account ought to be added to the framework shown in Table 2 (Round 1991). However the ramifications of this could be quite profound from an analytical standpoint, because the presence of transfer costs would weaken arguments in support of the existence of a single market and hence would make it less desirable to aggregate social accounts across member states for many practical purposes.

5. Income redistribution in the EC

Considerations of equity, alongside efficiency, underpin many areas of economic policy debate within the individual nations of the EC and they are potentially just as important in the context of the Community as a whole, especially in assessing the benefits and costs associated with integration. The subject is very wide-ranging indeed. But, just as there is wide variation between member states (and over time) regarding the extent to which equity and social issues form part of their current policy platform, so it is also true that the information base on which reliable comparisons can be made has been severely limited. Two relatively recent EC studies comparing poverty levels across EC member states utilized household expenditure surveys carried out in roughly similar time

Table 4: UK accounts 1990 in matrix format (£ billion)

	Production	Income generation			UK institutions (current A/C)			Combined capital A/C	Rest of world			Σ
		Employee compensation	Operating surplus	Net indirect taxes	H'holds	Corporate enterprises	General government		Intra EC	EC instit.	Extra EC	
Production					347.5		109.5	104.5	65.5		69.4	696.4
Employee compensation	316.8								0.1			316.9
Operating surplus	160.7											160.7
Net indirect taxes	71.0											71.0
Households		316.4	82.6			59.7	70.5		0.6		0.8	530.6
Corporate enterprises			70.8		37.2	46.2	12.5		1.9		7.1	175.7
General government			7.3	67.9	112.4	23.6	43.0			0.7		254.9
Combined Capital A/C					31.5	35.9	17.6					85.0
Intra EC	75.4	0.5			0.2	4.8	0.2	−13.0				68.1
EC institutions				3.1			0.3	−2.7				0.7
Extra EC	72.5				1.8	5.5	1.3	−3.8				77.3
Σ	696.4	316.9	160.7	71.0	530.6	175.7	254.9	85.0	68.1	0.7	77.3	

periods (Eurostat 1990). However there has been no attempt to integrate these data with other macro- and meso-level data on an EC basis. It has already been demonstrated in a developing country context how SAMs can provide a useful organizing framework for integrating data on incomes, production, and financial flows from many disparate data sources. So it is reasonable to argue that this is one of the specific contributions which an EC SAM could make.

Before proceeding further it would be helpful briefly to outline the distributional processes involved, and which therefore need to be captured in such an information base. In a distributional context one aim is to establish how different institutional sectors and, in particular, different households or societal groups in each of the member states of the Community, derive their income from primary or secondary sources. By 'primary' sources is meant deriving income through trade in factor services from income generated by productive activity of various kinds, or from abroad. By 'secondary' sources is meant the income that is redistributed between all the (domestic) institutions.

National governments play a crucial role in the redistributive process especially, but by no means exclusively, through fiscal transfers which are established in the national budget. However, national governments are not the only institutions to engage in redistributing income. For example, companies pay dividends to households (a transfer between institutions), and there may also be some income transfers between household groups although in the UK these transfers are probably not especially significant. Obviously, national governments and other institutions may influence income redistribution either directly or indirectly, but what is recorded in a SAM and the national accounts is the outcome of these effects and processes.

Table 4 illustrates the distributional features which can be incorporated in a SAM in the context of the UK module. It shows more detail in two of the main domestic accounts set out earlier in Table 1. The 'income generation' account is disaggregated into accounts for employee compensation and operating surplus, together with an account for net indirect taxes. Similarly, the current account of UK institutions is divided into separate accounts for households, corporate enterprises and government. This may not be the largest disaggregation of the UK domestic SAM that may be sustainable from published CSO sources but it does represent what can be achieved from readily available Eurostat sources and therefore what might be obtainable for all EC member states once Eurostat statistics are reasonably complete.

Reading through the SAM for the UK (1990) it can be seen that GDP in market prices consisted of £316.8 billion in employee compensation; £160.7 billion in operating surplus; and £71.0 billion in net indirect taxes. After allowing for transfers to and from EC institutions, the SAM shows (not at all surprisingly) that net indirect taxes (£67.9 billion) are paid to the government account, and employee compensation (£316.4 billion) is paid directly to households. Perhaps more surprisingly, the ESA accounts report that £82.6 billion of operating surplus was generated by unincorporated enterprises and hence formed a significant part of the primary income of households. Note that the total of the block of nine cell entries which intersect the three income-generation accounts sum to gross national disposable income, GNDI (£545.0 billion), allowing for a small statistical discrepancy.

The primary incomes of institutions are augmented by secondary (transfer) incomes shown in the adjacent block of cells which intersect the rows and columns of the institutions' current accounts. These cells of the matrix show, for example, the amount of transfers to households from corporate enterprises (dividends and interest) (£59.7 billion), and from government (social benefits) (£70.5 billion); and of transfers from households to corporate enterprises (interest payments) (£37.2 billion), and to government (taxes) (£112.4 billion). For UK institutions taken as a whole these entries must net out to zero and are only realized when the accounts are disaggregated. Of course, further disaggregation of the household sector and the factor accounts is desirable, as well as other parts of the SAM. Stone (1985) demonstrated what can be achieved in terms of a modest disaggregation of the UK household accounts in a SAM framework, using UK family expenditure survey data, and it would be useful if EC data could be harnessed in a similar way to examine intra-EC disparities. Stone disaggregated the household sector by income group and this could be replicated for each EC member state. Five income groups would thus lead to sixty separate household accounts at the EC level. But in common with developing country experience with SAMs, it might be preferable to disaggregate households in other ways too; say by occupational status or even by geographical region.

The redistributive mechanisms which lead to the outcome described above are not confined to the domestic policies of EC member states in isolation. There is also an international dimension in which the EC budget, though small relative to EC GDP, performs a modest redistributive function. For comparison, in 1990 the EC budget totalled approximately 1 per cent of EC GDP, whereas for the UK government, expenditure was about 21 per cent of UK GDP. Of course the two budgetary objectives are entirely different. Also, the redistributive impact of EC integration is not confined to the EC budget, any more than the UK budget is solely responsible for domestic income redistribution. Nor is the purpose of the EC budget only to do with redistributive objectives. Nevertheless it is interesting to observe the size of transfers between member states which directly result from their budgetary contributions and receipts. The pattern of these transfers can be read directly from the EC macro-SAM. In particular the estimates derived from the harmonized national accounts are essentially those recorded in the external transactions account for EC institutions shown in Tables 2 and 3.

These estimates need to be set alongside the accounts of the EC budget produced by the EC Court of Auditors for comparison and further examination. Following the same approach as Tsoukalis (1993) the net transfers from EC member states to the EC budget in 1990 are shown in Table 5. Estimates are also shown for years subsequent to the reform of the structural funds which took place in 1988. The total size of the budget in 1990 was ECU 43.3 billion which rose to ECU 53.8 billion in 1991, and which represented a substantial increase in real terms. As already noted, although the EC budget necessarily balances, some payments are absorbed by administrative costs and by development aid, so there is a residual which cannot be allocated to individual member states. In 1990 this amounted to almost 10 per cent of the total, although this has varied quite markedly over time. In 1988 and subsequently, the largest net contributor to the EC budget in absolute terms is Germany (pre-1991, the Federal Republic of Germany). The year 1988 is a useful base for comparisons because it marks the beginning of the Structural Fund reforms, which commits an increase in expenditure over the period 1988–93 and which constituted part of the 'Delors package' of reforms. However, the estimates for 1991 reveal a marked change in the net budget transfers from earlier years. Most notably, the abatement granted to the UK in respect of budgetary imbalances, negotiated and approved in 1988, resulted in a large decline in the UK's net contribution to the budget in 1991.

Tsoukalis (1993) normalized budget net transfers with respect to current market price GDP in order to provide a measure of the relative contributions of member states. Ireland and Greece are clearly the largest net beneficiaries, both in absolute terms and relative to the size of their GDP, and have remained so throughout the period 1988–91. Until 1991 Belgium and Luxembourg were the largest relative net contributors, but in 1991 they switched to become net beneficiaries. However, these figures are probably underestimates because, as Tsoukalis points out, Belgium and Luxembourg do benefit in other ways too, being the administrative centres of the Community and the seat of the EC institutions and, therefore, presumably the recipients of most of the (unallocated) administrative costs.

Applying the 1990 sterling/ECU exchange rate to the Court of Auditors' estimates of UK revenues and contributions via the EC budget gives figures that are close to those published in the Eurostat national accounts. For example the Court of Auditors report the level of UK contributions in 1990 to be ECU 6.4 billion while the Eurostat national accounts record ECU 6.3 billion. The figures for net transfers from UK amount to ECU 3.4 billion.

Although 1990 is the chosen base for the initial EC macro-SAM and therefore it is the size of the net transfers in that year which is relevant, it is worth noting the scale of some of the changes that are taking place. Italy became a net contributor in 1989, owing in part to the upward revision of the domestic product and its national accounts but their net contributions were relatively low in 1990. Similarly, although the total net contributions of France increased substantially from 1989 (in real terms too) these eased back in 1990, in common with those of Germany. Furthermore it should be noted that many of the reasons for the differences between the size and direction of the net transfers are due to the nature and size of their agricultural sectors. The EC budget is still heavily dominated by the CAP.

Table 5: Net transfers from the EC budget

	1988		1989		1990		1991	
	ECU bn	% GDP	ECU bn	% GDP	ECU bn	% GDP	ECU bn	% GDP
Belgium	−0.995	(−.78)	−1.124	(−.82)	−0.774	(−.51)	0.417	(.28)
Denmark	0.331	(.36)	0.174	(.18)	0.423	(.41)	0.346	(.34)
Germany	−6.107	(−.60)	−6.531	(−.60)	−5.550	(−.47)	−8.797	(−.75)
Greece	1.492	(3.33)	2.030	(4.13)	2.470	(4.80)	2.926	(5.64)
Spain	1.334	(.46)	1.376	(.40)	1.711	(.44)	2.295	(.59)
France	−1.782	(−.22)	−2.946	(−.34)	−1.805	(−.19)	−2.449	(−.26)
Ireland	1.159	(4.18)	1.341	(4.35)	1.893	(5.65)	2.358	(7.04)
Italy	0.124	(.02)	−1.429	(−.18)	−0.417	(−.05)	−1.387	(−.21)
Luxembourg	−0.067	(−1.18)	−0.065	(−1.02)	−0.060	(−.61)	0.160	(2.32)
Netherlands	1.150	(.60)	1.129	(.56)	0.368	(.17)	−0.538	(−.24)
Portugal	0.515	(1.46)	0.656	(1.60)	0.601	(1.27)	1.516	(3.23)
UK	−2.070	(−.29)	−3.354	(−.44)	−3.387	(−.43)	−0.666	(−.09)
Unallocated	−4.916	(−.12)	−8.743	(−.20)	−4.527	(−.10)	−3.819	(−.08)
Total budget	41.279	(1.02)	41.131	(.93)	43.325	(.91)	53.797	(1.14)

NOTE: 1. Net transfers equal receipts minus contributions expressed in ECU bn and a % of GDP (current prices and current exchange rates).
2. The estimates for Germany in 1991 refer to re-unified Germany. For 1990 and the years previously, the estimates relate to the Federal Republic of Germany alone.

Source: European Commission, Court of Auditors, Annual Reports for 1991 and 1992, Commission (1993), and Tsoukalis (1993)

6. Conclusions

The work of Nevin, Stone and others who pioneered the construction of regional social accounts at a subnational level bears a direct relevance to, and a comparison with, the accounting structure appropriate to describing structure and linkage in the European Community. In those early days, the emphasis was very much towards determining accounting aggregates and the size of the regional product and income in particular. In the intervening years the interest moved towards recording more disaggregation of the production sector and to input-output accounting in particular. The interregional input-output study for Wales was a forerunner in that field. Nowadays it is suggested that the policy and analytical concerns are much broader. Production, the 'engine room' of the economy, and production structure are still important of course, but some policy-makers and modellers are now interested in the process of income distribution in the economy and the role that markets of all kinds play in this process. The SAM has some special virtues as an information base in this regard.

The illustration of the possible structure of a European SAM and the representation of the accounts for the UK in the form of a macro-SAM to constitute a module of the European SAM is a first step in a long process. It permits some limited insights into the outcome of distribution and redistribution processes both within the UK and between it and the other member states through trade, transfers and via the EC institutions. In common with the early development of the regional accounts for Wales a possible next step might be to incorporate more detail on the production accounts using the harmonized EC input-output tables. However, further disaggregation of the institution accounts at an EC level is likely to be some way off and must await further harmonization of household survey results across member states.

References

Commission of the European Communities (1993). *European Economy*, Annual Economic Report for 1993, No. 54 (Brussels, Commission of the European Communities, Directorate-General for Economic Affairs 1993).

Department of Applied Economics, Cambridge (1962). *A Programme for Growth* 2 (Chapman and Hall, 1962).
Eurostat (1979). *European System of Integrated Economic Accounts* (ESA), 2nd edn. (Luxembourg, 1979).
Eurostat (1990). *Poverty in Figures: Europe in the Early 1980s*, Theme 3 Series C (Luxembourg, 1990).
Eurostat (1992), *National Accounts ESA, Detailed Tables by Sector, 1979–1990*, Volume 1: *Non-financial Transactions*, Theme 2 Series C, (Luxembourg, 1992).
Hanson, K. A. and Robinson, S. (1991). 'Data, linkages and models: US national income and product accounts in the framework of a social accounting matrix', *Economic Systems Research*, 3 (3) (1991), 215–32.
Hewings, G. and Jensen, R. (1989). 'Regional, interregional and multiregional input-output analysis', in P. Nijkamp (ed.), *Handbook of Regional and Urban Economics*, 1 (North-Holland 1989).
Nevin, E. T. (ed.) (1956). *The Social Accounts of the Welsh Economy, 1948 to 1952* (Cardiff, University of Wales Press, 1956).
Nevin, E. T. (ed.) (1957). *The Social Accounts of the Welsh Economy, 1948 to 1956.* (Cardiff, University of Wales Press, 1957).
Nevin, E. T., Roe, A. R. and Round, J. I. (1966). *The Structure of the Welsh Economy* (Cardiff, University of Wales Press, 1966).
Pyatt, G. (1988). 'A SAM approach to modelling', *Journal of Policy Modelling*, 10 (3) (1988), 315–88.
Pyatt, G. and Round, J. I. (1985). *Social Accounting Matrices: A Basis for Planning* (Washington DC, World Bank, 1985).
Pyatt, G. and Thorbecke, E. (1976). *Planning Techniques for a Better Future* (Geneva, International Labour Office, 1976).
Richardson, H. W. (1978). *Regional and Urban Economics* (Penguin, 1978).
Round, J. I. (1991). 'A SAM for Europe: problems and perspectives', *Economic Systems Research*, 3 (3) (1991), 249–68.
Stone, J. R. N. (1961). 'Social accounts at the regional level', in W. Isard and J. H. Cumberland (eds.), *Regional Economic Planning* (Paris, Organization for Economic Co-operation and Development, 1961), 263–96.
Stone, J. R. N. (1985). 'The disaggregation of the household sector in the national accounts', in G. Pyatt and J. I. Round, *Social Accounting Matrices: A Basis for Planning* (Washington DC, World Bank, 1985), 145–85.
Tsoukalis, L. (1993). *The New European Economy* (Oxford University Press, 1993).
United Nations (1968). *A System of National Accounts*, Series F Revision 3 (New York, United Nations Statistical Office, 1968).

4
Building Europe
JOHN WILLIAMS

1. Introduction

As recently as the mid-1980s the European ship seemed becalmed, perhaps even stranded. In the 1960s the European Economic Community (EEC) had made substantial advances, but thereafter the pace visibly slowed and then more or less halted in the 1970s and early 1980s. The explanation of this prolonged period of stagnation does not form part of the immediate purpose, although some strong and obvious candidates do present themselves. It is possible, for example, that the change resulted from the collapse in the early seventies of the post-war Bretton Woods settlement for the international economy; or the EEC may have experienced difficulty in digesting a substantially enlarged and less homogeneous membership from the original six to first nine and then twelve; and the disruptions of the two oil shocks of 1973 and 1979 obviously created a less favourable international environment. At all events, an enlarged Community seemed to have lost its way in a period of economic recession.

The position was decisively reversed from the mid-eighties when the European movement was given a new lease of life. The instrument for this transformation was the programme for the single economic market, the '1992' programme which was launched by the publication in 1985 of a European Commission white paper, *Completing the Internal Market* (1985). In place of negative and unseemly wrangling about budget contributions and sterile, divisive debates about the Common Agricultural Policy (CAP), the Commission pressed the more positive case for freer trade through the removal of non-tariff barriers (NTBs). The NTBs included border controls; differences in national regulations and standards; and the preferences given by national governments to their national producers when making their own expenditures. If all this sounded drearily technical it carried with it two compensating attractions: the removal of NTBs was an issue which did not divide the member states; and the 'single market' concept exactly fitted the economic liberalism of the 1980s.

The Commission enthusiastically set out to implement the proposals. To lend substance to this activity, sixteen volumes of specially commissioned research were published (European Commission 1988), along with a brief popularized version (Cecchini 1988). The aim was to indicate that removing the NTBs would carry with it large economic benefits for the Community. In fact, as several studies have demonstrated, the direct economic benefits of removing the NTBs were relatively small, and the claimed indirect economic benefits were uncertain because they rested on implausible assumptions, such as simultaneous co-ordinated reflation in all the member states (Cutler *et al.* 1989; Geroski 1988; Neuberger 1989). In part the economic benefits were limited because European free trade did not in fact depend on 1992. It already existed; tariff barriers between members of the Community had effectively been removed two decades before the 1987 Single European Act which was simply devoted (mostly) to facilitating the removal of the non-tariff barriers.

If the 1992 programme was as limited and restrictive as these comments are meant to convey the question arises: how is its vast impact and success to be explained? There is no doubting the success; not only in Britain but throughout Europe there was a vast outpouring of media comment and discussion around how companies and countries were, or were not, preparing for '1992'. The explanation largely lies in the nature of that success. The 1992 programme was brilliantly presented and pressed forward by the Commission as an economic text, but it carried with it a powerful political subtext. The essential objective was to promote European unity. If we look upon that as a desirable end it was, and is, much more for the Commission: the promotion of European unity is the *raison d'être* of the Commission.

By the early 1990s the Commission was attempting to repeat the success obtained from the approach which had been embodied in the single economic market strategy. Once again an explicitly economic programme was being pressed forward in order to secure a further leap towards European political union. By 1990, however, the economic instruments which were being proposed –

the creation of a European monetary union (EMU) and a single European currency – were much bolder and more dramatic, and their implicit political repercussions would be more explosive. The essential argument of this paper is that, whatever may have been the case in 1985, this is no longer the most appropriate way of building Europe. It is not appropriate, because European political union (EPU) now needs to be openly pursued, and not hidden behind an economic stalking horse; and it is not appropriate, because the economic forms being pressed by the Commission involve a deepening of the inequalities within Europe which will threaten the intended political unity. What is offered, then, is an exercise in old-fashioned political economy.

If it is a basic premise of this paper that excessive national and regional economic inequalities within the Community endanger European unity, it is necessary to try to understand the nature of existing inequalities and to attempt some assessment of existing and proposed solutions. To do this, the paper aims to address three main questions:

What is the pattern of trade and industry which has so far emerged in the European Community?

What mechanisms have existed within the Community for correcting or easing regional disparities?

Will the Commission's proposals for EMU make it easier, or more difficult, to tackle the problem of equitable economic distribution in Europe?

The organization of the paper is thus simple and straightforward: a section will be devoted to each of these questions and a final brief section will raise the issue of whether their examination suggests that the existing and proposed methods constitute the most effective way of building Europe.

2. Patterns of industry and trade

There are at least two good reasons why it is pertinent to begin with the historical question of what has so far emerged from the operation of free trade in Europe. The first rests on the simple fact that we have now experienced two full decades in which the European Community has been a free trade area (putting aside such qualifications as the temporary waivers allowed to new members like Greece and Portugal). The second reason

Table 1: Manufactured imports and exports at current prices as percentage of GDP

	1970	1978	1981	1985
West Germany				
Imports	12.0	14.3	16.9	19.3
Exports	17.6	21.1	24.0	27.7
UK				
Imports	12.8	18.8	15.8	20.0
Exports	14.5	19.6	15.9	17.1
Italy				
Imports	n/a	12.1	13.4	14.8
Exports	n/a	18.4	18.0	18.2
France				
Imports	n/a	12.5	14.6	15.6
Exports	n/a	14.6	15.9	16.7

NOTE: Manufactures correspond to SITC headings 5 to 8.

Sources: Eurostat Review *1977–85, Series 1A;* OECD, Compatible Trade and Production Data Base *1970–85, Paris OECD*

arises from the basic tenets of mainstream economic theory which would suggest that, over time, within a free trade area large differences in income and prosperity would automatically be ironed out (Padoa-Schioppa, 1987).

In looking at the pattern of trade and industry which has emerged, attention will be concentrated on manufacturing. Such an approach has obvious justifications. Some 80 per cent of European trade is visible trade, and 80 per cent of that visible trade is in manufactures. Moreover, as Table 1 shows, the total trade in manufactures (imports plus exports) now accounts for a significant proportion (32 to 47 per cent) of the total national income in each of the major countries. The combined effect of these considerations is self-evident: there is a close association between trade in manufactures and national prosperity in the main European economies.

In this context one central fact about the relative significance of the various European economies stands out very sharply: namely, that during this period the EC contained, in terms of trade competitiveness, just one world class economic power, West Germany. In 1989 West Germany had a larger surplus on its overall international trade than did Japan. The upheavals in eastern Europe in 1989–90 will in the short run reduce this, but once East Germany is, economically, absorbed and restored the position is likely to be reinforced. Apart from this global position, West Germany, which had only one-sixth of the Community's population, none the less accounted for 40 per cent of all manufacturing output and 35 per cent of all EC exports (Tables 2–5).

Some part of this overall economic dominance by West Germany did not depend on its position within the Community but reflected its overall strength within the international economy. For our purposes we need to concentrate attention just on trade within the EC to see how that trade has distributed and redistributed economic prosperity amongst the various member states. The results are shown in Table 6 and are pretty dramatic. The key points which emerge are: EC trade in manufactures has not been balanced; and there has been a characteristic pattern of surpluses and deficits. In particular, the first column of Table 6 gives the balance of each of the member states with West Germany for 1974, 1981 and 1987 (Greece, Spain and Portugal as late entrants to the EC are left out in order to emphasize the long-run trends). It shows that every country (except Ireland in 1987) consistently ran a deficit on their manufactured trade with West Germany and that these deficits tended to increase over time. (In parentheses the table – column 6 – also shows that Britain's record on intra-EC trade is almost an inverted image of the German record: Britain has had a deficit in manufactured trade with the EC since 1973; that deficit has consistently been larger than Britain's deficit on manufacturing trade with the world as a whole; and in 1987 Britain ran a deficit in manufactures with every other EC country, except Ireland.)

For this intra-EC trade the various EC countries are, to a considerable extent, in direct competition with each other. It would be an exaggeration to say that this trade is a straightforward zero-sum game, but it is substantially the case that output gained by trade by one country is partly output lost by other EC countries: an Audi sold is a sale lost for Fiat or Renault or Rover. At all events, the massive size of West Germany's surplus with the rest of the EC – 34 billion ECUs in 1987 – has obviously had a significant effect in determining the location of manufacturing production within the Community. Europe as a free trade area has been in existence for over two decades: the actual pattern of trade which emerged over

Table 2: The division of real manufacturing output and population between major EC countries

(a) Output	1970		1977		1985	
	ECU/bn	%	ECU/bn	%	ECU/bn	%
Belgium	10.2	3.6	13.4	3.9	15.3	4.3
West Germany	110.2	39.2	128.1	37.6	142.7	38.4
France	57.5	20.5	79.3	23.3	85.7	23.0
Italy	41.3	14.7	52.9	15.5	61.0	16.4
Netherlands	13.4	4.8	16.0	4.7	18.1	4.9
UK	47.2	16.8	50.3	14.8	47.8	12.8
EC12		100.0		100.0		100.0

(b) Population	1970		1977		1985	
	millions	%	millions	%	millions	%
Belgium	9.638	3.2	9.822	3.1	9.858	3.1
West Germany	60.651	20.0	61.400	19.6	61.024	19.0
France	50.772	16.8	53.145	16.9	55.170	17.2
Italy	53.661	17.7	55.955	17.8	57.141	17.8
Netherlands	13.032	4.3	13.856	4.4	14.488	4.5
UK	55.632	18.4	56.179	17.9	56.168	17.5
EC12	302.847	100.0	313.910	100.0	321.407	100.0

* Output is net output or gross value added at constant 1975 prices and exchange rates. Manufactures correspond to SITC headings 5 to 8.

Sources: Eurostat Review *1977–85*, Series 1A; European Commission, European Economy, Annual Report No. 38, November 1988

that period has tended to concentrate European manufacturing output and employment at the centre, and especially in West Germany. It is a tendency which has been accentuated by West German 'macro' policies: the government and the Bundesbank have kept a tight rein on the internal level of demand. As a result, German demand for imports and for domestic manufactures is less than would otherwise be the case. German manufacturing industry is thus pressed to seek part of its output growth through increased exports. A free trade Europe then allows them to manufacture in Germany, and distribute throughout the rest of the EC. Our immediate purpose, however, is less to provide explanations than to record the results of two decades of free trade in Europe.

Table 3: Manufactured exports (SITC 5 – 8) by country, as a percentage of EC12 exports

	1960	1970	1980	1987
Belgium/Luxembourg	9.6	10.4	9.2	8.6
Denmark	1.6	1.9	1.8	2.0
West Germany	31.1	33.2	32.1	35.4
Greece	–	0.2	0.2	0.5
Spain	0.7	1.4	3.0	3.6
France	15.5	14.6	15.8	14.5
Ireland	0.2	0.4	0.9	1.4
Italy	8.3	12.0	12.7	13.9
Netherlands	6.5	7.6	7.0	7.1
Portugal	0.5	0.6	0.6	0.9
UK	25.8	17.7	16.1	11.9

Source: Eurostat, *External Trade: Statistical Yearbook*, Series 6A, Table 7.

Table 4: National shares of EC extra-European manufactured (SITC 5 – 8) exports

	1960	1970	1980	1987
Belgium/Luxembourg	6.2	5.3	5.0	5.1
Denmark	1.7	2.6	2.2	2.7
West Germany	30.7	34.8	34.9	39.6
Greece	–	0.2	0.4	0.4
Spain	–	1.8	3.2	3.4
France	15.9	15.9	16.1	14.3
Ireland	–	–	0.4	0.8
Italy	8.1	11.8	13.2	14.2
Netherlands	4.5	4.5	4.1	4.4
Portugal	0.6	0.8	0.6	0.6
UK	32.1	24.1	19.6	14.4

Source: Eurostat, *External Trade: Statistical Yearbook*, Seriess 6A, Table 7.

From this factual, historical account three aspects which are relevant to the later argument need to be emphasized. What emerges is that: EC manufacturing industry and trade has been dominated by West Germany; this dominance results in a net transfer of output and employment to West Germany; and the actual history does not bear out the presumptions of orthodox economic theory – there has been no tendency for the imbalance automatically to correct itself. The last point is both important in

92 Building Europe

Table 5: National shares of EC12 intra-European manufactured exports (SITC 5–8)

	1960	1970	1980	1987
Belgium/Luxembourg	15.4	15.8	13.0	11.1
Denmark	1.4	1.3	1.5	1.5
West Germany	31.4	32.5	30.2	32.2
Greece	–	0.3	0.5	0.5
Spain	–	1.1	3.0	3.7
France	18.0	15.8	16.3	14.7
Ireland	0.5	0.6	1.3	1.8
Italy	8.5	12.5	12.8	13.7
Netherlands	9.9	10.4	9.2	9.2
Portugal	0.4	05	0.7	1.3
UK	14.3	9.1	11.4	10.0

Source: Eurostat, *External Trade: Statistical Yearbook*, Series 6A, Table 7.

itself, and needs to be borne in mind when we later consider the current reliance being placed by the Commission on the precepts of economics to justify its policies.

More immediately, the fact that two decades of EC free trade have been characterized by powerful centripetal forces represents a basic finding which has to be recognized when attempting to assess whether EC initiatives address the realities of EC inequalities. It leads directly to our second question.

3. Redistribution

What, then, are the existing mechanisms within the Community for correcting and easing regional and other disparities; and are these mechanisms adequate and appropriate?

The question is particularly relevant because many of those who are enthusiastic about the ideal of European unity, especially amongst social democrats, are uneasy about some of the accompanying features along the chosen path. Specifically, there is a natural anxiety that the strong stress being given to liberal market approaches will have unfavourable effects on social and distributional aspects. The Commission recognizes both these concerns and their legitimacy. Its frequently repeated response has been to assert that if some social groups, or regions, or countries,

Table 6: Matrix table of manufacturing trade balances* for eight of the EC12 countries

(a) 1974 manufacturing trade balances (ECU/m)

Reporting country	W. Germany	France	Italy	Netherlands	Belgium/Luxembourg	UK	Ireland	Denmark
France	−2,450.7	–	−88.5	−294.7	−853.1	202.5	47.7	91.4
Belgium/Luxembourg	−525.4	626.0	187.7	641.4	–	−535.2	17.2	216.1
Netherlands	−2,063.2	161.7	−8.6	–	−651.0	−218.8	52.7	109.3
W. Germany	–	2,313.9	1,331.2	2,035.6	447.2	1,575.0	140.7	874.6
Italy	−1,268.2	−419.1	–	−72.4	−140.4	168.5	42.9	54.4
UK	−1,439.4	7.6	−50.2	−125.1	247.2	–	501.2	185.4
Ireland	−128.9	−38.9	−34.1	−36.2	−23.3	−606.4	–	−16.6
Denmark	−864.5	−72.9	−50.3	−107.6	−128.3	−196.4	15.5	–

(Table 6 continued)

(b) 1981 manufacturing trade balances (ECU/m)

Reporting country	W. Germany	France	Italy	Netherlands	Belgium/Luxembourg	UK	Ireland	Denmark
France	−5,637.9	–	−711.9	−817.6	−2,266.8	957.4	17.5	−0.9
Belgium/Luxembourg	−2,008.6	1,802.4	517.7	−317.1	–	230.9	−59.9	180.4
Netherlands	−1,366.2	770.0	–	−35.3	−141.0	−45.0	112.0	112.0
W. Germany	–	5,306.5	1,607.7	3,249.5	1,199.6	3,499.4	85.3	1,006.7
Italy	−1,076.4	1,274.5	–	42.5	−533.0	726.4	6.7	117.7
UK	−3,606.4	−828.6	−508.4	85.4	−1,314.6	726.4	1,658.8	76.1
Ireland	−87.6	40.3	−16.7	−7.1	2.2	−1,754.0	–	32.7
Denmark	−965.9	−22.5	−117.0	−90.9	−278.5	−1.6	54.8	–

(c) 1987 manufacturing trade balances (ECU/m)

Reporting country	W. Germany	France	Italy	Netherlands	Belgium/Luxembourg	UK	Ireland	Denmark
France	−8,986.1	—	−2,852.2	−1,127.4	−2,096.9	2,165.4	−601.3	201.6
Belgium/Luxembourg	−3,872.9	4,069.2	1,637.7	593.9	—	544.6	−240.7	445.3
Netherlands	−5,684.7	1,400.3	962.7	—	−24.2	1,111.8	−200.2	233.3
W. Germany	—	9,176.5	3,312.0	6,013.7	3,202.6	10,290.2	−204.0	2,403.7
Italy	−2,820	3,573.8	—	−407.5	−1,244.6	1,998.1	−233.0	348.4
UK	−10,802.7	−1,584.3	−2,122.4	−1,534.4	−655.6	—	—	−179.1
Ireland	205.1	637.7	196.8	128.8	133.8	−686.11	—	5.1
Denmark	−2,328.5	−199.1	−354.3	−215.5	−439.3	82.1	−29.5	—

* Surpluses and deficits are calculated from the NIMEXE analytical tables where merchandise is classified into 'chapters'. Results approximating to SITC 5−8 can be obtained by adding together surplus/deficits in chapters 1 to 27 and deducting this total from the overall surplus/deficit of chapters 0 to 99.

Source: Eurostat External Trade: Analytical Tables, Series 6C

are disadvantaged, the EC regional and social funds will rectify the situation. And, if necessary, these funds will be increased in order to do so.

These reassurances are certainly beguiling, but they need to be examined carefully. There are good reasons for believing that the redistributional policies might not be accorded the priority necessary to convert their rhetoric into reality. Thus the Social Charter was initially proposed by the Commission in the early 1970s, but was still not in place in 1993. In contrast, the Single European Act was only passed in 1987 but by 1993 several hundred EC directives had already been issued to implement its objective of strengthening the liberal market basis of the Community. If nothing else, this suggests that a prudent scrutiny of the Commission's claims about redressing regional imbalance is justifiable.

The scale of the problem is indicated in Table 7, which shows that there are large disparities of wealth and poverty. *Per capita* income in the wealthiest regions of the EC is four or five times as great as that in the poorest regions. This represents a greater range of difference than exists in, for example, the United States (Eichengreen 1990; Swithin 1990). Two other features which are not explicit in the table need also to be noted. The first is that these inequalities tended to widen in the 1980s (European Commission 1991). The second is that they were accentuated, and to some degree overshadowed, in the 1980s and into the 1990s by mass unemployment even in the more prosperous countries. From a peak of 14.9 million (10.9 per cent) in 1985, unemployment fell slowly to 12.7 million (9.0 per cent) at the top of the boom in 1989, but then started to rise again.

Against this background, it is argued that existing EC policy was inadequate for the task which it was meant to confront. On the one hand, there is an uncomfortable disjuncture between the scale of the problem and the power of the Commission's proposed instruments. On the other, and perhaps more insidiously, the objective of curbing inequalities clashes with some major features of the Community's existing *a priori* philosophy, especially the attachment to a more or less unfettered market economy.

As might be expected, the central inadequacy is financial. The EC has three 'structural funds': the European Regional Development Fund (ERDF); the European Social Fund (ESF); and the 'guidance' section of the Agricultural Guidance and Guarantee

Table 7: Gross domestic product per capita in the EC (selected regions) in 1985

Rank	Country	Region	GDP, per capita (PPP) EC 12 = 100
1	Greece	Thrakis	43.2
3	Spain	Extremadura	46.6
5	Italy	Calabria	54.4
6	Portugal	Portugal	54.6
11	Spain	Andalusia	58.3
22	Ireland	Ireland	69.5
34	Belgium	Namur	80.9
35	France	Limousin	81.4
37	Holland	Friesland	82.4
49	UK	Northern Ireland	89.7
56	Spain	Madrid	91.1
60	UK	South Yorks	92.1
72	UK	Cleveland	94.6
127	Italy	Piedmont	110.6
138	France	Alsace	118.0
151	Italy	Valle D'Aosta	137.0
152	Germany	Oberbayern	142.7
153	Denmark	Hovedstads regionen	142.9
154	Germany	Berlin (West)	144.4
155	Germany	Bremem	148.7
156	Germany	Darmstadt	150.4
157	UK	Greater London	155.1
158	France	Ile de France	159.4
159	Germany	Hamburg	195.5
160	Holland	Groningen	237.4

Source: Padoa – Schioppa (1987)

Fund (AGGF). Of these only the ERDF is explicitly designed 'to contribute to the correction of the principal regional imbalances within the Community...' (Council Regulation 1787/84). The ESF was given 'the task of rendering the employment of workers easier and of creating their geographical and occupational mobility within the Community' (*Treaty of Rome*, Article 123), whilst Article 39 of the Treaty refers 'to improving productivity and technical progress in agriculture'. None the less both the ESF and the guidance section of AGGF have, in practice, operated in ways which bias their expenditure in favour of the poorer regions, although not as strongly as the ERDF.

If the structural funds can thus be seen to be addressing the problems of regional inequalities, where does the inadequacy arise? Whilst they are clearly to some extent redistributive, against this has to be placed the operation of the Common Agricultural Policy (CAP) scheme, the effect of which is to make a regressive transfer to the richer north European countries. Even more pertinent is the fact that the sum available for regional and redistributive purposes is modest. This is unavoidable when the total size of the EC budget is limited and when most of the expenditure goes on agricultural price support. The EC budget in 1988 accounted for only 1.1 per cent of Community GDP, and the target for 1992 was only 1.17 per cent. Moreover, 60 per cent of that EC budget was absorbed by the requirements of price support under the agricultural guarantee scheme and less than 20 per cent (16.9 per cent) was accounted for by the structural funds. The arithmetic is inescapable; after the CAP has taken its large slice of a small cake, there is not much left for all other purposes.

The Commission could reasonably say that that was the past situation, and point to the intention to double the size of the regional and social funds by 1993. It sounds a bold and grand programme and is certainly to be welcomed. But in judging how effective it will be, at least three broad considerations need to be briefly mentioned. Firstly, twice very little is still not very much. Secondly, the attainment of the Commission's target partly depends on there being a substantial reform of the CAP, and accumulated experience suggests that that is a process which shuffles rather than gallops. Thirdly, and crucially, the size of the resources has to be weighed against the scale of the problem. It is not only that, as has been shown, the pattern of EC trade has created disparities, nor that the Community contains several significant 'declining industrial regions'; there is also the fact that the enlargement of the EC in the 1980s brought in several countries with very low income levels. In this context the structural funds would need to be substantially enlarged even to stand still.

If the size of the structural funds is inadequate, it could also be argued that the objects of expenditure are inappropriate. As a matter of policy the bulk of the money has to be spent either on infrastructure improvements or on youth training. If each of these is desirable in itself, they are each subject to some qualification. Infrastructure improvement can be double-edged; building better transport facilities in Greece and Portugal not only makes it easier for them to send their goods to Germany and Holland, it also eases the transport of goods into Greece and Portugal. Similarly, for youth training to be effective requires not only that the right skills should be taught but also that there should then be skilled jobs waiting for them in their native countries. More fundamentally, with this policy and these instruments, everything depends on the Commission's implicit assumption that industry will voluntarily relocate from the centre to the periphery on a scale sufficient for any significant shift in the balance.

Neither the scale nor the choice of instruments is accidental; they reflect rather a particular interpretation of the nature and causes of the disparities, and also an attachment to liberal economics as the proper (only?) way to build Europe. Each of these presumptions is open to challenge. On interpretation, the fact of substantial divergences in prosperity within the EC raises the question: who is diverging from whom? The issue here is whether, or to what extent, the problems arise because of failure at the periphery, or because of success at the EC centre. The official view has no doubts about this: it is a problem of, and for, the periphery, where it manifests itself in two distinctive forms. In the underdeveloped south there is a large, low-productivity agricultural sector; in the north there are old, decaying, industrial regions; in both the levels of income are below, and the levels of unemployment above, the EC average.

The Commission, when referring to retardation at the periphery, mostly focuses on regional rather than national differences. This, for many purposes, is natural and sensible. It is also politically congenial: in the EC the discussion of regional differences is relatively uncontroversial since all the member states (rich and poor) have laggard regions. None the less, the concentration on the regions is distorting since it means that the long-established national success of West Germany is little registered. To say this is, given the background of the intemperate chauvinistic outbursts of recent years, to risk being branded a Tory 'Little Englander' – a melancholy fate for a Welshman writing from a quite different part of the political spectrum. The object here is more humdrum: not to make some large political statement, but to stress some persistent economic realities. West Germany has been the affluent centre of Europe (and a united Germany will, after a pause, be equally dominant); half of the ten wealthiest EC regions are in Germany and most of the rest are adjacent; and Germany's productive weight has already been indicated.

The argument which flows from this is, therefore, that the problem of European economic disparities is not simply one of peripheral failure or uncompetitiveness: it also arises from the centralization of production. And the prescription which would follow from this would be that any acceptable solution should also be aimed − not, certainly not, at reducing productive efficiency at the centre − but at securing the transfer of some of those skills and some of that production to the periphery.

In the same way, the instruments chosen − infrastructure and youth training − can also be challenged. The prominence of these particular instruments derives largely from the fact that they are consistent with the Commission's commitment to the assumptions of orthodox economics. On the basis of the Commission's interpretation, if some regions are less successful than others that must mostly be because the quantity or quality of their resources is worse. Hence the solutions: more infrastructure improves the overhead capital of the underdeveloped south; and more training improves the human capital of the north. There may be other ways, but each of these methods is acceptable because neither is essentially interfering with the market. Indeed, they can be said to be aimed at making the market work better, at 'making reality correspond with the assumptions of economic theory' as Beveridge neatly expressed it (Beveridge 1909, 321).

In addition, the Commission's approach − seeing the problem in terms of failure at the periphery and choosing the appropriate instruments − avoids the need to examine intra-EC trade. Such an avoidance is again both important and congenial for the Commission, for whom free trade within Europe is the ark of the covenant: free trade is the economic instrument which is seen as being essential for achieving the higher political goal of European unification. The avoidance is also necessary; it evades confronting even the possibility that the way in which free trade has operated in practice has been to produce substantial imbalance, which would be potentially politically divisive. Yet, as was demonstrated earlier, that imbalance has been the reality.

In this and the preceding section, the approach has been largely historical. The first section looked at the broad pattern of manufacturing trade and industry which had emerged out of two decades of free trade within the Community. Its broad finding was that trade had been dominated by West Germany, and that industry was concentrated at the centre. The present section looked at existing regional policies and their instruments, and found broadly that they were inadequate and inappropriate to the scale and nature of the problem. The next section turns more to the future by asking whether the Commission's proposals for EMU will ease or worsen the problems of unequal distribution within the Community.

4. Equity

When the 1992 programme to 'get Europe moving' was launched in 1985, consideration was given to an alternative plan based on pressing for monetary union. The alternative was explicitly and decisively rejected because it was recognised that it would be 'hopelessly divisive'; it was something for the far future. A measure of the momentum produced by the psychological success of the 1992 project is the fact that already by 1989 Jacques Delors, the president of the Commission, was able to take his earlier object of monetary union out of the closet and dust it down. The original Delors plan of 1989 envisaged progress to full EMU in three stages and was approved in principle at the Madrid summit in that year. The details are not necessary since the plan was still essentially a set of proposals to be negotiated by the member governments before they could be implemented and operated. Its philosophy and broad intent is, however, significant because it represents the Commission's next step forward, the official blueprint for building Europe. And a full statement of the underlying assumptions and objectives was provided in the Autumn of 1990 in a special number of the official journal (*European Economy*) (Commission 1990) devoted to a detailed justification of the Commission's plans for EMU and a single currency.

Considered at the broadest level, one striking feature was that the intention was to use precisely the same general strategy which had worked so well for the single market project. The attempt was made to carry the similarity down to a detailed tactical level by, as in the 1992 project, providing a specific timetable to pre-empt endless discussion, and to aim to have the whole scheme put in place in seven years – exactly the same period as had been set out in the 1985 proposals for 1992. Some of that detail was soon lost: EMU was not simply going to be an easy 'action replay'. It was, however, of much greater moment that the basic method was to be the same; an essentially economic programme was floated to push forward towards the desired political end. Moreover – and again just as before – the status of this second political project was completely unclear, as the stages and objectives of political union have never been defined in a specific and programmatic document equivalent to the report on EMU. This absence will be returned to later as part of the conclusion.

A feature of the *a priori* of the economic proposals for EMU is that the dominance of liberal economics is even more marked than it had been in the 1992 scheme. The hegemony of the market is to be even more strongly stressed whilst at the same time the market is given one single overriding objective. The sole declared aim of monetary policy is to be that of 'price stability'. The possibility of other objectives, either as additions or as alternatives, is simply not mentioned. If some of these objectives, like the maintenance of employment or balanced growth, might seem to be desirable in themselves their exclusion, or at least their lesser status, is meant to be irrevocable; price stability (and only price stability) is in this scheme to be explicitly written into the Constitution of the new central bank (the Euro Fed?), which is to be given – again constitutionally – total political independence.

The Commission's justification for EMU can also be seen to have become much more market-orientated than was the Cecchini report, which was the comparable justification for the 1992 programme. A particularly sensitive indicator is the balance suggested between reflationary (expansionist) policies and deflationary (contractionist) policies; this balance effectively indicates the weight which is being attached in the minds of policy makers to a policy of maintaining employment. Cecchini (1988, 100 – 1; see also European Commission 1988, 151 – 9) included as part of the beneficial package that it was claimed would flow from the single market, the notion of a co-ordinated European reflation. It is true that this represented a sort of add-on extra which would only appear at Stage 3 (beyond the 'medium term' of six or seven years). It was necessary because it was deemed essential for the

Commission to be able to present the 1992 programme as one which would eventually create jobs since it was recognized that in the short-run (Stage 1) there was likely to be a net loss of jobs which Stage 2 would not dramatically reverse (Cutler *et al.* 1989, 69 – 72). The failure to launch anything remotely resembling a 'co-ordinated European reflation', despite the high and rising European unemployment in 1992 and 1993, is itself a sufficient comment on EC priorities. The theoretical case for EMU presented in the special October 1990 issue of *European Economy* makes no such gestures, which presumably means that the Commission no longer thought them to be necessary. Once employment has been demoted as a specific objective of policy it was possible to be robust about the primacy of monetary policy. It is the reason why the main institutional requirement of the plan is for a politically independent central bank which has price stability as its sole objective: '... unless the central bank has political independence, board members with long and secure tenure, and statutes establishing an explicit duty to give priority to price stability', then monetary policy is vulnerable (Commission 1990, 22). It is the reason why provision is made for disciplining any member state which pursues 'loose' fiscal policy. Moreover, in operational terms 'looseness' is defined in an exceptionally restrictive manner: whatever the starting point and whatever the objects of expenditure, any rise in the ratio of debt to GDP is considered 'unsustainable' and any debt ratio above 100 per cent 'should imperatively be stabilized' (ibid., 103 and 109).

Redistribution through regional policy is also demoted in the intellectual case for EMU. For Cecchini, positive reference to the role of the structural funds was considered to be obligatory; it was thought essential that the EC should be presented as playing a significant role in redressing disparities. A semi-official report on the consequence of enlarging 'the Community to include Spain and Portugal and to create a market without frontiers by the year 1992', had concluded that market liberalization involved 'serious risks of aggravated regional imbalance' (Padoa-Schioppa 1987, ix and 5). It was to meet this perceived problem that the 1985 white paper had asserted that, after 1992, 'full and imaginative use will need to be made of the resources available through the structural funds' (Commission 1985, 8). This is incorporated into the Cecchini report where the Commission is presented as ready to use the funds to redress disparities, even if the fact that their instruments for doing so were inadequate was glossed over.

The case for EMU presented in *European Economy* avoids such gestures. Instead the scope and role of regional policy is to be severely constrained, essentially because any form of supranational redistribution in the EC is viewed with suspicion. It would involve 'risks of weakening incentives for production activity and creating a state welfare dependency' (Commission 1990, 227). The argument is almost exactly the same as that used by Malthus in the early nineteenth century against any form of assistance being given to the poor. The success of the weaker peripheral economies is now seen to depend entirely on their own commitment to 'generalized modernization', which is seen to 'extend very deeply and acquire socio-political as well as purely economic dimensions' and probably to require 'a comprehensive and credible change of regime' (ibid.). Essentially what this formulation means is that everything is to be reduced to the test of the market. Moreover, whatever the outcome, this monetarist market model is not at risk. If a weaker member state fails to catch up or keep up, that can only be because its own economic actors have failed to transform their behaviour to grasp the opportunities; they have only themselves to blame. If they experience greater economic prosperity, then that is a vindication of the theory.

The argument being made here is not that all this is going to happen. It clearly isn't; the inter-governmental conferences (IGCs) of the second half of 1990 and the first half of 1991 demonstrated that EMU was still a set of proposals to be negotiated and they would not emerge unscathed, as was confirmed by the Maastricht summit at the end of 1991, and the subsequent contortions to get it ratified. But the official version with its stress on sound money and the primacy of liberal economics does establish the terrain of discussion. It is the starting point for assessments for the future.

An underlying assumption in the present paper is that a stable European unity is unlikely to emerge if there are large disparities between regions and nations and interest groups. It is thus pertinent to ask whether the Delors proposals for EMU, as exemplified in the special issue of *European Economy*, make it easier, or more difficult, to tackle the problem of equitable distribution in the EC. In theoretical terms this version of EMU is set within a specifically monetarist problematic. In the original 1989 Delors report the sole declared aim of monetary policy was 'price stability' to be imposed by a politically independent central bank which would have this objective written into its constitution. *European Economy* then argued that an essential corollary of EMU was budgetary discipline. The members states would lose control over monetary policies and be greatly constrained as to which fiscal policy they could pursue. In practice, this meant that expansionary fiscal policies aimed at boosting employment or accelerating growth would be prevented or limited; the reality of fiscal discipline was the imposition of deflationary policies on the weaker peripheral economies.

There is very little appeal to evidence to support the beneficial claims made for this particular approach. The main empirical underpinning is provided by the use made of West German experience as an exemplar of these benefits. The solid basis for this is that Germany has clearly been the great European economic success. The Commission confidently attributes this economic success almost entirely to Germany's persistent pursuit of sound money, with the implication that what has been good for Germany will necessarily be good for the rest.

There are several problems with this interpretation. It could, for example, be argued that Germany, with its large social welfare sector, is not an economy which can reasonably be presented as fitting the free market stereotype. Moreover, whilst it is obviously true that monetary policy has been an important feature of modern Germany, it is still possible to question the legitimacy of abstracting monetary policy and monetary institutions from everything else in the economy. Germany has other distinctive national economic characteristics: the supportive relations between banks and industrial firms; a particular way of organizing industrial relations; and a long tradition of stressing education and vocational training.

More specifically, an interpretation which concentrates simply on Germany's monetary rectitude as an exemplar for EC-wide arrangements rests on a serious misreading of Germany's economic success. In particular it omits what the present writer would argue has been the essential active direct source of that success: namely, the superior productive competence of German manufacturing, and especially of German engineering firms. It is important to note that that is a success which is unexplained (is, indeed, inexplicable) simply by any orthodox theory of prices and costs.

It may be that German reunification has raised the question of whether this productive success will be disrupted. The judgement here is that the disruptions will be temporary and will have the short-term effect of improving the balance of payments of the other major EC countries with Germany. That is speculative, but it is clear that until 1990 German productive efficiency was the basis for the emergence, whether consciously or unconsciously, of a unique division of responsibility between public authorities and private capital. Whatever the intentions, the practice has been that the federal government and the Bundesbank have maintained restrictive fiscal and monetary policies which have constrained the level of domestic demand, and a competent manufacturing sector has evaded the contractionist consequences of that and created its own reflationary solution by finding markets in other European countries. It is instructive that, despite plummeting economic activity in Germany in 1993, the Bundesbank still clung to its restrictive policies; and, even more instructive, the orthodox belief in an independent European central bank modelled on the Bundesbank remained unshaken.

Be that as it may, what must be emphasized is that the historical German pattern makes it literally incredible for Germany to act as a model for all the other member states. To begin with, most of them lack the German level of manufacturing competence. Beyond that it is simply not possible for all the EC countries to secure economic success by running surpluses on intra-EC trade: they cannot all have surpluses with each other.

5. Efficacy

As a postscript we can perhaps add the additional question: is this the way to build Europe? In placing its faith in EMU, the Commission is again hoping to secure European political union as a by-product of an essentially economic policy. Apart from the fact that this is the strategy which worked so well in the 1992 programme where the single economic market concept was skilfully used to restore movement to the concept of a political Europe, the approach has a strong logical content. It is difficult to imagine EMU, especially as it moves towards a single currency or 'irretrievably locked' currencies, without a great deal of political integration of one sort or another. None the less it is highly questionable whether the very doctrinaire form of EMU espoused by the Commission will foster an integration which has the necessary stability. The Commission's monetarist scheme is one which pushes the burden of any necessary adjustment (which essentially means deflation, contraction and unemployment) on to the weaker peripheral countries which are to be disciplined to prevent them evading or easing the burden. Redistribution from richer to poorer countries is to be constrained, both for ideological reasons and as a simple consequence of the Community's income being kept low in relation to EC GDP. There are to be strong monetary institutions at the centre, but there are, despite UK phobias, no plans to construct a financially strong federal power.

In this context it is difficult to see how the Commission's regional and social rhetoric can be given any real substance. Specifically, given the scale of the problem with the EC now including several countries closer to Third World incomes and structures, it is hard to envisage how the resources available can reduce, or even contain, the disparities in income and employment. On past trends, there are good grounds for expecting that the result will be that the economic distribution of the costs and benefits of EMU within the EC will be highly unequal. And *that* represents a development which is divisive, and which can only endanger future European unity by increasing instability.

The argument of this paper rests on an overall value judgement that the trend towards European unity is desirable. To end with a brief suggestion of an alternative way of building Europe entails a further subjective view about the kind of Europe which is thought desirable. The proposal would be for a strong, democratic, federal European government which has substantial financial resources, reflects regional opinions and can make possible positive regional redistribution to lagging nations and regions. Any such objective would require a radically different approach; instead of relying on economics as the driving force (or stalking horse?) for political change, the ultimate political aim should be made explicit and constitute the starting-point. The IGCs of 1990 and 1991 rapidly exposed some of the dangers and illusions of relying on hard monetary policy as the road to unity. If there is to be a stable and cohesive Europe, all the national players must be seen to have a stake, to derive positive benefit and to exercise influence: for this, the most likely Community structure is one which is both effective and democratic.

It might seem that such a conclusion would be undermined by the outcome of the Maastricht meeting in December, 1991. Although the heads of government accepted the overall economic objectives (EMU, single currency etc.) of the Delors Plan, its implementation emerged in more ambiguous forms, which made it unsuitable for what had been Delors' basic purpose – the furtherance of political unity. Thus the conditions for monetary union were kept in their original stringent form but with the significant recognition that it was doubtful whether a majority, much less all, of the EC members would be able to reach these targets by the stipulated date of 1996. Indeed, a major feature of this summit meeting was the acquiescence by the Community in a 'pick and mix' philosophy allowing some members to go forward whilst others were still (presumably) striving to meet the various prerequisites. In the case of the social charter this was even carried to the extent of creating a 'new' Community of eleven, in order to accommodate (or isolate) Britain's intransigence.

Overall, the post-Maastricht lesson seemed to be that, in a period of general economic recession in Europe, several countries had reservations about a European economic policy based on a tight monetary stance with the suppression of inflation as the overriding objective. Such an approach carried with it a strong deflationary bias, particularly for the weaker, peripheral countries. The strategy of using economics to further European unity, which had seemed so effective in the 1992 programme, could no longer be counted upon. The reason for the earlier success was that, for all the hype, the economic aspects of 1992 were relatively innocuous; serious monetary union was, and is, a much more threatening prospect, more likely (as it has) to provoke disintegration than European unity. It thus seems more sensible to reverse the process: to make political unity the prior objective, the horse which will drag the economic cart along behind. And the framework for that political unity should be a strong federation with an effective federal budget able to pursue reflationary as well as deflationary policies.

References

Beveridge, W. (1909). *Unemployment: A Problem of Industry* (London, Longmans, Green, 1909).

Cecchini, P. (1988). *1992 – The European Challenge: The Benefits of a Single Market* (Aldershot, Wildwood House, 1988).

Cutler, T., Williams, K., and Williams, J. (1989). *1992 – The Struggle for Europe* (Oxford, Berg, 1989).

Eichengreen, B. (1990). 'One money for Europe? Lessons from the US currency union', *Economic Policy*, No. 10 (1990).

Commission of the European Communities (1985). *Completing the Internal Market*, White Paper (Brussels, European Commission, 1985).

Commission of the Europeam Communities (1988). *Research on the Cost of Non-Europe. Basic Findings*. 16 vols. (London, HMSO, 1988).

Commission of the European Communities (1990). 'One market, one money', *European Economy* (special issue) No. 44 (October 1990).

Commission of the European Communities (1991). *The Regions in the 1990s* (Brussels, European Commission, 1991).

Geroski, P. (1988). '1992 and European industrial structure in the twenty-first century' (mimeograph, London Business School, 1988).

Neuberger, H. (1989). *The Economics of 1992* (London, Socialist Group of European Parliament, 1989).

Padoa-Schioppa, T. (1987). *Efficiency, Stability and Equity: The European Community* (Oxford, Oxford University Press, 1987).

Smithin, J. (1990). *European Monetary Arrangements and National Economic Sovereignty: A Canadian Perspective* (Ontario, York University, 1990).

III SECTORS

5
The relevance of macroeconomics to agricultural problems

G. H. PETERS

1. Introduction

Agricultural economics is sometimes viewed as being wholly micro-based, especially within the context of highly developed countries. It is the study of a sector which can be very small in relation to the whole economy, and of the farms within it. Even if one extends subject boundaries to include backward-linking supplying sectors, and the forward-linked activities of food processing and distribution, the impression lingers that the issues, though they become more akin to those of industrial economics, remain micro-centred. The fact remains, however, that agriculture, like all sectors, operates within a macroeconomic framework and there is growing interest in the wider perspective.

The current debate runs in two directions. The farming consequences of macroeconomic developments, with much of the attention focusing on exchange rates and interest rates, have attracted considerable research. There is also another angle, partly generated by the costliness of agricultural policies in both Europe and the United States, and given a further twist by the central place which agriculture has assumed within the GATT Uruguay Round of negotiations, dealing with the effects of agricultural policies on the economy at large. There has, in short, been a deluge of literature in which macroeconomic themes have been stressed. Titles are easy to quote, although it is important to realize that the analysis under the title may be very different. One finds many pieces, often of American origin, on 'the effects of macro-policies on agriculture' (e.g. Kitchen and Monaco 1989). Not infrequently, however, there are other studies dealing with 'macroeconomic consequences of farm support policies' or 'economy-wide effects of agricultural policies'. Those are borrowed from Australian and OECD publications (Centre for International Economics 1988; OECD 1989–90).

2. The macroeconomy and agriculture

There can be few economists who are not fascinated by the intricate workings of the macroeconomy, and agricultural economists hardly need reminding of its importance. It is the interelationship between long-run growth, allied to the capacity of farmers to raise their own productivity, which is the prime factor in shaping the growth path of agriculture. Similarly, the birth of so much of agricultural policy resulted from the trauma experienced by farming as a short-run consequence of the great depression of the 1930s. The ground, to that extent, is familiar.

However, circumstances do alter. Thirty years ago, short-run macroeconomics, then very much of a Keynesian variety, could be relegated to the back burner. Around 1960 the macroeconomy was relatively stable. Unemployment was hardly an issue, inflation was modest, and exchange rates were governed by the Bretton Woods system. Some of the best-remembered flurries of macroeconomic interest in Britain occurred when devaluation became necessary (in 1949 and 1967) but, that apart, agriculture was locked into its own characteristic policy framework and little disturbed by extraneous factors. Events were 'made' within agriculture itself.

If there was British macroeconomic interest at the time it certainly did not come, as it were, 'downward' from major disturbance, but in the opposite direction. Problems of the macroeconomy appeared to stem from slow growth rather than instability, part of the cause being a balance of payments constraint. The argument was about the extent to which domestic farm output could help to break that constraint (Ritson 1977). It was not a question of what the macroeconomy might inflict on agriculture, but what agriculture might do for the macroeconomy.

A reminder of this background comes from Edward Schuh who wrote:

> Agricultural economics has grown up with a strong sectoral perspective, rooted in strong training in microeconomics. The theory of the firm has been our primary analytical tool. The theory of markets has not taken us much beyond partial equilibrium analysis

of agricultural markets. For the most part, we have little training in macroeconomics, and even less in the economics of general equilibrium. This perspective is less and less relevant to the kind of world which we now live in. Changes in the international economy and how individual countries relate to it, make it less and less relevant to think of agriculture as a sector of the economy. It is also less and less relevant to think about agriculture in the context of a closed economy. Instead it should be thought of as part of a well-integrated, open, international economy. (Schuh 1986)

He returned to the same theme in 1988 with the words:

Trying to understand the effects of macroeconomic policies on agriculture is of fairly recent vintage, although today it constitutes something of a growth area among agricultural economists. (Schuh 1989a)

There are many issues raised in these challenging comments. At the end of the first quotation, reference to an open international economy could simply be taken to mean that agricultural markets are interdependent on a global level, which is hardly a new theme. Schuh argued, however, that macro-events were impinging on agriculture in new and important ways. In effect, he was stating that the history of American agriculture should not be viewed solely in terms of the operation of commodity programmes. He was looking more deeply; in effect, viewing history as being a macro-feature with exchange rates being of particular relevance.

3. Exchange-rate economics

The theory of exchange rates can become complex. To establish basic terminology, assume a two-country world (B and A) with pounds and dollars as their currencies. If the exchange rate for B is expressed as the number of pounds required to purchase a dollar, devaluation of the pound then appears as an increase in the number of pounds involved. Should devaluation occur, B would tend to decrease imports from A, and to increase exports. Goods from A appear more expensive in B (more pounds are needed for a dollar), but for A, a dollar buys more pounds. The effects on trading sectors are obvious; advantages swing in favour of B. However, fixity of a nominal exchange rate as an aim of policy does not necessarily imply that incentives to trade remain unaltered. Constancy of the nominal value can disguise changes in the real exchange rate. The theory of purchasing power parity can be used as one illustration. Suppose that price indices are P_A and P_B, and that the fixed nominal exchange rate is E_n (number of pounds per dollar). Then the real exchange rate, E_r, relative to the base year of the inflation indices, is:

$$E_r = E_n . P_A / P_B$$

If country B has more rapid inflation, its real rate E_r diverges from E_n. The real exchange rate becomes revalued, and the nominal exchange rate can be described as overvalued, with consequent damage to producers of tradeable goods in B. If B residents can exchange pounds at a constant nominal rate per dollar, they will be anxious to do so; the pound buys less internally in B than it would purchase in A, if converted to dollars, since A inflation is lower. Imports are encouraged. Conversely, B goods will be less attractive to A and exports suffer. The effect will be felt as a trade deficit in B. By contrast, an undervalued currency (dollars in this case, for that is implicit) encourages exports and retards imports in A. Clearly if a nominal exchange rate is fixed for any length of time, when rates of inflation differ, there is a danger that it will become progressively misaligned. It is a feature of general application.

Nevertheless, generalized purchasing power parity changes are not the only feature which can cause divergence between real and nominal rates of exchange (Snape 1989). Theory stresses the key distinction between movements in the relative prices of tradeable and non-tradeable goods (a whole range of services for internal use, for example) within and between countries, caused by underlying productivity changes. A country which has particularly vibrant tradeable-goods sectors, with declining relative prices, could experience growing demand for its exports even with a nominally fixed exchange rate. Opposite effects would occur in a country with less well performing export and import replacing sectors which, even though it might be keeping inflation under control, could suffer the symptoms associated with an overvalued exchange rate. In the two cases foreign-exchange market effects would result, respectively, in pressure towards revaluation and devaluation of nominal exchange rates. There are obviously many examples in which such influences, added to those associated with differential rates of inflation, have forced adjustment to parities in fixed exchange rate systems, or have resulted in major variations in currency values under 'floating currency' regimes. The consequences for agriculture, where products are obviously tradeable, can be significant.

4. Experience in the US and the rest of the world

We turn first to the United States and the impact of exchange-rate effects. Significantly, a great deal also centres on the agricultural policy instruments in use. To see this, consider a country with a major export presence operating a large commodity programme. This can be caricatured as a single support price for a particular commodity, below which supplies will be withdrawn by the authorities. This is the US loan rate mechanism operated through the Commodity Credit Corporation. We can ignore other trappings of policy such as acreage-control arrangements and deficiency payments. The importance of the loan-rate scheme is that it provides an internal price floor, while at the same time setting the dollar-denominated price at which exports reach the world market. Should market conditions be such that prices received by farmers exceed the loan rate, for whatever reason, the favourable agricultural consequences become obvious. In an export situation much depends on the world market where, in turn, the exchange rate converts nominal dollars into foreign currency values. Following devaluation US prices perceived in world markets in other currencies fall, total demand (internal plus external) is enhanced and farmgate prices may rise. Conversely, dollar revaluation damages export prospects, pressing internal prices towards the loan-rate floor.

To support his case, Schuh argued that the farm income difficulties apparent in the 1950s and 1960s were caused by a real overvaluation of the dollar, which was only relieved when devaluation occurred in 1971, and when there was a further fall in the exchange rate when the international monetary system became one of the 'floating currencies' in 1973. The subsequent export boom lasted until there was a marked shift in internal monetary policy in 1979. Increased interest rates, in addition to affecting the costs of capital intensive agriculture, also raised the external value of the dollar, curtailing export demand. The resulting farm crisis of the early 1980s was only relieved by some decline in the exchange rate from 1985.

Despite its simplifications, this outline is sufficient to support Schuh's hypothesis that it has been the management of the US macroeconomy, reverberating through the dollar exchange rate and changes in interest rates, which underlies decades of American agricultural experience. It is not a story in which significant attention is given to potential changes in internal demand effects flowing from variation of personal incomes; elasticities are too low for that to be of importance, while internal redistributive mechanisms also cushion unemployed workers from income collapse. In short the internal scenario, even in the time of greatest difficulty in the early 1980s, was not one of 'agriculture in depression' in the style of the 1930s. The striking feature is the explanation of changing agricultural fortunes in terms of a set of variables which are external to agricultural policy *per se*. Adjustments in commodity programmes, of which there have been many over the years, do no more than lurk in the background.

It is not only in the United States that the fashion for analysing agricultural change in a broad macroeconomic setting has spread. Sector-specific policy – if it exists – should not, so the argument runs, be viewed in isolation, since it may be either reinforced or nullified by the indirect consequences of broader policies. There are numerous examples, including the Australian case (O'Mara 1990), though the setting is frequently in developing countries, which have become a major focus of analysis prompted by the World Bank. The *locus classicus* is the 1986 *World Development Report* (World Bank 1986). In this context broader policies may have a trade component (that is, the taxation of imports or of exports, or quantitative restrictions on trade) but also involve typical fiscal, monetary and (real) exchange-rate interplay.

A brief scenario runs along the following lines. Restrict imports of industrial goods to promote domestic activity. Use an overvalued exchange rate to make essential imports of key industrial goods appear cheap in local-currency terms. Sustain the overvaluation by external borrowing, and also use funds to expand public services. Run up a budget deficit, partly financed by monetary expansion. If all of this results in inflation, maintain continued overvaluation by slow adjustment of the nominal exchange rate. Simultaneously, through sector-specific policies, attempt to stimulate agriculture which, as is often the case, may be a major source of external finance. Not surprisingly the overvalued exchange rate hinders agricultural exports, and cheapens food imports. The end result is a collapse of agricultural incentive. If agricultural exports are taxed as one apparently obvious source of fiscal revenue the situation deteriorates further.

5. A European Community perspective

In the light of the previous sections, and given the pervasive analytic fashion, there must, at least, be some expectation that the history of European Community agriculture will have been influenced by macroeconomic developments. Indeed, given the complex agromonetary system which has been such a feature of the CAP, one might immediately expect the impression to be reinforced. However, while it is obviously true that operation of European instruments has been enormously complicated by a twenty-year history of exchange-rate disturbance, nevertheless agricultural management has always involved strong elements of policy choice, in which a frequent aim has been to guide agriculture through the macroeconomic currents.

The difference between the USA and the EC stems from a contrasting structural situation, and from the way in which that has conditioned policy instruments. If the USA, with export-dominated agriculture, was to support prices for major products, the older mechanisms adopted virtually had to affect external sales. Once a loan rate was in place, the extent to which prices received by farmers could rise above that level came to depend on the exchange rate, which in turn was dependent on macro-policy. Observers of the American scene will realize that these statements apply strictly to loan rates rather than to deficiency payments, and they apply most forcibly to loan rates which do not 'shadow' world prices, as they do under more recent arrangements.

European history is different; imports were more important and this resulted in a much stronger focus on internal prices as immediate targets. Blocking out movements in entry prices by variable levies insulated agriculture, hence on the revenue side any movement in external exchange rates which could affect entry prices became inconsequential. Similarly when exporting became more prevalent, the technique shifted to making compensatory changes in export restitutions as a bridge between internal and external price levels. Given the framework of policy there is less room for parallels between European developments and those in the USA. The type of roller-coaster ride experienced by American farmers (upwards in the late 1970s and downwards in the early 1980s for example), forced on them by exogenous macroeconomics, has not been nearly so obvious a feature. One gains the impression from Schuh's work that American agricultural policy can be thrown off course in meeting what might broadly be described as farm income objectives. The key issue is the extent to which any of this carries over into the Community. In a group of twelve nations there are too many specific cases to be considered for simple answers to be given. Hence my treatment will concentrate on providing impressions rather than on stating a definitive view. To illustrate basic principles, a little detail is needed. For CAP regimes to function, a unit of account must be denominated in some way. In the original six, forging the Community in an era of 'fixed' exchange rates in the 1960s, the problem was solved, in essence, by denominating the unit of account as the equivalent of the dollar and translating at central rates for currencies against that yardstick. When that no longer became possible from mid-1973, a currency 'basket' was used, made up from the currencies of those countries within the 'joint float', which by 9 March 1979 was transformed into the European Monetary System (EMS) with the European Currency Unit (ECU) as the denominating instrument.

This history hardly requires vast elaboration. The only important point to note is that no matter how a unit is fixed it must, by its nature, generally be 'external' when viewed from the vantage point of an individual member country. If this somewhat bald statement can be accepted (the invention of the agricultural ECU in 1984 will appear later), the crucial issue for farming becomes the rate at which the external denominator converts into national currency. It is crucial simply because for any commodity affected by a CAP regime the translation is total; similarly, any alteration in the conversion factor produces an effect on the revenue side which is complete. This feature distinguishes agriculture from other sectors; there appears to be nowhere to hide and no escape. As a basic proposition one can immediately infer that in a strong monetary union, with nominal exchange rates which are permanently fixed, and with those nominal rates determining agricultural conversions to common prices (i.e. green rates are not allowed to diverge) domestic agricultural output, and the income which it generates in any country, will be determined in a very rigid manner. Clearly the 'common' price level is a matter for Community choice but that is all; once it is agreed, the agriculture of any single country appears to be at the mercy of the domestic macroeconomic setting.

However, one major complication arose which had the effect of modifying the system. After 1969, and for more than twenty years, conversion of 'common' prices into national currency values was not necessarily accomplished using the denominated central rates. Instead countries in which devaluation or revaluation had occurred were given some freedom to substitute alternative 'green rates' of exchange to shift their internal agricultural and food prices to higher or lower levels than would otherwise have been the case. Divergences were sustained by the use of monetary compensatory amounts (MCAs) which acted essentially either as charges on imports, when positive, or as import subsidies, when negative (Peters 1980, Swinbank 1988). Hence there were 'common prices', set in terms of the unit of account, but their translation into national currencies involved an element of choice by each country. Effectively this meant that there was no true 'common market' in farm products.

Recognition of elements of the two contrasting situations in so much of Community history is not a matter of great difficulty. An overvalued green rate, relative to the national exchange rate, and the appearance of negative monetary compensatory amounts (MCAs) were indicators of the adverse case; an undervalued green rate and positive MCAs were the opposite. Of course we are now running backwards; the contemporary edge of the 'green money' controversy is dulled by the appearance of '1992' and by general efforts to eliminate MCAs. Much of the detail relating to MCAs and 'nationalization' of the CAP appears in Parris and Peters (1983). The point which needs emphasis is that, in addition to being a weapon of agricultural policy, the agromonetary system could be a distributional instrument and one of more general macroeconomic policy. This was inherent in its genesis in 1969 when German farmers were shielded from the consequences of a mark revaluation, while those in France were not, the escapees from franc devaluation being consumers. In addition to the distributional consequences, Germany was more successful in macroeconomic management; there was less need to bear down on inflation, by reducing food prices, than in France, where not raising them was a matter of importance.

We have British experience of a similar nature. When CAP regimes began to be phased in from February 1973 the pound had already become a floating currency (June 1972). It was obviously important to manage agricultural prices, against that background, to prevent exchange fluctuations disturbing major markets. The question became one of fixing the green rate (and later its commodity-specific values) in relation to the fluctuating market rate. They were initially close although, given the macroeconomic circumstances, the pound began a steep plunge which was not to cease until 1977. This was a complex period, because the phasing in of EC price levels was due only by January 1978. That, in fact, mattered little, especially to grain producers – the world market had 'taken over' with the producer return on wheat, for example, being 62 per cent above the guaranteed level in 1973–4. The progressively overvalued green rate was also academic; the bite came when the world market calmed from 1977. Though there was progressive green-rate devaluation it was insufficient to compensate for the market devaluation, and negative MCAs approached 40 per cent. Farming income was coming under increased pressure from cost increases, but in the inflationary circumstances of that disturbed era, green-rate devaluation was resisted; food-price moderation was regarded as an important prop to incomes policy, which was a major anti-inflationary weapon. In short, the policy choice was not exercised in agriculture's favour.

From 1979 in the early years of Conservative administration policy choice, in agromonetary terms, was exercised in the opposite direction. As in the USA, and for similar reasons, there was exchange-rate appreciation, but this was allowed to generate moderate positive MCAs for the first half of the decade of the 1980s; policy became temporarily protective. The interesting feature, however, was that the allowable MCAs were insufficient to shield farmers from the cause of exchange-rate appreciation, namely the upward swing in interest rates. There was a very distinctive change in the shares of net product accruing to 'farming income' and 'interest' elements (as conventionally defined), from the late 1970s into the early 1980s. That persisted; the interest share by 1989 had risen to 20 per cent of net product or almost three times the late 1970s level. Agriculture was not hit by the twin thrusts of exchange-rate appreciation and high interest rates, so damaging to manufacturing in the early 1980s, but it could not escape the latter which remained a continuous source of macro-induced pain. Subject to 'common prices' and other policy instruments having been set on a Community-wide basis − the element in the equation which has not been considered − one can hardly fail to recognize some affinity with Schuh's analysis. It can be pursued into land-market behaviour, where boom had been transformed into stagnation.

The trap of overvaluation was then dramatically eased by the events of September 1992, when sterling suffered a forced withdrawal from the exchange-rate mechanism with associated devaluation and the easing of interest-rate pressures. Sterling became a 'floating currency' with respect to 'narrow band' members of the ERM. However, there was also another factor of great importance. A green-rate mechanism remained in operation and it might be expected, therefore, that the British government would have a measure of choice in deciding whether or not to follow a fall in the exchange value of sterling by green-rate devaluation, which had been of importance on earlier occasions. Under provisions of the Single European Act (often spoken of as the 'single market' associated with 1992) that freedom was, to a large extent, removed and a rise in the institutional prices of farm products became virtually automatic. In short, British agriculture was expected to experience all of the favourable consequences of readjustment in the value of an overvalued currency, and similar effects were expected in Italy, which also left the ERM, and in Spain and Portugal, where parity adjustments occurred in September 1992 and May 1993.

There has been one other complex twist in the Community story. To go no further back than the beginnings of EMS/ERM in March 1969, nominal exchange rates between participating countries have not been rigidly fixed; the system has been one of adjustable pegs. It is well known that Germany and the Netherlands have experienced appreciating currencies against the remainder of the EMS group. Among the latter, the relative devaluations have frequently eased the pressures experienced by farmers; indeed the events of the period from September 1992 (including the further disturbance in the EMS of August 1993) to an extent continue previous episodes. The issue then shifts to the agricultural effects of revaluation. It is again complicated by possible divergence between 'green rates' and 'central rates', though here the issue concerns the latter, with the focus being on Germany. Though there has been an improvement in agricultural productivity it cannot match that of the industrial sector, and there has been considerable difficulty in protecting farmers from the consequences of a rising DM exchange rate, so often associated with adjustments in ERM parities.

The classic answer, of course, was the positive MCA, though the appearance of such a device (and of negative MCAs in the opposite case) had the effect of splitting the Community into areas of greater or lesser agricultural protection and destroying any pretence that there was a 'common market'. The answer, devised in 1984, was the complex 'switchover' mechanism (Swinbank 1988), which absolves any revaluing country from the difficulty of erecting an MCA barrier. Basically what is involved amounts to nothing more than raising all of the ECU-denominated institutional prices within the many CAP commodity regimes, in proportion to the degree of appreciation of the leading currency (the coefficient used over the years since 1984 now cumulates to some 16 per cent). Hence farmers in revaluing countries do not suffer the fall in prices denominated in domestic currency which they would otherwise experience on general currency appreciation. Technically this has been done not by operating directly on institutional prices but by defining 'agricultural central rates' (or 'agricultural market rates' for those with floating currencies), which differ from the normal values by the agricultural coefficient. The effect, however, is similar to what could have been achieved by operating on the regime prices. References to the 'green ECU', which are often seen in agricultural reporting, relate to this mechanism.

One consequence has been of great significance in moves toward internal Community freedom of trade in agricultural products. Devaluations within the system were welcomed by the farmers affected, but revaluations were resisted or countered by positive MCAs. Given the switchover mechanism it has been easier to move towards a 'single market'. However, there is a suspicion, which is often emphasized in the United States, that the Community agricultural price levels relative to the rest of the world have been allowed to drift upwards as the DM has revalued.

Against this brief sketch of a vastly complex area are there pointers? Can we say that agricultural-sector management, directly impinging at the farm level, is prone to be blown off course by extraneous macroeconomic forces? This is a matter which must be distinguished from the technical issue of the manner in which policy is handled; that has been unbelievably complicated by exchange-rate behaviour. It is also one which must be distinguished from the way in which policy choice has been exercised, even though there may have been macroeconomic considerations which were borne in mind when choices were made. Tolerance of negative MCAs is one example in which agriculture has not been favoured; but that is a choice. Similarly, use of positive MCAs, or the adoption of switchover, is a reaction decision. Choice or reaction are opened by an initiating move, but that is not to be equated with helplessness. To search for the latter we can, however, note the very clear British examples of the importance of interest-rate effects. One can say that Schuh's fashion is not irrelevant, but it needs some adaptation.

However, that is not the end of the story. Agricultural policy also has costs; in this context, particularly, those which impinge on the Community budget. It is becoming evident that there may be relationships between costs and macroeconomic effects which influence world price levels. There are, of course, many reasons to account for open-endedness in budget costs; agricultural supply and demand conditions worldwide are obvious. To add to that, however, remember that the dollar/ECU relationship is market dominated; it is a floating-rate arrangement. Schuh (1986) made one assertion that an appreciation of the dollar has the effect of raising 'world prices', especially for grain. Since export restitution payments, in that sector, are an important budget element, such a move, specifically that associated with the dollar appreciation of the early 1980s, had an effect; it 'bailed the EC out of its costly commodity programs'. It was the reversal towards dollar devaluation post-1985 which made Community budgeting a matter of greater complexity; there was a view expressed by the Commission that a 10 per cent depreciation would itself raise CAP costs, on balance, by up to one billion ECU. Hence, quite apart from variability in world agricultural markets *per se* (one immediately thinks of the 1988 US drought), the volatility of the 'float' as between dollar and ECU means that the power simultaneously to control internal CAP price levels and budget costs is curtailed (Meester 1987).

One must also ask another macro-related question. It is often contended that the general depressed state of world markets, which was only temporarily adjusted by the US drought, is the consequence of protectionism, allied to export subsidization. That can hardly be totally denied. Nevertheless many of the countries which figure as importers (the newly industrializing nations, or those with oil revenues, and a surprising number of less developed countries) have felt the draught of the recession of the early 1980s which has been perpetuated by the hangover of debt problems. We no longer tend to think in terms of 'agriculture in a depression' as a developed country phenomenon – insulation occurs – but it may well be one of the macroeconomic influences which is currently operating at a global level.

6. Macroeconomic consequences of agricultural policies

We now change tack, reversing the direction of causation. The object is to consider the broader consequences, specifically of agricultural policies, on the economy at large. A focus on policy is deliberate; it should be obvious that in some circumstances a disturbance in agricultural markets may, if agriculture is important enough, itself be a source of macroeconomic problems. Deliberate policy, however, is quite another matter. Here it is protectionism and its consequences which form the main item on the agenda.

In section two there was a reference to the contribution which agricultural expansion might make to breaking balance of payments constraints. The focus there was on the net effect on the external situation, rather than on unqualified 'import saving'; resource costs were involved, and resources have potential alternative uses in exporting sectors. It was natural to think in that way (Moore and Peters 1965), since we were told by the 1947 Agriculture Act to consider the output level which 'in the national interest it is desirable to produce in the United Kingdom'. Josling (1969) took the argument a stage further; he remained interested in exchange savings associated with alternative configurations of policy (deficiency payments, variable levies, minimum import prices) but he also showed that the 'economic cost' of agricultural policies can be measured more systematically. In the simplest format (i.e. one involving the assumption that a pound is always counted as a pound regardless of the parties involved), an agricultural policy has a welfare impact which is the algebraic sum of producer, consumer, and taxpayer effects. Out of this has grown a voluminous literature which suggests that developed world agricultural protectionism is expensive. For example:

> Rice protection alone is estimated to have cost Japanese society $2.9 billion – 0.6 per cent of Japan's GNP. The costs of the CAP to the EC were $15.4 billion in 1980, or 0.6 per cent of GNP. Even traditional agricultural producers were not immune ... the United States lost almost $4 billion in total agricultural support in 1984–85. (World Bank 1986)

This quotation was chosen since its authorship (and dating) were influential, though similar sentiments have been expressed elsewhere. It has not been academic number-swopping; it has become the intellectual foundation for the very serious business of GATT Uruguay Round negotiations, which began in 1986 and were originally timetabled to reach a conclusion in December 1990. Major disagreement on agricultural issues between the European Community and the United States resulted in the Brussels meeting ending in stalemate, though efforts to rescue the Uruguay Round resulted in the final agreement of December 1993. The reforms in the CAP introduced by Commissioner McSharry in 1992 provided the basis for an eventual agreement. They are not directly related to any of the agromonetary arrangements described in section five, which effectively stand, but do attempt to lower Community price levels (notably in the critical grain sector), or reinforce production quotas, compensating farmers by a system of direct payments which is not related to output.

My main concern is not the negotiation details of GATT; it is with methodology. Hence the brief excursion into older British controversies (that will reappear); a method of analysis (Josling's) which is now almost commonplace grew out of what, to the world at large, was a somewhat parochial issue. It is, of course, not at all the same thing as the 'Schuh' fashion for analysing macroeconomic effects on agriculture. The phrase 'macroeconomic consequences of farm support policies' signifies an exercise in what might be more aptly thought of as the economics of resource allocation, or trade and welfare policy. Interestingly, however, there is a strong echo in the first Schuh quotation in section two concerning partial and general equilibrium.

Research on policy costs, and the closely related issue of the effects of trade liberalization, has become an art-form with its own methodological style. It is an exercise in counterfactual hypothesis, using a simulation approach, where the test bed may be the world agricultural economy, distinguishing countries or groups of countries in greater or less detail. Major commodity groupings also appear, again at various levels of aggregation. In important cases (Tyers and Anderson 1988, and the many examples quoted by World Bank 1986) the boundaries of the models employed are agriculture-related only. Using 'appropriate' supply and demand elasticities, models are calibrated to reproduce an existing base-year situation, and then re-estimated to derive post-liberalization effects, or in some cases to look at more limited reductions in protection. Exercises are strictly 'partial equilibrium' in nature, though they can become extremely complex, since simulations may run across so many commodity/country interrelationships. Some are 'static' (i.e. time paths in reaching new equilibria are not considered), and the 'before' and 'after' situations must be interpreted 'as if' the initiating change had somehow occurred; others incorporate more 'dynamic' elements. From this material emerge the familiar 'welfare' effects, simulated impacts on 'world prices', and sometimes estimates of the degree to which the latter might exhibit decreased variability (Gardner 1989; OECD 1989–90).

The results, according to Gardner (1989) have brought 'the calculation of economic benefits and costs out in the open', helping, possibly, in 'removing one area of troublesome recalcitrance in pushing the world toward an overall liberal trade regime'.

Nevertheless, there are important issues to be borne in mind. The first is that the ammunition is less explosive than it might appear. This is implicit in the World Bank quotation − billions of dollars of 'loss' from protectionism evaporate quickly, when viewed in relation to GNP or to population. For example, the net welfare effect of world liberalization on EC12 for 1980−2 is placed by Tyers and Anderson at $7.5 billion (1985); with population at 318 million this is $24 per person, although their 1995 'projection' is admittedly higher ($17.6 billion). Obviously the combined 'consumer and taxpayer' effect alone is larger ($42.8 billion, or $91.3 billion projected, or some $135 per head of total population for 1980 – 2) but the view which one takes of this depends entirely on whether it is felt that 'producers' should be compensated for their loss. If that rule is adhered to, any move towards liberalization is hardly enough to shake the economic foundations. It is, of course, what one would immediately suspect; even gross protection of a small sector must have a similarly small overall impact.

The second problem is deeper. If there is a suggestion from 'partial equilibrium' results that gains are possible, how is it envisaged that they are to be realized? The obvious answer is via reallocation of resources; one moves from an implicit expression of faith (the gains will appear somehow!) to exploration of tangible possibilities, or in short from partial to general equilibrium where the 'markets' considered extend beyond the boundaries of agriculture. A resource flow out of farming (or associated food processing) must affect markets for erstwhile intermediate inputs, and for labour and capital; it will have external consequences (either more food imports or less exports, and induced trade flows in non-agricultural sectors operating, potentially, through real exchange rates); it will affect the terms on which non-agricultural sectors are able to acquire inputs or sell output as they expand to take up the slack. This is the field for (computable) general equilibrium modelling, where many more interrelationships are considered than in an agricultural 'elasticities' model, and where the theoretical structure can incorporate optimizing behaviour in producing and consuming sectors. Collections are readily available from the Centre for International Economics (1988) and OECD (1989 – 90).

It is never easy to get to the heart of CGE models in order to trace through the many behavioural relationships which they incorporate; models can become a 'black box' in which one is forced to trust the judgement of authors. The important point, once again, is that it often does not appear difficult to run 'liberalization' scenarios which have dramatically serious effects on agriculture, potentially large savings in government budgets when support expenditure is initially large, but minimal 'economy wide' consequences. For example, Robinson, Adelman and Kilkenny (CIE 1988) simulate the behaviour of the United States economy from 1986 to 1991. Using sector income as a measure, on a number of agricultural policy change scenarios, the maximum impact on farming is a reduction of some 18.9 per cent (unilateral cessation of support), though a fall of only 4.4 per cent could accompany multilateral liberalization (world prices rise). The results, and those of Hertel, Thompson and Tsigas in the same collection, produce the type of suggestion common from 'partial' analysis. Protectionism is best attacked multilaterally; it is an inefficient method of support; and the savings of governmental expenditure alone provide an accessible source of compensation payments. However, while the usefulness of such results is granted, the economy-wide effects, after allowing for modelled reallocations are minuscule. Surprisingly, in the work of Robinson *et al.*, they actually suggest a minor fall, of about 0.4 per cent, in non-agricultural real income.

Similar effects appear in the latest WALRAS modelling exercise of OECD (OECD 1989–90) of multilateral liberalization based on 1986–8 levels of support, which are to be read 'as if' they refer to long-term consequences. The results, in brief, are that agricultural output is severely affected except in the cases of New Zealand and Australia (note the Canadian and USA consequences); in relation to real income, economy-wide, this shows through most in New Zealand again, but fades elsewhere. The dimensions are less than a year's normal growth. It must be noted also that the actual impact of the 1993 GATT agreement is likely to be even less, since it by no means achieves the 'full liberalization' commonly assumed in the modelling exercises reported here.

It must be stated, however, that more dramatic results can be found. Stoekel and Brechling (CIE 1988) perform a retrospective counterfactual exercise for the four major EC countries (Germany, UK, France and Italy) through the 1980s. The GDP results (a 3 per cent gain for the first two countries, less elsewhere) are larger, though they put more weight on the employment impact, suggesting that three million jobs would have been preserved had protection been removed. It appears in the following way. To support one sector others must be 'taxed', either directly or indirectly through food prices. As the transfer is 'extracted' from the economy at large, it has a first-round effect of reducing real wages. This then encounters real-wage resistance (i.e. nominal wages are forced upward), and it is that inflexible adjustment which forces a contraction in employment. This is a 'classical'

Table 1: Multilateral liberalization simulation 1986–8: OECD 'WALRAS' model

Percentage changes

Real income			
EC	1.4	Canada	1.3
Japan	1.1	New Zealand	2.7
USA	0.3	Australia	0.8
Agricultural output			
EC	−18.7	Canada	−16.7
Japan	−24.2	New Zealand	7.9
USA	−7.0	Australia	4.4

Source: Martin et al., 'Economy-wide effects of agricultural policies in OECD countries: simulation results with WALRAS', Table 5. The source contains comparisons with the RUNS and IIASA models; the former providing EC real-income effects more than double those in WALRAS, other countries being aggregated. IIASA has tiny effects, the largest (1.1%) being for Japan. Full references appear in Martin et al.

mechanism, rather than an explanation of unemployment along Keynesian, demand deficiency, lines. Frankly it is difficult to see how the sea-change which occurred in unemployment levels in the 1980s was, in any sense, caused by agricultural protection. The reasons appear to lie in general deflationary policies. At the very least, one could retort by arguing that protection of agriculture has been ongoing for decades and that it was associated, up to the 1980s, with remarkably low unemployment levels.

7. Conclusions

A large proportion of this essay has dwelt on the 'Schuh fashion' for interpreting agricultural history as being, at least, conditioned by macroeconomic side-effects. Though interpretation can be difficult, and needs to be interwoven with analysis of inherently variable agricultural market conditions and of policy aims and interactions, it is compelling material. It has certainly forced agricultural economists to alter their views concerning the wider forces which impact on the farm sector. In the world context, the question raised is whether agricultural markets will recover from the currently low level of prices – which is in part a symptom of the 1980s and which may be exacerbated should the recessionary tendencies evident in 1991–3 become more serious. Within the European Community the budgetary costs of the CAP, which pose such a problem, are partly related to the levels of international prices, and also tied in with the relative values of the dollar and the ECU. My second theme, the backwash from agricultural policy to the macroeconomy, has been desperately cursory. Some of it ('partial' analysis) will have been familiar; the expansion (into general equilibrium) is beginning to flood. My own view remains equivocal. There is certainly a sense in which partial equilibrium results leave unanswered questions about reallocation pathways and potential effects (the same questions that arose, in principle, in early British debate); but I sit uneasily between admiration of potentially valuable model-building arts and suspicion. We know that there are 'costs of protection' (the fact that their magnitude has been played down is realism, rather than conversion to the protectionist cause), but we should be wary of what could be regarded as a search for a needle in a macroeconomic haystack, namely the damaging effect of agricultural protection on unemployment and the general macroeconomic balance.

Note

This is a substantially revised version of the author's presidential address to the Agricultural Economics Society, March 1991 (Peters 1991).

References

Centre for International Economics (1988). *Macroeconomic Consequences of Farm-Support Policies* (Overview and seminar papers), (Canberra, Centre for International Economics, 1988; London, Trade Policy Research Centre, 1988). For citations of Hertel, Thompson and Tsigas; Robinson, Adelman and Kilkenny; Stoekel and Brechling.

Dixit, Praveen M., *et al.* (1989). 'Global implications of agricultural trade liberalization', in United States Department of Agriculture' *Agricultural Food Policy Review*, (Washington, ERS, 1989), Agricultural Economic Report No. 620, 253–274.

Gardner, B. (1989). 'Recent studies of agricultural trade Liberalization', in Maunder and Valdes, 361–79.

Josling, T. (1969). 'A formal approach to agricultural policy', *Journal of Agricultural Economics*, 20 No. 2, 175–91.

Kitchen, J. and Monaco, R. (1989). 'Effects of macro-economic policies on agriculture', in USDA, *Agriculture Food Policy Review* op. cit.

McCrone, G. (1962). *The Economics of Subsidising Agriculture* (London, George Allen & Unwin, 1962).

Martin, J. P. *et al.* (1989–90). 'Economy-wide effects of agricultural policies in OECD countries: simulation results with WALRAS', in OECD *Economic Studies*, loc. cit.

Maunder, A. H. and Renborg, U. (1986). *Agriculture in a Turbulent World Economy* (IAAE Spain 1985), (Aldershot, Gower, 1986).

Maunder, A. H. and Valdes, A. (1989). *Agriculture and Governments in an Interdependent World* (IAAE Argentina, 1988), (Aldershot, Dartmouth, 1989).

Meester, G. (1987). 'Budget constraints and international realities in the CAP', *European Review of Agricultural Economics* 14, No. 1 (1987), 37–42.

Moore, L. and Peters, G. H. (1965). 'Agriculture's balance of payments contribution', *Westminster Bank Review* (August 1965).

O'Mara, L. P. (1990). 'Exchange rates, interest rates and agriculture: a macro-economic view from down under', in T. Grennes, *International Financial Markets and Agricultural Trade* (Boulder, San Francisco and London, Westview Press, 1990), 160–213.

Organization for Economic Co-operation & Development (1989–90). 'Modelling the effects of agricultural policies', *O.E.C.D. Economic Studies* (Special issue) 13 (Winter). Specific citation is of Martin *et al.* but the volume has a useful general overview of many modelling exercises.

Parris, K. P. and Peters, G. H. (1983). 'Agricultural commodity trade in a regime of floating exchange rates', *World Agricultural Economics and Rural Sociology Abstracts*, 25 No. 4 (1983), 241–69.

Peters, G. H. (1980). 'The green pound: a simplified expository analysis', *Journal of Agricultural Economics*, 31 No. 1 (1980), 113–20.

Peters, G. H. (1991). 'Agriculture and the macro-economy: Presidential Address', *Journal of Agricultural Economics*, 42 No. 3, September 1991, 231–49.

Ritson, C. (1977). *Agricultural Economics: Principles and Policy* (London Crosby Lockwood Staples, 1977), chapter 7.

Schuh, G. Edward (1974). 'The exchange rate and US agriculture', *American Journal of Agricultural Economics*, 56 No. 1 (1974) 1–13.

Schuh, G. Edward (1986). 'The international capital market as a source of instability in agricultural commodity markets', in Maunder and Renborg, op. cit., 83–90.

Schuh, G. Edward (1989a). 'Macro-linkages and agriculture; the United States experience', in Maunder and Valdes, op. cit., 533 – 41.
Schuh, G. Edward (1989b). 'Exchange rates and pricing: impacts on national economies, food consumption and agriculture', in Helmuth and Johnson (Editors), *1988 World Food Conference Proceedings* (Ames, Iowa State University Press), 77 – 89.
Snape, R. H. (1989). 'Real exchange rates, real interest rates and agriculture', in Maunder and Valdes, op. cit., 519 – 32.
Swinbank, A. (1988). *Green 'Money', MCAs and the Green ECU*, Agra-Europe Special Report No.47 (Tunbridge Wells, Agra-Europe, 1988).
Tyers, R. and Anderson, K. (1988). 'Liberizing OECD agricultural policies in the Uruguay Round', *Journal of Agricultural Economics*, 39 No. 2 (1988), 197 – 216.
World Bank (1986). *World Development Report 1986* (Oxford, Oxford University Press, 1986) chapters 4, 5 and 6.

6
The Common Transport Policy and its impact on peripherality in the European community

J. HUGH REES*

1. Introduction

In the light of the current debate on the future of the European Community, this paper takes a retrospective and prospective look at the Common Transport Policy (CTP) with a view to examining whether it is simply the gradual application of the necessary basic rules for a customs union. The argument is advanced that in practice it has become something more than a common transport competition policy and now presents a balance between competition and wider socio-economic objectives. The subject is especially appropriate in view of Ted Nevin's interest in EC regional analysis; hence the question of the CTP and its impact on peripherality will be given special attention.

2. The Common Transport Policy

It is hardly necessary to stress the importance of efficient transport for any economic union; indeed, customs barriers, together with transport costs, are *the* great barriers to closer integration. It was clear from the very beginning of the European Community that its development depended to a large degree upon the fluidity of trade and travel between its regions. However, although an efficient transport sector is vital, efficiency in the transport sector has been shown to need more than the creation of the proverbial English 'level playing field' and then standing back to watch the players get on with the game. Over time, it has been found that transport is a very difficult pitch to level. To the extent that there has been a greater rate of success in implementing a CTP in recent years, this is due to the fact that the initial, rather doctrinaire, approach to policy development has given way to a more modulated strategy that recognizes the peculiarities of the transport sector.

The first steps towards the creation of the CTP can be traced back to 1955; in that year the European Coal and Steel Community (ECSC) – the forerunner of the EEC devoted to creating a free market in coal and steel products – agreed to establish international through rates for goods by rail.[1] In March 1957 the Treaty of Rome setting up the EEC was signed. Title IV of the treaty, articles 75–84, set out in very general terms what form the CTP should take. However, as the articles of the title were rather general, it was four years later, in 1961, that the Commission presented to the Council of Ministers a first comprehensive memorandum which laid down the guidelines for organizing the transport sector. Hardly suprisingly, the ideas set out by the Commission were developed directly from the basic principles of the Treaty of Rome. The principal objective was to promote the unification of the transport market, and to that end the following aims were identified:

free choice of the means of transport by users;
equality of treatment for modes of transport and for carriers;
financial and commercial independence for transport enterprises;
co-ordination of transport infrastructure.

In practice these became the key objectives that the CTP has followed ever since. It is evident that there was a considerable influence from the 'competition' aspects of the treaty. Again this is not surprising as the Community is a free-trading area and as such, competition rules are an essential ingredient for success. However, this paper aims to show there is more to achieving these objectives than simply ensuring free competition. Moreover, even after many years of experience, it is clear that these objectives can be interpreted in a number of ways and they do not simply require the application of the free-market philosophy of Adam Smith to the transport sector. However, these rather general objectives have played a key role in the course of development of Community policy as the very diverse nature of member states' priorities led to differences of opinion regarding their application. These differences existed even amongst the original six members of the Community (Belgium, France, Germany, Italy, Luxembourg and the Netherlands). Hence, as the Community has expanded, the differences have certainly not diminished. In the period since 1957, the European Court of Justice has been called upon on several occasions to adjudicate on differences in interpretation. For the future, the increasing acceptance of the importance of the external consequences of transport may make a Community transport policy even more difficult to develop, although majority voting has now become the norm in the Council of Ministers on transport matters.

Even in the light of the various judgements handed down by the Court of Justice, it has not been easy to establish an operational strategy to implement the objectives of the CTP. However, from this it should not be concluded that the founding fathers of the Community considered transport unimportant or that they did not devote much thought to it. Indeed, the Treaty of Rome created only two specific policies, agriculture and transport; all other sectors, except those covered by the earlier ECSC and nuclear treaties, are only subject to the general provisions set down in the treaty, i.e. the free movement of goods, people, services and capital, and objectives concerning competition, social policy, monetary policy, etc. The problem, rather, was that transport was, and is, very important (6 to 7 per cent of GNP) and views on 'the' right transport policy differ substantially; hence the lack of specific objectives in the treaty has been of particular importance.

With hindsight and in the light of the very specific nature of transport, it might have been preferable for the treaty to have set down a clear set of specially tailored objectives for transport that eliminated the risk of difficulties concerning the extent to which the general rules of the treaty apply. Indeed Nevin (1990, 194) commenting on the CTP, concluded:

> For all practical purposes the common 'policy' in transport amounts to no more – but equally no less – than the application to it of prescriptions for full and free competition contained in Article 85, and the rights of establishment contained in Article 52.

This view is based on a broad interpretation of the meaning of competition rules. Practice has shown that the special nature of the transport sector and the number of interfaces with other policies imply that a successful policy has to be based on more than a direct reliance on free competition.

Although for economists it is sometimes a difficult and trying experience, occasionally it is useful to look at legal texts in some detail, and it is rewarding to compare the transport title of the Rome treaty with that of agriculture. Agriculture is often regarded, particularly in the UK, as the 'black hole' of the Community consuming vast sums for little benefit to anyone but the farmers. This view may have overtones of the sometimes insular attitude of the UK to the Community, and an impartial observer might be excused for wondering whether the results of the UK's approach to agriculture were really that much more successful than the CAP. However, leaving this point aside, it is interesting to note that in the agricultural title there is a clear and unambiguous reference made to the specific nature of the sector, and the need to take this into account in framing the general policy (see Articles 38–41 of the treaty). For the transport sector, the only reference is that in Article 61(1), concerning the freedom to provide services which should be granted under the transport title. In the transport title itself, only vague references to subsidies (Article 77) and the economic situation of transport (Article 78) can be found. This shortcoming of the transport title has been the result of much argument in the Community, and even now a debate is going on about possible revisions to the title to clarify the matter.

3. Stages in the development of a Common Transport Policy

Admitting these general problems with the transport title, what purposes should it then serve? A generally accepted starting point is that it should aim to ensure that the economic and social development of the Community is promoted by efficient transport services. In doing this it should:

(a) take account of the distinctive features of the transport sector;
(b) create the conditions for a transparent (i.e. non-discriminatory) and efficient market in the transport sector.

The fields covered by the transport title are rail, road, inland waterways and sea and air transport; transport by pipeline was not considered to be important at the time of the development of the treaty, and the question of the transmission of electrical energy and gas are covered under energy policy.

The development of common principles has to give special attention to the basic freedoms of the Community; in particular, as transport is a service industry, to the removal of restrictions on the freedom to provide services throughout the Community by any organization – private or public. In fact considerable progress has been made in this area, although it has become clear that the application of the freedom-to-provide-services principle cannot simply be limited to those services which receive a direct payment, as there are many 'indirect' elements that seem vital for its effective application.

Among the other areas which have to be considered for the efficient operation of transport services are, notably:

technical rules concerning transport operations;
fiscal questions affecting transport;
social and safety matters;
infrastructure planning and financing.

If this interpretation of the scope of the treaty is accepted, it clearly goes beyond the direct application of competition rules, and as such this interpretation has not won universal approval from member states. Indeed, it has been contested by a number of member states with regard to the question of infrastructure and safety matters. Despite this opposition it is clear that slowly, but surely, transport policy has moved to encompass these areas.

The argument is continuing, but in the two fields mentioned, the exclusion of a Community element from national plans seems difficult to justify on transport grounds. Unfortunately, these particular areas are sometimes considered to be questions of national sovereignty, where any ceding of authority to the Community would have wider consequences. Given the high rate of growth of international traffic, the scope to produce benefits by a degree of Community planning of resource allocation on main international routes is evident. The success or otherwise of applying this notion will be examined later.

4. European transport activity

The most important transport mode in terms of traffic flow in the Community is road transport. However, to obtain an overall picture of European transport is not easy. Although transport is one of the key sectors of 'services', EC-wide information is variable. Even at the level of measurement there is a problem. Passengers are not homogeneous and freight tonnage even less

Table 1: Transport in the EC

(a) Freight *(million ton kms)*

Mode	1975	1980	1985	1989	
Road	475	599	611	798	
Rail	177	194	155	150	
Waterways	98	105	87	95	
Sea	85	90	95	100	(est.)
Air	1	7	1	1	
TOTAL	836	995	949	1144	
(Index)	(100)	(119)	(113)	(137)	

(b) Passengers *(million passengers kms)*

Mode	1975	1980	1985	1989
Road	1949	2306	2440	2961
Rail	200	209	215	232
Air	34	48	56	72
TOTAL	2183	2563	2711	3265
(Index)	(100)	(117)	(124)	(150)
GDP constant prices (index 1975 = 100)	100	116	125	171

Source: EC transport statistics

so, yet statistics based on these measures are universally quoted, with few if any caveats attached. Leaving these problems aside, it is evident that there has been a very substantial growth of road transport in the last three decades. This has resulted in road transport becoming the dominant mode in terms of both passengers and freight. The railways have constantly lost market share and in the freight market, with the decline of the basic industries, even actual rail volumes have decreased. In this situation it is certainly not surprising that the road-transport sector was the major concern of Community policy and the future of this sector remains the major preoccupation for the CTP in the 1990s.

Policy in the road-transport sector

The road-transport sector presents an excellent illustration of the problems posed by the polarization of views on liberalization in the Community. In the 1930s and 1940s, European governments found it necessary to control the development of bus and lorry operations. This took the form of erecting entry barriers, and imposing controls on the existing operators with regard to factors such as prices etc. Starting in the 1950s, this regulatory system came in for increasing criticism, and new proposals were put forward that stressed the benefits of removing controls unjustifed on direct economic grounds: this 'liberal' approach was adopted in the treaty. The problems inherent in the regulatory corset that most Community members relied upon became increasingly apparent in the 1960s, when the initial success of the Community led to the rapid development of international trade. With the growth of the new motorway system and the decreasing real costs of road haulage there came to be constant pressure for relaxation. These problems were first tackled on the basis of bilateral agreements between member states to limit the controls on their own firms.

Even so, the international road haulage operator in the 1970s faced many hurdles:

(a) a firm has to be established in a member state: however, the laws on establishment varied considerably from the relatively strict to the almost non-existent;
(b) the technical standards imposed on nationally registered vehicles varied considerably as to their initial requirements and the degree of subsequent control;
(c) laws in the social field (driving hours), fiscal (road and fuel taxes), not to mention customs regulations, were very different.

The existence of these national regimes in the member states led to the argument that liberalization could not progress until harmonization had advanced to the point where competition could be said to be 'fair'. This argument is at first sight attractive. However, behind the veneer of objective realism supporting this argument, the reality was that this view was often advanced to impose as many restraints on the process of liberalization as possible. To a large extent the industries of those countries with so-called strict controls benefited from a quasi-monopoly situation and were unenthusiastic about changes that would open up their markets. A first step to resolving the problem came with the adoption, in 1968, of a system of Community quotas, which gave the holder the right to move freely between the member states and also to undertake what is termed triangular traffic, for example, a UK haulier moving goods from France to Belgium.

The development of a quota system presented the first opportunity for progress. However, with the rapid development of road haulage the situation regarding market access became increasingly resented. The net result of the national regulations was to protect the local hauliers. This naturally resulted in higher prices on the protected markets than on those which have been freed from controls. An illustration of this can be seen in Germany. On the basis of the figures that are given in Europa Transport,[2] it can be seen that in the 1980s the prices charged by the German road haulage industry constantly increased by a higher amount than those of its neighbours in the Netherlands, where the market was much more competitive. It is also interesting to note that the average public German haulage firm has between one and five vehicles and does little international business, while in the Netherlands the average firm has three times the number of vehicles and does a great deal of international business.

The real impetus for the development of a Community policy did not come until the 1980s. Until that date the member states opposed to liberalization had argued that further progress could not be made before there had been agreement on a high level of harmonization of technical and other matters affecting competition. This argument was finally settled by two events:

(a) the development of the concept of the 'single market' galvanized thinking about how the Community should develop. In the field of land transport the Commission estimated[3] that the liberalization of the road-haulage industry would reduce haulage rates by an average of 5 to 10 per cent and in West Germany (as it then was) by as much as 20 per cent;
(b) in addition to this gradual awareness that the current situation was costly and inefficient, in 1985 the Community Court of Justice handed down a judgement in case No. 13/83[4] that had very wide-reaching implications. The Court's main findings were that the Council: had failed in its obligations under the treaty to provide for the principle of the freedom to provide services in transport; and should remedy these failings in what it described as a 'reasonable period'.

This 'reasonable period' has widely come to be considered as 1992, the completion of the single market. The judgement made it clear that further progress on liberalization did not have to await harmonization. The immediate result of this was that the Council was finally able to adopt, in 1988, a proposal to abolish, from January 1993, all EC quotas, both bilateral and Community-wide. This was accompanied by a first step in the development of cabotage services on the basis of an annual number of authorizations. However, at the same time the Council also called for measures to be enacted that provided for action to be taken in the event of a crisis occurring in the industry. This measure provides for the Commission to:

> take measures to prevent any further increase in the supply of capacity in the market affected through limits on the increase in the activity of existing hauliers and restrictions on access to the market for new hauliers. (Article 4(4)).

This is interesting, because it specifically authorizes the Commission to intervene in the market 'through measures to prevent any further increase in the supply of capacity'. This provision thus explicitly accepts that the market may be incapable of recognizing the existence of a crisis and reacting to the situation through the play of market forces. The Council has accepted a proposal that would allow any haulier licensed in an EC country to participate in international haulage in the Community. The final result should be a more efficient, liberalized industry and one where the public authorities (the Commission) retain considerable power to intervene to correct any malfunctioning of the market mechanism. As it is clear that widespread evasion of Community rules on driving hours, weights and dimensions, speed limits, etc., occurs in road haulage, new measures have to be devised to make policies self-policing as far as is possible. This implies that measures such as speed limiters for heavy vehicles, or establishing that freight forwarders are held responsible for the illegal acts of their transporters, could be introduced.

Again in the freight market the Council has acted to intervene in the market to stimulate the demand for combined transport, 'combined transport' being the use of road and rail — or waterways — in conjunction with one another. In view of the dominant position that has been achieved by road transport, the development of combined transport, which is desirable from an environmental viewpoint, is not easy. As market failures discourage private economic agents from contributing significantly in this area, Community initiatives have been taken to stimulate the development of a viable system.

These initiatives have taken the form of ensuring that the maximum freedom from restrictions in licences etc. is obtained, and that aid can be provided both for investment and to assist with the operation costs of services in very difficult situations e.g. in Alpine transit. Indeed, the Alpine area has turned into a kind of 'test bed' for the very likely forthcoming debate over how environmental factors should be included in transport. The success of the Commission in encouraging the development of combined transport will be particularly important for the UK, as the Channel Tunnel will allow combined transport services to operate efficiently for the first time. A whole series of other measures have also been enacted and the main legislative acts are shown in an annex.

Community railway policy

There are currently fourteen main railway companies in the Community and they show a large variation in size, efficiency and operational policy. However, since the inception of the Community, their key features have been:

(a) an inherently national outlook with limited contacts with other countries;
(b) a considerable degree of public involvement and hence a lack of managerial autonomy;
(c) an almost militaristic-type management structure, concentrating heavily upon railways operations but not responsive to commercial needs.

To the end of the 1940s, the railways were able to maintain a virtual monopoly in many inland markets. As a *quid pro quo* of this situation, the railways were saddled with a number of burdens in the shape of public-service obligations to provide uneconomic services or special fares. This situation could only continue as long as the railways had core markets that were profitable and could subsidize the other operations. In the 1950s and 1960s these core markets were increasingly attacked by road transport, and the financial situation of the railways became serious. The twin imperatives of the Community were, therefore, to ensure that the general subsidies being given to the railways were not used to discriminate in favour of certain producers, and to establish a system whereby the subsidies were made transparent.

In the late 1960s a number of legal provisions were approved by the Council that: first, attempted to devise a common transparent framework for railway accounts; and, second, identified those areas where the railways could legitimately receive state aid. To the extent that these measures were limited in their objectives, they can be said to have achieved a measure of success. Even if they did nothing to tackle the fundamental problems of the railways, they did create a clearer framework for the sector. However, it has become evident that, in spite of the potential technical advantages of the railways, they are increasingly failing to attract the traffic that they should be carrying. Even on long distances, where the economies of scale are important, the railways have lost business. In order to tackle this situation, the Commission proposed a number of measures that were designed to encourage the development of railways. These measures were largely unsuccessful at the Council, where the very political nature of the railways made it very difficult to take action.

Only in the last year or so has there been a realization that there should be an active Community railways policy. The codification of the railways' debts and various accountancy provisions in the 1960s and 1970s did little to make the railways more attractive to the user. In the last few years there has, however, been a realization that the railways are capable of making a much greater contibution to Community transport than is currently the case. In this way they could also help to resolve the supply problems of transport. Faced, as seems certain, with a steady increase in the demand for transport, partly as a result of the single market, the generation of more and more road traffic poses increasing problems. On the environmental level, the external costs of road transport are increasingly recognized as being very high. In Germany, a recent study for the Ministry of Transport[5] has produced figures that indicate that the railways and the inland waterways have substantially lower external costs than road transport. However, the problem is quite simply to produce railway services that will attract the customer who faces a free choice among alternative modes of transport.

The Commission proposals to tackle this problem show again how the principles of free competition may be combined with a policy of intervention, wherever this is needed as a result of market imperfections. The basic elements have been to:

(a) open up the monopoly rights of the existing national railways to infrastructure;
(b) create a contractual framework, within which the member states can arrange to purchase services from the railways (social services);
(c) allow the national railways as much autonomy as possible in their relationship with the state, notably by the creation of a realistic capital structure;
(d) encourage the development of a Community network of high speed train services through aid for infrastructure and work on technical harmonization;
(e) stimulate the use of the railways for freight services by a series of measures to create a European system of combined transport.

The Council of Ministers had made considerable progress with these proposals and the first steps to open up the railway system were made in June 1991. Further action to develop high-speed and combined transport systems is planned in the near future.

Inland waterways

Inland waterways are no longer important in the UK but, as seen in Table 1, their share of the European freight market is still large. The waterways, like the railways, have the potential to carry additional traffic and are also environmentally friendly. However, the waterway industry has a number of special characteristics that distinguish it from other sectors of transport. The waterways:

(a) are still largely artisanal with the majority of vessels being the personal property of the captain;
(b) suffer from severe swings in the demand cycle. This is partly due to natural features, such as water levels of the rivers, and partly due to the fact that much of their traffic is linked

to the ports, where the number of boat arrivals fluctuate, and to seasonal agricultural movements.

The joint effect of this rather particular structure has been the development of a market-control system for much of the industry (but not the Rhine where no controls exist),[6] designed to share traffic on an equal basis in terms of difficulty. This system, which is known by the French name of 'tour de rôle', is a handicap to the more efficient sections of the waterway fleet which are required to wait their turn like anyone else. However, the situation is complex and as recent research[7] tends to indicate, the sector of the market governed by the 'tour de rôle' appears to act as a safety value for the unregulated sector. This observation is based on the evidence that vessels move from the 'free' sector to the 'tour de rôle' sector when the former suffers from any crisis.

In the light of this situation, which had led to chronic overcapacity in the sector, the Commission proposed a scheme to stimulate the withdrawal of vessels from the fleet, combined with provisions to limit the entry of new capacity, until demand and supply were brought more into equilibrium. This was to be funded by a levy on vessels in the industry which would pay off the interest-free loan granted by the member states to finance the action. Following approval of the Council in 1989, the results of the action proved to be successful, with 12 per cent of the dry cargo and 9 per cent of the tanker fleet being withdrawn. The question now remains of how to handle the question of the 'tour de rôle', which appears to offend against the competition laws of the treaty but reflects a real problem in the industry. One avenue that might be explored is to consider whether a 'crisis management' system, as has been put in place for the road haulage industry, could operate. Such a system would require that effective indicators are developed to pinpoint potential problems before they occur and that some form of rapid intervention system is devised.

Air policy

Community air policy really began to move following the court judgement of 1984 in the 'nouvelles frontières' case that the competition rules in the treaty were applicable to civil aviation. Until then, the article of the treaty relating to maritime and air (Article 84(2)) had been interpreted by member states as if civil aviation and maritime were excluded from the general provisions covering land transport. The first objectives of the Commission were to:

ensure the introduction of competition rules into civil aviation;
introduce controls on categories of agreement that potentially affect prices and capacity;
encourage the development of inter-regional air services.

The basic regulations introduced a certain amount of competition in an economic sector which, in the past, was entirely managed according to national rules. However, these provisions did not go very far and in 1989 the Commission put forward a new series of proposals. These new proposals would greatly enlarge the scope for the so called 'fifth freedom' rule in the Community (the fifth freedom being the right to pick up passengers in an intermediate country). The Commission also proposed that the first steps be taken to introduce cabotage into air operations. However, this right would be restricted to services involving the country of establishment of the airline and one of the airports involved must be below category one (that is the principal national airports). The Commission also proposed certain derogations from the competition rules of the treaty (Articles 85 and 86). These derogations would cover the joint planning and co-ordination of capacity, sharing of income, tariff agreements, time slots, etc. They met a need for legal security felt by airlines, whilst encouraging them to abandon previous agreements of a more restrictive nature.

Overall, the results of the Commission's efforts on the aviation front have begun to produce favourable results, although further progress is necessary. For the peripheral regions the policy should result in a wider range of services although it is noteworthy that there has been a trend in the USA, after deregulation there, for the smaller airports to be restricted to links to/from one given 'hub' airport.

Maritime policy

In the same way that air policy only started to develop in the mid-1980s, the maritime sector also did not see any important proposals until that date. The initial attitude of the member states that no Community policy was necessary, was radically affected by the severe downturn in activity in the maritime sector in the earlier 1980s (approximately 25 per cent reduction of traffic), as well as

the inclusion of new maritime countries. Between 1980 and 1988 the tonnage of the EC fleet dropped from 116.8 million to 58.3 million. Some of this reduction has been due to 'flagging out', but even so there has been a real reduction in the Community fleet. In 1989, the Commission proposed the following:
 the creation of a Community register (flag), EUROS;
 the establishment of cabotage and other possibilities for vessels with the EC flag.
The Council of Ministers has, by mid-1991, held a number of discussions on these proposals, but there has been no agreement as yet. To the extent that many peripheral regions depend heavily upon sea transport, this failure is disappointing.

5. Transport infrastructure measures

The need for action to ensure that the Community has the transport infrastructure it requires was stressed in the Commission's original memorandum from 1961. However, it was not until 1976 that the Commission made a first proposal in this area. In this initial proposal, the Commission put forward the argument that there exists a 'Community interest' in certain projects that goes beyond members' direct national interests. This idea could be translated into practice by citing the case of Luxembourg. This comparatively small country is the scene of a large number of transit movements between other members of the Community. If the Luxembourg authorities undertook a cost/benefit evaluation of the competing projects in the transport sector, they would have every interest in ignoring the costs and benefits of non-residents. This problem can be remedied if the Commission were to act as the banker for the non-resident users of the roads and 'compensate', through grants, the Luxembourg authorities for the benefits that accrue to non-Luxembourg residents. If this form of transfer payment could be organized, the total benefit of the Community could be increased and no one made worse off. This is a fairly simple illustration of the Commission's ideas. In practice, the richer member states were concerned that this principle, if widely applied, would benefit mainly the poorer, peripheral, regions; they maintained the view that the regional fund existed for just this situation. In reality, however, the regional fund is devoted to regional matters and is not applicable within the broad context of transport policy.

A five year (1988–1992) action programme delivered to the Council in 1988 included five main priorities that were aimed to be achieved:

(a) the elimination of bottlenecks;
(b) the integration of areas which geographically are either landlocked or situated on the periphery of the Community;
(c) the reduction of costs associated with transit traffic, in co-operation with any non-member countries concerned;
(d) the improvement of links on land/sea routes.
(e) the provision of high quality links between the major urban centres, including high-speed rail links.

The Council has finally, at the end of 1990, approved a multiannual programme worth ECU 328 million. Although the amounts are not significant, this programme does represent a breakthrough and it is now planned to continue developing subsequent programmes and specific actions in favour of high-speed and combined transport services. The programme is to be superseded, now that the Union (Maastricht) Treaty is approved, by the development of 'Trans-European networks' (TENS). The TENS will be based upon the new Article 129 of the treaty and will serve as the key guideline for Community investment in the field of transport infrastructure.

6. Regional objectives in the field of transport

In examining the importance attached to regional policy in the context of the CTP, it should be recalled that the Rome Treaty made no express provision for such a policy. Only since the Single Act (1987) has there been a specific reference in the title concerning 'economic and social cohesion'. If the logic of the treaty is followed, the objective seems to be that the free play of market forces would lead to a redistribution of wealth and economic activity, that would eventually lead to a reduction of regional disparities. In practice, this market-led process does not seem to have resulted in any great reduction in regional differences.

It is clear from the above that the principal objective of the Rome treaty was to introduce free competition in the Community. However, the fact was recognized very early on that certain types of transport services could not be profitable. The profitable services were largely in urban areas, but rural or regional passenger services were also covered by the transport provision. The difficulty with the competition aspects of the treaty is, quite simply, that their application might produce lower-cost services overall, but that these services might be restricted to areas where demand (and hence potential profits) were initially high. Moreover, it is clear that transport companies in the Community have very varied cost structures. In general, the cost of labour in the peripheral regions is lower than in the centre of the Community. This fact should allow, say, the road-haulage companies established in these regions to compete successfully for business. While this might be the case, it does not provide the level of services that these regions need in order to compete.

Any form of regional policy (and it should be noted that regions may be whole countries or even areas of otherwise rich countries) is based on the notion that the regions are relatively backward economically, and that this difference is likely to create difficulties in achieving a successful economic union. In the past, the physical nature of many industrial processes meant that they were tied to one geographical zone. Today this is less true, but on the other hand a more complex relationship seems to exist between transport and economic development.

Overall, it is clear that the cost of transport both directly and indirectly (such as in terms of time) has decreased since the 1960s. Transport costs now commonly vary between 3 to 5 per cent of total production costs. However, although this can be said to indicate a certain success for the CTP, the situation still remains that transport costs to and from the centres of the Community vary widely. Firms established in peripheral regions have to face transport costs as much as double those in more centrally placed locations. This is typically the case of firms in say Ireland, Greece or Portugal. However, the implications of this situation are not as clear or as straightforward as might be expected. It is not the role of the Community to ensure that every region has comparable transport costs to those in the centre of the Community. This argument would be equivalent to trying to eliminate geographical differences between regions. It might cost more to transport tomatoes from Portugal to northern Germany than to haul them from, say, the Netherlands. However, it is to be expected that the obvious climatic benefits of Portugal can compensate for this difference. Also, in practice, the subsidies (often concealed) for national growers may alter these differences, but again this is not directly a transport policy matter.

Overall, the steady reduction of barriers to transport efficiency have clearly benefited the peripheral regions throughout the 1970s and 1980s. That this is the case is borne out by the movement of large vehicle-manufacturing plants to Southern Italy or Spain. The firms that have made those moves have been able to ensure that the production costs of their plants, including transport, are competitive with those in the older industrial regions.

For the future there are possibly two major opposing forces that will come into play in determining the role of transport in the configuration of many peripheral regions. First, on the negative side, there is a likelihood that the Community will develop closer links with eastern Europe, where costs are even cheaper than in the peripheral regions of the Community. This is now a real possibility in the case of some agricultural products, but when a semblance of an operational infrastructure is re-established in the east, it will also become a very real possibility for industry, too. Second, on the positive side, modern industry does not depend on the external economies of scale that characterized classical industrial regions. New technologies, as experience in the USA has shown, can be established anywhere, and the criteria for location include points where the peripheral regions score well – climate, quality of life, etc. However, this is not to say that transport is unimportant. Accessibility will continue to be a key element in the choice of location and therefore good transport infrastructure will be vital. As was noted earlier, the Council of Ministers has been reluctant to accept any attempt to develop a hierarchy of European routes for infrastructure. Today, under increasing pressure from lack of resources and the realization that there is a crisis in view, that attitude is changing. The Council has already accepted an outline plan for the development of high-speed railways (that is, with speeds over 200 kph) and the Commission has proposed similar plans covering roads, waterways and combined transport. If the Council accepts these plans and, of course, finds the means to turn them into reality, they can be very important for the peripheral regions. Already, there is some anxiety in certain regions, notably Ireland and Greece, that their special transport situation – Ireland with the sea link, Greece with the problem of Yugoslavia – will mean that they are disadvantaged by these moves. These fears have been, or should be, resolved by the action of the so-called 'cohesion fund', again set up under the Maastricht treaty, much of which will be devoted to transport infrastructure.

To conclude on this point, it has to be admitted that a direct regional objective for the CTP has not been readily accepted by the Council of Ministers. However, the general benefits of the increased efficiency of transport have had a positive effect on the peripheral regions by reducing their transport costs. For the future, the possible development of new high-speed passenger railways and combined transport will be important because of the fact that railway services require long distances to be economic, and because of this, will offer particular benefits to those areas situated relatively further from the main population centres. It yet remains to be seen whether the financial means to realize these plan will be made available.

7. The next steps in the development of the common transport policy

This paper has attempted to demonstrate that the CTP cannot be based solely on a competition policy. Even in the first decade of the policy there were measures that recognized, however tentatively, that the nature of transport operations requires Community policy to be flexible and to take account of external, indirect factors. In the 1990s with the completion of the single market, the question of whether the existing policy is satisfactory for the post-1992 Community has come even more to the fore. Clearly the future policy of the transport sector will be largely influenced by what is decided in relation to Community powers as a whole. However, it can be argued that the CTP, as it has emerged after a long thirty years of development, is already a flexible tool. If, as has been claimed,[8] transport is too cheap, the means exist to incorporate social and external cost factors in the fiscal and cost structure already in place. It may, however, be argued that the pricing weapon is too blunt-edged or too unreliable to produce the results that are desired.

For instance, a move positively to encourage the use of environmentally friendly means of transport – notably the railways and waterways – has been urged as a rapid means to reduce nuisances. This type of policy is advocated in the latest Commission white paper on transport;[9] it would require changes to the current approach but it has to be said that a return to regulatory policies, especially in view of their notable lack of success in other areas, has to be very carefully considered. It seems, as is often the case, that the European model of free-market economics which combines the incentives of competition, where this is shown to be in the general good, together with a certain degree of intervention, where market forces can be shown to be inefficient, can provide the answers. As was noted in the section on road haulage, it will be important for the future to attempt to design policies that are self-policing: if this can be achieved, the existing policies look capable of taking account of the post-1992 situation. Against this scenario it appears that the sometimes maligned CTP is not too far from what will be necessary and already provides examples of how such an approach could be adopted in the Community. If changes are to be introduced in the Community as a whole, it is clear that many different arguments have to be evaluated. However, the CTP shows that a liberal dose of pragmatism is capable of producing policies that serve to enhance the welfare of the Community as a whole, and as such may be a model for progress of a more general nature.

Notes

*The Commission of the European Communists does not necessarily endorse the views expressed by the author in this paper.

1. For details of all acts of the Communities see 'Directory of Community legislation in force and other acts of the Community institutions'. European Communities, Brussels-Luxembourg (June 1992).
2. See Commission of the European Communities (1990).
3. 'Research on the "cost of non-Europe" – basic findings of the research: an illustration of the road haulage sector'. Series documents, Office for Official Publications of the European Communities.
4. Case No. 13/83. *Official Journal of the European Communities*, C144 (13 June 1985).
5. Study undertaken for the Bundesministerium für Verkehr, Bonn 5 (German Ministry of Transport) 1990 (German text).

6. 'Convention of Mannheim 1862'. This lays down that navigation of the Rhine should be free from all controls and charges.
7. 'European inland waterway transport: economic problems and policy options'. NEA and PLANO, 1991, for the Transport Directorate of the EC (unpublished).
8. 'Transport in fast changing Europe.' Group Transport 2000 Plus. Report submitted to the EC, December 1990 (unpublished).
9. 'The future development of the Common Transport Policy'. Internal Commission paper (COM (92) 494 final).

References

Nevin, Edward. *The Economics of Europe* (Basingstoke, Macmillan, 1990).

Commission of the European Communities (1990). *Europa Transport: Analysis and Forecasts 1989* (Directorate-General for Transport, Brussels, 1990).

IV REGIONS

7
Labour-market flexibility in western Europe

DAVID BLACKABY and ROBIN BLADEN-HOVELL

1. Introduction

Since 1960, most countries in western Europe have suffered from sizeable increases in unemployment. Even countries in which, in the 1960s, unemployment was as low as one or two per cent, experienced unemployment well into double figures in the 1980s. Moreover, as Holmlund and Lofgren (1990) and Dreze and Bean (1990) note, although these increases in unemployment have in the main been associated with a general weakening of inflationary pressures in most countries, inflation itself continues to be a problem throughout much of Europe. The persistence of substantial inflationary pressures, accompanied by historically high levels of unemployment, suggests that many European economies may have become less flexible during the 1970s and 1980s, particularly in terms of their labour-market performance. This apparent reduction in labour flexibility led Giersch (1985) to characterize these economies as suffering from 'eurosclerosis' — implying that their labour markets were incapable of adjusting to the big supply shocks of the 1970s.

The purpose of the current paper is threefold. First, we trace out the varied labour-market experiences of Europe since 1960. The outline drawn in this respect is deliberately kept broad-brush in nature and concentrates on the major developments within Europe over the period. Even so, the discussion is augmented by evidence, drawn notably from Japan and the United States, for the purpose of comparison. Second, we examine the principal theoretical developments which offer either a partial or complete explanation of the European experience. Three main factors are emphasized in this section: the potentially beneficial effects of centralized wage bargaining for labour-market performance; the role of unemployment duration and the reduction of capital accumulation over the 1970s in raising the natural rate of unemployment; and, finally, the role of skills-mismatch in prolonging the period of adjustment back towards full employment. In the final section of the paper, we draw an analogy between regional labour markets within a single country and the situation of Europe as it moves closer towards a single market and complete monetary union. The emphasis here is placed primarily on the policy implications for Europe and, in particular, the possible effects on labour-market performance. A summary of the main results, together with concluding comments, completes the paper.

2. Labour-market experience within Europe

Although labour-market performance has varied considerably across Europe over the last thirty years, the underlying trend in unemployment has been one of almost continuous increase. Moreover, the pattern emerging has been in sharp contrast with that experienced by our major OECD partners. In Japan, for example, unemployment has remained low throughout the period, while in the United States, the general resilience of labour markets has been demonstrated by the fact that the unemployment fluctuations which have occurred have not been accompanied by an upward trend.

Within Europe, the principal periods of increasing unemployment coincide with the impact of significant supply shocks in the 1970s, together with an apparent loss of effectiveness for traditional stabilization policy. Indeed, the fourfold increase in oil prices which accompanied the 1973 – 4 OPEC oil shock marked, in effect, a watershed as regards general economic development throughout Europe. In general, the post-war experience prior to this shock had been characterized by fast growth and high employment. Following the shock, however, a substantial downturn in economic activity occurred, associated with a sharp rise in unemployment and a surge in the underlying inflationary pressures. The principal developments, in terms of the unemployment experience of the major European countries and their OECD partners over the period, are shown in Table 1. With the sole exception of Italy, these figures refer to the standardized rate of unemployment produced by the OECD. Values for the final year, 1989 – 90, are based on unemployment forecasts produced by the OECD.

Table 1: Unemployment rates in OECD countries

	1960–68	1969–73	1974–79	1980–85	1986–90
EC members					
Belgium	2.35	2.38	6.32	11.28	10.27
Denmark	1.46	0.95	6.02	10.00	9.33
France	1.69	2.52	4.52	8.32	10.20
Ireland	4.98	5.76	6.77	11.64	15.50
Italy	3.64	3.95	4.37	6.15	7.63
Netherlands	1.14	2.02	5.05	10.05	9.46
Spain	2.42	2.74	5.27	16.58	19.00
West Germany	0.71	0.84	3.20	5.95	6.04
United Kingdom	2.62	3.39	5.04	10.48	8.80
Other European countries					
Austria	1.96	1.40	1.78	3.23	3.33
Finland	1.83	2.34	4.53	5.60	5.10
Norway	2.01	1.66	1.82	2.55	3.11
Sweden	1.64	2.22	1.88	2.83	1.89
Switzerland	0.06	0.01	1.08	1.92	2.37
Rest of OECD					
Australia	2.17	2.04	5.02	7.64	7.40
Canada	4.71	5.56	7.17	9.88	8.26
Japan	1.36	1.22	1.93	2.42	2.52
New Zealand	0.16	0.28	0.67	4.17	6.06
United States	4.74	4.86	6.86	8.00	5.79

Source: Nickell (1990)

Note: With the exception of Italy, these figures refer to OECD standardized rates: Italian figures are based upon estimates constructed by the US Department of Labour. Rates for the final year 1990 are based upon OECD forecasts.

Table 1 reveals that, almost without exception, the unemployment experience over the period can be subdivided into three main intervals: 1960–73, 1974–9 and 1980–90. The division at each point coincides with one of the oil-price shocks, OPEC I and OPEC II, which were administered in 1973–4 and 1979 respectively. Unemployment remained low and remarkably stable across Europe prior to the first of these shocks. The largest average increase in unemployment over the period 1960–73 occurred in the Netherlands, and even here it measured less than one percentage point. Following OPEC I, however, unemployment began to rise substantially throughout Europe. In West Germany, for example, the oil-price shock was followed by a threefold increase in unemployment; in Denmark the increase was more than twice that.

Moreover, the increase proved particularly persistent and withstood the various attempts of policy-makers throughout the world to ameliorate the situation[1]. Unemployment worsened further following OPEC II. By now, membership of the newly formed European Monetary System meant that the external constraint, for much of western Europe, had tightened considerably. As a result, demand management over the period 1980–90 has been dominated by the need to apply sharp disinflationary pressure. For the rest of Europe only the nordic countries, together with Austria and Switzerland, appeared capable of containing the effects of the two oil-price shocks. In comparison with the European experience, unemployment in the United States peaked in the early 1980s and has subsequently fallen back towards the levels experienced before OPEC I. Japanese unemployment has remained low throughout.

The unemployment picture across western Europe, then, is not universally poor; wide diversity continues to exist in unemployment rates. Over the period 1986–90, for example, unemployment ranged from 1.9 per cent in Sweden to 19 per cent in Spain. Generally speaking, unemployment is highest on the southern and western peripheries of Europe, with regions lying furthest from the centre of Europe experiencing the highest levels of unemployment (see Figure 1). There is a marked contrast between the unemployment rates of southern Italy, Spain, Portugal, Turkey, Ireland and the UK and those of Norway, Sweden and Finland. Explaining the difference in performance of these nordic countries from that of their southern counterparts is, therefore, likely to contribute to our understanding of the unemployment problem within Europe.

3. General theoretical background

The varied unemployment experience of European economies throughout the 1970s and the 1980s has led to a reappraisal of the theory of unemployment and, in particular, of the link between unemployment and wages (see Nickell 1990 for a comprehensive survey of the literature). The major supply shocks

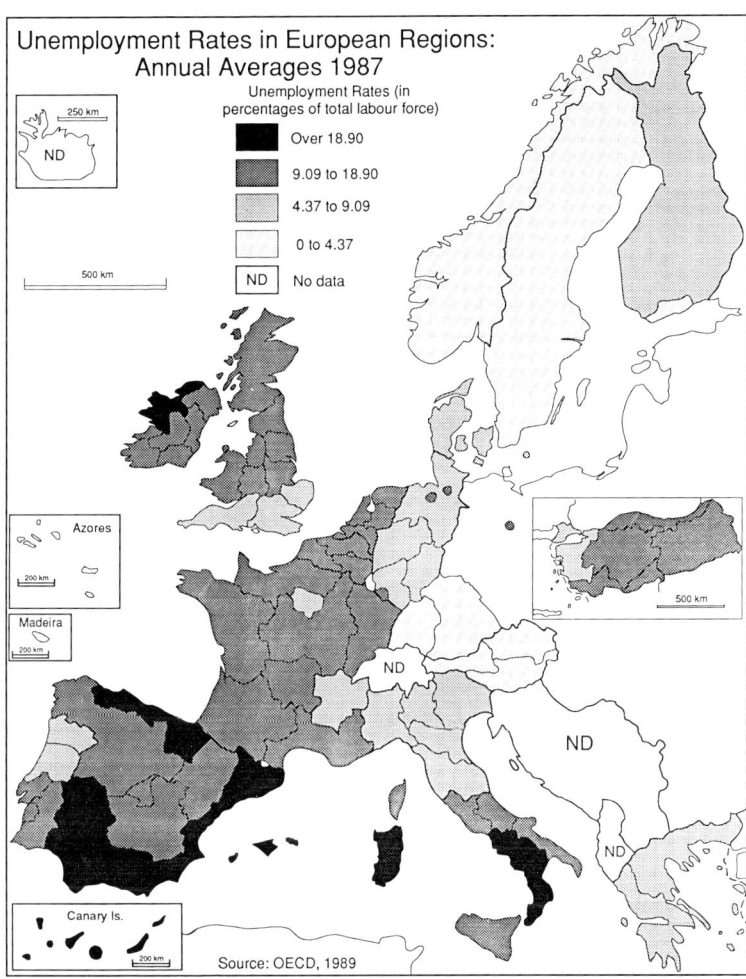

Figure 1. Unemployment rates in European regions: annual averages 1987

of the period, initiated by higher commodity price, affected all countries, yet the employment impact has varied considerably. It was observed, however, that a number of countries, which included Norway, Sweden and Austria, were relatively successful at holding down their unemployment levels over this period. As a result, economists began to look for particular features of the labour markets concerned, which may have been responsible for their superior performance. The work of Bruno and Sachs (1985), for example, found a strong relationship between centralization in wage bargaining and the capability of an economy to sustain and generate employment. Subsequent work by Barro (1988) and Layard (1989) found similar support for the view that centralized bargaining and labour-market flexibility were positively related. Calmfors and Driffill (1988), however, have questioned whether this relationship is linear. Instead, they present a theoretical model and empirical evidence to support the view that the relationship is non-linear and, in particular, U-shaped. At one extreme, employment is highest in those countries where bargaining is undertaken by a small number of large institutions, and where the actions of individual members are integrated and monitored in order to avoid cheating. Moreover, within such a system, institutions are unable to pass on their wage increases to others, because each represents a large element of the total workforce. In these circumstances the maxim that 'one member's wage increase becomes another member's price increase' manifestly holds. However, Calmfors and Driffill also note that at the opposite extreme, where a large number of independent small unions and firms set wages in a competitive environment, low unemployment might also prevail. In their model, the worst possible scenario occurs in the situation in which bargaining is undertaken by a limited number of medium-sized organizations which are sufficiently large to reap the benefits of individual market power, whilst remaining unconstrained in their ability to pass increases on to others.[2] In this context, Norway and Sweden are most commonly seen as countries benefiting from the centralization of wage bargaining, with Austria and Switzerland offered as additional examples. However, the evidence supporting the claims of the latter pair has been questioned in some quarters. Rowthorn and Glyn (1987), in particular, suggest that the low levels of unemployment achieved in these countries

Table 2: Union membership densities in European countries, 1970 to 1985

	1970	1980	1985
EC			
Denmark	–	78.2	83.5
France	22.0	18.7	16.5
Germany	33.0	37.4	38.0
Italy	34.8	48.6	41.4
Netherlands	36.5	32.9	27.5
UK	45.2	52.0	44.7
Non-EC			
Austria	–	52.4	53.3
Norway	–	54.8	55.1
Sweden	67.6	79.7	82.8
Switzerland	29.2	31.4	29.6

Source: Henley and Tsakalotos (1991)

have been obtained by their either exporting the problem abroad or by simply ignoring it in the official statistics.

Soskice (1990) has also drawn attention to a number of problems with the analysis of Calmfors and Driffill. He argues that a number of countries are incorrectly classified, that there are major problems with unco-ordinated company-level bargaining, that the pushfulness of unions at local level is neglected, and that the effect of wage restraint on unemployment is different in open and closed economies. The emphasis is also different from that of Calmfors and Driffill, in that the level at which co-ordination takes place is stressed, rather than the formal location of bargaining. Both theories, however, emphasize the importance of co-ordination and bargaining structures rather than union densities. Table 2 reveals that at a European level, union densities are general, higher and more stable in the more corporalist European economies outside the EC.

In addition to the relatively high employment levels, a number of other favourable labour-market characteristics have been associated with the Scandinavian countries.[3,4] Freeman (1988), for example, finds wage dispersion is lower than in decentralized economies, which, as noted by Rowthorn (1990), is not wholly surprising, given that economic policy has encouraged the squeezing of differentials. The male-female wage differential is also lower than in most other countries which, whilst being a laudable outcome in itself, is also likely to reduce the level of resource misallocation which follows upon discrimination. Drawing these factors together, Rowthorn (1990) sees the major achievement of the nordic countries as being their ability to combine full employment with comparatively well-paid jobs, which has reduced inequality. He notes that:

> ... if it is to mean anything at all, the term 'full employment' must surely signify not any old job at any old wage, but a reasonable job for all at a wage reasonably close to the average. (Rowthorn 1990, 18)

Overall, Rowthorn sees Sweden coming closest to this aim, with the other nordic countries also doing well by international standards. An alternative institutional feature, highlighted in the search for factors influencing labour-market performance across Europe, is the varied nature of the benefit system in different countries. The hypothesis most often expressed is that high levels of unemployment benefit reduce the opportunity cost of unemployment, thereby reducing the incentive for individuals to find employment.

Both Burda (1988) and Layard (1990) find an important role for the benefit system in explaining the variance of unemployment across countries. In terms of behaviour within Europe, for example, Layard notes that:

> The main reason why unemployment remained so high in Britain and most EC countries was that the benefit system permitted unemployed individuals, however demoralized, to maintain their families even if they failed to obtain work year after year. (Layard 1990, 8)

Burda also finds a strong positive relationship between the 'generosity' of the benefit system and long-term unemployment rates across countries.

A recent OECD (1991) study, however, suggests that this relationship is far from straightforward. As indicated in Table 3, both Greece and Spain have experienced relatively high levels of long-term unemployment, yet neither country has a particularly high benefit-to-earnings ratio. Conversely, Australia, where the replacement ratio has remained relatively constant through

Table 3: Long-term unemployment and the replacement rate in 1989

	Unemployment in excess of:		Replacement rate:	
			short-term	long-term
	26 weeks	52 weeks		
EC members				
Belgium	84.8	74.7	47	45
Denmark	46.0	22.6	64	53
France	59.9	41.6	57	47
Ireland	85.1	71.9	43	38
Italy	84.2	68.2	–	–
Netherlands	69.3	56.3	68	58
Spain	66.9	51.3	62	27
West Germany	68.1	52.3	58	54
United Kingdom	64.3	49.3	41	41
Rest of Europe				
Finland	–	–	58	45
Norway	18.2	9.1	62	30
Sweden	22.7	8.7	85	39
Rest of OECD				
Australia	44.9	28.0	36	36
Canada	22.2	8.0	59	35
Japan	44.2	23.3	29	0
United States	12.5	7.4	32	5

Source: OECD (1991), Employment Outlook, Paris

time, has a much lower incidence of long-term unemployment than many European countries.[5,6]

More detailed evidence from microdata sets, which allow researchers to analyse unemployment spells within countries whilst holding constant many individual characteristics, generally indicate that the duration of unemployment is relatively inelastic to the level of benefit. Surveying eight studies for the Netherlands, Groot and Jehoel-Gilsbers (1990) note that a significant role for the benefit system is found in only one. Their work suggests that it is not the level of benefits (which they consider a push-factor), but rather the expected wage (a pull-factor) that is responsible for determining re-employment. In the UK, research by Atkinson et al. (1984) fails to find any significant role for benefits, although Lancaster (1979), Narendranathan *et al.* (1985) and Nickell (1979) do. However, even where a significant effect is obtained, the response of unemployment duration with respect to the replacement rate is found to be relatively inelastic, with estimated values ranging between 0.18 and 0.36.[7]

Research on the issue of unemployment duration is important in many respects, not least because of the contribution which increased duration has made to raising the overall level of unemployment across Europe. Within the European Community, for example, the rise in unemployment over the 1970s and 1980s arose mainly through a reduction in outflows from the unemployment pool and, hence, an increase in the average length of an individual's unemployment spell. Indeed, commenting upon this characteristic, the OECD notes that:

> ... if rates of outflow from unemployment in North America were comparable to those in many European countries, unemployment rates there would easily have exceeded 20 per cent. (OECD 1990, 13)

One popular explanation for the reduction in outflow from unemployment in Europe is that the employment security provisions, introduced in a number of cases under pressure from trade unions, have increased the effective hiring and firing costs for labour. In this context Bertolila and Bertola (1990) argue that the high levels of unemployment are due to low job creation rather than excessive job destruction. Moreover, the oil shocks of the 1970s substantially increased the degree of uncertainty faced by firms and have thereby reduced job turnover. The result of combining increased uncertainty with high hiring costs is to make firms hesitant to increase employment, even in relatively prosperous times, owing to the high costs involved in subsequently shedding labour in a downturn. Increasing the cost of labour also reduces employment through capital/labour substitution and an output effect arising from lower profits.

Hiring and firing costs, in conjunction with bargaining, also play an important role in generating economic rent in a number of models. These typically emphasize the importance of insiders, as against outsiders, in wage and employment determination.[8] The models were developed because it was felt that the conventional natural-rate framework was unable to explain fully the unemployment experiences of the period.[9]

In the work of Blanchard and Summers (1987), Gottfries and Horn (1987) and Lindbeck and Snower (1988), the pivotal role traditionally given to unemployment in wage determination is questioned.[10] The basic premise of the insider – outsider model is that wages are set by bargaining between employees and employers. Individuals, or unions acting on behalf of employees, negotiate over wages whilst securing the employment of insiders; unemployed outsiders play no role in wage determination. In such models, unanticipated reductions in aggregate demand or supply may well have permanent effects on employment. A deflationary shock, for example, may reduce the number of insiders and employment fails to return to its original level as conditions improve, because the smaller group of insiders may choose to negotiate wage gains rather than allow employment to increase to the benefit of outsiders. As a result the equilibrium rate of unemployment would rise, following the demand shock.

This effect has been termed 'hysteresis' in the literature.[11] It emphasizes the importance of past levels of unemployment for the determination of the natural rate.[12] Early examples of this approach frequently contained no effect whatsoever for unemployment on wage determination.[13] Later modifications, however, did incorporate a variety of mechanisms through which such an effect could operate.[14] These mainly include 'fear' and 'threat' effects. High unemployment is likely to reduce dramatically the job prospects of individuals who are currently working but who potentially may be laid off. As a result, union negotiators may demand more conservative wage increases at times of high unemployment. Also, during periods of high unemployment, a firm's threat to replace its workforce may be more credible, although the credibility of this threat may itself depend upon the size of hiring and firing costs faced by the firm. These costs, as we have already noted, tend to be higher within Europe than in North America. Not surprisingly, therefore, Blanchard and Summers (1986) find much stronger evidence of a hysteresis effect for Germany, France and the UK than they do for the United States.

Increased duration has also featured in a number of explanations for the apparent inflexibility of the wage-rate response to unemployment over the 1970s and 1980s. This approach typically emphasizes the deficiencies of aggregate unemployment as a measure of excess supply within the labour market. Layard and

170 Labour-market flexibility

Nickell (1986) in particular drew attention to the macroeconomic implications arising from high levels of long-term unemployment. The essence of their argument is that the long-term unemployed represent a less effective supply of potential labour than their short-term counterparts. Thus one of the few benefits commonly associated with higher levels of unemployment – that it reduces inflationary pressure – may fail to materialize if unemployment is predominantly long-term in nature.

Two possible explanations of why the long-term unemployed may cease to compete successfully for vacancies have been put forward. Firstly, in response to feelings of frustration and hopelessness, many of the long-term unemployed may spend less time looking for work than do individuals who have only recently become unemployed. Indeed, Moylan *et al.* (1984) and Jackman and Layard (1991) offer evidence that increased duration reduces the search effectiveness of unemployed workers. Secondly, there may be reticence on the part of employers to employ individuals who have experienced a long spell of unemployment, owing to the fact that their human capital may have depreciated.[15] Moreover, employers screen job applicants on the basis of their unemployment duration, using this as an indicator of the worker's quality. Meager and Metcalf (1987), for example, find evidence among British firms of applicants being rejected on this basis.

In a recent survey of the unemployed-duration literature which used microdata sets, Devine and Kiefer (1990) conclude that the evidence adduced for a duration effect was sensitive to specification. In particular, they note that the empirical finding that re-employment probabilities decline as duration lengthens – the so-called negative duration-dependence effect – may in fact be due to a failure to control fully for heterogeneity of the workforce in empirical studies.

Support for the Layard and Nickell hypothesis has been obtained from a variety of sources. Layard and Nickell themselves report evidence from time-series studies for the UK, with the finding that the greater the proportion of long-term in total unemployment, the weaker is the overall inverse relationship between unemployment and earnings.

Supporting evidence for the Layard and Nickell proposition has also been widespread across Europe. Coe (1988), for example, found that the proposition appeared to hold in Germany, France, the United Kingdom, Austria, Finland and the Netherlands. Eriksson, Suvanto and Vartia (1990) also report supportive findings for Finnish data. Holmlund (1990), however, finds little support for the proposition using Swedish data though, as he points out, long-term unemployment in Sweden is relatively unimportant as compared with OECD countries.

Similarly, the evidence obtained from cross-section data sets concerning the effect of unemployment duration on wage determination is generally supportive. Positive support for the hypothesis is reported by Blackaby and Manning (1990) using UK data drawn from the General Household Survey and Nickell and Wadhwani (1990), based upon a study of firm-level data for the UK. In contrast, Blanchflower and Oswald (1990) find little support for the hypothesis, but instead favour a specification for the relationship between wages and unemployment which emphasizes the role of non-linearities.

Blackaby, Bladen-Hovell and Symons (1991) using a pseudo-longitudinal data set constructed from the Family Expenditure Survey 1980 – 6, also find support for the Layard and Nickell hypothesis. The principal advantage of this approach over conventional time-series analysis is that it offers an opportunity to control for a number of personal characteristics considered significant for wage determination. This may be particularly important during a recession, when it is likely that the least able and qualified individuals will lose their jobs first. As a result, real wages may initially rise during a recession – a sort of real wage 'batting average' effect due to the elimination of the tail-enders in the workforce. In time-series work, however, failure to control for such characteristics may be captured by the long-term unemployment variable, because the proportion of long-term unemployed tends to increase throughout the recession. This movement mirrors the increase in the average level of human capital characteristics of those members of the workforce in employment as unemployment increases.

The long-term unemployment premise also produces 'hysteresis' type results. An individual's stock of human capital is likely to fall during a period of unemployment, and as a result a temporal disequilibrium situation may become structural. An additional source of hysteresis within the economy has also been identified by a number of authors, including Malinvaud (1980) and Modigliani *et al.* (1986). In contrast to the preceding analysis, the approach they suggest emphasizes the role of demand-side factors in raising the full-employment level of output in a recession and thereby motivating the persistence in unemployment that has been so widely observed. Central to their argument is the notion that Europe is essentially suffering from a capital shortage.

The argument is based upon two observations. The first is that throughout the 1970s, profit rates across Europe were dramatically reduced as a result of adverse demand and supply shocks. This had the effect of reducing the rate of investment, the proportion of gross fixed-capital formation in GDP falling by between 20 per cent and 30 per cent. Over the same period, the average life of the capital stock has fallen, the combined impact being to reduce the aggregate level of capital accumulation. Under these circumstances maintenance of full employment requires that relative-factor prices move against labour. In reality, however, precisely the opposite has occurred and the subsequent increase in unemployment may be thought of, in effect, as coming about as a result of the capital constraint.

Critics of the capital-gap framework, however, typically point out that a fundamental flaw with the approach lies in the fact that it involves no obvious form of market failure in itself. Bean (1989), for example, notes that, provided that increases in labour demand are not dissipated in the form of higher wage demands, increased demand and higher levels of capacity utilization should encourage firms to expand capacity via increased investment. The mechanism may take some considerable time to operate, but any capital constraint which occurs must be, at most, a transitory problem.

One factor which may potentially extend the time horizon needed for this adjustment process to operate is the availability of an appropriate skill-mix among the workforce. We therefore turn to consider the role of worker mismatch in explaining the persistence of European unemployment. The idea that the structural characteristics of the unemployed — defined variously in terms of occupation, industry or skills — are important, has long been recognized. Layard and Nickell (1986), for example, address the issue within the context of the UK labour market, whilst Layard, Nickell and Jackman (1991) examine the problem across a range of OECD countries. In the European context, the argument is relatively straightforward. Since 1970, fundamental changes in industrial structure and work practices have shifted production techniques away from mass production to those requiring a more flexible form of specialization among the workforce. As a result, the relative demands for labour have been altered in favour of skilled workers; maintenance of full employment among unskilled workers, therefore, requires that the relative wage for this group should fall. However, this adjustment mechanism may be impeded in two respects – where unskilled wages exhibit downward inflexibility, or where the skilled–unskilled differential is rigid. In either of these situations, changes in the pattern of labour demand will produce unemployment among unskilled workers.

Unfortunately, solid evidence concerning the extent of worker mismatch within the economy is extremely difficult to come by. Certainly casual evidence does suggest that one characteristic of the current European situation is a disproportionate incidence of job loss among unskilled workers. Anecdotal evidence regarding a skills shortage developing during the previous recovery also seems to support the general premise. At a more formal level, however, the evidence of mismatch is considerably weaker. Layard *et al.* (1991), for example, find little evidence of an index of worker mismatch increasing through time. Broadly consistent evidence from a wide range of countries including France, Germany, the Netherlands, Austria, Finland and Norway is also reported by Jackman and Roper (1987). Under these circumstances, it is extremely difficult to maintain the notion of mismatch as a primary cause of persistent unemployment within Europe.

4. Regional labour markets: the policy implications for Europe

The European labour market is currently more of a concept than a reality, though recent moves towards both a single market and monetary union within Europe increase the possibilities for treating labour markets within Europe in a manner analogous to regional labour markets within a single country. Three factors, in particular, operate to bring this about. First, complete monetary union within Europe implies a single currency and, therefore, a single monetary policy. Second, to the extent that budget deficits require monetary financing, a complete monetary union will also reduce fiscal autonomy. These factors combined severely restrict the opportunities for individual countries to offset the effect of asymmetric shocks. Finally, under the regulations governing the operation of the single market, free movement of labour across national boundaries is guaranteed, implying that labour-market conditions in one country may spill over directly into labour markets located in neighbouring countries. The analogous problem within a single country is the spill-over effects which may occur between regions.

Completing the single market within Europe may adversely affect labour markets for a variety of reasons. Enhanced competition among producers located in different nations, for example, should result in a movement towards a greater degree of specialization as the least efficient businesses are removed from the market. As a consequence, resources will need to be reallocated within Europe in line with the emerging pattern of production. Regional — which in this case may involve areas as large as countries — unemployment is likely to feature as one aspect of this adjustment process. Indeed Anderton et al. (1991) see high unemployment in countries belonging to the ERM as a consequence of attempting to obtain nominal convergence with Germany through a policy of deflation, probably resulting in 700,000 lost jobs in France and approximately one million in Italy. To date European integration, rather than reducing unemployment through expansion of the internal market, has resulted in unemployment increasing in the Community, relative to other European and OECD countries.[16] The passage to European monetary union is likely to place further adjustment costs on already disadvantaged countries on the periphery of Europe which are especially inflation-prone. As a result, Begg and Mayers (1991) expect real disparities in the EC to widen further during the 1990s as in the 1980s.[17]

Although economic theory suggests that any regional unemployment differentials which develop in this way should disappear through the process of migration, the evidence from the United States suggests that removing barriers to migration alone may be an inadequate response to this problem within Europe. Here, in particular, we would draw attention to the heterogeneity of both language and culture which may effectively limit the extent to which intra-EC labour flows can occur. As a result, regional unemployment differentials that come about through the process of structural adjustment may persist for quite some time (see Ermisch 1991).

Three additional factors have also been identified as contributing to the non-convergence of regional unemployment differentials in the United States. Murphy and Hofler (1984), for example, highlight the role played by the sectoral composition of employment, together with differences in both education and training. They suggest that the latter, in particular, may give rise to substantial labour market rigidities. For Topel (1984), however, it is experience that matters, with experienced workers typically being found to invest more in region-specific skills and, therefore, less likely to migrate. Of these, differences in education and training may prove to be particularly important in the European context. Evidence gathered by the National Institute of Economic and Social Research suggests that major differences exist between the provision of education and training across Europe, with Britain, in particular, having one of the least well-trained and educated workforces.[18]

The problem which these wide disparities pose for Europe, as it moves closer towards complete monetary union and the single market, cannot be overstated. Labour-market imbalances induced by the adjustment process are likely to put considerable strain upon the emerging system and lead to calls for 'regional devaluations' within Europe. In the United States such pressures are contained through the provision of substantial inter-regional transfers, which limit regional unemployment differentials by offsetting part of the decline in regional income and relaxing the severity of the external constraint. Whether sufficient political foresight currently exists within Europe to implement such fiscal federalism remains, as yet, to be seen.

5. Conclusions

Since the 1970s, the European countries (especially the members of the European Community) have experienced large increases in unemployment. This has particularly been the case in a number of the less prosperous countries on the periphery of Europe. These increases in unemployment have, of course, involved large economic and social costs. Hence policies are desperately needed to solve the problem.

A move toward centralization and co-operation across economic institutions should also perhaps be a long-term aim, given the relative success of Scandinavian countries in holding down unemployment. This system seems to have been particularly successful in avoiding rises in unemployment following supply-side shock such as oil-price increases in the 1970s. Real-wage decreases can be managed without a price-wage spiral and resulting unemployment. However, as Nickell (1990) points out, there is little evidence that such institutions can successfully be transported across national boundaries.

Competitive theory suggests that regional unemployment differentials should disappear as a result of the migration of labour and capital; hence labour-market intervention is unnecessary. Evidence suggests, however, that this process is not happening, or is taking place so slowly, in much of Europe that additional action is necessary. Indeed alternative theories have developed, emphasizing virtuous and vicious circles of development rather than convergence to equilibrium. In particular, Nevin (1990) has questioned whether the process of migration actually leads to the elimination of wage differentials:

> Labour mobility tends to be highest amongst the young and skilled, so that the exporting country may be weakened rather than strengthened by the process. (Nevin 1990, 266)

In this case, migration is likely to lead to divergent development. Indeed, a number of other changes taking place in Europe may also encourage this.

The benefits arising from integration of the European market after 1992, and eventual monetary union, may not be evenly distributed across regions. Traditional means of alleviating such problems such as exchange-rate movements and fiscal measures, are likely to become increasingly constrained and less effective within the European Community, as the process towards integration continues to create complex interdependencies between countries. Indeed centripetal forces (see Cowling 1990) are at work pulling industry increasingly towards the richer regions at the centre of Europe. As a result, Nevin (1990) argues that:

> ... the emergence of greater regional inequalities would make some form of regional policy essential to the success of a monetary union. (Nevin 1990, 288)

Given the existence of wage and skill differentials across Europe, this regional policy may be most effectively directed towards human-capital developments, especially if aimed at the long-term unemployed (since the possible inflationary consequences are reduced as these individuals have effectively dropped out of the labour market). This in itself, however, may not be enough, because the general levels of skill accumulation suggests that the vintage approach (of training the young and the unemployed), may no longer be sufficient, and so training policy needs to be directed across the whole workforce. The notion of a once-and-for-all career preparation is becoming less appropriate. Rather, workers need continually to upgrade their skills in order to keep pace with, and encourage, the diffusion of technology, if Europe is to compete successfully and so avoid high levels of unemployment in the future. Such labour-market policies would also speed up adjustment when in disequilibrium, by reducing the influence that past unemployment has on future unemployment.

Acknowledgements

We are grateful for helpful comments on earlier drafts of this paper from M. J. Artis, K. Clark, I. Jeffries, D. Leslie, P. D. Murphy, R. Naylor and E. Symons. All remaining errors are, naturally, our own.

Financial support from the Welsh Funding Councils and the ESRC (research award R00232754) is gratefully acknowledged.

Notes

1. A clear example of this is Belgium, where government borrowing increased to 16.4 per cent of GDP in 1981, and France, where the PSBR rose to 13 per cent of GDP following OPEC I.
2. Blanchflower and Freeman (1990) also note that countries with centralized wage-setting behaviour have small union/non-union wage mark-ups, thereby giving management less incentive to appease such organizations. On the whole, unionization rates in Europe are above the average for OECD countries, and higher in small countries than they are in the larger ones.
3. Centralized bargaining appears to have been particularly successful in avoiding increases in unemployment following adverse movements

178 Labour-market flexibility

in the terms of trade. In effect, the system manages to bring about the necessary reduction in real wages, without resorting to a wage-price spiral and consequent increase in unemployment.

4. This has also been the case in Germany to some extent, where guest workers (*Gastarbeiter*) have been encouraged to return home during periods of rising unemployment.
5. Indeed, for Layard the benefit system ranks as one of the five most important factors, the other four being unions, employers' organizations, mismatch, and active labour-market measures.
6. See also Heylen (1991) for further evidence.
7. Such values are, of course, noticeably lower than the unemployment elasticities reported by Minford (1983) using time-series data. Recent work by Wadsworth (1991) using the labour-force survey shows that workers eligible for unemployment compensation engage in more extensive job search than their ineligible counterparts. Hence one outcome of the unemployment benefit system is to maintain a larger labour force than would otherwise exist.
8. Bertola (1990), for example, compares ten countries, eight of them European, in terms of job security. Of these, he finds that Italy has the most restrictive firing practices, whilst the United States has the least.
9. The response to this in a number of countries has been to introduce legislation designed to reduce firing costs. In addition, firms and workers have enhanced 'flexibility' by increasing the scope for part-time employment. Many of these part-time workers are not covered by job-security legislation.
10. Empirical research on the Phillips curve found that, in a number of countries, the actual and natural rates of unemployment were highly correlated. As a result, critics of the natural rate have tended to argue that the concept itself is vacuous.
11. The effect may usefully be distinguished from persistence in unemployment which might be expressed in terms of a random walk model, $U_t = U_{t-1} + e_t$. Hysteresis, on the other hand, might be expressed as $U_t = \beta U_{t-1} + e_t$.
12. This possibility was first recognized by Phelps (1972). He observed that 'the transition from one equilibrium to the other tends to have long, lingering effects on the labour force, and these effects may be discernible in the equilibrium unemployment rate for a long time. The natural rate of unemployment at any future date will depend upon the course of history in the interim' (Phelps 1972, 123).
13. See Blanchard and Diamond (1990) for a summary of these models and a discussion of their importance within the European context.
14. Indeed, the evidence that unemployment does depress real wages is considerable. Summarizing the evidence from time-series studies, Holmlund (1991) concludes that 'the unemployment elasticity of

real wages is in general rather small and varies across countries; there is some tendency for the elasticity to be higher (in absolute value) in countries with more centralized bargaining institutions (such as Sweden, Norway, Finland and Austria)' (Holmlund 1991, 14). When estimating cross-section earnings functions for the UK, Blackaby and Manning (1987) find a role for unemployment in depressing earnings; they find the elasticity of earning with respect to regional unemployment to be small (-0.16) but significant. Similar estimates have been found for a number of European countries by Blanchflower and Oswald (1991). For a useful summary of recent research adopting this approach, see Blanchflower and Oswald (1990).
15. For a theoretical rationale of why firms should adopt this approach, see Blanchard and Diamond (1989).
16. The costs of too rapid an integration process were noted in the Commission of the European Communities report (1977). Increases in unemployment have both economic and social costs; the relationship between unemployment and poverty, for example, is well established. For a discussion of poverty within the EC see Commission of the European Communities report (1989).
17. Regional discrepancies have grown in the European Community from 1973, reversing the tendency towards convergence that was evident since the 1950s (Commission of the European Communities 1989).
18. For further details of this research, see Prais (1989).

References

Anderton, R., Barrell, R. and in't Veld, J. W. (1991). 'Macroeconomic convergence in Europe', *National Institute Economic Review*, (November 1991) 51–62.

Atkinson, A. B., Gomulka, J., Micklewright, J. and Rau, N. (1984). 'Unemployment benefit, duration and incentives in Britain: how robust is the evidence?', *Journal of Public Economics*, 23 Nos. 1/2, 3–26.

Barro, R. (1988). 'The persistence of unemployment', *American Economic Review: Papers and Proceedings*, Nos. 78, 2, 32–37.

Bean, C. (1989). 'Capital shortages and persistent unemployment', *Economic Policy*, 8 (April 1989), 11–54.

Begg, I. and Mayers, D. (1991). 'Social and economic cohesion among the regions of Europe in the 1990s', *National Institute Economic Review* (November 1991), 63–74.

Bertola, G. (1990). 'Job security, employment and wages', *European Economic Review*, 34, 851–86.

Bertolila, S., and Bertola, G. (1990). 'Firing costs and labour demand: how bad is eurosclerosis?', *Review of Economic Studies*, 57 No. 3, 381–407.

Blackaby, D. H., Bladen-Hovell, R. C. and Symons, S. (1991). 'Unemployment duration and wage determination in the UK: evidence from the Family Expenditure Survey', *Oxford Bulletin of Economics and Statistics*, 53 No. 4, 377–400.

Blackaby, D. H. and Manning, N. (1987). 'Regional earnings revisited', *The Manchester School*, 55 No. 2, 158–83.

Blackaby, D. H. and Manning, N. (1990). 'The north-south divide: questions of existence and stability', *Economic Journal*, 100 No. 401, 510–27.

Blanchard, O. J. and Diamond, P. (1990). 'Unemployment and wages: what have we learned from the European experience?' (Employment Institute, 1990).

Blanchard, O. J. and Summers, L. (1986). 'Hysteresis and the European unemployment problem', in S. Fisher (ed.), *NBER Macroeconomics Annual* (Cambridge, Mass., MIT Press, 1986).

Blanchard, O. J. and Summers, L. (1987). 'Hysteresis in unemployment', *European Economic Review*, 31 No. 3, 543–60.

Blanchflower, D. G. and Freeman, R. (1990). 'Going different ways: unionism in the US and other advanced OECD countries' (Centre for Economic Performance, discussion paper No.5, 1990).

Blanchflower, D. G. and Oswald, A. (1990). 'The wage curve', *Scandinavian Journal of Economics*, 92 No.2, 215–36.

Blanchflower, D. G. and Oswald, A. (1991). 'US and European wage curves', paper presented to the Econometric Study Group, Bristol University, 1991.

Bruno, M. and Sachs, J. (1985). *The Economics of Worldwide Stagflation*, (Oxford Basil Blackwell, 1985).

Burda, M. (1988). 'Wait unemployment in Europe', *Economic Policy*, 7, 391–426.

Calmfors, L. and Driffill, J. (1988). 'Centralization of wage bargaining and macroeconomic performance', *Economic Policy*, 6, 13–61.

Coe, D. T. (1988). 'Hysteresis effects in aggregate wage equations', in R. Cross (ed.), *Unemployment and the Natural Rate Hypothesis* (Oxford Basil Blackwell, 1988).

Cowling, K. (1990). 'A new industrial strategy: preparing Europe for the turn of the century' *International Journal of Industrial Organization*, 8, 165–83.

Devine, P. and Kiefer, N. (1990). 'The empirical status of job search theory', paper presented at the world meeting of the Econometric Society, Barcelona, 1990.

Eriksson, T., Suvanto A., and Vartia, P. *et al.* (1990). 'Wage setting in Finland', in L. Calmfors (ed.), *Wage Formation and Macroeconomic Policy in Nordic Countries* (Oxford, Oxford University Press, 1990).

Ermisch, J. (1991). 'European integration and external constraints on social policy: is a social charter necessary?', *National Institute Economic Review* (May 1991), 93 – 108.

European Commission (1977). *Report of the Study Group on the Role of Public Finance in European Integration* (Brussels, European Commission, 1977).

European Commission (1989). *Employment in Europe* (Luxembourg, European Commission, 1989).

Freeman, R. B. (1988). 'Labour-market institutions and economic performance', *Economic Policy*, 6, 64 – 80.

Giersch, H. (1985). 'Eurosclerosis' (Department of Economics discussion paper No.112, University of Kiel, 1985).

Gottfries, N. and Horn, H. (1987). 'Wage formation and persistence of unemployment', *Economic Journal*, 97 No. 4, 877 – 86.

Groot, W., and Jehoel-Gilsbers, G. (1990). 'The influence of unemployment benefit levels on the duration of unemployment', CURE Working Paper, 1990.

Henley, A. and Tsakalotos, E. (1991). 'Corporatism and the European labour market after 1992', University of Kent discussion paper 91/7, 1991.

Heylen, F. (1991). 'Long-term unemployment in the OECD countries: the relevance of structural labour market and labour-market policy characteristics', report 91/258, Studiecentrum voor Economisch en Sociale Onderzoek, 1991.

Holmlund, B. (1990). *Wage Formation in Sweden – Theory, Evidence and Policy* (Stockholm, Timbro Press, 1990).

Holmlund, B. (1991). 'Unemployment persistence and insider – outsider forces in wage determination', OECD working paper, No.92, 1991.

Holmlund, B. and Lofgen, K. G. (1990). *Unemployment and Wage Determination in Europe* (Oxford, Basil Blackwell, 1990).

Jackman, R. and Layard, R. (1991). 'Does long-term unemployment reduce a person's chance of a job? A time series test', *Economica*, 58, 93 – 106.

Jackman, R., and Roper, S. (1987). 'Structural unemployment', *Oxford Bulletin of Economics and Statistics*, 49 No. 1, 9 – 36.

Lancaster, T. (1979). 'Econometric methods for the duration of unemployment', *Econometrica*, 47 No. 4, 939 – 56.

Layard, R. (1989). 'European unemployment: cause and cure', Centre for Labour Economics, discussion paper No. 368, London School of Economics, 1989.

Layard, R. (1990). 'Understanding unemployment', Centre for Economic Performance, discussion paper No.4, London School of Economics, 1990.

Layard, R. and Nickell, S. (1986). 'Unemployment in Britain', *Economica* 53 (Special issue on unemployment), S121 – S169.

Layard, R. Nickell, S., and Jackman, R. (1991). *Unemployment: Macro-*

economic Performance and the Labour Market (Oxford, Oxford University Press, 1991).
Lindbeck, A. and Snower, D. (1988). *The Insider-Outsider Theory of Employment and Unemployment* (Cambridge, Mass., MIT Press, 1988).
Malinvaud, E. (1980). *Profitability and Unemployment* (Cambridge, Cambridge University Press, 1980).
Meager, N. and Metcalf, S. (1987). 'Recruitment of the long-term unemployed', Institute of Manpower Studies, report No. 138, 1987.
Minford, P. (1983). *Unemployment: Cause and Cure* (Oxford, Basil Blackwell, 1983).
Modigliani, F. et al. (1986). *Reducing Unemployment in Europe: The Role of Capital Formation* (Brussels, Centre for European Studies, 1986).
Moylan, S., Miller J. and Davies, R. (1984). 'For richer, for poorer?', DHSS Cohort Study of Unemployed Men, Department of Health and Social Security research report No. 11, 1984.
Murphy K. and Hofler, R. (1984). 'Determinants of geographic unemployment rates: a selectively-pooled simultaneous model', *Review of Economics and Statistics*, 66, 216–23.
Narendranathan, W., Nickell, S. and Stern, J. (1985). 'Unemployment benefits revisited', *Economic Journal*, 95 No. 2, 307–29.
Nevin, E. (1990). *The Economics of Europe* (London, Macmillan, 1990).
Nickell, S. (1979). 'Estimating the probability of leaving unemployment', *Econometrica*, 47 No. 5, 1249–66.
Nickell, S. (1990). 'Unemployment: a survey', *Economic Journal*, 100 No. 401, 391–439.
Nickell, S. and Wadhwani, S. (1990). 'Insider Forces and Wage Determination', *Economic Journal*, 100 No. 2, 496–509.
OECD (Organization for Economic Co-operation and Development) (1989). *Employment Outlook* (Paris, OECD, 1989).
OECD (1990). *Employment Outlook* (Paris, OECD, 1990).
OECD (1991). *Employment Outlook* (Paris, OECD, 1991).
Phelps, E. (1972). *Inflation Policy and Unemployment Theory* (London, Macmillan, 1972).
Prais, S. J. (1989). 'Qualified manpower in engineering: Britain and other industrially-advanced countries', *National Institute Economic Review*, (February 1989), 76–83.
Rowthorn, R. (1990). 'Wage dispersion and employment: theories and evidence', Department of Applied Economics, working paper No. 9001, University of Cambridge, 1990.
Rowthorn, R. and Glyn, A. (1987). 'The diversity of unemployment experience since 1973', Applied Economics discussion paper No. 40, University of Oxford, 1987.

Soskice, D. (1990). 'Wage determination: the changing role of institutions in advanced industrialized countries', *Oxford Review of Economic Policy*, 6 No. 4, 36–61.

Topel, R. (1984). 'Equilibrium earnings, turnover and unemployment evidence', *Journal of Labour Economics*, 2 No. 4, 500–22.

Wadsworth, J. (1991). 'Unemployment benefits and search effort in the UK labour market', *Economica*, 43, 13–27.

8
The impact of the European Community on regional policies in Wales
D. ROY THOMAS

1. Introduction

In the period leading up to UK entry into the European Community there was considerable apprehension in Wales about its likely impact on UK regional policy. In retrospect, it might appear that there was some basis for this apprehension. The period since UK accession has seen a progressive erosion in regional policy in the UK, and one of the themes explored in this paper will be the extent to which this can be attributed to EC membership. The other main theme will be an examination of the relationship between developments in UK regional policy and the evolution of regional policy at the European level.

2. Regional policy at the time of UK entry

At the time of UK accession to the EC, regional policy in Britain was in one of its most active phases. The whole of Wales was designated as an assisted area. The two highest-category areas, special development areas (SDAs) and development areas (DAs) covered, respectively, 25 per cent and 60 per cent of Wales's working population. The value of the incentives available to firms in these areas was also higher than had been available in any previous package. For a typical manufacturing project with a plant:buildings expenditure ratio of 4:1, the combined effect of regional development grants (RDGs) and tax savings from capital allowances, reduced the cost to firms of investing in DAs (on a DCF basis) by over 50 per cent (*Trade and Industry*, 27 April 1972, 147). The differential in favour of DA investments was also at an unprecedented level. To attain an equivalent after-tax DCF rate of return, a firm investing in an ordinary area would have required a before-tax level of profits 32 per cent higher than for a comparable DA investment (Thomas 1972).

In addition to RDGs which were available only in DAs, firms throughout Wales were eligible for regional selective assistance (RSA). Although total expenditure on RSA in Wales in the 1970s averaged less than one-quarter of the amount paid out in RDGs, the discretionary element in RSA allowed the Welsh Office to make very substantial assistance available to individual projects which it was particularly anxious to attract.

Apart from investment incentives, all manufacturing firms in DAs received an automatic labour subsidy in the form of the regional employment premium and, in many cases, a rent subsidy, since the rents paid by firms occupying government factories were substantially below the levels needed to provide a commercial rate of return on factory building. Positive financial inducements to locate in the assisted areas were reinforced by a system of negative controls. At its peak in the mid-1960s, the refusal rate for Industrial Development Certificate (IDC) applications in the Midlands and the South East reached 25 per cent. Moreover, this almost certainly underestimates the severity of IDC policy at this time, since in many cases firms held back from making a formal application if they believed this would be unsuccessful.

3. The decline in UK regional policy

The period following the UK's accession to the EC witnessed a progressive run-down in British regional policy. By the mid-1970s, IDC policy was effectively in abeyance, although it was not until 1981 that IDC controls were formally suspended. The dismantling of regional financial incentives began with the repeal of REP at the end of 1976. The following year saw the start of a gradual erosion in the value and the scope of the RDG scheme. In 1977, RDGs were withdrawn from mining and construction projects. Two years later in 1979, the rate of grant in DAs was reduced from 20 per cent to 15 per cent. The next major change came in 1984 when DA coverage was drastically reduced. As a result, the areas in Wales eligible for RDG assistance now covered barely one-third of the working population, compared with 86 per cent in 1978. The 1984 reforms also saw major changes in the RDG system itself. In particular, replacement and modernization investments were specifically excluded, and (except in the case of small firms) a £10,000 cost-per-job limit imposed. In

1988, the scheme itself was terminated, and RDGs were abolished altogether.

In the meantime, the conditions governing the payment of RSA had also been considerably tightened. In 1979, new RSA guidelines were introduced which meant that assistance would only be made available if it could be shown that this was necessary to enable a project to proceed as planned. In 1984, a further restriction was introduced, namely, that a project had to be of benefit not only to the assisted area but also to the United Kingdom as a whole. In effect, this meant that a firm which diverted part or all of its activities to an assisted area would no longer be eligible for selective assistance, unless it could be shown that the relocation would result in a net increase in jobs. Finally, in 1993, there was a further reduction in DA coverage to just over 15 per cent of the working population (although over one half of the population continued to reside in Intermediate Areas where a lower level of RSA was available).

The net effect of these changes has been a substantial reduction in government expenditure in Wales on regional preferential assistance (see Figure 1). Indeed, by the early 1980s, expenditure in real terms had fallen to around one half of its mid-1970s level.

4. The role of the EC in the decline of UK regional policy

UK accession to the EC had both a direct and an indirect influence on the direction of British regional policy. In the case of the abandonment of IDC policy, the influence was mainly indirect. Although there is nothing in the Rome treaty to prohibit the use of negative controls, fears that firms refused IDC applications might transfer their activities abroad, or suffer a loss in competitiveness by being forced to expand in existing premises, were considerably heightened as a result of EC membership.

In the case of regional financial incentives, the effect of UK accession has been much more direct. Section 3a of article 92 of the Rome treaty gives specific dispensation to member states to provide 'aid intended to promote the economic development of regions where the standard of living is abnormally low, or where there exists serious under-employment'. However, the Commission was given extensive legal powers under Article 93 of the treaty to monitor and control the types of regional assistance each member state can provide. In particular, the treaty empowers the Commission to determine which areas should be eligible for assistance, to set limits on the amounts of assistance that can be made available, and to determine which types of assistance are permissible.

The Commission's approach towards regional aid provided by member states has been governed by four main criteria, namely that aid should be transparent, degressive, selective, and related to need.

By *transparency* is meant that the value of any aid should be calculable with certainty. The way the Commission measures the value of an incentive is by reference to its net grant equivalent (NGE) (essentially its present value), expressed in relation to the initial cost of an investment. In the case of investment incentives, the Commission has taken a firm view that grants are preferable to investment allowances, on the grounds that in order to take full advantage of accelerated depreciation, a firm needs to have sufficient profits to make full use of the capital allowances at its disposal, and clearly profits are subject to uncertainty. Although free depreciation was not specifically a regional incentive since it was available post-1972 throughout the UK, nevertheless its removal in the 1984 Finance Act was very much in line with the Commission's thinking. An alleged lack of transparency also explains, in part, the Commission's opposition to labour subsidies. Although it is not difficult to estimate the present value of labour subsidies, the Commission would no doubt argue that future employment levels, once again, are subject to uncertainty, and in the case of an unconditional subsidy (such as the regional employment premium, REP) it is not clear how the present value of the subsidy could be related to investment costs.

The Commission's main objection to ongoing labour subsidies, however, is not so much that they are 'opaque', but that they violate the principle of *degressivity*. Basically, this implies that the aim of regional financial assistance should be to remove locational shortcomings, rather than simply to compensate firms for locational disadvantages. In other words, the aim should be to create the conditions in which, ultimately, the assistance can safely be phased out.

The *selectivity* criterion is designed to ensure that any distortion in inter-state competition resulting from state aids should be minimized. The basic principle is that financial inducements should be set at the minimum level necessary to achieve their stated objectives. Thus, regional assistance should not be available to finance projects or investments that would be undertaken without any financial support. The selectivity criterion effectively rules out blanket subsidies such as REP. It also implies that any investment incentives should be confined to new projects or expansion projects, and should not be available on an ongoing basis to finance replacement investments which, the Commission would argue, firms have to undertake as a matter of course. The imposition of cost-per-job limits is very much in line with the selectivity criterion, as indeed is the more general movement witnessed in the UK away from automatic subsidies towards more discretionary forms of assistance.

The final principle that has guided the Commission's thinking on regional aid is that there should be a close *relationship* between the level of incentives available in different areas and the severity of the problems faced by those areas. The first steps towards implementing this principle were taken by the Commission in 1971, and by 1975 a system of differentiated limits had been introduced. These took the form of NGE ceilings expressed either in relation to the initial cost of an investment or to the number of jobs created. In the case of the UK development areas, the NGE ceiling was set as 30 per cent of the initial investment or 5,500 ECUs per job created, compared with 75 per cent and 13,500 ECUs in Ireland and the Mezzogiorno. In the early years, the Commission seems to have been somewhat reluctant to enforce these limits. In the UK, for example, as was indicated earlier, the value of the incentives available to manufacturing firms investing in the DAs remained well above the Commission's 1975 limits throughout the 1970s. Nevertheless, the Commission has brought pressure to bear on member states to scale down the level of their assistance, and to concentrate help in areas of greatest need. Indeed, in written evidence to the Welsh Affairs Committee, the European Policies Research Centre at the University of Strathclyde goes so far as to suggest that the influence of the European Commission has been the single most important factor behind the tightening of regional grant regimes in many EC countries, and that the efforts of DG IV (the competition directorate) have 'led to a systematic reduction in spatial coverage of designated assisted areas' (House of Commons 1988, 2, appendix 17).

The Commission has also exerted a decisive influence on the *types* of regional assistance provided by member states. As was indicated earlier, REP effectively violated all the Commission's regional policy criteria, and it was the Commission which eventually insisted that it be abolished. The switch from item-related to project-related assistance introduced in 1984, and the decision to exclude replacement investment from RDG eligibility also seem to have been prompted by EC pressure. Indeed, the Department of Trade and Industry (1983, para 19) acknowledged that the decision to exclude replacement investment was the result of an undertaking to this effect it had given to the Commission. An assurance was also given in the 1983 green paper that account would be taken of EC limits in setting the rates of grant for the revised RDG scheme (ibid., annex B, para 6). It is clear from the evidence of the DTI to the Committee on Welsh Affairs that the Commission was also involved in the decision to abolish RDGs in 1988 and to place greater reliance on selective assistance: 'We certainly consulted them [the European Commission], indeed had their approval for the change, which is with the grain of much of their thinking in Brussels' (op.cit., Q344).

Although the European Commission has undoubtedly exerted a considerable influence on the direction of UK regional policy, there are a number of other factors, largely unrelated to EC membership, which have contributed to the run-down in policy. By the mid-1970s the economic environment had become much less favourable to the operation of regional policy. The deceleration in economic growth following the first OPEC oil price rise, coupled with the structural decline in manufacturing employment – dating back in the case of the UK to 1965 – considerably diminished the scope for influencing the location of manufacturing activity, upon which UK regional policy had traditionally relied. By the mid-1970s the traditional micro and macro arguments for regional intervention had also come to be viewed with increasing scepticism.

On the micro side, the view that regional policy can contribute to a more efficient spatial allocation of resources had come to be regarded as highly dubious. In particular, the problems in the car industry following its dispersal away from its west Midlands base, cast considerable doubt on the results of earlier empirical work by Luttrell (1962) and others, which had suggested that inter-regional cost differences were insignificant. The externality arguments in favour of regional policy advanced in the Barlow Report (1940) were also increasingly being called into question. By the mid-1970s, concern about congestion costs, arising from the increasing concentration of the population in industrial conurbations, was rapidly giving way to a concern over the increasing dereliction of inner-city areas, brought about by the drift of population *away* from the major conurbations. In the meantime, the rise in monetarist orthodoxy was also undermining the main *macro* argument in favour of regional policy, namely that by diverting activity away from labour-shortage areas, regional policy can improve the terms of the trade-off between inflation and unemployment. The rationale behind traditional regional policy was further undermined by an argument which rapidly gained ground in the aftermath of the 1979 – 81 recession, that the post-war policy of diversifying the industrial structure of declining regions had succeeded only in creating, within these regions, a branch-plant syndrome which was highly damaging to their entrepreneurial potential and to their capacity for indigenous growth (see, for instance, Regional Studies Association, 1983).

It is clear, therefore, that the erosion in UK regional policy that followed the UK's accession to the European Community cannot be wholly attributed to EC membership. Indeed, if the UK had not entered the EC, the decline in policy might have been even more pronounced. The conservative governments of the 1980s had little real commitment to regional intervention, and seem to have regarded regional policy as little more than a political expedience, and a leverage to attract foreign investment and European Regional Development Fund grants. The main stimulus to inward investment in the UK has stemmed from EC membership. The retention of regional incentives by the Thatcher government, therefore, could well have been due, in part, to a desire to maximize the UK share of inward investment by overseas companies seeking a manufacturing base within the EC. A further factor was the availability of Regional Fund grants. One of the reasons for the establishment of the fund in 1975 was precisely to reduce the UK's net budgetary contribution to the Community. In order to qualify for Regional Fund assistance, however, member states are normally expected to provide matching funds from their own resources. In addition, grants have mainly been restricted to areas that governments have designated as assisted areas for their own regional-policy purposes.

In order to maximize its 'take' from ERDF, therefore, the UK government has been obliged to maintain its own regional-development programme. As we shall see in the next section, the actual benefits Wales has obtained from European regional assistance have been relatively insignificant, and it could be argued that ERDF's most important contribution during the 1980s was to help ensure the survival of the UK's own regional policies.

5. EC regional policy

The main instruments of EC regional policy are the three structural funds: the European Regional Development Fund, the Social Fund and the guidance section of the Agricultural Fund (EAGGF). Of these, only the ERDF was set up specifically to deal with regional imbalances. However, the Social Fund, which is mainly devoted to supporting industrial training, and the guidance section of EAGGF, which assists programmes to improve the incomes of hill farmers, both operate with a definite regional bias. One other source of structural spending has been the grants paid under European coal and steel provisions to assist the resettlement and retraining of redundant coal and steel workers. ECSC loans have also been available to promote alternative employment in coal and steel closure areas. The other main source of loan assistance has been the European Investment Bank, which from the outset has operated primarily as a regional development bank.

Figure 1 shows EC grant allocations for structural spending in Wales over the period 1973–92. These do not include grants, notably from the Social Fund, negotiated on a UK basis, where the Welsh element cannot readily be identified. Although Figure 1 indicates that the value of EC structural spending in Wales has increased relative to UK regional expenditure, the scale of EC assistance has remained quite small, and by 1988 amounted to less than 0.4 per cent of Wales's GDP. Moreover, the benefit to Wales from the ERDF component (around 90 per cent of total *identifiable* spending in 1987–8) has been largely illusory. In the case of aid for industrial projects (which, up to 1988, accounted for around 30 per cent of total ERDF spending in Wales), ERDF receipts were used simply to reimburse the UK government for expenditure on regional assistance it had already incurred. The

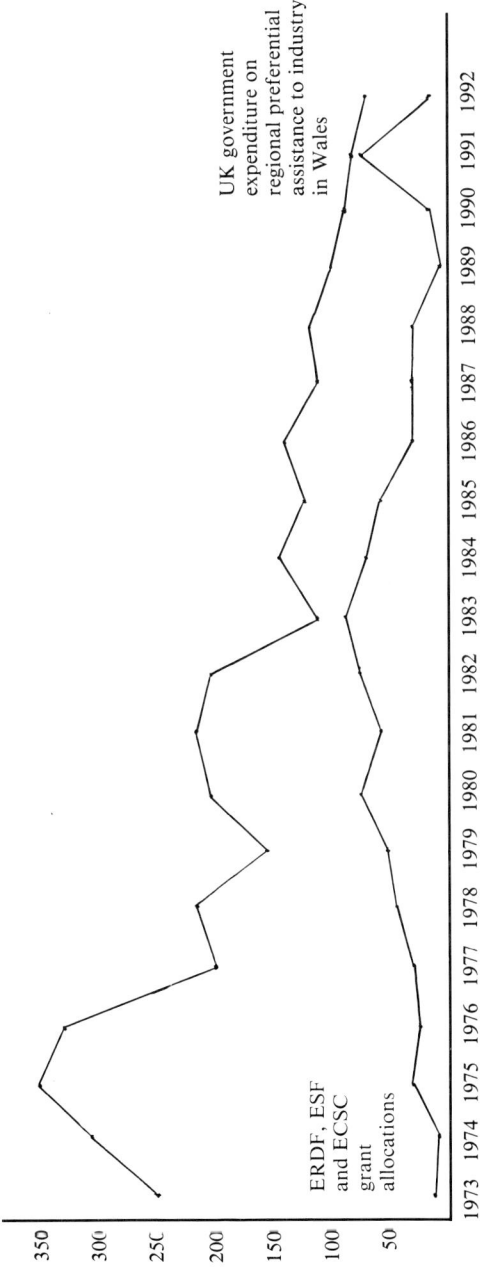

Figure 1: Regional-policy expenditure in Wales 1973–92, at constant 1985 prices

NOTES: UK government expenditure includes regional development grants, regional enterprise grants, regional employment premium, selective financial assistance and expenditure by the WDA and DBRW on land and factories.
EC grant allocations are grant expenditures allocated to Wales by the European Regional Development Fund the European Social Fund and the European Coal and Steel Community. Since payments lag allocations this series overstates the value of EC grant aid. On the other hand, grants negotiated on a UK basis (notably from the ESF), the Welsh element of which cannot readily be identified, are not included.
The series are not directly comparable. UK government expenditure relates to financial years and EC expenditure to calendar years.

Sources: Welsh Economic Trends, Regional Trends, and annual reports of Industry Act.

government, while conceding that in the case of *individual* industrial projects there never has been any 'additionality', has always maintained that ERDF receipts are fully taken into account in determining overall regional spending. This claim is impossible to refute, but it has become less plausible as the UK grant regime has become more selective.

The bulk of ERDF assistance to Wales up to 1988 was in respect of local authority infrastructure projects. In this case, any grants received were passed on to the relevant local authority. Once again, however, there was no local additionality, since no adjustment was made to a local authority's capital spending limits to take account of the receipt of an ERDF grant. In very few instances, therefore, did ERDF aid enable local authorities to proceed with projects which they would not otherwise have been able to undertake. Moreover, it is not entirely certain that local authorities in receipt of ERDF grants obtained any benefit from the resulting saving in loan charges. There is at least a suspicion that this saving was taken into account by central government in determining local authority revenue-support levels.

As in the case of industrial projects, the UK government has always insisted that the projected level of ERDF grants for infrastructure projects is taken fully into account in its expenditure planning. However, the problem with overall additionality in this context, as the Department of the Environment conceded in its evidence to the House of Lords select committee in 1988, is that some of the benefits of ERDF assistance are likely to accrue to areas for which it was clearly not intended: 'It is rather ironic at present that places like Esher get in effect a small percentage of ERDF' (House of Lords 1988, Q372).

6. The 1988 structural reforms

It is clear from the previous section that the direct benefits obtained by Wales from EC regional policies up until 1988 were relatively insignificant and largely illusory. The period since 1988, however, has witnessed major changes in the EC's structural operations, and in the final section of the paper I shall examine to what extent our earlier conclusions need to be modified in the light of these changes.

A key feature of the 1988 reforms has been a substantial increase in the scale of the EC's structural operations. Between 1988 and 1993, structural spending increased from £5 billion to £9.2 billion at 1988 prices. As a percentage of the total Community budget, this represents an increase from 17 per cent in 1987 to 27 per cent in 1992. Although clearly this is a substantial increase, its significance should not be exaggerated. The increase can largely be accounted for by the increase in the size of the Community and the structural problems of the new member states. Indeed, expressed as a percentage of Community GDP the increase has been quite modest — from 0.2 per cent in 1988 to 0.3 per cent in 1993. Moreover, as we shall see shortly, the whole of the increase in expenditure has been concentrated on the Community's poorest regions.

The increase in the scale of the EC's structural assistance has been accompanied by major reforms in the operation of the structural funds. These reforms have been characterized by four main features: concentration, programming, partnership and additionality.

A central feature has been the *concentration* of resources on six specific objectives. Three of these are explicitly regional: the development of structurally backward regions (objective 1); the conversion of declining industrial regions (objective 2); and the development of rural areas (objective 5b). The main priority was accorded to the objective 1 regions — Greece, Portugal, Southern Italy, most of Spain and the whole of Ireland — which were allocated 80 per cent of the total funds available. The territorial boundaries of the objective 2 and 5b regions were to be determined by the Commission using a common set of criteria, thereby, hopefully, ensuring that assistance would be concentrated on areas of greatest need.

In the early period of the operation of the ERDF, assistance was provided entirely for individual projects approved by the member states. However, from 1984 onwards, there was a switch in emphasis towards *programme* assistance. By 1988, 22 per cent of ERDF grants were allocated to programmes drawn up by the ERDF in consultation with national and local governments. The 1988 reforms carried this process a stage further. Under the 1988 regulations, member states were required to submit multi-annual regional development plans, to which the Commission would respond by drawing up a community support framework. This was a document setting out a strategic framework within which specific integrated programmes would be developed, to which *all* the structural funds, the EIB, central and local government, and regional and local development agencies would contribute. The aim was to put together a co-ordinated package of mutually reinforcing measures, and to produce the maximum synergistic effect by ensuring complementarity between Community, national and local initiatives.

The 1988 reforms were also designed to establish a *partnership* between the Commission, national governments and regional and local authorities. The basic idea was to get away from the previous rigid separation between applicants and decision-makers, and to ensure that those responsible for implementing programmes at the local level would be fully involved, from the outset, in programme planning and execution.

The final feature of the 1988 reforms was *additionality*. From the early days of the ERDF, there was a general acceptance that member states had a moral obligation to ensure that any assistance provided by the Community would result in an increase in expenditure over and above what would otherwise occur. Article 9 of the 1988 regulations, however, introduced for the first time a legal requirement to this effect. In addition, the requirements for the co-financing of programmes were designed to ensure that *conditionality* – the principle that resources provided by the Community should be matched by an equivalent commitment of resources by national or local authorities – would be built into the programmes from the start.

7. The 1988 reforms: an assessment

The heavy concentration of assistance on the objective 1 regions was built into the 1988 regulations, and this was more or less implemented according to plan. At the objective 2 level, however, things have not worked out quite as one might have expected. After a considerable delay of some twelve months, the areas in the UK eventually designated as objective 2 regions were areas that corresponded very closely to the UK assisted areas. Moreover, the UK was allocated an 'indicative allowance' of 38.3 per cent of the total funds available for objective 2 purposes. Although this allowance was merely 'indicative', and, therefore, subject to some uncertainty, it is clear that there was not quite as clean a break with the old 'national quota' system of allocating funds between member states as one had been led to expect.

The coverage of areas eligible for assistance in the UK also turned out to be somewhat more extensive than one might have anticipated. Objective 2 regions covered 35 per cent of the UK population, and the objective 5b regions a further 2.6 per cent. If one adds in Northern Ireland (an objective 1 region), then over 40 per cent of the UK population resided in areas that were eligible for assistance − a higher percentage than pre-1988. The only parts of Wales that were excluded were the Colwyn and Monmouth travel-to-work areas.

Within the UK context, therefore, the notion of concentrating assistance in areas of greatest need appears to have gone by the board. In real terms, the amount of funds available per head of population in objective 2 regions of the UK actually fell. As a result, the actual rates of grant paid in these areas have been well below the maximum 50 per cent level laid down in the 1988 regulations. All of this suggests that the funds available have been dispersed too widely. At least as far as the UK is concerned, therefore, the outcome of the 1988 reforms appears to have been *less* rather than more concentration.

There has also been very little indication hitherto that programme assistance has led to a more co-ordinated approach to regional development. There appears to have been very little co-ordination between the structural funds at Community level. The Social, Regional Fund, and Guidance directorates have fought strenuously to retain their independence, and the directorate set up to co-ordinate structural operations (DG XXII) appears to have made very little headway. In evidence to the House of Lords select committee, the Welsh Office reported in 1991 that it had yet to see any evidence of co-ordination at the Community level (House of Lords 1992, Q407). The picture is broadly similar at the local level. The monitoring committees set up to implement programmes have invariably dealt with applications for Social Fund and ERDF assistance quite separately. Indeed, in a recent review of Community structural policies, the Commission itself acknowledges that 'the approach taken is based on what is eligible... instead of being focused on designing programmes made up of mutually supporting measures' (Commission 1992, para 4.4). In the same document (para 4.2) the Commission also admits that efforts to secure the best combination of grants and loans had proved to be totally ineffective. The European Investment Bank has been entirely sceptical of the whole 1988 exercise from the outset. In its evidence to the House of Lords Select Committee in 1988, the EIB dismissed programmes as nothing more than 'a collection of disparate projects' (op. cit., Q49), and to all intents and purposes the bank has played no part in programme formulation or implementation, at either the Community or local levels.

The aim of ensuring complementarity between Community, national and local initiatives has proved even more elusive. While an element of co-financing has been built into development programmes, there is little evidence of any fundamental change in attitude on the part of applicants, who have continued to concentrate their efforts on maximizing their 'take' from Community sources rather than developing a more integrated approach.

Difficulties in achieving greater co-ordination can be attributed in part to the failure to realize another of the key aspects of the 1988 reforms, namely the establishment of a genuine partnership between Community, national and local agencies. In retrospect, it is perhaps not entirely surprising that attempts to adopt a tripartite approach have run into difficulties. There have always been fundamental differences in the attitudes of the different partners towards EC regional policy. Indeed, the history of the ERDF has been characterized by a constant struggle on the part of the Commission to wrest control over the operation of the fund from national governments. In the pursuit of this struggle, the Commission has taken every opportunity to enlist the support of regional and local authorities, who throughout have acted as willing accomplices. The 1988 proposals, that regional and local agencies should be fully involved in every single stage of programme development and implementation, represent a further stage in this power struggle. Not surprisingly, local authorities warmly endorsed the 1988 reforms, while at the same time expressing doubts over whether central government departments would be willing to relinquish power (House of Lords 1988, Q521). For their part, central government officials were highly sceptical of the value of the proposed changes, and anticipated that they would result only in 'an unnecessary increase in bureaucracy' (ibid., para 42).

In retrospect, the concerns expressed by both local-authority representatives and central-government officials have been amply borne out by events. There is little reason to doubt the accuracy of TUC allegations that the government has resisted the spirit of the 1988 reforms by seeking to restrict the inputs of local authorities (Bowen and Mayhew 1991, 349), or of similar allegations by a Welsh member of the regional committee of the European parliament that the Welsh Office has tried to dictate its terms with the result that 'the partnership principle in Wales has not worked very well' (House of Lords 1992, Q452). Equally, however, as we shall see shortly, events have amply confirmed the worst fears of central government officials regarding an increase in bureaucracy. Closely tied up with the partnership principle was the declared intention of the Commission, in 1988, to decentralize decision-making in line with the principle of subsidiarity. Once again, this does not appear to have materialized. In its evidence to the 1991 House of Lords inquiry, the Welsh Office alleges that 'some at desk-officer level in Brussels have not yet been able to feel that they can let go' and, as a result, 'the idea that Brussels would delegate most of the day-to-day management has not been realized' (op. cit., Q407). The Commission itself has subsequently acknowledged that there has been excessive participation by its officers in the detailed implementation of regional programmes (Commission 1992, para 3.2).

As was indicated earlier, the final feature of the 1988 reforms, additionality, is a concept that has been around since the early days of the ERDF. The fact that since 1988, additionality has been a legal requirement, does not necessarily make it any easier to enforce. The main problem from the outset has been that additionality is almost impossible to demonstrate, since there is no way of knowing what government spending on any given programme would be without EC support. In recent years, the Commission's main concern has been to try to ensure that Community funds reach the areas for which they were intended, but it has had difficulty in obtaining data from several member states to enable it to monitor the extent to which this is being achieved (ibid., 4.7).

The main culprit in this regard seems to have been the UK government. As was indicated earlier, it is clear that pre-1988, some of the EFDF funds allocated to the UK were not being spent in the way that had been intended. The 1988 regulation making additionality a legal requirement led to a protracted dispute between the UK and the Commission, which eventually decided to withhold £109 million in regional aid that had been set aside to support projects in Britain's coalfield areas. The Treasury insisted throughout the dispute that the UK government was 'abiding by the letter and the spirit of the law' (House of Lords 1992, Q534), and that any misunderstanding on this score was entirely due to the intricacies of the UK local authority financing system (ibid., Q550)[1]. These assurances failed to satisfy the Commission, which early in 1992 threatened to withhold a further £800 million in aid. This appears to have been sufficient to persuade the UK government to comply fully with the Commission's requirements, thereby bringing the dispute over additionality to an end. However a further dispute arose during 1993, with the EC once again threatening to withhold funding for UK projects. The main problem this time has been conditionality, with many local authorities having difficulties in providing the matching funds needed to comply with EC requirements because of the expenditive ceilings imposed by the UK government.

Most of the ideas behind the 1988 reforms are highly commendable, and they may well eventually bear fruit. However, experience to date has not been very encouraging, and it would be difficult to disagree with the comment made by the Welsh Office to the House of Lords Select Committee (1992, Q407) that 'the hopes and aspirations of 1988 have got bogged down'.

One of the main problems has been the cumbersome and protracted nature of the procedures laid down in the 1988 regulations. These require plans, community support frameworks (CSFs) and then programmes to be written, negotiated and approved before any funding can be committed. To implement these procedures at the local level a two-tier committee system was established for all three areas in Wales – Clwyd, industrial south Wales, and Dyfed, Gwynedd and Powys – where integrated development programmes have been agreed. This consisted of a CSF monitoring committee, which was supposed to take an overview of the operation of the programmes that fall within the CSF, and a programme monitoring committee responsible for programme implementation. Each committee is chaired by a Welsh Office official, meets up to four times a year, and has a membership of up to ninety 'sponsors' or 'participants', representing every public body that has any conceivable interest in any of the CSF programmes, from European Commission directorates to district councils. The sheer size of these committees makes them extremely unwieldy and wholly unsuitable for carrying out some of the tasks they are expected to perform, notably the crucial task of deciding which projects should be supported and included within any given programme.

Given the complexity of the procedures, it is hardly surprising that both the Welsh Office and the Scottish Office have found that the numbers required to administer the new schemes have trebled. The increase in administrative effort on the part of local authorities may well have been even greater. The House of Lords committee is not alone in wondering whether all of this activity can be justified, given the limited resources available: 'regions covered by objectives 2 and 5b sometimes receive comparatively small sums of money for a disproportionately large bureaucratic effort' (House of Lords 1992, para 123). This view has recently been endorsed by the Commission itself, which now acknowledges that the 1988 reforms have resulted in an 'administrative overload which is difficult to justify' (Commission 1992 op.cit., para 4.2).

An inevitable consequence of increased bureaucracy has been long delays in programme approval and implementation. In the case of the Dyfed-Gwynedd-Powys integrated programme, which was originally submitted under the pre-1988 arrangements, it took four years before the programme was fully approved. It is not unusual for CSFs to take over twelve months to be drawn up, and there have also been long delays in payments during the implementation of programmes. Not only are these delays unacceptable in themselves, but they have also put in jeopardy some of the principles underlying the 1988 reforms. In particular, the delays have made it difficult in practice to apply the principle of joint financing. Special provisions have had to be made for Community assistance to be paid retrospectively, with the result that member states have continued to regard this assistance as a reimbursement of their own expenditures.

Whether these shortcomings will be rectified when the Community's structural operations are revamped in 1994 remains to be seen. At the time of writing, there is considerable uncertainty about the future direction of EC regional policies. From the outset the rationale for EC regional policy has derived from the need to prepare the weaker regions of the Community for the increased competition arising from closer economic integration (Tsoukalis 1991, 217). Thus, the doubling of resources for structural spending in 1988 was a direct response to the signing of the Single European Act two years earlier. By the same token, the so-called Delors II package, which envisaged a doubling in structural spending in the EC's poorest regions over the period 1993 – 7, coupled with a 50 per cent increase in objective 2 regions, was originally put forward as a precondition for the establishment of Economic and Monetary Union. Since then a number of countries have encountered difficulties in ratifying the Maastricht Treaty, the ERM has effectively collapsed and the European-wide recession has removed any possibility of any of the major countries being able to meet the Maastricht convergence criteria. As a result, it is now generally expected that progress towards EMU will be considerably retarded. Despite this, the EC has somewhat surprisingly succeeded in gaining acceptance for a substantial part of the original Delors II proposals. The promise of EC aid for the East German Länder and the addition of Merseyside and the Highlands and Islands of Scotland to the list of objective 1 regions helped to overcome the resistance of the German and UK governments to increased structural spending, and it was agreed at the Edinburgh Summit in December 1992 to increase the objective 1 budget by 60 per cent by 1999. At the time of writing, the designation of objective 2 and objective 5b regions has still to be announced, although there is considerable optimism in Wales that the EC emphasis on the income per head criterion (as opposed to unemployment) will mean that almost the whole of Wales will continue to be eligible for assistance from the EC Structural Funds post-January 1994.

8. Conclusions

At the time of UK accession to the EC, there was a firm commitment within the UK to the concept of regional policy. The pressure from Brussels was towards cutting regional spending. In the years that followed, the UK's commitment to regional policy weakened but, in the meantime, the opportunity to tap into Community funds opened up by the emergence of an EC regional policy, helped to ensure that at least the vestiges of a UK regional policy survived the Thatcher years.

The 1988 changes in the structural funds have made EC regional aid a much less attractive proposition from the standpoint of the UK government. The increased concentration on lagging regions has meant that not only the UK, but those parts of the UK such as Wales which benefit from objective 2 funding, have effectively become net contributors to the Community's structural operations, and it is likely that the UK's net contribution will increase still further in the years ahead. In the circumstances, it is perhaps not surprising that the UK government has for some time set itself firmly against any further substantial increase in structural spending (see House of Lords 1992, Q617 and Q628).

The increase in administrative demands arising from the 1988 reforms, the pressure from Brussels to devolve responsibilities to regional and local authorities, and the insistence on additionality have all combined to diminish still further both the attractiveness of EC regional aid to the UK government, and the incentive on its part to persevere with its own regional programme in order to maximize its take from EC regional funds. Any inclination on the part of the UK government to cut back still further on its regional spending, however, is likely to be firmly opposed by the Commission. In recent years, the pressure from Brussels has been towards an increased commitment on the part of member states towards reducing regional disparities.

The wheel, it appears, has come full circle. Not surprisingly, this has been reflected in a transformation in local authorities' attitudes in Wales towards the EC. Widespread apprehension has largely given way to enthusiastic endorsement. No longer is the EC seen as a threat to regional policy, but as one of its principal upholders.

Note
1. The government's case was not exactly helped by an argument advanced by the Secretary of State for Industry that since no additional funds were being allocated to the UK as a result of the 1988 reforms, there was no need to demonstrate additionality (ibid., Q767).

References

Barlow Report (1940). *The Distribution of the Industrial Population*, Cmnd 6153 (London, HMSO, 1940).

Bowen, A., and Mayhew, K. (1991). *Reducing Regional Inequalities* (London, Kogan Page, 1991).

Commission of the European Communities (1992). *Community Structural Policies: Assessment and Outlook*, 84 final, (Brussels, 1992).

House of Commons (1988). *Inward Investment into Wales and its Interaction with Regional and EEC Policies*, Committee on Welsh Affairs, session 1988 – 9, 1st report (London, 1988).

House of Lords (1988). *Reform of the Structural Funds*, Committee on the European Communities, session 1987 – 8, 14th report (London, 1988).

House of Lords (1992). *EEC Regional Development Policy*, Committee on the European Communities, session 1991 – 2, 4th report (London, 1992).

Luttrell, W. F. (1962). *Factory Location and Industrial Movement*, vol. 1 (London, National Institute of Economic and Social Research, 1962).

Thomas, D. R. (1972). 'The new incentives to invest: liquidity and profitability aspects', *Scottish Journal of Political Economy* (1972), 273 – 86.

Tsoukalis, L. (1993). *The New European Economy: The Politics and Economics of Integration* (Oxford, Oxford University Press, 1993).

9
Agriculture and the rural economy of Wales

G. O. HUGHES, D. I. BATEMAN and P. MIDMORE

1. Introduction

Agriculture is in a state of crisis, unprecedented since the 1930s. Its most immediate and highly publicized symptoms are the reductions that have taken place in farming incomes in the past decade and international pressures, through GATT, for even more reductions. The causes of these pressures, though, go deeper and are comparable in their significance with the reasons that led, for instance, to the repeal of the Corn Laws in 1846, or the permanent introduction of agricultural support in the UK in 1947. In short, the cause is that existing policies have simply become outmoded. The objectives of post-war policy (established for the UK in the 1947 Agriculture Act and for the EC in the 1957 Treaty of Rome) have either been achieved and surpassed, or have failed to be met at all, or have come to be seen as inadequate. Thus, the time is ripe in the 1990s, as it was in the 1840s and in the 1940s, for a sea-change in agricultural policy.

This paper explains why there is a need for a major reform of policy; it discusses both the changes that are likely and those the authors believe are desirable, and considers how they might affect a region such as Wales.

It begins by discussing the economic significance of agriculture to the economy of Wales. On the one hand, there is the view that 'agriculture is the backbone of the rural economy', whereas, on the other, there is the view that agriculture, now only 2 per cent of Welsh GDP, no longer matters. Which, if either, of these views is correct has direct significance for policy – in the EC no less than in the UK – since agriculture continues to take about two-thirds of the total EC budget.

In section two, we discuss what has been happening in the Welsh agricultural economy, and the implications of existing trends for the future. Since agricultural policies have been important in determining the prosperity of Welsh agriculture, the nature of policies and the level of protection they provide are described in section three. We point out that important, and perhaps radical changes are taking place in these policies, and discuss their implications for Wales. Finally, in section four, we provide some ideas as to the future direction that agricultural policy might sensibly take.

2. The role of agriculture in the Welsh economy

Traditionally, the figure that attracts attention when discussing this subject is the contribution of agriculture to GDP — the 2 per cent referred to earlier. Another measure frequently used is the proportion of the total labour force employed in agriculture, which for Wales is estimated at between 4 and 5 per cent. This raises the question of why one should select one input alone as indicative. If land had been selected, for instance, the magnitude of our indicator changes dramatically, since the proportion of land in agriculture in Wales is about 80 per cent. This extreme example makes the point that the relevant measure will vary, depending on the objectives of the study. If the focus is on the role of agriculture in relation to the environment, for example, then land use is the proper measure. In the present context, the focus is on the role in the economy. It will be argued that for this purpose neither share of GDP, nor of employment, nor of land use is adequate.

Agriculture's gross product in Wales has been estimated at about £400 million for 1990 (Welsh Office 1991), and it is this figure that is used to estimate the share of Welsh GDP contributed by agriculture. However, this is an inadequate measure of the contribution of agriculture to the economy. Firstly, it is the much larger figure of the value of sales of agricultural output (£883 million in 1990) that indicates how much spending power is being attracted into the economy by the existence of agriculture. In Wales as a whole, even this figure is relatively small (under £350 per head of population), but for the largely rural area of mid-Wales the figure is over £1,200 per head.

Secondly, there are multiplier effects. Midmore (1987) has used input-output analysis to estimate type 1 and type 2 multipliers for Welsh agriculture. The type 1 multipliers measure backward linkages, which are the effects on industries supplying agriculture with its inputs of a change in agricultural output. They were estimated for eight different farm enterprises, and ranged in value from between 1.08 and 1.92 for employment and 1.1 to 2.12 for income. The type 2 multipliers include the additional effects of farm household expenditures, and were between 1.11 and 2.03 in the case of employment, and 1.18 to 2.67 for income. In addition to the usual and well-known deficiencies in such estimates, there is the further problem that traditional input – output approaches assume that economic activity is demand-driven. This ignores supply-led effects, which can be important. For instance, the immediate effect on parts of Wales of the introduction of milk quotas was the closure of dairy-processing plants. Thus, the full multiplier effects may be greater than Midmore's estimates would suggest.

Much of the confusion that arises about agriculture's contribution to employment exists because of the use of different sources of data, and a failure to appreciate what each source measures. One mistake frequently made is to use the Department of Employment's statistics. These are inadequate because they do not include the self-employed who predominate in agriculture. A second source of information on agricultural employment is the decennial population census, but this ignores the complexities of agricultural employment, and records only those whose primary occupation is in agriculture. The third and most comprehensive source is the Ministry of Agriculture's (MAFF) annual census, which distinguishes eighteen categories of labour, and includes all those working in agriculture, regardless of whether or not it is their main occupation. Even so, definitional changes in the MAFF census have meant that trends over long periods of time are difficult to establish. Nevertheless, the comprehensiveness of MAFF's data has enabled us to make estimates of total agricultural employment in terms of full-time equivalent jobs (FTEs).

These estimates suggest that agriculture accounts for only about 5 per cent of FTEs in Wales – rising to 8 per cent when an allowance is made for employment multiplier effects. However, in rural Wales (Dyfed, Gwynedd and Powys) its contribution is significantly greater, with 16 per cent of FTEs being directly contributed by agriculture, increasing to between 20 and 25 per cent when an allowance is made for agriculture's multiplier effects. As far as Wales is concerned, there is a further reason for attaching importance to agriculture. This is its cultural significance. There has been much discussion, mostly inconclusive, as to whether there is such a thing as rural culture and, if there is, whether it can and should be preserved. These things are hard to quantify. But in Wales the Welsh language constitutes a cultural value that clearly does exist, that can (with problems) be measured, and that is recognized as being worth preserving.

An indication of agriculture's cultural importance was revealed by an analysis of the results of the 1981 census of population (Jones 1989). This showed statistically significant differences between the employment structure of the Welsh- and non-Welsh-speaking populations, and that the correlation was particularly strong in the case of agriculture. The above-average age of the agricultural labour force and the declining number of Welsh speakers may partly explain this situation. However, other factors also need to be considered, such as the predominance of family farms, the growth of owner occupancy, the lack of alternative employment opportunities, and the capital constraints facing new entrants.

The evidence presented thus suggests that concern with agriculture is not just persistent rural fundamentalism but has a genuine basis for two reasons. Firstly, because a significant decline in agriculture could cause a localized slump in an area as large as mid-Wales; and, secondly, because further decline could have implications for the survival of the Welsh language. Having concluded that agriculture is important to the rural economy of Wales, the next question to ask is what is happening to it? This is the subject of the next two sections, which discuss existing trends and likely changes in policy.

3. Trends in output, income and employment

In Wales, agricultural output consists of only three products of any importance, which, given the physical constraints on producing alternatives, makes it particularly vulnerable to change, compared with more diversified areas of production. These are milk (33 per cent of output); cattle and calves (26 per cent); and sheep and lambs (26 per cent). Together, these three account for 85 per cent of all Welsh agricultural output. In rural Wales, the concentration is even greater: thus, it is estimated that in the area covered by the Development Board for Rural Wales (DBRW), 94 per cent of output is from these activities.

Milk production is a labour-intensive occupation and it is estimated that it provides 14,000 job equivalents in Welsh agriculture – some 30 per cent of all jobs. The multiplier effects are also important, with a type 2 employment multiplier of 1.4. Cattle production represents about 18 per cent of the job equivalents in Welsh agriculture and its multiplier effect is estimated at 2.03. In terms of jobs within agriculture itself, the sheep sector is slightly more important than cattle production (21 per cent of job equivalents), but the multiplier effect is smaller, only 1.53. Thus all three sectors, but particularly cattle and milk production, have a strong capacity through their multiplier effects to influence the rural economy.

During the 1980s and, especially, in the last years of the decade, agriculture's problems have multiplied, with the result that it is now facing its most serious crisis since the 1930s. Milk production has been seriously restricted by EC milk quotas, cattle production has been virtually static, and the considerable expansion in sheep production, stimulated by the introduction of an EC common policy for sheepmeat in 1980, is coming to an end as the EC seeks to control the growth of output and its expenditure on this sector.

For all three of these activities real product prices have fallen during the 1980s. This is hardly surprising. Both theory and empirical evidence suggest that this is the norm for agriculture. However, the decline in real prices recently experienced has been particularly severe, as the EC's policy-makers have become more determined to control output and expenditure. Indeed, in the UK, price falls would have been even larger, but for the compensating rises provided by devaluations of the green pound. Consequently, the real value of Welsh agricultural output has declined during the 1980s, especially since 1987. This, combined with rising input prices, has resulted in a 14 per cent decline since 1980 in the real value of the net product (the sum available for paying the incomes of farmers, farmworkers and landlords, as well as interest on borrowed capital).

The decline in agriculture's net product is not simply a continuation of a long-term trend; a longer series available for the UK, but not for Wales, shows a very different picture. It is the result of the increasing pressures put on farmers by policy-makers trying to reduce the budgetary costs of agricultural surpluses. When such pressures occur, it is farmers themselves who are most immediately affected and it is their incomes that have fallen most. In the longer term, farmers can only respond to this by cutting where they can and, in the process, other agricultural income-earners also suffer.

The effect on the part of agriculture's net product available as a reward for labour has been even more pronounced than that on the net product itself. Total labour payments (i.e. to farmers, family workers and employees) in Welsh agriculture fell by 25 per cent in real terms during the 1980s; and the residual amount available for farmers and their spouses, after all other labour payments had been met, actually fell by 50 per cent. The squeeze on incomes was especially severe in the latest years as output restrictions, price restraint, inflation and high interest rates took their toll.

The increasing impact of interest rates on farm-labour incomes over the decade underlines the fact that predicting in the agricultural field depends not only on being able to forecast the behaviour of agricultural markets themselves, and government policy towards agriculture, but also the effects of government macroeconomic policies on interest rates, exchanges rates and the like.

In the long run, it is the level of labour income from farming that is the main determinant of the number of people who can be employed in agriculture. If incomes drop significantly, pressure falls initially on farmers rather than on farm workers, because it is the farmers' income that is the residual. The fall in farmers' incomes might lead them, in the first instance, to pay lower rents if they could but, since most are owner-occupiers, this is not a possibility. Their second choice might be to cut workers' wages, but this is usually impracticable too, so the number of farmworkers has to be cut instead. If even this step proves insufficient to maintain farmers' own incomes, then sooner or later the farmers may be forced to take the third step, to follow their workers out of the industry. What evidence is there that this has been happening?

In Wales, as in other countries, there has been a long-term decline in the absolute and relative importance of agriculture as a source of employment. This is well documented by the census of population. In 1851, agriculture was the principal employment of one-third of the labour force in Wales and, in the counties of

Dyfed, Powys and Gwynedd, the proportion was as high as 44 per cent. By 1981, these figures had fallen to 3.6 and 10.5 per cent respectively. Between 1851 and 1971 (the last census before the establishment of the DBRW), the working population of mid-Wales fell by 52,000 or nearly 40 per cent. Of that drop, 47,000 were in agriculture. Thus, without making any allowance at all for multiplier effects, it was the decline in agricultural employment that accounted for most of the decline in the total working population. Given this background, it is hardly surprising that the rural areas have had problems of adjustment.

There have been two factors contributing to change: technical change, which has raised the labour productivity of agriculture, as well as shifting certain activities away from agriculture and into other industries; and changes in the level of agricultural output itself.

Technical changes will continue, though their effects are unpredictable. Over much of the long period of agricultural-employment decline, the effects of technical change were reinforced by a decline in output, as the UK came to depend more heavily on imported foodstuffs and allowed her own agriculture to contract. Since 1939, however, output expanded, to some extent diminishing the downward pressures on agricultural employment. Now this effect appears to have been reversed again.

MAFF statistics on agricultural employment in Wales since 1977, converted to FTEs, are given in Table 1 (1977 has been taken as the base year, because definitional changes at that time make comparisons with previous years difficult). One of the most striking and unexpected features of these data, until the last two years, has been the relative stability of the total number of persons in employment. This is surprising, given agriculture's long-term decline as a source of employment and the decline in farming income during the 1980s. It means that income per person has fallen substantially. It also raises the question as to whether agriculture's decline, after continuing for a century or more, has finally bottomed out, or whether the impact of agriculture's latest and deepest recession has yet to be felt, and further decline is inevitable in the 1990s, re-establishing the long-term trend.

Although there has been no definite downward trend in employment in the 1980s, there has been a very clear trend in the structure of the agricultural labour force. The marked

Table 1: Agricultural Employment, Wales (thousands)

Year	Total persons	Total FTES
1977	64.9	48.8
1978	67.1	49.6
1979	65.5	48.8
1980	62.9	47.1
1981	63.2	47.2
1982	63.0	46.9
1983	62.7	46.2
1984	64.1	47.4
1985	65.8	47.7
1986	65.0	47.2
1987	63.0	45.6
1988	63.2	45.6
1989	62.9	45.4
1990	61.5	44.4
1991	61.0	43.6

Source: Agricultural Census, *Welsh Office Agriculture Department*

drop in farm incomes was accompanied not by the reduction in the numbers employed that might have been expected, but rather by a shift from full-time to part-time working. The number of regular full-time workers has declined dramatically (30 per cent since 1980); so also, to some extent, has the number of full-time farmers. In contrast, part-time working has expanded from 13 to 17 per cent of the labour force. This suggests that there may be a good deal of adjustment in the pipeline – the extent depending on the strength of the pressures on farm incomes in the 1990s.

If we allow for the different trends in the agricultural labour force by converting part-time, seasonal and casual workers to FTEs, we find that there is stronger evidence of a decline in total employment, particularly since 1985. Thus, between 1977 and 1985, FTEs fell by only 2 per cent. After 1985 this accelerated, suggesting that since then, the movement to part-time has been unable to compensate for the loss of full-time employment, and that we may see a significant fall in total persons working in agriculture in the 1990s.

In conclusion, it would appear that from the war until the early 1970s agricultural employment declined continuously, as technical change more than compensated for any increase in output. Following entry to the EC in 1973, agriculture had a particularly prosperous period in which output expanded considerably and agricultural employment stabilized. The prosperity was in any case short-lived, and from the early 1980s the industry has been under financial pressure. This has had a marked effect on its ability to provide whole-time jobs, with possible implications for the level of population who can be regarded as economically committed to rural areas. Up to the mid-1980s, the decline in whole-time opportunities has been compensated by an increasing need for casual and part-time workers; this also has implications regarding the need to provide complementary part-time jobs in rural areas. Without some provision of part-time, off-farm employment, the alternative may be a fairly radical restructuring of holding sizes, with fewer farmers operating much larger farms. Finally, the most recent two years provide evidence that the new-found determination of policy-makers to control agricultural surpluses may be causing a re-establishment of the downward trend in total agricultural employment − a trend which may become more evident if agricultural output really is forced down to new low levels − requiring greater provision of full-time jobs in rural areas, as well as part-time ones. Whether these trends will continue will depend critically − at least in the short term − on government and EC policy. The next section analyses the pressures that are likely to drive this policy in the long term.

4. The changing role of government

UK and EC policies have been a critical factor in determining the prosperity of agriculture. In this section of the paper we describe the nature of these policies and the level of protection they afford to agriculture in Wales. We highlight the fact that important and radical changes are taking place in these policies, and discuss their implications for Wales.

From the repeal of the Corn Laws in 1846 to the 1930s, British agriculture was largely unprotected from foreign competition. Some government support was provided in the 1930s, but it was in the period following the Second World War that a large and comprehensive system of support was established. This provided government-guaranteed prices for output (the so-called deficiency payments) and also input subsidies. Thus, whilst producers' incomes were supported, consumers could still benefit from the lower food prices available on world markets. When the UK joined the EC in 1973, agricultural support was continued under the Common Agricultural Policy (CAP), but in a fundamentally different way. Now the domestic market is protected by variable tariffs which raise domestic market prices substantially above those on the world market, thus transferring much of the cost of agricultural support from taxpayers to consumers. Nevertheless, despite this shift of emphasis, there still exists a substantial cost to taxpayers under the CAP, because of internal support for the market through EC purchases at predetermined prices, and various direct output and input-related payments to farmers.

Although the methods of agricultural support changed in the UK as a result of joining the EC, the objectives remained broadly similar (compare the 1947 Agriculture Act with the 1957 Treaty of Rome). A review of the reasons given for policy suggests the following main objectives. Firstly, one of the most long-established objectives has been to provide better incomes for farmers which, it is argued, in a free market, would fall to unacceptable levels and show too much instability. A second objective has been to maintain population in rural areas. Thirdly, there was the objective of increasing domestic food production (and its technical efficiency) for reasons of food security, although balance of payments considerations were important in the UK before EC membership. Finally, and more recently, it was decided to promote environmentally sensitive agriculture.

As a result of this long history of government intervention, Welsh agriculture is highly dependent on public support. The level of public expenditure on agriculture in Wales is relatively easy to measure from government statistical sources. Quantification of market-price support (for example, through trade barriers) is very much more difficult, because it requires estimates of what prices and output would be in the absence of the CAP. It is estimated that identifiable public expenditure on agriculture in Wales has been running at about £110 million per annum in recent years. This is about 12 per cent of Welsh agriculture's total annual receipts. The addition of market-price support would significantly increase this figure, since the markets for milk, beef and lamb, on which Welsh agriculture overwhelmingly depends, receive substantial protection in this way.

The quantification of market support for agriculture has been the subject of considerable research in recent years (OECD 1990). One measure that has been developed has been the producer subsidy equivalent (PSE). This incorporates, within a single figure, the value of all the various elements of agricultural support, direct and indirect, market or otherwise, so that inter-country and inter-product comparisons can be made.

The PSE can be expressed in money terms or as a percentage of production valued at farmgate prices. There are a number of generally recognized problems with this approach (Peters 1988). For example, PSEs make no allowance for the fact that, in the absence of support, world prices would rise substantially — one estimate suggests by 20 per cent were the EC to abandon support, and as much as 30 per cent were this to be the case for 'all industrial market economies' (Tyers and Anderson 1988). Nevertheless, the PSE does represent a more comprehensive approach than just measuring identifiable public expenditure on agriculture, and its values are now widely quoted. In the case of the EC, the OECD's estimate of the PSE in 1990 was $82 billion or 48 per cent, compared with an OECD value of $176 billion or 44 per cent. Japan's was $31 billion or 68 per cent, and the United States' was $36 billion or 30 per cent.

An application of OECD estimates of the EC's commodity PSEs to Wales suggests that the value of agricultural support in Wales could be as much as 58 per cent of the average value of total output between 1988 and 1990, or about £500 million. The dependence of rural Wales on agricultural support is further illustrated by estimates made for the DBRW's area. Out of a total output of £259 million (1988), identifiable public expenditure on agriculture was estimated at £50 million and the PSE level of support at £160 million. By comparison, identifiable public expenditure within other sectors of the DBRW area was estimated at only £8 million (Bateman 1991).

The preceding discussion has highlighted the importance of public support to Welsh agriculture. There are now intense pressures to change the CAP on grounds which include: wasteful overproduction; an ineffective incomes policy; the environmental costs of intensive agriculture — which policy has helped to create;

and immense international pressure for a substantial reduction in CAP support. It is now widely accepted that a radical change of policy is essential. In July 1991, the EC Commission published proposals for a reform of the CAP (the MacSharry Plan) and on 21 May 1992, the EC Council of Ministers reached an agreement on these proposals. This agreement, which is a slightly watered-down version of the MacSharry Plan, has been described as historic, and is the culmination of a long process of reform begun in the mid-eighties. It brings to an end a period of considerable uncertainty about the future direction of policy for at least the next three years, and probably for the rest of the decade.

The 1992 agreement has four principal components: a substantial reduction in price support for agricultural products; supply controls such as set-aside (taking land out of production) and quotas; direct payments to farmers as compensation for lower prices and production controls; and the so-called 'accompanying measures' which have a variety of objectives but, in particular, the promotion of environmentally sensitive farming. A further and interesting new development in policy has been the introduction of the principle of cross-compliance. This means that in some cases farmers can only receive EC support provided they accept certain conditions, for example, provided they agree to set aside land from production, or to farm in an environmentally beneficial way. Environmental conservation will play a bigger role in agricultural policy, and farmers in Wales can expect more opportunities to obtain income in this way. However, its potential should not be exaggerated. For example, if the present environmentally sensitive areas schemes, operating in the Cambrian mountains and the Lleyn peninsula, were extended to the whole of Wales, the level of payments to farmers would only be a small percentage of the current value of market support. Thus, environmental support for agriculture is only likely to be a partial solution to the cuts that could occur within traditional agriculture.

Potentially, Welsh farmers could benefit from discrimination in favour of 'poorer regions'. However, although mid-Wales already qualifies for some special assistance under EC legislation, rural Wales must compete for EC funds with other, much poorer, EC regions. In this respect, most of Wales falls within the EC's less favoured areas (LFAs) and the continuation of this policy will be important for Welsh farmers faced with a decline in other traditional methods of support.

An important additional uncertainty for farmers in Wales is the future of milk marketing. This is because of the abolition of the Milk Marketing Board, whose policy of paying all producers the average price of milk has benefited farmers in Wales and other remote areas, who would otherwise have had to sell their milk in the lower-priced milk processing market.

In conclusion, the short-term prospects for Welsh agriculture are very much better than could have been envisaged at the time of the publication of the original MacSharry proposals. This is firstly because the 1992 agreement provides compensation for price cuts and production controls until 1996. Secondly, and rather fortuitously, it is because of the UK's swift and unexpected departure from the ERM. This has been extremely beneficial for farmers. On the one hand it has allowed a large fall in interest rates, and on the other hand, it led to a substantial devaluation of the green pound as a result of sterling's depreciation, thus causing a significant increase in the value of EC agricultural subsidies. The fall in the UK's rate of price inflation has been a further bonus, because farm incomes have traditionally been subject to a cost-price squeeze as input prices have inflated faster than output prices.

We are, however, more pessimistic about the longer-term prospects for Welsh agriculture for a variety of reasons. The EC market will become more open and there will be less opportunity to dispose of EC agricultural products on world markets at subsidized prices. With only limited growth in the consumption of agricultural products, this will mean a more competitive environment for EC farmers. It may also mean that further efforts are needed to control production and the EC now has the policies in place to do this. A tightening of quotas is quite likely in the future. It is very uncertain whether further compensation would be provided if this were to happen or, even, whether the compensation provided by the 1992 agreement will continue after 1996. In the longer term there are likely to be further pressures, both internally and externally, for a reduction in domestic support. In this respect, the switch in the provision of support from consumers to taxpayers, as a result of the reduction in price support and increases in direct payments, makes support more explicit and thus more vulnerable to EC and UK budgetary and fiscal policies. Environmental conservation and some opportunities for on-farm diversification will provide welcome, but only limited compensation, and will not prove to be the panaceas that some suppose.

Therefore, although there remains considerable uncertainty as to the overall outcome of the various policy changes described, we would expect the long-term effects of future policy changes to be much more serious than anything experienced in the 1980s. Consequently, we anticipate a decline in full-time agricultural employment, a further polarization of farm holdings structure between the small and the large, and an accelerating need for additional sources of income, other than farming, in the rural areas of Wales. Thus, it may be necessary for the government to develop policies which will help farm households to remain viable by diversifying their sources of income, not only on the farm, but by the provision of full and part-time work within travel to work distance of their farms.

5. From agricultural to regional policy?

So far it has been explained why EC agricultural-policy reform is necessary and the recent changes in policy have been discussed. In this section, we consider what policy changes should be made, and whether the changes that are taking place in the CAP are moving policy in the right direction. Policy objectives were reviewed in the previous section. These objectives have had different weights at different times and these may well change again. At present, it would appear that the main objectives are likely to relate to rural incomes and society, and the natural environment.

The principal criticisms of policy that can be made by economists, however, are not that objectives of policy are undesirable, since these are for society to decide, but that the price-support policies that have been used to achieve them have been costly and not very successful. There are a variety of reasons for this conclusion. Firstly, price policies have resulted in substantial overproduction. Secondly, since the amount of support largely depends upon the volume of production, the largest farmers have benefited the most, yet, presumably, these are the least in need. Moreover, economic theory, with some empirical support

(Traill 1982), suggests that price policies do not provide long-term protection for farmers' incomes, because farm subsidies are capitalized into higher land prices. Thus landowners (who are not necessarily farmers) are the ultimate beneficiaries of government policy. It also seems logical that if income support is provided on welfare grounds, the total income of farm families, regardless of source, should be taken into account in formulating policy. Thirdly, although there is a *prima facie* case for believing that price-support will help to maintain rural employment, it is not necessarily the most effective employment policy. Furthermore, in this respect, the effectiveness of price-support policy has been reduced by the existence of subsidies on capital investment in agriculture. Fourthly, there is strong evidence that policy has had detrimental effects on world markets by reducing trade in agricultural products, increasing price instability, and retarding the growth of trade in other products (Tyers and Anderson 1988). Fifthly, agricultural price policies have encouraged intensification and ignored its environmental effects. Sixthly, food security provided by a high level of output is illusory if it is dependent upon high levels of imported inputs. Finally, a variety of different sources suggests that the real resource costs of policy are high (Winters 1987). What kind of policies ought to be adopted? The preceding criticisms suggest that they should incorporate a number of features.

Farm-income support, if desirable, should be provided by direct payments unrelated to output levels. This would enable support to be directed to where it would have the greatest effect and would be less costly than the present, indiscriminate, blanket approach to income support. Such a policy change would allow support prices to be moved nearer to world levels, avoiding overproduction, and promoting GATT. A clear statement to this effect, with a timetable, would enable farmers to plan their response. Accompanying this policy should be 'adjustment policies' designed to alleviate hardship and to promote adjustment, for example, retraining, financial and other assistance for diversification, and so on.

If support for rural communities is an objective, then what is required is not an agricultural policy *per se*, but a new regional policy that can be directed to the problems of areas where traditional industries are declining, whether the area is Merseyside or mid-Wales, and whatever the industry. The regions in which agriculture is the focus industry are getting, and will continue to get, fewer, but this is not a reason for ignoring it where, as in mid-Wales for example, it is still of central importance. What has been conspicuously lacking in existing approaches to rural-development policy has been an integrated approach. In the UK, this is a reflection of the institutional framework, in which agricultural policy has been MAFF's responsibility, whilst rural policies are the responsibility of the Department of the Environment. A particular example in Wales is the DBRW which, despite its title, has had no remit for agriculture. Ideally, the structure of policy-making should facilitate an integrated approach in which the linkages between sectors are recognized and exploited; and in which the allocation of public expenditure between agriculture and other rural activities is made on a rational basis. This, for example, would be one that would ensure that (*ceteris paribus*) the cost of the last job created (or retained) was the same across all forms of employment. Intuitively, it seems likely that the cost of jobs retained in agriculture exceeds the cost of creating new jobs in industry but, surprisingly, this has never been formally quantified.

The illogicality of failing to adopt a more integrated and rational approach is increasingly being recognized and discussed at EC levels. In Wales, the responsibility of the Welsh Office for a wide range of affairs could be advantageous in developing such an approach.

The question of how the environmental externalities of agricultural production should be handled by policy-makers is one of growing importance. There are various considerations, but the ownership of property rights in land is paramount. If they are deemed to belong to a farmer or landowner (for example, the right to destroy a landscape), then compensation should be paid if they are prevented. Alternatively, if property rights belong to society (and the 'Polluter Pays Principle' holds), then a farmer or landlord would have to pay for damage to the environment, not be compensated for restraining himself. The corollary of the 'Polluter Pays Principle' is that if farming generates positive externalities, the farmer should be paid by society for them. It is this idea that is the basis of proposals (Jenkins 1990) for a system of conservation-management payments to replace current price-support policy, and this, and the

'Polluter Pays Principle', would probably command widespread support. Finally, if the government wishes to reduce the instability of agricultural prices and incomes, greater consideration should be given to alternative policies, like insurance schemes and futures markets. As far as the national food security arguments for agricultural support are concerned, the potential risks and policies should be re-evaluated. Current policies are almost certainly an expensive and inappropriate means of securing this end (Winters, 1988).

The prospects for the kind of desirable changes in policy that have been outlined are now better than they have ever been. The recent developments in policy, described in the preceding section, suggest that there will be a significant shift from price support to a more integrated and discriminatory (selective) approach to the problems of agriculture and the rural economy in the 1990s. This will require a re-emphasis of the Nevin tradition of regional economic research: not only in its methodological aspects, like regional input-output analysis and in the construction of regional accounting frameworks that include the environment, but also in the expansion, design and analysis of regional policy itself which, in recent years, has been a neglected feature of agricultural and economic policy in general.

References

Bateman, D. I. *et al.* (1991). *Future Agricultural Prospects in Mid Wales* (Newtown, Powys, Development Board for Rural Wales, 1991).

Commission of the European Communities (1991). *The Development and Future of the Common Agricultural Policy*, COM(91) 258 Final/3 (Brussels, 22 July 1991).

Jenkins, T. N. (1990). *Future Harvests: The Economics of Farming and the Environment* (London, Council for the Protection of Rural England/World Wide Fund for Nature, 1990).

Jones, M. E. (1989). 'The linguistic implications of agricultural change in Wales' (University of Wales M.Sc. dissertation, 1989).

Midmore, P. (1987). 'The impact of farm prosperity on the rest of the Welsh Economy' (Aberystwyth, Department of Agricultural Economics, The University College of Wales, 1987).

OECD (1991). *Agricultural Policies, Markets and Trade: Monitoring and Outlook 1991* (Paris, OECD, 1991).

Peters, G. H. (1987). 'The interpretation and use of producer subsidy equivalents', *Oxford Agrarian Studies*, XVII (1987), 186–218.

Traill, W. B. (1988). 'The effect of price support policies on agricultural investment, employment, farm incomes, and land values in the UK', *Journal of Agricultural Economics*, XXXIII No. 3 (1988), 369–85.

Tyers, R. and Anderson, K. (1988). 'Liberalizing OECD agricultural policies in the Uruguay Round : effects on trade and welfare', *Journal of Agricultural Economics*, 39 No. 2 (1988), 197–216.

Welsh Office (annual). *Farm Incomes in Wales* (Cardiff, annual).

Winters, L. A. (1987). 'The economic consequences of agricultural support: a survey', *OECD Economic Studies*, No. 9 (1987), 7–54.

Winters, L. A. (1988). 'The national security argument for agricultural protection', Centre for Economic Policy Research Discussion Paper Series, No. 287 (London, CEPR, 1988).

V INTERNATIONAL PERSPECTIVES

10
VERs: theory and estimation with reference to EC imports from Japan

ALI M. EL-AGRAA

1. Introduction

In standard texts, there is a full discussion of the economic effects of the imposition of tariffs and import quota restrictions (hereafter simply quotas). It is stated there that under very strict conditions the two are equivalent, but if the foreign suppliers are organized while the home importers are not, the area representing tariff revenue will be taken over by the foreign exporters as excess profits (or rent). Hence, the equivalence of tariffs and quotas breaks down when certain imperfections are introduced into the model. Moreover, quotas have been known to be less efficient than tariffs. They prevent the importer from taking advantage of technical progress abroad and this increases instability overseas, thus deterring foreigners from being innovative. Also, as the importing country grows, quotas become increasingly restrictive since imports are not allowed to grow with income, whereas under tariffs they are. Because of these factors, international organizations have been very strict about the adoption of quotas. The General Agreement on Tariffs and Trade (GATT) permits their use in emergencies, provided they come under international surveillance and are not discriminatory. However, quotas are bound to attract retaliation and result in the payment of compensation. For these reasons, countries have become reluctant to use them and have instead resorted to the use of voluntary export restraints (VERs).

As long ago as 1935, Japanese industry voluntarily agreed to restrict its exports of textiles and clothing to the US. From 1968 to 1974, the US imposed VERs on imports of Japanese and European steel. In response to demands made on it by the European Community (EC) and the US in 1981, Japan declared VERs on its car exports for the period 1981–3. However, this historical development is often forgotten since what seems to capture the imagination is the present situation. Today, VERs limit: (i) exports of clothing by the less developed countries (LDCs) to western Europe and North America; (ii) Japanese car exports to France, Italy, the UK and the US; (iii) Japanese and EC steel exports to the US; (iv) Asian exports of consumer electronics to several LDCs; and (v) the export of several agricultural products, for example feedstuff (cassava) exports by Thailand to the EC.

Although VERs have been widely used, and now seem to be a permanent feature of Japanese car exports, particularly to the EC and US, the term itself is still surrounded by mystery. VERs are obviously a form of protectionism, since putting a limit to the amount a country can export can hardly pass as free trade. However, people do not generally equate VERs with protectionism since what they are familiar with are tariffs and quotas, both imposed by the importing country – but in the case of VERs we have a policy instrument which is controlled by the exporting nation, thus adding to the mystery.

The aim of this paper is to explain the real nature of VERs and the estimates of their costs with reference to EC imports from Japan. Before doing so, however, it may be useful to make general comparisons between VERs and tariffs, recalling that quotas are simply specific restrictions on the quantity imported. As Hamilton (1985) has suggested, it is sometimes helpful to consider a protectionist measure as a set of constraints on the free flow of international trade. Thus a VER is a measure by which the importing country imposes an upper limit on foreign supply (constraint I), defined by commodity category such as cars (constraint II), by source of supply (constraint III), in volume rather than value terms (constraint IV) and for a specified period of time (constraint V). Moreover, as we have already seen, the exporting country administers the restraint on the supply of exports.

In comparison, a tariff also limits foreign supply. It is defined by commodity group (such as cars of a specific horsepower) which is a narrower definition than a commodity category as is the case with VERs. A tariff is not defined by source if it is a most-favoured-nation (MFN) tariff, but is defined by source if it is a preferential tariff. According to GATT, MFN tariffs are imposed on all sources of import supply, while in the case of economic integration (for example, the EC; see El-Agraa (1983, ch. 11; 1987; 1989a, ch. 11; 1990) for details), member nations remove tariffs on mutual imports and retain or create common tariffs on imports from non-partners; thus their tariffs are preferential tariffs, since they are applied against some nations to the exclusion of others. However, a preferential tariff is very rarely export-country-specific (since it applies against all non-partners), whereas a VER always is. Typically, a tariff is defined as a percentage of the value of the goods imported (*ad valorem* tariff) and is not related to the volume of the traded goods as is the typical VER. Finally, a tariff is usually imposed on a permanent basis. In addition, the importing country administers the tariffs and collects the tariff revenue.

It follows from this brief comparison that it would be difficult to explain the economic implications of VERs without an understanding of the effects of the imposition of tariffs, since the two are closely interdependent. Moreover, it is also obvious that VERs are closely related to quotas, which are in turn related to tariffs. Therefore, it is useful to consider all three together. However, since economists are familiar with the analysis of tariffs and quotas, we can go straight to an analysis of VERs.

2. The economic effects of VERs

In spite of the long history of VERs, their theoretical analysis has been both recent and rare. Using partial equilibrium techniques, Takacs (1978) compared them with alternative trade impediments in terms of their equivalence. Murray *et al.* (1983) made a more general analysis of the equivalence of quotas and VERs. The theoretical attempts made by Falvey (1979) and Rodriguez (1978) were used by Feenstra (1984) to show that Japanese VERs on car exports to the US induced a shift towards higher-quality exports. Feenstra also estimated the size and analysed the economic effects of this shift. Some calculations of the costs of VERs were made by Morkre and Tarr (1980), Jenkins (1983), Hindley (1985) and Digby *et al.* (1988). A comprehensive analysis of the political economy of VERs was undertaken by Jones (1984).

This paper is confined to a partial equilibrium analysis of the effects of VERs. However, most of the conclusions are maintained in a general equilibrium framework except in two special

228 VERs: theory and estimation

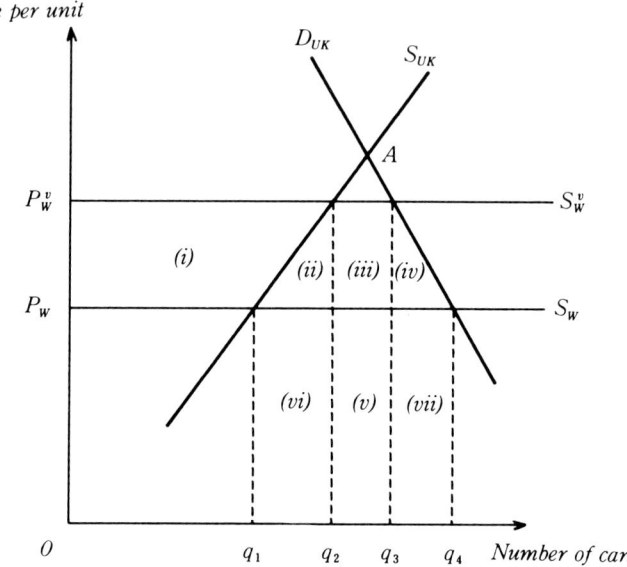

Figure 1: The international UK car market with fixed world prices

cases and under certain circumstances: (i) when a different definition is adopted (a fixed price for the imported product); and (ii) when 'rent-seeking' activity is incorporated into the model. For a full analysis see El-Agraa (1989b).

To analyse the economic effects of VERs, consider a partial equilibrium diagram (Figure 1) where $P_w S_w$ is the world's perfectly elastic supply curve for cars (i.e. at price OP_w consumers in, say, the UK can buy any number of cars they wish). S_{UK} is the UK's domestic supply curve and D_{UK} is the UK's domestic demand curve. Under free trade conditions, consumers in the UK plan to buy Oq_4 number of cars, produce (domestically) Oq_1 and import the difference ($q_1 q_4$) from the rest of the world (hereafter referred to as Japan) at a total cost of areas (vi) + (v) + (vii), i.e. the number of cars imported ($q_1 q_4$) multiplied by the world price of cars (OP_w).

Assume that VERs do not affect the relative prices of exports and imports (the terms of trade), that is, assume the supply and demand forces in the UK have an insignificant impact on the world market for cars. Recall that with a VER on UK car imports, the

UK government asks the exporting country, Japan, to limit the number of cars it will sell in Britain. Suppose the VER is equal to q_2q_3. Because Japan is asked to control this number, and because no tariffs are involved, it follows that Japan will charge the UK importers the full UK domestic prices, P_w^v. Hence the UK will pay areas (iii) + (v) to Japan instead of just area (v). Thus, what was a tariff revenue for the UK becomes excess profit to the Japanese car exporters. This is the outcome reached with a quota when the foreign suppliers were organized into a cartel and the UK importers were perfectly competitive. Therefore, a VER is less harmful to Japan than the imposition of tariffs or, under specific circumstances, a quota by the UK.

3. The large-country case

The importing country

So far, we have assumed that the UK is too small to affect the world price of cars, that is, the terms of trade. This is a very unrealistic assumption, but it can easily be remedied. In Figure 2, S_{UK} and D_{UK} are as in Figure 1, but S_{W+UK} is the total world supply curve, including the UK's; the supply curve for the world excluding the UK's is the horizontal difference between S_{W+UK} and S_{UK}. Note that the world supply curve slopes upwards to the right, thus disposing of the assumption of a fixed world price. Under free trade conditions, imports by the UK are equal to q_1q_4. A VER equal to q_2q_3 results in a UK domestic price of P_w which leads to excess profits to Japanese exporters of areas (a) + (b). Hence the analysis is no different from before, except for the fact that the VER has reduced the world price from P_w to P_w^*. There is therefore a terms of trade effect (gain) which in this case accrues wholly to the exporting country. However, if this Figure were about tariff imposition, area (b) would have been an extra tariff revenue for the UK government.

The exporting country

To complete the picture, we need to look specifically at the exporting country (Japan) itself. For this purpose, consider Figure 3, where S_w is Japan's export supply curve and D is the UK demand

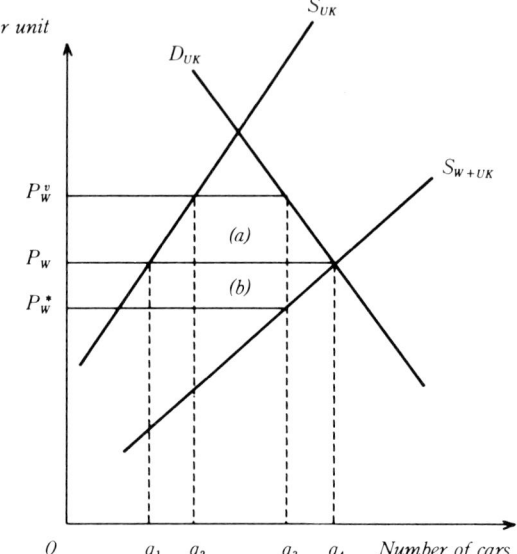

Figure 2: VERs – The large-country case.

for imports, that is, the demand for these exports, not the total UK demand for cars; this curve is the horizontal difference between D_{UK} and S_{UK} in the previous figures.

Under free trade conditions, Japan will export $0^*q_2^*$ (equal to q_1q_4 in Figure 1) at price P_w. The VER restricts the supply of exports to $0^*q_1^*$ (equal to q_2q_3 in Figure 1), leading to excess profits of areas (a) + (b), with area (b) representing the terms-of-trade effect which in this case goes to Japan. However, if this were a quota, area (b) would become a gain to the UK, provided the UK importers were organized into a cartel and the Japanese exporters were perfectly competitive.

4. Upgrading

As already indicated, a VER is specified in units of a commodity category such as a number of cars or tons of steel. However, it has already been pointed out that each commodity category may contain different types or grades of quality each with its own price, for example, 'cars' could be an average Toyota or Volkswagen

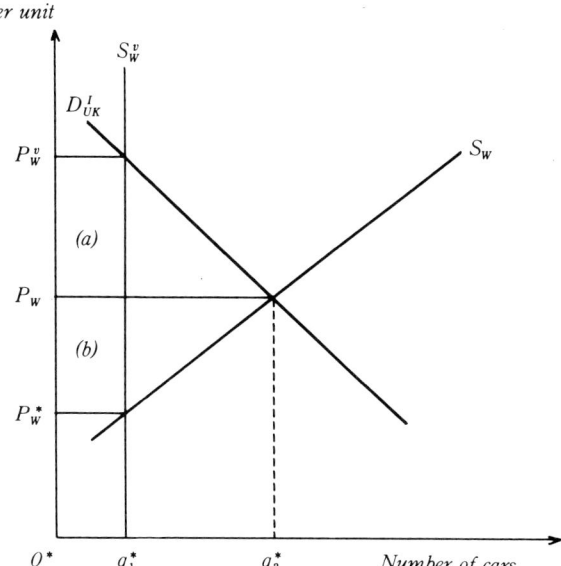

Figure 3: VERs – The exporting country.

or a prestige Jaguar or Rolls Royce, with the price difference counted in tens of thousands of pounds. Since a VER is specified in physical units, the increase in the money price generated by the VER will be the same for all units within the same commodity category, irrespective of the grade or quality. It follows that the more expensive and usually high-quality items will have a lower *ad valorem* money price increase than less expensive, mostly low-quality items. In terms of effective protection, this means that the VER will afford higher effective protection for the lower-priced items within the same commodity category: a $250 dollar charge per car is insignificant when the car is priced in the world market at $750,000, and fairly substantial for a car priced at $15,000.

Since the exporter will normally be interested in minimizing the deterioration in his relative competitive position, a VER will encourage him to change his mix of the commodity subjected to the VER to bias it towards the higher-priced, higher-quality grades. In short, natural commercial instincts will encourage the exporter to respond to the adoption of a VER by increasing the number of sophisticated items within the same category.

This characteristic of a VER has thus been labelled upgrading or trading-up.

The only detailed empirical investigation of this phenomenon was made by Feenstra (1984). He considered Japanese exports of passenger cars to the US in 1980−1 both with and without the US adopting a VER. He split the rise in the price in Japanese cars in the US into three components which were attributed to: (i) inflation, (ii) the tariff equivalent of the VER and (iii) improved quality. After adjusting for inflation, he found two-thirds of the price increase to be due to the upgrading of Japanese cars in terms of increased horsepower, more use of automatic steering, etc. Thus his finding was that US consumers were granted sufficient better quality to compensate for two-thirds of the price rise brought about by the VER.

Hamilton (1985) drew attention to the fact that quality upgrading was not what the US consumer necessarily desired. He argued that, had consumers wanted improvement in quality before the VER was imposed, producers would have provided it, but most likely at a higher asking price. He concluded that the welfare effects for the US consumer were therefore ambiguous, even if the price had increased by only two-thirds of the actual price increase.

5. VERs and the pattern of trade

In the context of the EC it is appropriate to ask about the economic effects of a VER imposed by members of an economic union, customs union (CU), free trade area (FTA), etc. Recall that in any such union, member countries can discriminate against non-member nations, that is, a VER can be adopted by the UK against car imports from Japan, but such a trade policy would be declared illegal against Germany (G) since the UK and G are both members of the EC. In short, a VER by a member of an integrated area, by distorting relative prices, may affect the pattern of world trade.

Hamilton (1985) used a partial equilibrium diagram for this purpose. In Figure 4, S_w, S_{UK}, D_{UK}, P_w and P_w^v are as before. S_{UK+G} is the joint supply curve of the UK and G; it is needed, since the VER cannot not be applied to G exporters. Note that the diagram has been drawn in the most simplified way since the UK is assumed to be small.

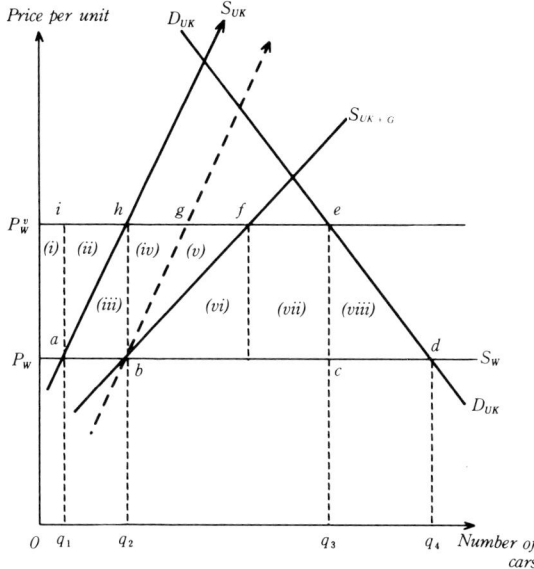

Figure 4: VERs and the pattern of trade.

Under free trade conditions, British consumers will plan to purchase Oq_4 cars while UK domestic producers will plan to make Oq_1 cars, hence the UK will plan to import the difference, q_1q_4, of which q_1q_2 will come from G, the EC partner country, and q_2q_4 from W, the rest of the world. Assume then that the UK government wants to increase domestic production to Oq_2 and decides to achieve this by the adoption of a VER against Japanese imports. Therefore, UK imports will have to be limited to q_2q_3. The implication of this, is that the VER will have to be equal to fe since a total amount of imports equal to q_2q_3 will require a domestic price increase to OP_W^v, but at this price G's exports to the UK will be equal to hf. Thus the VER under these conditions will distort the pattern of trade.

To put it differently, the actual effect of the VER is to reduce Japanese exports to the UK from bd ($=q_2q_4$) to fe and to expand WG exports to the UK from ad ($=q_1q_2$) to hf; the line drawn parallel to S_{UK} shows that G has increased its exports to the UK by gf. It follows that imports from the EC partner country have increased both relative to their share in the UK market and in absolute terms. The implication of this, is that if the VER is replaced by a tariff or quota and applied proportionately on all sources of import supply to the UK (that is both G and W maintain their share in the UK import market), imports from G would be equal to hg ($=ab$).

Whether the import restriction takes the form of a VER, tariff or quota, the UK domestic producers experience a welfare increase equal to areas (i)+(ii). G increases its welfare on initial exports by areas (ii)+(iii), which is equal to areas (iii)+(iv), since areas (ii) and (iv) are equal by construction. G's welfare increase on the new exports is equal to area (v). Hence, G's total welfare increases by areas (iii)+(iv)+(v). The VER results in excess profit or rent for W equal to area (vii).

6. Empirical estimates for the EC

There is a paucity of empirical research on the costs and benefits of VERs. One of the main reasons for this is the difficulty of obtaining data on which to make estimates. For example, tariffs create a difference between the international and domestic prices, while VERs raise the price the exporter may charge. This in itself does not create a difficulty for measurement; rather it is the fact that tariffs are set by governments and are accessible to the public, but VERs are not available from official sources and will not be known to governments of importing countries. Hence information on VERs is surrounded by obscurity. Also, upgrading or trading-up generates problems since its impact will not be captured by simple aggregation.

In spite of this, empirical estimates of the costs of VERs for the EC have been attempted. Here, we shall concentrate on the two by Hindley (1985) and Digby *et al.* (1988). Hindley's study covers four groups of commodities, but is limited to the UK, while that by Digby *et al.* covers all EC VERs, but is confined to cars, which are included in the Hindley exercise. Thus, in considering both studies, we will at least be able to compare their results for the car sector.

Hindley started his analysis by stressing the three possible categories of VER benefits: (i) a higher level of employment; (ii) the avoidance of adjustment costs; and (iii) increased profits for the domestic firms. He suggested that owing to the trade diversion effects discussed above, VERs may have no impact on employment since partner countries may increase their exports to the home country after the adoption of a VER, and that even if a VER enables an increase in employment, changes in the rate of exchange will eliminate this possibility: the favourable impact of a VER on the balance of payments will have to be counteracted by a currency revaluation in order to maintain balance-of-payments equilibrium. With regard to adjustment benefits (protection which eliminates redundancies disposes of the possibility of loss of output brought about by the fact that workers made redundant in one sector may not find an alternative job immediately, or at all), he is also sceptical, since the same could be claimed for the contraction of any sector due to changes in demand or technology. Finally, whatever happens to domestic employment, Hindley agrees with the proposition that a VER will increase the profits (or reduce the losses) of domestic producers, but he stresses that this is likely to be a small percentage of the cost of the VER upon the consumers of the protected sector; all exporters of the item will get a higher price as well as the domestic producer, but when the domestic producer has a small share of the market, there is a clear loss for the nation as a whole. He concluded from these observations that the benefits of VERs are of dubious sign and magnitude, except for the increase in the profits of the protected firms. Indeed, he suggested that some of the benefits might more appropriately be counted as costs.

To be more precise, Hindley indicated that the increase in the price of the product under consideration is a clear cost of the VER. But there are two other costs as well. The rise in the price of the product protected by the VER will make some purchasers switch to buying a product combination which is inferior to the combination they would have chosen in the absence of the VER, and the income needed to compensate them for this is a cost of the VER; this can be estimated in terms of the amount of consumers' surplus lost. The second cost element is the extra charge that has to be paid to domestic factors of production to increase the output of the product subjected to the VER.

Hindley then selected four industries for his estimates; he decided it would be too costly to study all VERs adopted by the UK. The four industries are: video cassette recorders (VCRs); motor cars; woven garments; and non-leather footwear. For the latter two a domestic elasticity of supply of unity is assumed. These products were selected because they are significant in international trade and, in the case of VCRs and woven garments, are representative of even larger product groups (consumer electronics and clothing) which are heavily subjected to VERs. Also, VERs tend to influence trade either with the LDCs or with Japan, hence the selection of garments and footwear (affecting trade with the LDCs) and VCRs and motor cars (affecting trade with Japan) represents the actual geographical incidence of VERs. Finally, the selection represents a blend of VERs adopted by the UK without direct reference to the EC (motor cars and footwear) as well as one directly involving the EC.

The four chosen industries themselves operate under different technologies and production conditions, and these may affect the methodology for estimation. With regard to the effect of a VER on domestic production, the structural classification of the domestic import-competing industries is important; while the UK footwear and clothing industries may be classified as being near to perfectly competitive, the same cannot be said about the British motor and the EC VCR industries. Therefore, it can safely be assumed that a VER will raise the UK's production of footwear and clothing, but no such *a priori* claim can be made with respect to the UK car and the EC VCR industries. Also, a VER on the car and VCR industries may encourage foreign exporters to establish production facilities within the UK and the rest of the EC (for example, Nissan in the UK), but this is unlikely in the case of the other two industries. This raises problems regarding the benefits of the foreign investment enticed and the calculation of later costs since foreign investment is likely to affect both the structure and magnitude of the costs and benefits over time. Finally, there is a problem created by the extent of substitutability: domestic substitutes for cars and VCRs are more likely to be seen as different products by the consumer ('Video 2000' is not treated as equivalent to a Japanese VCR, whereas no such drastic distinction is held regarding footwear and clothing). Therefore, while Japanese motor cars and VCRs must be treated as imperfect substitutes for UK and EC domestic production, the other two industries can be handled as perfect substitutes.

The main results of the Hindley study are shown in Table 1, from which Hindley draws attention to the following points:

(i) The losses are for the UK as a whole. Hence, the benefits to UK residents (domestic producers setting a higher price) have been deducted from the costs of the VER to UK consumers and potential consumers, so the actual costs are higher than those shown in the table.
(ii) The estimates are for the costs of protection by VERs only. All four industries are also protected by tariff imposition; hence the calculations underestimate the costs to the UK.
(iii) The 'jobs created or maintained' relate to the specific industry under consideration, not to the whole of the UK economy. Hindley draws attention to the fact that the economy as a whole will experience less extra employment than the specific industry.

With these qualifications in mind and the fact that the garment sectors studied amount to only 30 per cent of the protected sectors, Hindley suggests that the total cost to UK consumers of protection by VERs in the four industries is nearer to £1 billion per annum and may be in excess of this figure.

He stresses that even if the job-creation estimates are taken at face value, the costs per job created or saved in the sector subject to the VER is very high, exceeding the average rate in the relevant sector. For example, the lowest figure of £7,500 per annum in the footwear industry compares with an average gross earning of £5,146 per year in 1982, the year on which this particular calculation is based. Since even stronger conclusions apply in the case of the other three industries, one can state the general consideration that abandoning the VERs would make it possible to continue to pay UK workers who lose their jobs their current wage rate and still make a net benefit for the UK as a whole, so the UK could save a large sum of money by dismantling VERs.

The aim of the Digby *et al.* (1988) study is to analyse the effects that the removal of the French, Italian and British VERs would have on the sale of Japanese cars; these are, respectively, 3 per cent and 11 per cent share of the market and an insignificant quota. They rightly assume that there are no VERs in West Germany or the rest of the EC and that the VERs employed by the US are peripheral to their analysis. They expect to find supporting evidence for three propositions concerning VERs: (i) by limiting the availability of certain cars, VERs raise their prices; (ii) the revenue that would accrue to the importing country from tariff imposition

Table 1: Costs to UK consumers of VERs and quotas

Sector	Cost to consumers per annum	Jobs created or maintained in industry	Cost per job per annum
VCRS	£80m	Less than 1100 by end of 1985	At least £80,000 in 1983 alone
Motor cars: Assuming that differences between UK and other EC prices would persist in the absence of VERs.	£175m	(i) 13200 if Ford and Vauxhall car production is assumed to increase as a result of the VERs.	£13,250
		(ii) only BL production increases.	£31,500
Assuming that differences would not exist in the absence of VERs.	In excess of £500m	Nil or negative	
Woven trousers, shirts and blouses	£52m	4000	£13,000
Non-leather footwear	£28m	3700	£7,500

Source: David Greenaway and Brian Hindley (1985) 'What Britain pays for voluntary export restraints'. Thames Essay, No. 43, 25.

is, in the case of VERs, received as an extra element of price for the exporting firm; and (iii) the VERs have 'anticompetitive effects', since non-Japanese firms selling in the markets subject to the VERs will realize that they can sustain higher prices there due to the VERs restricting the Japanese firms' ability to compete.

The study employs an empirical model, which is based on the theory of quantitative trade restrictions under conditions where economies of scale in production exist, and there is imperfect competition in the market; thus the model is not directly comparable with the one employed in the theoretical section. They justify the assumption of imperfect competition by the relatively small number of car producers, some evidence of significant economies of scale in the industry and the apparently high degree of product differentiation within the industry. Moreover, they rightly assume that since the VER itself affects the market, the modelling approach must accommodate market structure.

The numerical parameters of their model were based on 1985 data. The model incorporates seven markets: France; West Germany; Italy; the UK; the rest of the EC (RoEC); Japan; and the rest of the world (RoW). It identifies eight groups of car producers: French; German (minus US multinationals); Italian; UK (minus US multinationals); US multinationals in Europe, i.e. Ford and General Motors (F/GM); Japanese; the rest of the Eastern Hemisphere (RoEH); and the Western Hemisphere (WH). Table 2 gives the car sales in each country and a matrix of market shares.

The results of the Digby *et al.* study (see Table 3) indicate that the removal of the three EC VERs would increase Japanese car sales in Italy by 13,864 per cent! Also, the equivalent effect in the French market would be about 586 per cent and would be about 57 per cent in the UK. Realizing that the percentage changes for France and Italy may be grossly exaggerated, Digby *et al.* are quick to point out that in France and Italy one observes the same pro-competitive effect of the removal of the VER as they saw in the case of the UK: 'the biggest price reductions among the non-Japanese producers are, in each case, by the market leaders, who in France and Italy are the respective domestic producers' (Digby *et al.* 1988, 16). The results also show that the removal of the VERs has less proportionate effects on the sales of domestic products than on the sales of non-Japanese foreign producers: 'a policy

Table 2: The world market for cars in 1985

	F	G	I	UK	RoEC	J	RoW
Sales (million cars)	1.77	2.38	1.75	1.83	1.20	3.10	18.22

Market shares (in volume terms)

	F	G	I	UK	RoEC	J	RoW
France	63.4	7.2	16.8	9.4	16.5	0.0	4.2
Germany	9.2	46.6	10.8	8.7	15.4	1.3	3.5
Italy	6.2	4.6	59.5	3.6	6.4	0.1	0.1
UK	1.8	0.4	1.4	18.3	1.4	0.1	0.1
F/GM	12.5	26.2	7.3	43.1	26.5	0.1	0.8
Japan	3.0	13.1	0.2	10.9	23.3	98.4	16.9
RoEH	3.9	1.6	4.0	6.0	10.4	0.1	3.6
WH	0.0	0.2	0.0	0.0	0.1	0.0	70.9
Total	100.0	100.0	100.0	100.0	100.0	100.0	100.0

Source: C. Digby et al. (1988, 17)

instrument that is sold to the public as a means of preserving domestic employment has a bigger proportionate effect on the employment of importers (and, of course, a big effect on the profits of domestic producers)' (Digby et al. 1988, 17).

The welfare gains for the EC as a whole are calculated by adding up the net sum of consumer surplus in the markets from which VERs have been removed, plus the increases in tariff revenues and the profit reductions for EC producers. They amount to £333.3m. Note that the Japanese also gain about £165.7m, but the net effect is more favourable to the EC.

These results are obtained on the understanding that the product range of each firm remains unaltered after the removal of the VERs, and that the number of firms also stays the same as a result of this change in policy. The authors found it impossible to obtain acceptable estimates of the consequences of a change in this presumption, without the availability of information on how the pattern of consumer demand is likely to change when the product varieties also change. However, they are confident that granting more scope for firms to react to the policy change would reduce the impact of the removal of the VERs. On the

Table 3: The effects of the removal of all EC VERSs when model and firm numbers are held constant

Percentage change in prices

	F	G	I	UK	RoEC	J	RoW
France	−2.1	0.0	−0.9	−0.5	0.0	0.0	0.0
Germany	−0.4	0.0	−0.5	−0.3	0.0	0.0	0.0
Italy	−0.4	0.0	−2.1	−0.2	0.0	0.0	0.0
UK	−0.1	0.0	−0.1	−0.8	0.0	0.0	0.0
F/GM	−0.8	0.0	−0.6	−1.6	0.0	0.0	0.0
Japan	−26.1	0.0	−52.3	−7.5	0.0	0.0	0.0
RoEH	−0.1	0.0	−0.1	−0.2	0.0	0.0	0.0
WH	0.0	0.0	0.0	0.0	0.0	0.0	0.0

Percentage change in sales

	F	G	I	UK	RoEC	J	RoW
France	−4.6	0.0	−16.4	−5.8	0.0	0.0	0.0
Germany	−15.1	0.0	−18.7	−7.1	0.0	0.0	0.0
Italy	−15.3	0.0	−8.9	−8.1	0.0	0.0	0.0
UK	−16.9	0.0	−21.2	−4.3	0.0	0.0	0.0
F/GM	−12.8	0.0	−18.6	1.4	0.0	0.0	0.0
Japan	585.6	0.0	13863.9	56.5	0.0	0.0	0.0
RoEH	−16.8	0.0	−20.9	−8.0	0.0	0.0	0.0
WH	−17.5	0.0	−21.7	−9.3	0.0	0.0	0.0

	F	G	It	UK	RoEC	All EC	J
(i) Percentage change in:							
production	−3.8	−3.0	−7.9	−5.2	−2.1	−3.7	−7.9
value of product	−4.8	−3.1	−9.4	−5.7	−2.6	−4.3	−7.3
(ii) Sterling change in:							
profits	−137.1	−60.5	−126.8	−19.7	−70.9	−415.0	165.7
consumer surplus	201.3	0.0	248.2	116.0	(0.0)	565.5	0.0
CET revenue	65.1	0.0	91.0	26.7	(0.0)	182.0	
Change in sum of *(ii)* as percentage of base consumption	2.5	−0.9	4.2	2.0		1.3	2.5

Source: C. Digby et al. (1988, 17)

other hand, they believe that if their model allowed for collusion between firms, their estimates would understate the costs of the VERs. This is because some observers have attributed the prevalence of large price differentials between the UK and other European car markets to collusive behaviour among non-Japanese producers.

It may be worth noting that the net effect for the UK is a saving of £127.8m; the sum of consumer surplus and CET revenue (though this is an EC 'own resource'), minus the loss to Ford and GM. If the loss in profits for the US multinationals is to be included in UK's welfare, on the understanding that it will be reflected in the earnings of UK workers, the net effect for the UK will come down to £94.8m. In comparison with Hindley's estimate of £175m, this represents a much lower increase in welfare. The large difference between the two figures may come as a surprise, especially when the two studies employ similar demand elasticities. However, Hindley assumed that Japanese car sales would double after the removal of the UK VER, while Digby *et al.* assumed that they would increase by only 56 per cent. Thus, the two estimates may not be so different.

7. Conclusions

One should not end without asking why VERs are being adopted rather than alternative policies, when empirical evidence suggests the existence of net losses for the importing countries. A very important reason is that for all intents and purposes the rules of GATT forbid the use of quotas and tariff increases (usually VERs are introduced on top of tariffs), but VERs do not come under the rules of GATT. Also, VERs can be applied in a discriminatory way, hence they are most effective for dealing with the problems of the importing country; for example, if the UK seeks to restrict the import of Japanese cars rather than, say, German or Italian cars. Moreover, because of the excess profit accruing to the exporters from the VER, exporting countries naturally prefer VERs to tariffs or quotas, that is they have an incentive to entice importing countries away from these policy instruments. Finally, because VERs are not permanent, they give the exporting country the option of pressurizing the importing country (when the time comes) to remove the restriction, or to change or relax the definition of VER categories in a way that suits their needs. These two attractions to the exporting country make them offer VERs to dissuade the importing countries from the imposition of permanent tariffs or semi-permanent quotas.

References

Digby, C., Smith, A. and Venables, A. (1988). 'Counting the cost of voluntary export restrictions in the European car market', Discussion Paper 249 (London, Centre for Economic Policy Research, 1988).

El-Agraa, A. M. (1983). *The Theory of International Trade* (Beckenham, Croom-Helm; New York, St. Martin's, 1983).

El-Agraa, A. M. (ed.) (1987). *Protection, Cooperation, Integration and Development: Essays in Honour of Professor Hiroshi Kitamura* (London, Macmillan; New York, St. Martin's, 1987).

El-Agraa, A. M. (1989a). *International Trade* (London, MacMillan; New York, St. Martin's, 1989).

El-Agraa, A. M. (1989b). 'The theory and estimation of VERs', *Fukuoka University Review of Commercial Sciences*, 34 No. 2/3 (1989).

El-Agraa, A. M. (ed) (1990). *The Economics of the European Community* (Oxford, Philip Allan; New York, St. Martin's; New Delhi, Heritage Publishers, third edn., 1990).

Falvey, R. E. (1979). 'The composition of trade within import-restricted product categories', *Journal of Political Economy*, 87 (1979).

Feenstra, R. (1984). 'Voluntary export restraints in US autos, 1980 – 1: quality, employment and welfare effects', in R. E. Baldwin and A. O. Krueger (eds.), *The Structure and Evolution of Recent US Trade Policy* (Chicago, University of Chicago Press and National Bureau of Economic Research, 1984).

Hamilton, H. (1985). 'Economic aspects of voluntary export restraints', in D. Greenaway (ed.), *Current Issues in International Trade* (London, Macmillan, 1985).

Hindley, B. (1985). 'Motor cars from Japan', in D. Greenaway and B. Hindley, *What Britain Pays for Voluntary Export Restraints*, Thames Essay No. 43 (London, Trade Policy Research Centre, 1985).

Jenkins, G. P. (1983). 'Costs and consequences of the new protectionism', in G. P. Jenkins (ed.), *Canada in a Developing World Economy* (Oxford, Oxford University Press, 1983).

Jones, K. (1984). 'The political economy of voluntary export restraint agreements', *Kyklos*, 37 (1984).

Morkre, M. and Tarr, D. (1980). *Staff Report on Effects of Restrictions on United States Imports: Five Case Studies and Theory* (Washington DC, Federal Trade Commission, 1980).

Murray, T., Schmidt, W. and Walter, I. (1983). 'On the equivalence of import quotas and voluntary export restraints', *Journal of International Economics*, 14 (1983).

Rodriquez, C. A. (1978). 'The quality of imports and the differential welfare effects of tariffs, quotas and quality controls as protective devices', *Canadian Journal of Economics*, 12 (1978).

Takacs, W. E. (1978). 'The nonequivalence of tariffs, import quotas and voluntary export restraints', *Journal of International Economics*, 8 (1978).

11
The European Investment Bank and African development finance companies
MICHAEL NEVIN

1. Origins of the European Investment Bank

The European Investment Bank (EIB) was established on 1 January 1958, principally as an instrument for financing regional development within the European Community. Its shareholders are the member states of the Community, who also guarantee its borrowings and nominate its board of directors.

During the first quarter-century of its existence, between 1960 and 1985, the EIB lent 22.5 billion ECU within the EEC, of which 16 billion, or over 70 per cent, was provided for regional development. Although EIB's loans have been supplemented by grants from the European Regional Development Fund (ERDF) since 1975, in gross terms EIB loans remain the most important source of funds for regional development within the EC.

During the 1960s and 1970s, the EIB's activities in assisting less favoured regions within the Community was extended to areas outside the Community with which it had historic links. These areas included nations geographically close to Europe in North Africa and the Middle East, and the former colonies of EC member states in Africa, the Caribbean and the Pacific. The rationale for EIB assistance to these areas was similar to that which had applied to the poorer regions of the Community. They suffered from a shortage of finance capital to fund development projects because of their imperfect access to the world's capital markets. The EIB could add value by acting as a middleman, borrowing on international capital markets at the finest rates available.

2. The Lomé Conventions

The formal link between the European Community and former

French and Belgian colonies in Africa and the Pacific began in the 1964 with the signature of the first Yaoundé Convention. The lifetime of this Convention, which was signed by eighteen African states, ran from 1964 to 1969 when it was succeeded by the second Yaoundé Convention which ran to 1975. Under the terms of the Convention, the ex-colonies were provided modest amounts of financial assistance and were granted preferential trading terms with the Community.

The relationship between the European Community and Africa was significantly extended following Britain's entry into the European Community in 1973. The second Yaoundé Convention was succeeded by the first Lomé Convention signed in 1975, under which the scope of the Community's links was extended to former British colonies in the African, Caribbean and Pacific (ACP) regions, and the amount of financial support given to them was significantly increased. More than forty ACP states signed the first Lomé Convention, and the number of signatories increased to sixty-six under Lomé II. Over the same period, the value of the financial assistance provided by the Community increased substantially, from less than ECU 3.5 billion under Lomé I (1976–80) to ECU 5.5 billion under Lomé II (1981–85) and ECU 8.5 billion under Lomé III (1986–90). The Community's aid package under the Lomé Conventions comprised the following elements:

(i) grants and special loans administered by the European Development Fund (EDF) for investment in agriculture and social infrastructure, which comprised approximately two-thirds of the total aid package under Lomé II and Lomé III;

(ii) STABEX funds administered by the EDF to stabilise the export earnings of the ACP states, which comprised just over 10 per cent of the total aid package under Lomé II and Lomé III;

(iii) a special finance facility for minerals (SYSMIN) administered by the EDF, which comprised approximately 4 per cent of the total aid package under Lomé II and Lomé III;

(iv) risk capital and own resource loans administered by the EIB, which between them comprised approximately a fifth of the total aid package under Lomé II and Lomé III.

In total, the financial assistance allocated by the European Community under the first three Lomé Conventions was made up as follows:

Table 1: European Community financial assistance to the ACP states under the first three Lomé Conventions (million ECU)

	Lomé I	Lomé II	Lomé III
European Development Fund			
grants	2,150	2,999	4,860
special loans	446	525	600
STABEX	377	634	925
SYSMIN	–	282	415
Sub-total:	2,973	4,440	6,800
European Investment Bank			
risk capital	99	284	600
loans	390	685	1,100
Total:	3,462	5,409	8,500

Sources: European Commission and European Investment Bank

3. EIB constraints on lending

The figures given in Table 1 overestimate the amount of aid actually disbursed under each Convention, because in practice the EIB's loans on own resources were not fully committed. There were three main reasons for this.

The first reason was the limitations placed on the sectors to which EIB was permitted to lend. In its operations under the Lomé Conventions, the European Investment Bank is empowered to lend to projects in the industrial, mining and tourism sectors. In recent years, the definition of these sectors has been broadened to include economic infrastructure such as electricity, telecommunications and water supply. The European Commission through the European Development Fund (EDF) is responsible for Community aid to all other sectors. Despite the wider definition of sectors to which EIB may lend, an insufficient volume of projects was identified to absorb all the EIB loans theoretically available to the ACP states.

The second reason for EIB's failure to commit the total of funding available related to its stringent lending criteria. The signatories to the Lomé Convention comprise many of the world's poorest states. The bank's Twenty-Five Year Review (EIB, 1983) commented that,

> Out of seventy-three countries in the world which had a per capita income of less than US $1,000 per annum in 1980, forty-nine were ACP countries; of the thirty-four countries with per capita incomes of less than $370, twenty-five of them were ACP. (EIB 1983 79)

Yet despite the extreme poverty of many of its Lomé Convention clients, the EIB's statute required it to maintain a highly conservative lending policy. Article 18(3) of EIB's statute (1986) states that:

> When granting a loan to an undertaking or to a body other than a member state, the Bank shall make the loan conditional either on a guarantee from the member state in whose territory the project will be carried out, or on other adequate guarantees. (EIB 1986)

In practice, the EIB interprets 'adequate guarantees' to mean first-class guarantees, which are defined as guarantees from large blue-chip corporations or credit-worthy sovereign governments. Very few governments in the ACP states were deemed sufficiently credit-worthy for their guarantees to be acceptable. Therefore, the EIB was unwilling to lend from its own resources in these countries. The EIB's own resources constitute the funds it raises directly from the capital markets through bond issues, or from its shareholders through equity subscriptions. It excludes funds managed by the EIB on behalf of the European Community, for which it is not directly liable.

The third reason that EIB failed to commit the full allocation of funds relates to the minimum economic size for an EIB loan.

One of the main factors enabling the EIB to maintain low lending rates is its extremely low administrative overheads. The EIB's 1989 Annual Report (1989) indicated that its administrative costs, at ECU 77 million, represented only 0.16 per cent of the value of its loan portfolio, which was ECU 47,672 million at 31 December 1989. This extremely low overhead was achieved through the EIB's policy of placing large loans with high-quality clients who required little appraisal or monitoring. Indeed, other multilateral lending agencies have on occasion criticized EIB for putting insufficient effort into its appraisal missions, and tending to ride on the back of other lenders such as the World Bank. This enabled EIB to derive considerable economies of scale.

In a 1985 analysis of the accounts of nineteen international development banks (Nevin 1985), I established that the relationship between the average size of loans made by development banks and their proportionate administrative overheads is of the form:

$$a = \alpha + L^\beta$$

where a which equals the administrative overheads as a proportion of portfolio value (which equals the total administrative costs divided by total loan portfolio); L = average size of lending operation, US$ million (which equals total portfolio value divided by the number of lending operations which comprise it).

An examination of the 1981/2 accounts of a cross-section of nineteen international development banks indicated that the best fit for α was 4.33 and for β was -0.5, with an R^2 of 0.88.

The relationship indicates that, at early 1980s prices and costs, substantial economies were reaped by development banks as they increased the average size of individual loan operations up to approximately US$5 million, but as the size of the loan increased beyond this sum there was more limited scope for further economies by spreading administrative overheads over a larger loan size. The practical problem faced by the EIB in many of the smaller ACP states in which it operated was that there were few large projects requiring capital investment of a scale sufficient to justify a loan of $5 million or more.

In summary, EIB was constrained from committing the full amount of its own resource loans agreed under the terms of the Lomé Conventions by three factors:

(i) limitations on the sectors to which it was permitted to lend;
(ii) its own strict lending criteria;
(iii) the minimum economic size for a lending operation.

However, it should also be added that these problems could have been overcome, at least partially, by a more proactive and aggressive approach by the EIB's senior management. In practice,

EIB's senior management adopted a highly conservative lending policy, and were unwilling to take a lead in the identification, preparation or appraisal of viable development projects in Africa. Their normal approach was to wait until a sponsor or another international institution had done most of the necessary preparatory work, and then seek to place a large project loan backed by a first-class guarantee from the borrower and cross-default clauses with other more powerful lenders such as the World Bank. The consequence was that EIB's effectiveness as an agent for the development of African, Caribbean and Pacific economies was much more limited than its impact on regional development within the Community itself.

In the European context, EIB proved an effective medium for recycling funds from the wealthier to the less favoured regions of the Community. By lending only to first-class borrowers, it did not need to provide for bad debts; by lending in large sums, it secured significant scale economies and achieved lower administrative overheads than any comparable institution. It was thereby able to lend at rates lower than those that any commercial bank could offer.

However, in the Lomé Convention countries, the EIB did little lending on its own resources to the majority of Caribbean and Pacific islands because they were too small and had few projects large enough to be economic for direct EIB operations. A major constraint on EIB loans to many African states was their poor credit rating. These problems were partly overcome by the introduction of risk capital. Risk capital is a highly flexible instrument, which can be used to finance equity investments (either directly or through recipient governments), feasibility studies, and conditional or subordinated loans. The repayment of a risk-capital loan is only triggered if the cashflows of the project for which it is advanced are sufficient to service it. Risk capital is quasi-equity, carrying no fixed obligation to pay, and as such the burden of servicing it can never result in the insolvency of a borrower.

Because of its flexibility, risk capital has proved a popular financing mechanism for the Lomé Convention countries. Consequently, the proportion of the total Lomé aid package allocated to it has increased substantially under each Convention. The Lomé I risk-capital allocation of 99 million ECU represented less than 3 per cent of the aid package; the Lomé II allocation of 284 million ECU represented just over 5 per cent of the total; and the Lomé III allocation of ECU 600 million just over 7 per cent. Under Lomé IV, the amount of aid allocated to risk capital has increased further to ECU 825 million. Risk capital has proved a useful instrument for addressing the twin problems of excessive indebtedness and poor credit-worthiness. By providing a source of quasi-equity funding, it reduced the degree of gearing or leverage in project financing. It thereby enhanced the security for any debts raised within a funding package.

However, another mechanism was required to channel EIB funds to projects that were too small for a direct EIB loan. This mechanism was the global loan operation.

4. Global loan operations

Global loans comprise credit lines from the EIB to national development finance companies (DFCs), which then allocate funds from them to small and medium sized enterprises to finance specific projects in the industrial, mining and tourism sectors. The DFCs to which EIB has advanced global loans during the lifetime of the Lomé Conventions fall into three main categories: development banks, development corporations and government agencies.

Development banks

Development banks seek to fill a gap in the financial system of most sub-Saharan countries by lending to private enterprises for terms in excess of five years, to complement short-term lending by commercial banks. Development banks also occasionally take minority equity stakes in the companies to which they lend, but never become actively involved in their management. Examples of development banks of this type include Indebank in Malawi, the Tanganyika Development Finance Company, and the Development Bank of Zambia.

Development corporations

Development corporations undertake lending operations in the same way as development banks, and in addition act as a nursery for new ventures. Unlike development banks, development corporations often take an active role in promoting new enterprises, which may involve taking a majority equity stake in them. Development corporations may also provide serviced sites of commercial and industrial buildings which they lease to private companies. Examples of such development corporations include the Botswana Development Corporation (BDC) and the Lesotho National Development Corporation (LNDC).

Government agencies

Government agencies effectively act as channels for government funding into projects appraised and controlled by government, and undertake only a limited appraisal of the investments in their portfolio. Apart from administering the loan accounts, their role is very limited, and so their overheads tend to be low. An example of an agency of this type is the Agricultural and Industrial Bank of Ethiopia.

In the lifetime of the first two Lomé Conventions between 1976 and 1986, the EIB did not attempt to influence the form or management policy of the DFCs to which it advanced global loans. The DFC was used by the EIB as an intermediary for European development assistance to small and medium-scale enterprises (SMEs) to which it would be impossible for EIB to lend directly. The procedure by which the EIB channelled finance through DFCs involved making specific allocations to individual enterprises. In order to make an allocation from a global loan, a DFC had to submit a full appraisal report on the project to the EIB in Luxembourg, where it was vetted by an economist, a loan officer and a technical expert prior to approval. Upon approval, the DFC could draw down that part of the global loan corresponding with its commitment to a borrower.

Allocations from global loans, whether drawn from the EIB's own resources or from risk capital, typically financed investments in machinery and buildings. Risk-capital allocations have occasionally been used to finance the construction of industrial buildings for rental – for example, those of the Lesotho National Development Corporation. A DFC could also use risk-capital global loans to take minority equity stakes, to finance studies, or to extend conditional or subordinated loans to its borrower. No global loan allocation could be used to finance working capital.

Under the first Lomé Convention and in the early part of Lomé

II, repayment tended to be on a back-to-back basis, with the EIB repaid by the DFC as the DFC was repaid by the final beneficiary to which it had on-lent. After 1982, the popularity of annuity repayments increased, under which the EIB was repaid by the DFC according to an amortization schedule defined at the time of loan signature. The terms of amortization have varied considerably, within a range of six annual annuities following a four-year grace period (a ten-year term) to ten annuities following a five-year grace period (a fifteen-year term). Since most DFCs on-lent for periods of less than fifteen years, this implied that the DFC had some room to recycle global loan funds within the lifetime of its loan from EIB.

Under the terms of the finance contracts between EIB and national DFCs, EIB stipulated a maximum on-lending margin which the DFC as intermediary was permitted to earn. The permitted margin or spread between the EIB's lending rate and the DFC's on-lending rate varied between 4 per cent and 8 per cent under the first two Lomé Conventions.

The variations in the terms under which global loans were provided represented an attempt by the EIB to respond flexibly and pragmatically within the constraints of the Lomé Convention to the differing needs of African DFCs. However, in practice the variations in the terms of different global loans often appeared to have little rationale and injected administrative complexity into their operation without obvious benefits.

A particular problem arose with foreign exchange risk cover. Since EIB lent in ECU, while the DFC on-lent in the local currency, arrangements had to be made to cover the risk that the local currency would depreciate in relation to the ECU. In different cases, this foreign-exchange risk cover was provided by the final beneficiary, the DFC itself, or the national government of the country in which the DFC was located. None of these options proved entirely satisfactory. Where the final borrower took the foreign-exchange risk and a large devaluation of the local currency occurred, the borrower typically reacted in one of two ways. Either he repaid early to avoid further exposure, if the funds were available; or he experienced great difficulty in repaying at all, where funds were not available. Whatever option the final borrower took, the effect on the DFC's loan portfolio was inevitably adverse. Early repayment by credit-worthy borrowers reduced the size of a DFC's portfolio, while non-repayment by insolvent borrowers reduced its quality and led to an arrears problem. A number of African DFCs which attempted to pass on the foreign-exchange risk to the final borrower consequently ran into problems because of these factors, including TDFL in Tanzania, NIDCS in Swaziland, Indebank in Malawi and DFCK in Kenya.

On the other hand, where the DFC directly accepted the foreign-exchange risk, it laid itself open to potential foreign-exchange losses which were very difficult to predict or control. African DFCs also found it difficult to limit their exposure to foreign-exchange risk because of the absence of forward markets in foreign exchange for even short periods, let alone terms in excess of five years for which DFCs typically lent. An alternative solution would have been for the government itself to accept the foreign-exchange risk, either directly or through the Central Bank, in return for a premium. However, few governments were prepared to cover the foreign-exchange risks of DFCs.

A full list of EIB global loans to African DFCs between 1976 and 1986 is given in Table 2, in alphabetical order by country. This shows that during the lifetime of the first two Lomé Conventions, the EIB committed a total of ECU 218.3 million in twenty-seven global loan operations to national DFCs in Africa, and a further ECU 7.6 million to regional DFCs. Of this amount, ECU 74.1 million was committed under Lomé I and ECU 151.8 million under Lomé II. This constituted almost exactly a fifth of EIB's total commitments in Africa during the period.

Not only did the value of EIB's lending to DFCs increase during the lifetime of the first two Lomé conventions, but its scope was extended. Under Lomé I, EIB's commitments were overwhelmingly to DFCs in anglophone Africa (ECU 65 million, or nearly 90 per cent of the total), and the bank acted as a pure financier, providing credit lines but not seeking to influence management structure, personnel or policy. Under Lomé II, often reluctantly, the EIB was forced into a more active role, partly as a consequence of the problems experienced by the DFCs it first supported under Lomé I. It extended its DFC activities in francophone Africa, and in a limited number of cases played a catalytic role in setting up or restructuring DFCs in countries where no suitable intermediary existed.

By the end of Lomé II in 1986, the EIB held shares in

twelve African DFCs : the Banque Nationale de Développement Economique in Burundi; the Banque de Développement des Comores; the Caisse de Développement in Djibouti; the Banque Internationale pour le Commerce et l'Industrie de Guinée; the Liberian Bank for Development and Investment; the Development Bank of the Seychelles; SINDECO in Swaziland; the Tanganyika Development Finance Co. Ltd. in Tanzania; SOFIDE in Zaire; the Development Bank of Zambia; the Zimbabwe Development Bank; and BOAD.

5. An evaluation of global loan operations in Africa

From the point of view of both the EIB and the recipient country, global loans proved a useful means of placing economically sized loans which would help a range of small and medium scale enterprises. They also may have had higher economic value-added than direct lending operations. In an unpublished 1980 analysis of forty-two direct loans made by EIB under the first Lomé Convention and fifty-five allocations from global loans to eight DFCs, an EIB economist, Stephen McCarthy (McCarthy 1980) established that:

(i) the average project size of direct EIB operations, at 69 million ECU, was twenty times that of indirect operations through national development finance companies, at 3 million ECU;
(ii) the average economic rate of return (ERR) estimated at the time of appraisal was 20 per cent for global-loan allocations, compared with 14 per cent for direct loans (no data were available on the ERR actually achieved on completed projects, since the EIB only exceptionally carries out *ex post* economic evaluations of the projects which it finances);
(iii) the average capital cost per job for global loan allocations was 29,000 ECU, compared with 36,000 ECU per job in direct operations.

The popularity of global loan operations is attested by their growth during the 1970s and 1980s. In countries where suitable DFCs did not exist, the EIB often played a role in setting one up, in co-operation with other international development finance institutions. However, by the late 1980s an increasing number of DFCs were experiencing financial problems of some degree. The quality of their loan portfolios was deteriorating as a result of

Table 2: EIB commitments to African DFCs under the first two Lomé Conventions, 1976–1986

Country	Borrower	Loan amount '000 ECU	Convention	Window	Signature date Year	Signature date Month/Day	Notes
Botswana	Botswana Development Corporation	4000	Lomé II	Own resources	1983	9.06	
Burundi	Banque Nationale de Développement Economique	500	Lomé I	Risk capital	1979	10.09	
Burundi	Banque Nationale de Développement Economique	1300	Lomé II	Risk capital	1982	12.17	
Burundi	Banque Nationale de Développement Economique	846	Lomé II	Risk capital	1984	12.28	EIB shareholding in the DFC
Chad	Chad Government Global Loan	2000	Lomé II	Risk capital	1985	8.21	
Comoros	Banque de Développement des Comores	161	Lomé I	Risk capital	1981	12.29	
Congo	Banque Nationale de Développement du Congo	4000	Lomé II	Own resources	1983	10.13	Loan to govt to buy shares
Djibouti	Caisse de Développement du Djibouti	450	Lomé II	Risk capital	1982	7.16	EIB shareholding in the DFC
Djibouti	Caisse de Développement du Djibouti	50	Lomé II	Risk capital	1983	3.23	
Ethiopia	Agricultural & Industrial Development Bank	500	Lomé II	Risk capital	1982	12.17	For studies only
Guinea	Banque Internationale pour le Commerce et l'Industrie	2100	Lomé II	Risk capital	1985	10.25	
Guinea	Banque Internationale pour le Commerce et l'Industrie	605	Lomé II	Risk capital	1985	10.25	EIB shareholding in the DFC
Ivory Coast	Crédit de la Côte d'Ivoire	3500	Lomé I	Own resources	1980	11.12	
Ivory Coast	Compagnie Financière de la Côte d'Ivoire	3500	Lomé I	Own resources	1980	11.12	
Ivory Coast	Compagnie Financière de la Côte d'Ivoire	5000	Lomé II	Own resources	1982	12.14	
Kenya	Development Finance Company of Kenya Ltd	2000	Lomé I	Own resources	1976	10.27	
Kenya	Development Finance Company of Kenya Ltd	5000	Lomé I	Own resources	1979	5.22	
Kenya	Development Finance Company of Kenya Ltd	8000	Lomé II	Own resources	1982	11.18	
Kenya	Industrial Development Bank Ltd	5000	Lomé I	Own resources	1977	11.08	
Lesotho	Lesotho National Development Corporation	3000	Lomé II	Risk capital	1981	12.17	
Lesotho	Lesotho National Development Corporation	3000	Lomé II	Risk capital	1985	8.13	
Liberia	Liberian Bank for Development and Industry	338	Lomé I	Risk capital	1978	3.16	EIB shareholding in the DFC
Liberia	Liberian Bank for Development and Industry	2500	Lomé I	Own resources	1978	3.16	
Liberia	Liberian Bank for Development and Industry	3500	Lomé II	Own resources	1984	5.08	
Liberia	Liberian Bank for Development and Industry	1500	Lomé II	Risk capital	1984	5.08	
Madagascar	Bankin'Ny Indostria	8000	Lomé II	Risk capital	1984	9.19	
Malawi	Investment and Development Bank of Malawi Ltd	3000	Lomé I	Own resources	1977	11.03	
Malawi	Investment and Development Bank of Malawi Ltd	5000	Lomé I	Own resources	1980	9.17	
Malawi	Investment and Development Bank of Malawi Ltd	4000	Lomé II	Own resources	1985	10.14	
Malawi	Investment and Development Bank of Malawi Ltd	2000	Lomé II	Risk capital	1985	10.14	
Mauritius	Development Bank of Mauritius	3000	Lomé I	Own resources	1977	9.08	
Mauritius	Development Bank of Mauritius	4000	Lomé II	Own resources	1982	11.12	
Mauritius	Development Bank of Mauritius	500	Lomé II	Risk capital	1982	11.12	
Nigeria	Nigerian Industrial Development Bank	25000	Lomé I	Own resources	1978	12.14	
Nigeria	Nigerian Industrial Development Bank	40000	Lomé II	Own resources	1983	6.30	

Table 2 (continued)

Country	Borrower	Loan amount '000 ECU	Convention	Window	Signature date Year	Month/Day	Notes
Rwanda	Banque Rwandaise de Développement	700	Lomé II	Risk capital	1983	10.13	Studies & shares only
Seychelles	Development Bank of the Seychelles	580	Lomé II	Risk capital	1978	10.21	EIB shareholding in the DFC
Seychelles	Development Bank of the Seychelles	1000	Lomé II	Risk capital	1982	5.14	
Seychelles	Development Bank of the Seychelles	3000	Lomé II	Risk capital	1985	9.16	
Somalia	Somali Development Bank	250	Lomé I	Risk capital	1980	6.03	
Swaziland	National Industrial Development Corporation of Swaziland	2000	Lomé I	Own resources	1980	12.16	
Swaziland	National Industrial Development Corporation of Swaziland	1000	Lomé I	Risk capital	190	12.15	
Tanzania	Tanganyika Development Finance Co Ltd	5000	Lomé I	Own resources	1978	12.18	
Tanzania	Tanganyika Development Finance Co Ltd	2500	Lomé I	Risk capital	1977	3.10	Convertible bonds*
Uganda	Uganda Development Bank	7500	Lomé II	Risk capital	1982	9.20	
Uganda	Uganda Development Bank	2500	Lomé II	Risk capital	1982	9.20	Loan to govt to buy shares
Zaire	Société Financière de Développement Zaire	1096	Lomé I	Risk capital	1977	11.15	Subordinated loan
Zaire	Société Financière de Développement Zaire	98	Lomé I	Risk capital	1977	11.15	EIB shareholding in the DFC
Zaire	Société Financière de Développement Zaire	38	Lomé I	Risk capital	1980	12.18	EIB shareholding in the DFC
Zaire	Société Financière de Développement Zaire	6000	Lomé II	Risk capital	1981	9.08	
Zaire	Société Financière de Développement Zaire	12000	Lomé II	Risk capital	1984	12.18	
Zaire	Société Financière de Développement Zaire	155	Lomé II	Risk capital	1984	12.18	EIB shareholding in the DFC
Zambia	Development Bank of Zambia	2500	Lomé I	Own resources	1978	8.31	
Zambia	Development Bank of Zambia	548	Lomé I	Risk capital	1978	8.31	EIB shareholding in the DFC
Zambia	Development Bank of Zambia	6500	Lomé II	Own resources	1981	9.30	
Zambia	Development Bank of Zambia	1500	Lomé II	Risk capital	1981	9.30	
Zimbabwe	Zimbabwe Development Bank	4500	Lomé II	Risk capital	1983	12.07	Loan to govt to buy shares
Zimbabwe	Zimbabwe Development Bank	442	Lomé II	Risk capital	1983	12.07	EIB shareholding in the DFC
	Subtotal, loans to national DFCs	218257					
Regional	Banque de Développement de l'Afrique Centrale (BDEAC)	500	Lomé II	Risk capital	1984	10.02	For funding feasibility studies
Regional	East African Development Bank	500	Lomé II	Risk capital	1985	3.02	For funding feasibility studies
Regional	Banque Ouest Africaine de Développement	5000	Lomé II	Own resources	1981	10.15	
Regional	Banque Ouest Africaine de Développement	1620	Lomé II	Risk capital	1981	10.15	EIB shareholding in the DFC
	Total	225877					

NOTE: *Converted into ordinary shares in 1986.

rising arrears in debt servicing, caused in part by devaluation and consequent foreign exchange losses.
  Among the criticisms made of global loans were the following:

(i) The extent to which they genuinely added value, by helping to finance projects which would not otherwise have got off the ground, was not clear. Since funds were allocated only to the best projects, the suspicion is that for the most part EIB finance merely crowded out other sources of finance, rather than adding to the real level of investment in African economies.
(ii) The main benefit for the recipient is likely to have been short-term savings in interest payments. Since the interest charge on EIB loans was lower than that on any alternative source of finance because of the interest subsidy, firms which were able to gain access to it got a competitive edge over firms which could not.
(iii) In the longer term, this advantage was attenuated by the foreign-exchange risk carried on ECU-denominated loans. In the context of IBRD/IMF structural adjustment loans, many African currencies were sharply devalued against the ECU during the 1980s, leaving those who borrowed in ECU exposed to large foreign exchange losses which wiped out any short-term benefits from low interest rates.

  The EIB's philosophy has traditionally been to play a largely passive role in the management of DFCs to which it lends. An EIB appraisal mission of a DFC typically lasts a week, complemented by more detailed desk research in Luxembourg. The broad-brush nature of the appraisal reflects the fact that the EIB regards DFCs principally as conduits to channel EIB funds as cheaply as possible to small and medium-scale enterprises. While such an approach may have been adequate where the DFC was well established and well run, in cases where a DFC was newly established, or was facing problems because of poor management or a difficult economic environment, this passive approach was not sufficient to ensure that global loan funds were used effectively.
  Of the twenty-seven national DFCs with which EIB was involved in sub-Saharan Africa in late 1986, less than half a dozen were sufficiently strong in financial and managerial terms for the EIB's passive approach to be pursued with confidence.

In the late 1980s, I undertook an analysis of the accounts of twenty-seven African DFCs to which EIB had advanced global loans. This analysis suggested that:

(i) the accounting standards used by different DFCs varied widely;
(ii) in particular, DFCs had widely different treatments of provisions for bad debts, and it was usually the least solvent DFCs which were most guilty of underprovision;
(iii) although the performance of DFCs was related to external economic conditions over which they had little control, the key factor in the success of a DFC is the quality of its management;
(iv) a general conclusion was that government-owned DFCs, as a group, tended to be less profitable than DFCs in which a substantial stake is held by international development institutions, particularly those of the Interact group of European institutions, which comprises European development finance institutions such as the Commonwealth Development Corporation of the UK (CDC), Caisse Centrale of France and DEG of Germany;
(v) while this may reflect the fact that the profitability targets of government-owned DFCs weres often lower than those owned by international development institutions, it also suggested that the internal management of Interact-owned DFCs tends to be more professional and rigorous than that of government-owned DFCs.

Table 3 summarizes the comparative profitability of the DFCs examined. It is clear from the table that, while not all the Interact banks performed outstandingly well, none were real disasters; the real disaster stories, such as the Ugandan Development Bank, NIDCS in Swaziland and LBDI in Liberia, were all government-owned development banks. Other government-owned DFCs, such as NIDB in Nigeria and AIDB in Ethiopia, were saved from insolvency only by government support.

There was also a correlation between the performance of DFCs and the general economic environment of the country in which they operated. DFCs in African countries with comparatively high per capita income performed better than those in the poorest ACPs. For example, in Botswana and Mauritius (both of which have

Table 3: Key performance indicators of African DFCs to which EIB lent under the first two Lomé Conventions, 1976–86

Country	Borrower	Ownership	Net profit as a % of own funds, 1984	Administrative expenditure, % of balance-sheet value, 1984	Total 1984 balance-sheet value '000 ECU
Botswana	Botswana Development Corporation	Government	11.5	6.1	24585
Burundi	Banque Nationale de Développement Economique	Govt/CCCE/DEG	1.4	3.1	18935
Chad	Chad Government Global Loan	Government	N/A	N/A	N/A
Comoros	Banque de Développement des Comores	Government	N/A	N/A	N/A
Congo	Banque Nationale de Développement du Congo	Government	N/A	3.2	79305
Djibouti	Caisse de Développement du Djibouti	Government	N/A	7.8	3850
Ethiopia	Agricultural & Industrial Development Bank	Government	-9.7	0.4	783820
Ivory Coast	Compagnie Financière de la Côte d'Ivoire	BICI Bank	1.6	1.5	28705
Kenya	Development Finance Company of Kenya Ltd	Interact Group	2.7	4.5	45830
Kenya	Industrial Development Bank Ltd	Government	10.2	2.4	76850
Lesotho	Lesotho National Development Corporation	Government	-2.9	9.8	18000
Liberia	Liberian Bank for Development and Industry	Government	-23.1	6.1	36150
Madagascar	Bankin'Ny Indostria	Government	5.4	3.5	266710
Malawi	Investment and Development Bank of Malawi Ltd	InteractGroup	15.7	8.3	21470
Mauritius	Development Bank of Mauritius	Government	11.2	1.7	49540
Nigeria	Nigerian Industrial Development Bank	Government	3.2	4.6	509460
Rwanda	Banque Rwandaise de Développement	Government	1.6	2.8	37655
Seychelles	Development Bank of the Seychelles	Government	3.8	2.6	6854
Somalia	Somali Development Bank	Government	0.4	5.1	21535
Swaziland	National Industrial Development Corporation of Swaziland	Government	0.0	3.7	20690
Tanzania	Tanganyika Development Finance Co. Ltd	Interact Group & TIB	14.6	3.4	28100
Uganda	Uganda Development Bank	Government	-114.3	5.7	19010
Zaire	Société Financière de Développement Zaire	Interact, IFC & others	8.9	4.0	70560
Zambia	Development Bank of Zambia	Government	16.1	1.6	85400
Zimbabwe	Zimbabwe Development Bank	Interact, IFC & others	N/A	N/A	N/A

Note: No figures are available for: Chad Government Global Loan, Banque de Développement des Comores or Zimbabwe Development Bank, as these banks were only just commencing their operations in 1984.

high per capita income by African standards), the government-owned DFCs achieved good results. However, where an Interact DFC and a government DFC were operating in the same country, the Interact DFC generally performed better. For example, the Interact-owned Tanganyika Development Finance Company performed better than the government-owned Tanzania Investment Bank in Tanzania; in Kenya, the Interact-owned Development Finance Company performed better than the government-owned Industrial Development Bank; while in Malawi the Interact-owned Indebank performed better than the government-owned Malawi Development Corporation.

The reasons for the superior performance of the Interact group of national DFCs appear to include the following:

(i) DFCs with a significant Interact participation had boards of directors which included professional development bankers. They may have applied more rigorous criteria in project selection than the political appointees of government-owned banks, and in particular have been more prepared to reject projects which had powerful political support but were unlikely to be financially viable;
(ii) governments tended to place less emphasis than the Interact institutions on the financial results of its DFCs. The priority of governments was the social impact of DFC operations, including job creation and the promotion of high-risk start-up projects that might not have got off the ground without DFC support;
(iii) executive management may have had less autonomy in government-owned DFCs. In the case of the Interact group of DFCs, the board set the overall policy framework but then left executive staff to implement it with minimal interference in day-to-day management. This was not always true in the case of government-owned DFCs;
(iv) salary levels in government-owned DFCs tended to be linked with civil service levels, whereas in the Interact group of DFCs there was a greater freedom to pay market rates, so that a higher calibre of staff could be recruited.

However, DFCs with no government involvement often suffered from government regulation of interest rates, which were kept too low for the DFC to be profitable.

The EIB's own lending policies often compounded this problem. The EIB used DFCs as a channel to get EIB funds to private enterprises in Africa as cost-effectively as possible. Since the object of global loans was to help the development of private enterprise rather than to develop the DFCs, the EIB placed limits on the on-lending margins which the DFCs were permitted to earn. Depending on the circumstances of individual DFCs, these margins varied between a minimum of 4 per cent and a maximum of 8 per cent, which the EIB deemed sufficient to cover the administrative overheads of the DFC. Thus, in a case where the EIB lent to a DFC at 5 per cent and allowed a 5 per cent onlending margin, the final borrower would be charged a rate of interest of 10 per cent by the DFC.

In some cases, EIB's maximum permitted on-lending rate lay below the minimum lending rate stipulated in an IBRD credit line with the same institution. The EIB's approach to interest rates thus sometimes ran directly contrary to that of the IBRD. While the IBRD was pressing for higher interest rates in order to encourage local saving and capital formation, the EIB placed an upper limit on the interest rates that DFCs were permitted to charge under its global loans in order to maximize the benefits of its global loan operations to small- and medium-scale enterprises.

There is some evidence that the EIB's policies in this regard contributed to the financial problems of some African DFCs. In an independent analysis of the financial performance of DFCs, George Gondicas concluded that the main reason for the financial problems of the DFCs was the inadequate spread between their borrowing and on-lending rates. In particular, he stated that:

> ... the spreads allowed to DFCs....have been inadequate, allowing for inadequate cash flow and profits. The most important factor [in the financial distress of many DFCs] is the inadequacy of spreads. As the present experience shows, the concentration of DFCs in the long term financing of the industrial sector is a cyclical and risky business which can only be maintained if the spreads are adequate to create ample provisions. (Gondicas 1984)

6. Conclusions

Towards the late 1980s, a certain disillusionment was evident in the World Bank and elsewhere with regard to development finance companies (IBRD 1985). This was caused by the problems faced by DFCs in many countries, both in sub-Saharan Africa and elsewhere in the world. The prescription recommended was to switch the focus of global loans from DFCs towards commercial banks.

The wheel had turned full circle. DFCs had been set up in the quarter-century between the late 1950s and the early 1980s because of the perceived failure of commercial banks to finance long-term investment in the world's developing economies. The subsequent history of DFCs has to some extent borne out the caution of the commercial banking sector. Lending long-term to private enterprise in fragile economies is a high-cost and high-risk operation. Even in the most prudently managed DFCs, administrative overheads are likely to be at least 3 per cent of portfolio value and bad debt provision well in excess of 1 per cent of portfolio value is likely to be required each year.

However, it seems most unlikely that commercial banks will perform any better than DFCs in these respects. The counsel of despair advocated by some economists and international development bankers — of abandoning the DFCs and switching resources to commercial banks — is therefore misconceived. What is required is action to develop the DFCs into key elements in the embryonic long-term capital markets of the countries in which they operate.

The analysis of this paper strongly supports the central thesis of *Capital Funds in Underdeveloped Countries* (Nevin, 1961) written thirty years ago: namely, that the development of a stable indigenous market for long-term capital is a critical factor in the development process. External capital flows will not provide sufficient finance to meet the needs of economic development, and far more could and should be done to mobilize local sources of finance. The policies adopted by EIB towards its global loan operations may have hampered rather than helped that process.

There are two reasons for this conclusion. Firstly, global loans provided an apparently cheap and readily available source of external capital for economic development, and thereby diverted attention from the paramount need to develop the internal capital markets of the ACP states. Secondly, the terms under which global loans were provided — particularly the strict limits on the spreads allowed DFCs and their exposure to foreign-exchange risk — often undermined the longer-term viability of DFCs by preventing them from building up their own capital base and lending capacity.

The central implications of the experience of EIB's relationship with African DFCs under the Lomé Conventions include the following:

(i) Treating DFCs as mere vehicles for channelling funds to SMEs is fundamentally misconceived. The object of assistance should be to help the DFCs to build themselves up as key elements within the long-term capital markets of African economies.

(ii) Experience indicates that the traditional EIB approach of funding SMEs through global loans, involving an initial one-week appraisal mission of the DFC itself, followed by a commitment of funds and their disbursal through a desk exercise to vet each proposed allocation, is suitable only for a minority of well-established and financially sound DFCs. In the case of less well established DFCs, this traditional approach would imply that EIB either does not lend at all, or it accepts in advance that a high proportion of its funds will be channelled to firms and projects that eventually collapse – and may ultimately threaten the solvency of the DFC itself.

(iii) A preferable approach would be to adopt a more active role: taking shares and assisting with the institutional development of DFCs, particularly alongside other Interact institutions such as Caisse Centrale of France, DEG of Germany, FMO of the Netherlands and CDC of the United Kingdom, in the light of the historical evidence that DFCs wholly or partly owned by the Interact institutions have performed better than government-owned ones.

(iv) The economic value of EIB global loans is likely to be higher where they are complemented with technical assistance to ensure good management. For this reason, consideration should be given to reinforcing an EIB shareholding with at least observer status on the board of directors. Interact directors have proved valuable because of their experience and independence of judgement, and because they have acted as a buffer between executive management and political nominees.

(v) With regard to the spreads that are permitted to DFCs, there is a strong case for not putting any constraints on DFC spreads but allowing them to charge whatever the relevant market rate of interest is, taking account of the status and credit-worthiness of the borrower. Wider margins should not be a cause for concern, provided that the funds generated are used to build up the DFC's capital base and recycled for further development lending rather than swallowed up by wasteful administrative overheads.

References

European Investment Bank (1983). *25 Years, 1958–1983*, (Luxembourg, European Investment Bank, 1983).
European Investment Bank (1986). *Statutes and other provisions*, (Luxembourg: European Investment Bank; text updated to 1 January 1986).
European Investment Bank (1989). *Annual Report, 1989*, (Luxembourg: European Investment Bank, 1989).
Gondicas, G. (1984). 'Development finance institutions : their record, problems and prospects' (paper presented to a policy seminar for chief executives of development banks sponsored by the Industry Department and the Economic Development Institute of the World Bank, September 1984).
International Bank for Reconstruction and Development (IBRD) (1985), 'Financial intermediation policy paper' (IBRD Industry Department, 8 July 1985).
McCarthy, S. (1980). 'The economic impact of EIB operations under Lomé I' (Internal memorandum of the European Investment Bank, April 1980).
Nevin, Edward, (1961). *Capital Funds in Underdeveloped Countries* (London and New York, Macmillan, 1961).
Nevin, Michael, (1985). 'Dilemmas in Development Banking', *Savings and Development*, No. 4 (1985), Milan.

12
Capital funds in reforming socialist economies

ALAN R. ROE

1. Introduction

In the late 1950s, Ted Nevin spent a period as banking adviser to the government of Jamaica, and produced a concise but timely book encapsulating the problems of newly emerging financial systems. It was entitled *Capital Funds in Underdeveloped Countries* (CFUDC) (Nevin 1961).[1]

There were three elements of the international context of that time which seem to have conditioned what was included and also what was excluded from CFUDC. First, it was the era of the 'winds of change', when colonial arrangements were still providing the institutional structures, including financial structures, in most underdeveloped countries. Second, it was a period when the Bretton-Woods institutions seemed likely to succeed in one of their primary objectives, namely to defend a fixed-exchange-rate system. Self-evidently this success derived from the low and stable inflation rates which generally prevailed at that time. Third, it was a period when 'development economics' did not really exist as a subject. However, the few economists who ventured into this field generally espoused an articulate and unashamed scepticism about the effectiveness of unhindered market forces as a basis for rapid solutions to the problems of underdevelopment.

The first of these contextual factors resulted in CFUDC emphasizing as a main theme that the cause of economic development could be served positively by the creation of new monetary arrangements and institutions and the reform of the old. This would involve, in particular, reforms to remove the main disadvantages of dependence on colonial currency systems and expatriate banks. The second of the contextual factors resulted in issues of monetary and exchange-rate stability being given little attention in the development of the main theme. It was underdevelopment and poverty which were seen as the main problems to be addressed; general economic stability was a matter of much lower concern. The caveat about the dangers of improvident governments and the need for proper prudential regulation were all there (Nevin 1961, 40) but were not presented as reasons for holding back from the 'bolder and more positive policy' in the financial area which underdeveloped countries were argued to need. Finally, the third contextual factor resulted in CFUDC providing a convincing set of reasons for proactive government involvement in most aspects of the financial reform and institution-building which emerging countries were argued to need. The most obvious need was for direct government involvement in the creation of new central banks. However, arguments, based mainly on divergencies between private and social rates of return, were also developed to support the case for direct government involvement in agricultural credit, small-business finance, development finance companies and selective credit allocations.

If a wise prophet had materialized in Kingston, Jamaica, in 1959, there are two aspects of his prophecies about the international financial situation of the 1990s which might have surprised the author of CFUDC. The first would have been the prophecy that the practical implementation of financial reforms in the UDCs would have been so poor, in the intervening thirty years, that severe monetary instability would become commonplace in the developing world;[2] commonplace to the point of replacing poverty alleviation as the main concern of a new generation of development economists. The second would have been the prophecy that in the early 1990s there would be a dozen or more middle-income European economies just embarking on financial-sector reforms, far more substantial even than those analysed in CFUDC, and from an even more primitive base.

Inspired by this idle fantasizing, the purpose of this paper is to write a very short sequel to CFUDC, namely 'Capital funds in reforming socialist economies (CFRSE)'. Because it has to be short, it focuses only on some of the fundamental differences of the task facing the financial reformers or engineers in the two different contexts. The objective of the analysis is to highlight features of the solution which are radically different in the eastern European case.

2. The inherent contradiction and initial conditions

The emerging UDC economies of the 1950s, although administered by colonial governments, generally had productive sectors owned and operated by private-sector agents and motivated by profit. It was entirely appropriate in contemplating their future development and diversification to expect this strong private-sector influence to continue. It was also appropriate to identify and analyse the market failures which future public policy needed to take account of and correct. By contrast, in the emerging RSE economies of the 1990s, there is at least forty years of experience of active government intervention in all markets, and a consensus that this intervention has been a dismal failure. Thus, in the RSEs, it is the failure of public policy and bureaucratic intervention and not the failures of free markets which are reckoned by the new generation of reformers to be in need of correction.

The certainty in 1959 that active government intervention was required to produce the reformed financial sectors needed in the UDCs, is replaced by an equally strong conviction in the 1990s, at least on the part of many eastern Europeans, that the maximum possible freedom is what is now required. The contradiction inherent in this is obvious. The reform of the RSE financial sectors certainly cannot be achieved by the unhindered workings of market forces. So the eastern European practitioners who have just espoused the free-market message will now be asked to back off from this and accept a degree of direct government intervention, yet to be defined, in order to restructure hopelessly inadequate financial systems.

This is a confusing message, and not least because it flies in the face of western experience that sound regulatory systems take a long time to develop and gain consensus. In particular, the knowledge and wisdom about appropriate financial-sector regulation and control which has been built up in the West, and even in the UDCs, has been influenced by a process of learning-by-doing as well as the lessons from numerous episodes of financial crisis and collapse. In eastern Europe, by contrast, the practitioners are being asked, almost overnight, to replace one code of failed interventionist practice with a new interventionist code which is imported from elsewhere and of which they have no experience. Not surprisingly, it is possible to find much confusion as well as many influential people in the reforming countries who are resistant even to the most modest intrusion of regulation on otherwise free financial systems – for example the introduction of prudential regulations for the new banks.

Apart from this most troublesome contradiction, three aspects of the initial conditions facing financial-sector reformers in the RSEs are essential to an understanding of the constraints on their behaviour. They are:

(i) Serious macroeconomic instability. This is manifested initially in repressed inflation (i.e. excess demands for real commodities, matched by excessive money balances). However, as commodity market liberalization has got underway in Poland, the former Yugoslavia, Bulgaria and more recently the former Soviet Union, repressed inflation has given way to levels of open inflation or even hyper-inflation.

(ii) A pattern of allocation of resources to productive activities which is unsustainable as controls are lifted, subsidies removed and relative prices adjusted. The main example of this in all the RSEs is a very high weight of non-viable, technology-backward, environmentally unacceptable and financially loss-making industrial enterprises.

(iii) A large accumulated overhang of bad debts from the non-performing parts of the productive sector to the banks. In most RSEs this arises from the long-established 'cultural' tradition of eastern European banks, that they exist as a part of the social support mechanism to productive sector enterprises, and not as arm's-length evaluators of financial profitability. In short, the banks have been complicit in providing the enterprises with their 'soft-budget constraint'.[3]

With this essential background, the remainder of this paper attempts to analyse the same four main aspects of financial sector development that were considered in CFUDC. These are: the currency system; the role of central banks; the commercial banks; and the creation of non-bank credit institutions.

3. A stable currency

The UDCs analysed in 1959 were 'handicapped', according to

the judgements of that time, by the linking of their currencies to those of metropolitan countries, and especially through the colonial currency-board systems involving near 100 per cent sterling backing for local currencies. By contrast, the RSEs in the 1990s have not benefited from a legacy of stable currency arrangements from their former colonial master. All the reforming countries have encountered inflationary problems and several countries, especially Poland, Hungary and the former Yugoslavia, far from holding net overseas assets are burdened with substantial net external debts.[4] However, a number of crucial aspects of their necessary move to stable prices and currency are already evident.

First, repressed inflations will be, or have already been replaced by open inflation or even hyper-inflation as a consequence of initial price-liberalizing reforms and the ending of subsidies. The 600 per cent and 3,000 per cent inflation rates in Poland and Yugoslavia respectively, and the hyper-inflation in Russia and the Ukraine after 2 January 1992, are obvious examples. These inflationary surges will be financed initially by the dishoarding of the monetary overhangs or 'forced savings' accumulated from the past. The artificial price stability of the pre-reform years which provided some comfort to holders of large domestic currency balances has ended, thereby releasing a flood tide of accumulated spending power. Although this effect is theoretically stoppable by recourse to a confiscatory monetary reform, the RSEs have been strongly advised to avoid this apparently soft option.[5] Where it was tried, as in the confiscation of large-denomination notes in the Soviet Union early in 1991, it was assessed as a destabilizing measure resulting in intensified capital flight.

Beyond the initial stimulus to inflation arising from liberalization and dishoarding, the general consensus seems to be that large fiscal deficits, broadly defined, are the main perpetuating factors in inflation.[6] Accepting that this is the case, the second main point to make is that fiscal restraint, and the associated moderation of monetary expansion and so inflation, is far from being the moderately straightforward technical task which it may appear to be in the West. Thus strictures such as those in *The Economist* that 'it is vital that efforts to close the officially measured budget deficit should be supported by strict monetary control. Mr Yeltsin's officials understand this but they are not doing anything about it'[7] are true, but not particularly helpful.

This is partly because the 'officially measured fiscal deficit' is patently misleading as a measure of fiscal, and so monetary, pressures on inflation. Roberto Rocha (1991) for example, in an analysis of the Yugoslavian inflation of the late 1980s notes that the small fiscal surpluses realized during that period led to the conclusion that the fiscal situation was not a fundamental influence on inflation. Rocha goes on to observe that a broader view of financial balances would have revealed the true source of the Yugoslavian inflation problem, namely a major decline of enterprise profits from the equivalent of 10 per cent of GDP in 1981 to an overall negative amount by 1988.

The key to avoiding this possible confusion, as emphasized by, among others, Fry and Nuti (1991), is a linguistic one. Enterprise 'profits' in the western jargon can reasonably be regarded as a main source of government 'tax revenue' in the pre-reform RSEs. This is because of the tradition of automatic syphoning off of enterprise profits as state revenue. Symmetrically, enterprise losses in the pre-reform economies were financed either by direct transfers from the state or by officially directed credit from the captive banking system. In the context of liberalizing reforms, this automatic linking of profits, taxes and credit is an explosive cocktail. In particular rapid privatization, if it can be achieved, including even disorderly spontaneous privatizations,[8] will rapidly remove corporate profits from the control of the state. Since these lost revenues cannot be replaced by a 100 per cent corporate tax rate — scarcely a secure basis for establishing new capitalist economies — new fiscal arrangements need to be developed rapidly to replace the loss or decline of the government's main revenue source. The urgency of this problem is intensified by the fact that the difficulties of the reform period will almost certainly erode the profitability of those enterprises which remain within the ambit of state control, and this will further erode the tax base. The loss of captive CMEA markets; overvaluation of currencies in, for example, the former East Germany; the confusion, disorientation and demotivation of bureaucrat managers are all reasons for expecting that this collapse of profits will be a serious problem.

The conclusion which emerges from this part of the analysis is simple, but also paradoxical. Specifically, monetary stability in the

RSEs requires early attention to two matters, namely fiscal reform and banking and credit reforms, which have been regarded traditionally as medium-term objectives in the UDC context. Fiscal reform and the establishment of new tax bases are needed early on, to provide the replacement for the 100 per cent syphoning off of corporate profits as government 'revenue'. Banking and credit reform is needed early on to replace the automatic link between enterprise losses and credit extended – which is a sure-fire recipe in a liberalized economy for monetary instability. In other words, the obvious first step in the sequencing of reform, namely the creation of a stable economy, will need to be pursued in the RSE context in parallel with fiscal and financial reforms![9]

The second of these matters is discussed further below. We can conclude this section by a brief examination of the other possible techniques – additional, that is, to fiscal restraint – for achieving monetary stability.[10]

The second policy instrument is the nominal exchange rate. There is a broad-based agreement that convertibility for current-account transactions of residents is an essential early element of reform, because of the important influence which international prices must be allowed in restoring some rationality into long-distorted domestic price structures. Thus convertibility has been implemented in most of the early-stage reforming countries, and is seen as an important instrument directed at the industrial restructuring of these countries. If its role is viewed only in this light, then well and good.

However, the trade liberalization implicit in this move to convertibility has necessarily required early and large discrete devaluations in all cases, in order to avoid serious losses of reserves. Having accepted the need for these initial devaluations, the RSEs have generally found it very difficult to sustain subsequent exchange-rate policies in such a way as to concentrate narrowly on the medium- and longer-term objective of stimulating a new industrial structure more closely oriented to comparative advantage. Indeed, the use of the nominal exchange rate to provide a brake or 'nominal anchor' for inflation has been a substantial temptation. In Poland, in particular, the periodic pegging of the nominal rate, in 1990 and 1991, after the initial large devaluation, merely led to substantial real-exchange-rate overvaluation at various times, and so to confused signals to already bemused enterprise managers, about the importance really attaching to improved dollar export earnings.

In the light of these experiences, it should be stressed as a basic proposition that a nominal anchoring of the exchange rate can merely provide policy-makers with breathing space in which to attack the fundamentals of inflation causation with more vigour. If the fundamentals are not dealt with, the use of this instrument will be destabilizing, as the 1970s experiences in several South American economies amply testifies. A nominal exchange-rate peg certainly cannot compensate for the inadequacies of other stabilization policies.

A related and final issue relates to the inadequacy of foreign reserves, and the pressures which this creates to float or crawl the nominal exchange rate. In the case of the Russian Republic in particular, it has been strenuously argued that in the early stages of reform, floating has created a destabilizing undervaluation of the currency (i.e. far too large a fall in real wages). This in turn has brought forth the recommendation, evocative of the CFUDC recommendation in 1959, that a stabilization or guarantee fund should be provided by western governments to help defend a 'reasonable' value for the rouble and other RSE currencies. This idea has become controversial and mainly because of perceptions in western governments that a stabilization fund, like a nominal exchange-rate anchor, will have a reasonable chance of succeeding only if the fundamentals of inflation correction are broadly in place. With the credibility of a Russian economic reform in serious doubt, the provision of large stabilization funds could merely become a way of financing equally large amounts of capital flight, without achieving the desired effect on the exchange rate.

4. The role of the central bank

The analysis of CFUDC took issue with the proposition that the new central banks in the UDCs should have mainly traditional objectives and especially 'the control of the commercial banking system with the objective of stabilizing the economy' (p. 23). Instead, Nevin argued that any 'central bank must meet the most urgent needs of the monetary situation in which it comes into existence and develops' (p. 24). In the UDCs, their appropriate main function was argued to relate primarily to that of assisting the process of economic growth and capital formation. It can be added, as a personal observation, that other functions such as 'regulation, direction and the guidance of credit institutions', could be more easily de-emphasized at that time, because of the built-in prudential constraints associated with expatriate banking systems.

Probably the major difference between the tasks of new central banks in the UDCs and the RSEs is that central banks in the UDCs were typically established to deal, among other things, with the *future possibility* of monetary instability and banking-sector distress. By contrast, in the RSEs the new central banks are being born in an environment already characterized by extreme instability and high levels of banking-sector distress. Our central proposition is that the new institutions cannot be expected to deal fundamentally with the pre-existing situation, but they must be set up to ensure significant and growing authority over that situation as it evolves.

In particular, in considering the role of the new central banks it is important to recognize Nevin's guidance to the UDCs, namely '... no-one proposes to create a central bank merely because of what it can perform in the next year or two; its establishment is essentially a long-run matter in which the responsible authorities naturally and properly look to the growth and development of its functions over generations into the future' (p. 25).

The application of this advice in the RSE context requires some standing back from the immediate monetary turmoil to define a vision of what the new financial system should be like and how central banking development can contribute to its achievement. That vision for the future of the RSEs' financial systems, though difficult to achieve, is clear enough in outline. It is one in which most, if not all, allocation of credit is achieved through market and profit-orientated banks. It is a vision in which banks, whether organized with universal licences or on a specialist basis, provide credit on an arm's-length basis to their clients, and entirely give up the roles of automatic credit provision and support to ailing clients which they are presently required to discharge. It is a vision in which a reasonably competitive banking system results in the banks themselves succeeding, and occasionally failing, depending on their skills in balancing the risks and returns of the different types of loans they make. Finally, it is a vision in which the government itself is moderately successful in limiting its own demands on credit and so in establishing the pre-conditions for monetary stability.

This being accepted, it is relatively uncontroversial to recommend that all the new central banks should be established as the pre-eminent, and largely independent, financial institution in their respective countries, with responsibility to regulate, supervise and also aid the sound development of the remainder of the financial system. The legislative authority of the new banks would include:

(i) rules relating to central bank regulation and supervision of commercial banks including capital asset requirements;
(ii) rules governing central banking support to the government;
(iii) arrangements to enable effective central-bank management of domestic money and currency stability; and
(iv) arrangements to provide a central-bank role in long-term financial-sector institution-building and development.

This longer-term view of the role of the new central banks is easy to describe. What is far more difficult, is to determine what part of this role they can and should try to take on in the distorted and disequilibrium conditions presently characterizing the transition. The danger here is that premature efforts by new central banks to establish their influence in the four areas listed, but in circumstances clearly non-conducive to this, may establish modes of behaviour which could adversely affect their long-term success. In particular, some early failures could easily undermine the strong authority and respect in the rest of the financial community which central banks need for their sustained long-term success.[11]

What seems to be needed, but has not as yet been attempted seriously, is a phased introduction of the practices of western European central banking, with each phase being started only when transitional conditions have improved to the point of allowing it a reasonable prospect of success. Wherever possible, pre-announced timetables for the enforcement of particular types of measure might also be used to enhance the credibility of the central banks. The purpose of all this would be to leave the private-sector agents and institutions in no doubt about the pivotal long-term role of the central bank while, at the same time, preserving some scope for a flexible approach in the shorter term.

The remainder of this section of the paper draws on some important examples to illustrate this basic idea.

The taxation of the financial system

It is apparent from what was said earlier that the RSEs in their reforming state will be characterized by shortages of fiscal revenues, and that these shortages could exacerbate problems of monetary instability. In this situation it is predictable that policy pragmatism will result in significant taxation of the financial system, including the holdings of monetary balances. This will be achieved through a variety of methods including continued recourse to the inflation tax as a means of financing budgetary and enterprise deficits; high reserve requirements imposed on banks; and the syphoning off of possible excess liquidity in commercial banks caused by credit ceilings. The new central banks may need to go along with this pragmatism during the transition period, but they should not accept it as a long-term fact of life. Indeed, they should actively work to draw attention to the distortions associated with this approach and explain the long-term damage to/repression of the financial system which will result.

This public position could be supported, in turn by clear benchmarks relating to the central banks' own policies. In particular, it would be possible to establish clear targets to eliminate reserve requirements surplus to reasonable prudential requirements within, say, eight years and to eliminate any taxation element of commercial-bank deposits with the central bank within a similar time frame.

This approach would establish the new central banks unambiguously as advocates and defenders of a soundly based and untaxed banking system and would reconcile this position with the more pragmatic position required of them during the transition. Since the basic condition required to achieve the proposed targets of low reserve requirements would be an effective new system of general taxation, the same approach would also establish the new central banks as important advocates for the rapid introduction of tax reform.

Financial support to the government

Central-bank legislation in many countries includes clear limits on the amounts, the terms and the methods whereby central banks can lend to government. The new legislation in the RSEs should certainly include some such restrictions, although enforcement should not be anticipated to be possible for some time. It is naive to imagine that new central banks established for only one or two years can use brand new and untested legislation to stem the tide of a monetary expansion, arising from fiscal deficits that even determined reforming governments are unable to control. As Nevin himself noted, laws relating to monetary restraint are ultimately dependent for their effectiveness 'on the good sense and probity of the government of a territory and on nothing else' (p. 40).

What seems to us important in the evolutionary circumstances of the RSEs, is to establish monetary laws which have credibility and authority and are not overturned every few months because they cannot deal with the immediate instabilities. This again argues for a phased and pre-announced withdrawal of central banks from the business of providing automatic credit to government. The transition period involved needs to be long enough to enable the government to reduce its deficit to amounts not requiring much monetary financing, and establish and foster securities markets which can provide it with some realistic and market-based alternative sources of financing.

Supervision and regulation of the commercial banks

It is widely accepted that a major weakness in all the RSEs prior to reform has been the subordination of annual credit plans to the real production and other targets of the centrally planned system. The emerging market economies all need to replace this passive system of credit provision with one dependent on commercially based credit allocations organized by reasonably competitive banks. One role of the new central banks in this new set of arrangements will be to ensure, first, that this transformation is actually achieved and, secondly, that the commercial actions of the banks are properly regulated and supervised in order adequately to safeguard depositors' funds.

The change in banking and business attitudes required by this transformation is absolutely fundamental, and the difficulties of achieving it should not be underestimated. The new central banks will be critical since they must play the leading role in defining and then enforcing the regulatory context for the new arrangements. These rules should include:

(i) uniform accounting guidelines which can provide a proper basis for assessing the quality of commercial-bank portfolios. Ideally these will involve detailed loan-quality classification and not the more arbitrary reporting of loan arrears;
(ii) limits on large exposures especially if the commercial banks became active in privatization issues and so became partial owners of, as well as bankers to, productive sectors.

There is absolutely no reason why the definition and implementation of these rules should not begin at a very early date. The fact that most of the commercial banks in the RSEs will presently fall dismally short of acceptable standards is not a reason for holding back from the definitions of what these standards are. Indeed, the new central banks will make a valuable contribution to financial reform if they can document systematically the extent to which commercial banks are presently undercapitalized, burdened with non-performing debts and so on. This basic information-gathering will serve to define both the scale of financial-sector restructuring which is needed, and the dates by which a real enforcement of the new standards can be attempted with any prospect of success.

Enforcement of the new rules should involve substantial powers to the central bank, both to gain access to bank information on lending structures and quality, and also to intervene directly to arrest tendencies to bad practice. Critical to all this should be the power of the central bank to replace the managements of those banks unable to comply with the new commercial orientations of lending referred to earlier. This is a doubly important element in the RSEs, since not only will inexperienced bank managements be prone to the normal commercial risks of bank lending, but in the transitional years the traditional pressures to lend to bolster loss-making activities will undoubtedly be present.[12]

What these three examples illustrate is that strongly constituted central banks in the RSEs can begin immediately to establish the standards of good practice which should underpin a modern market-orientated banking system. They argue that the turmoil of the present transition period is not a reason for constructing the new central banks on a pragmatic or trial-and-error basis. Indeed, such an approach is a sure-fire recipe for perpetuating the present distortions of RSE financial systems in the longer term. The present turmoil can be used as an argument to delay the full implementation of the new arrangements, provided that clear targets are established to guide all decision-makers about when such aspects of the new system will be enforced. We believe that this might be done consistently, with the new central banks gaining recognition early on as the unchallenged leaders and opinion formers of financial-sector reform. This can provide such certainty as is possible in an inherently uncertain situation; help to define a clear route-map for reform; and provide leadership in critical supporting functions such as the training of bank managements.

5. The new commercial banks

The analysis of CFUDC was preoccupied with the ways in which colonial commercial banking systems could be reformed, to provide both the quantities of credit and the sectoral allocations of credit required to support the more rapid development of the countries concerned. In the RSEs by contrast, aggregate shortages of credit have never been a problem, because of the primacy of production planning over credit planning. On the contrary, the problem of focusing narrowly on production targets was that loss-making firms were never closed – western concepts like bankruptcy and redundancy were regarded as wasteful – and credit allocations were as likely to favour the loss-makers as the profit-earners. Nor have there been any reservations in the RSEs about the use of selective credit allocations of the type advocated in CFUDC. Credit allocation has been pervasive and a core element of the centrally planned systems.

Commercial bank reform none the less has a pivotal role to play in the overall reform programmes of the RSEs. It is a non-negotiable element in the establishment of market economies that reasonably efficient and profit-motivated banks be established to intermediate between savers and borrowers; and to enforce market tests of viability on at least the larger of all new productive-sector investments which are proposed.

We argued earlier that monetary stability in the RSEs will require the early establishment of soundly based banks which can eliminate the automatic financing of enterprise losses associated with the traditional banking systems. This, in turn, means that the banks have to start defending the security of their depositors' funds instead of defending, as in the past, the survival of their enterprise clients, irrespective of the cost. The cultural attitude associated with this new approach represents a radical departure, since it involves active and often difficult decision-making on the part of the banks, rather than the passive application of the planners' decisions as in the past. It is a reasonable proposition that bank managements brought up in the old system are unlikely to be suited well to the new, and that a whole new generation of commercial bankers will need to be trained.[13]

The most immediate problem of commercial-bank reform is how to deal with the legacy of non-performing loans and the associated under-capitalization of the existing banks. This situation has to be cleaned up, since both bank and borrower behaviour is likely to be distorted quite severely so long as it persists. Banks, for example, will have incentives to extend further credit to failed businesses in an effort to avoid the writing down of large losses. Borrowers who are unable to repay existing debts will have few inhibitions about extending their borrowings even at much higher interest rates. The result, as experienced in other contexts, could be an explosion of lending, largely allocated to failed businesses, and at real interest rates which would crowd out businesses with viable new investment possibilities.

How should the restructuring of the existing banks be organized? Closure of the worst of the loss-makers is a possibility but not realistic in most cases, given the very large size of most of the RSE banks. In some large banks the non-performing loans account for over a third of all deposits and something like five or six times total capital, implying large losses of depositors' funds in the event of closure. The Hungarian National Savings Bank, for example, is reputed to have losses equivalent to 3 per cent of GDP.

Thus a first step in restructuring will normally be the recapitalization of the banks and the associated reconstruction of a base of profitability. The full writing off of unrecoverable loans is ruled out by the same reasoning that rules out bank closure. Instead, the banks probably need to be allowed to sell their non-performing and non-recoverable loans to the government, or an appropriate government agency, in return for a transfer of government securities. Valuations need to be realistic and to recognize the almost valueless nature of the underlying assets being transferred. The transfer itself recognizes the ultimate responsibility of the state for the accumulated bad debts. The fiscal implications are unavoidable, but are limited to the interest on the securities being provided to the banks. This is likely to be small, relative to the many other new fiscal burdens which the RSEs are having to accept, and especially improved social provision in areas such as health, housing, unemployment benefits and the environment.

The reforms which established commercial banks would need to accept as the *quid pro quo* for new capital would include the accounting and informational reform associated with the new standards of central-bank regulation discussed earlier. Additionally, the banks would need to agree programmes of action to deal with non-performing but recoverable loans and in most cases avoid the further extension of loans to the debtors involved. Above all, the banks would need to reorganize their own loans-appraisal and monitoring systems to establish commercial criteria in the pre-eminent position.

As was noted earlier, much of this reorganization will be easier to achieve if new senior management teams are in place. The managers of the pre-reform banks are not necessarily to blame for the accumulated problems, but they are inevitably implicated in the failed system which caused these problems, and they will rarely have the motivation or abilities to implement the necessary reform.

Even when reforms are underway, the central bank could still use the sanction of management replacement as its main instrument of ensuring that reforms go in the right direction. This recognizes that traditional sanctions such as penal reserve requirements depend for their effectiveness on the profit motive, and so will not work if bank managers are finding it difficult to respond to that motive.

The issues of bank ownership are also relevant to the success of bank restructuring. The original owners of the banks need to recognize that their investments will have been completely lost in most cases and that they have no legitimate voice in the future of the banks. Bank employees might be argued to be candidates for acquiring an ownership stake. However, this raises the question of divided loyalties, since employees would find it difficult to co-operate in the acute surgery often needed as part of bank reform.

Most likely institutional investors, including foreign joint-venture partners, will provide the main source of new capital injections for the reconstituted banks.

Beyond the scope of this paper, but an essential complementary step to bank and financial-sector restructuring, is the parallel restructuring of commercial enterprises. The viewpoint adopted here is that early attention to the establishment of a soundly based banking system (including an authoritative central bank), will immeasurably ease the task of productive-sector restructuring. This is because it can provide a fixed point of commercially-motivated funding which will help to support viable restructuring investments, but even more important, to deny credit to non-viable loss-makers. Except in the case of very large firms for whom special regimes will be needed, this will help to de-politicize and decentralize difficult decisions about industrial success and failure. In the process, the new banks ought to provide an important way of economizing on the human resources needed to implement the massive real-economy restructuring which all the RSEs face.

The only remaining point to consider in this section relates to the types of bank to which the RSEs should aspire, once the immediate imperative to restructure banks is dealt with.

Two main concerns have been expressed in this context about the directions in which RSE banking reform is pointing so far. The first of these is that the reformed banks are being constituted with universal licences which extend well beyond traditional banking functions to embrace brokerage work, the writing of insurance and the provision of other financial services. This tendency is normally justified by the chronic shortages of relevant trained staff and the probable economies of scope to be reaped from a universal banking approach. However, Millard Long, among others, has drawn attention to the tradition of highly segmented banking, both functionally and geographically, in the pre-reform economies and the narrow scope of the experience-base of most RSE bankers which has resulted from this (Roe 1992). In these circumstances, the offering of universal licences creates obvious dangers evocative of those which have resulted from the liberalization of the US savings and loan industry.

Are these inexperienced bankers really going to be able to deal with the wide range of technically demanding tasks implicit in a universal banking licence? A solution to this problem, and one which would also enhance the chances of effective central-bank control, would be to require banks to run their various financial-services operations through subsidiary companies having separate managements and accounts. Although this might reduce the economies of scope and scale, it would have the merit, as Long notes, of allowing commercial failure in one area without threatening the stability and reputation of a bank as a whole.

A second concern associated in particular with Mayer (1991) is that US and UK advisors to the RSEs are encouraging popular participation in corporate security holdings, and the emergence of active stock markets to work alongside, and to some extent in competition with, banks. Mayer suggests that the RSEs might be better advised to adopt 'insider methods' of corporate control as found in Germany and Japan, in which banks are active in both corporate ownership and monitoring. He argues that this is a more realistic model in the light of the enormous task of enterprise restructuring now required. In particular, it could enable the formation of 'control groups' of linked enterprises and banks working together to transform and restructure identified subsets of enterprises, and avoid the social waste associated with bankruptcy and closures.

Although Mayer's reservations are valid, the practicalities of applying his suggestion ring some important warning bells which also need to be taken seriously. Above all, a close ownership and working link between enterprise and banks is precisely the situation which has caused the passivity in credit allocation referred to earlier. In the early years of reform when basic commercial cultures need to be transformed, it seems important to do everything possible to create arm's-length relationships between banks and their clients. The new banks initially will need to say 'no' more often than they say 'yes', and it is hard to see how this can be achieved with cross-ownership and insider approaches.[14]

Additionally, there is no real evidence from the experience of West German banks in their new East German joint ventures that they have found it easy to work with the banking culture in the reforming economy, or have been any less committed to an arm's-length relationship with enterprises than have bankers from other countries.

In view of these ambiguities about the real differences between commercial-banking practices from different western countries, our own view is that it would be dangerous to advocate a strong 'insider' system as superior to any other. In particular the notion that pervasive bank-ownership stakes in industry are the norm in Germany is wrong, and the recommendation that significant bank ownership of industry should be encouraged in the RSEs is fraught with dangers.

6. Developing non-bank financial institutions

The analysis of CFUDC was clear that a range of specialized financial intermediaries additional to banks were both necessary for reasonably rapid development, and unlikely to emerge in the short- or medium-term future without proactive government encouragement. Lying behind this view was the idea that many important areas of productive potential in the UDCs would be insufficiently profitable to bring forth adequate financing from banks and other established private-sector institutions.

With the benefit of thirty years of hindsight, the optimism with which these ideas for government-propelled diversification of the financial system were put forward seems misplaced. In the interim many countries in the developing world have accumulated a sorry catalogue of failed development-finance companies, agricultural-credit organizations and other specialist banks.

The RSEs and those who would advise them have learnt something from this record, to the point that there is little apparent advocacy of the type of financial-sector diversification analysed by Nevin. However, Mayer is correct to point out that there is a significant advocacy for security markets, and significant legislative and other steps have already been taken in this direction. The Budapest Stock Exchange, for example, was opened in 1990 and both Poland and CSFR have plans for their own stock exchanges.

Notwithstanding Mayer's reservations, there are good reasons for believing that the active promotion of security markets will be beneficial to long-term economic development in the RSEs. The government itself will need a broader range of financing mechanisms to help it avoid the monetary consequences of its own residual deficits. Thus markets do need to be established for government securities, in order to enhance their liquidity and render them more attractive as assets to hold in institutional or private portfolios.

The supply side of securities markets is also likely to be boosted by the various privatizing mechanisms which are being designed and slowly implemented in all the RSEs. Apart from the spontaneous privatizations which now are generally discouraged, two main routes for privatization are being developed. The first is the direct sale of larger firms to the highest bidder which is the preferred approach in Hungary, the former East Germany and Poland. The second is the mass 'give-away' of shares to the public at large which is the preferred route in the CSFR and is also gaining support in Romania and Poland.

The direct-sales approach is less conducive to the development of an enhanced supply of marketable securities. However, it is also an approach which is likely to result in an unacceptably slow pace of privatization. The main reason for this is the inherent problem of valuation of assets, but an important second major factor is the shortage of potential domestic buyers with adequate accumulations of capital. Where such wealth does exist it is widely perceived to belong in the hands of the 'nomenklatura' of the old order or the semi-criminals of black-market regimes, who are generally regarded as unfit to become the new owners of market-orientated capitalist firms. Thus the pace of privatization based on direct sales has been disappointingly slow, with only handfuls of firms being sold compared to the several thousand on offer in all the reforming countries.[15]

The obvious riposte to the second of the two problems just indicated is to arrange the securitization of the companies to be privatized with the initial ownership of shares being allocated by voucher systems or some other 'give-away'. Three disadvantages of this approach are commonly referred to. The first is that fiscal receipts from privatizations organized in this way will be negligible. This seems to be a non-issue, given the slow pace of privatization based on direct sales. The second is Mayer's point that widespread share ownership could result in companies being sold, in effect, as accumulations of financial securities with little real interest of the new 'owners' in the long-term performance of the company. The third disadvantage is related to the informational and other difficulties which small shareholders may have in wisely investing in, and subsequently trading, their vouchers.

The reality here is that the governments of all the RSEs face a stark and difficult choice. If they regard the rapid privatization of productive assets as the *sine qua non* of reform, then they will have to resort to some form of 'give-away', accepting all the implications just referred to, including the securitization of enterprise assets.

Alternatively if governments downplay the urgency of privatization, then they obviously have the luxury of slow and steady progress towards the achievement of direct sales. Such an approach has several advantages. Above all, it allows time to establish realistic valuations for the enterprises being divested; it does provide some capital receipts to the government to compensate for the loss of revenue receipts already referred to; and it does provide an opportunity to screen potential new owners to ensure that they possess at least the basic prerequisites for managing the enterprises competently. But it also fundamentally delays the emergence of true market economies in which a critical mass of productive sector enterprises, including a reasonable population of the larger ones, are under private ownership and control.

Some analysts do indeed argue that rapid privatization is the *sine qua non* of economic reform. Hinds, in particular, has argued strenuously that neither economic stabilization measures nor new incentives to restructure and raise the efficiency of productive sectors can possibly work, until there is a strong 'advocate of the interest of capital' established in the system (Hinds 1991). Such advocacy will not be there while the major part of productive enterprises remains in state ownership, or in various states of limbo under some temporary form of official control. Hinds's argument is further reinforced by those many people who see private ownership of productive assets, on a dispersed basis, as the strongest guarantee that a return to socialist systems can be avoided.

The view adopted in this present paper is that arguments such as those advanced by Hinds are of critical importance to the ultimate success of economic reform. Thus without in any way predicting that his view will gain the ascendancy, the plans of the reformers should be presaged on the basis that a significant proportion of state-owned productive assets will be transferred to private-sector ownership within a relatively short period of time. Strategies for financial-sector reform should take this on board and anticipate the creation of a relatively large supply of commercial, as well as government securities in the medium-term future. The orders of magnitude here are potentially very large. In the case of Poland, for example, it is reckoned that the market value of the top 500 companies would be about US $30 billion, equivalent to 40 percent of GNP.

Having taken this line, the next issue to consider is whether the *demand* for securities will be commensurate with the potentially large supply and, as a subsidiary question, whether benefits can arise from satisfying that demand. Several points need to be made in this context. First, the portfolio diversification available both to individuals and institutions in the pre-reform economies has been extremely narrow. At the risk of some oversimplification that choice has been one between money balances, inventories of real commodities[16] and, for a selected few, foreign-currency assets. Admittedly high savings rates have been achieved, but this is largely a consequence of the forced saving implicit in scarcity economies, rather than because of the inherent attractiveness of saving itself or the assets in which savings might be held. In the future this has to change. The transition period will see a collapse of domestic savings as commodity markets are liberalized. The recovery of these rates in the medium term will depend upon the availability of attractive incentives to save. The special circumstances of rapid privatization provide a unique opportunity to create such incentives in the form of well-packaged portfolios of commercial securities.

Similarly, the transition periods of the reform process are obviously characterized, especially in the former Soviet Union, by large-scale capital flight. This has to be corrected, first and foremost, by successful programmes of macroeconomic stabilization. But assets into which the non-fleeing capital might move also need to be established. Little benefit will be achieved by merely re-creating the monetary overhang; by creating a property boom; or by further stimulating inventory accumulation!

A second important point in this connection relates to the change in insurance and social-security arrangements which will be necessary in most of the RSEs. In general this will shift responsibility for these arrangements from state-owned enterprises, which have normally discharged this responsibility on a non-funded basis, towards the state itself or to commercially operated life-insurance and pension companies, which will need to create and manage appropriate investment funds. In the light of the seriousness of the fiscal situation already referred to, the larger the share of the new activities which the private funds can obtain the better, provided that these are soundly managed. However, this success, if it occurs, will create a potentially very large demand for domestic-investment outlets. The more diversified and attractive these are, the faster this type of business can be built up.

The final point on this topic of the demand for corporate securities relates to capital transfers from western as well as Japanese and other Far Eastern sources. It is a reasonable presumption that there are many overseas investors who may not wish to invest directly in individual enterprises in the RSEs, but who may be very interested in a portfolio of such investments as part of a globally diversified portfolio. The benefits of so-called 'country funds' is already well established through the experiences of Taiwan, Mexico, India and other countries. The first effort along these lines in the RSEs has been in Hungary with the creation of the US $80 million Hungary Fund in 1989. Because such funds have achieved high degrees of credibility, and because they transfer well established fund-management techniques from abroad, they can probably play a small but catalytic role in the overall process of diversifying RSE financial sectors.

Additional to the interrelated need to establish securities markets, insurance and pension funds, and country funds, any scenario which anticipates substantial dependence on 'give-away' approaches to privatization will also call for the emergence of various other fund-management arrangements. There is a general view in countries such as the CSFR, Poland and Romania, where this has been considered, that allocations of small blocks of shares in individual enterprises, to individual small investors, is not advisable. Instead the allocation of claims to particular portfolios, segmented possibly by sector or by size of enterprise, might be anticipated. This has the advantage that the management of the portfolios could be assigned to trusts in which appropriate professional expertise could be concentrated. Additionally to working as portfolio managers in the manner of, say, unit trusts in the UK, the RSE trusts could be asked to take initiatives in arranging the restructuring of enterprises within their charge. This could include *inter alia* the search for joint-venture partners to inject new capital and management into enterprises; the closure of chronic loss-makers; the organization of appropriate mergers with other local firms; and the identification and remedying of obvious management weaknesses in particular enterprises.

Because these trusts would be answerable to the ultimate shareholders of the component enterprises, they might avoid some of the evident disadvantages associated with the retention of the ownership of enterprises under the state, pending the search for direct buyers. Equally, if the trusts were well funded they could recruit competent management teams, including those with appropriate overseas experience, and this would dilute one of the criticisms of 'give-away' privatizations, namely that it may not assure a reasonable level of enterprise governance. Additionally, if it were shares in the trusts and not in the individual companies which were made marketable through the new securities markets, then one of the concerns of Mayer could be answered. Specifically an incentive structure for the managers of trusts could be constructed, which would encourage them to focus their efforts on raising the efficiency and profitability of the companies under their supervision. They would be expected to maintain a supervisory management competence in relation to all their companies and so would have, from the outset, a broader concern for the long-term performance of the enterprises than do some portfolio managers in western financial institutions.

7. Conclusions

Ted Nevin concluded his book with an epilogue instead of a concluding chapter, noting that this could do little more than repeat a series of individual points made in the body of the text.

Similarly, our review of the four main issues of financial reform in the RSEs has touched on a variety of matters which do not lend themselves to concise summary. Thus we can use this final section to note just two broad themes.

First, the present turmoil and uncertainties of the transition stage of reform contain the danger that efforts to rebuild new financial systems will be based on short-term pragmatism and will be subject to frequent changes of direction. This paper has stressed the considerable dangers of this pragmatic approach and, above all, the danger that it can serve only to aggravate rather than soothe the existing levels of uncertainty in the reforming economies. The paper has also suggested an alternative, in which a vision of the future financial system of each country is defined and a route-map drawn to indicate the feasible steps in working towards its achievement. Particularly important in all this is the role of a strong, independent central bank set up to act as the advocate of that new system, and regulate and supervise its component parts as they evolve. We have been at pains to suggest that provided the route-map is reasonably clear, there need be no contradiction in the central bank operating with varying transition periods for the achievement of the ultimate standards of financial soundness and good practice to which the new system must ultimately aspire.

Second, attention has been drawn to the serious shortages of skilled and experienced managers which can constrain many aspects of this reform process. This fact has been argued to enhance the importance of the financial sector in these economies and to support the case for early action on financial-sector reform. In particular, the paper has argued that the early development of commercially-orientated banks can provide a limited set of decision points for guiding resource allocation, and so can be extremely important in expediting the massive process of industrial restructuring and the reform of attitudes to industrial management more generally. In particular, the early reliance on banks in this process can serve to remove the process from the political sphere as well as from the *ad hoc* decision-making which is likely otherwise.

Similarly the concentration of portfolios of privatized-enterprise assets in a limited set of privatization trusts, could help more rapidly to achieve the enhanced levels of private ownership in the RSEs which many see as the prerequisite of a mixed-market economy. Furthermore, with proper design they could do this consistently, with the preservation of adequate corporate management and governance.

Notes

1. This followed his Ph.D. research published as *Mechanism of Cheap Money: A Study of British Monetary Policy, 1931–1939*, University of Wales Press, 1955.
2. Wise prophets are notorious for simplifying their messages for the sake of effect. Obviously this particular exponent of the art failed to draw attention to the exogenous events in the international environment such as oil and debt crises, which may have complicated financial reform in many countries.
3. It is important to our subsequent argument to note that they are not the only element contributing to soft budgets. Other institutions involved are the government itself through direct fiscal support, and related enterprises through intra-enterprise credits.
4. These three countries all have accumulated external debts equivalent to 30 per cent of GNP or more. This may not seem particularly high, but it none the less imposes a high debt-service burden because of small hard-currency export earnings.
5. See Nuti (1991). He refers to the strong association of such reform with post-Second-World-War Stalinist policies in many of the colonies of the USSR.
6. This is certainly a reasonable presumption, since in the absence of markets for state bonds, the tradition in most of the RSEs is one involving the automatic financing of state budget deficits by monetary expansion.
7. *The Economist*, 14–20 December 1991, 69.
8. 'Spontaneous' privatizations are sales of firms or their assets from below (for example to former managers and other insiders). The experiences in Hungary, Poland and Yugoslavia have shown that it is profitable enterprises which are most likely to be sold in this way and that the benefiting insiders will also include the 'nomenklatura' of the old regimes.
9. It is recognized that full fiscal reform inevitably takes time. However, some first steps on reform are needed early on as, for example, with the crude value-added tax introduced in the Russian reform programme in 1991/2.
10. Wages polices are not considered here but are discussed in detail in Kornai (1990).
11. A basic problem here is that while there might be broad agreement that central banks need to be 'independent', there are likely to be many different interpretations of how the scope of the central-bank work should or might be limited. Eccentric interpretations of this are also possible in the unique circumstances now being encountered in the RSEs.
12. A major issue here is how active central banks should be through their 'lender of last resort' function in preventing the collapse of 'sound' enterprises in financial difficulties. If this work is well

done, it serves an important welfare-enhancing role. If badly done, it easily becomes the passive credit provision of the pre-reform system.
13. This of itself is not a reason for being pessimistic about banking reform. In the old East Germany, large numbers of Deutsche Bank and other western-trained bankers are already working in new joint ventures. Equally, new banks set up in Portugal after 1984 when banking was liberalized achieved success very quickly in spite of policies involving no recruitment of bankers from the nationalized banking system.
14. Additionally it is easy to overstate the closeness of the bank – enterprise links in the German model, as well as the benefits which supposedly arise from this. For a well researched but sceptical view see Edwards and Fisher (1991).
15. For example, 7,500 in Poland and many more in Romania.
16. In some cases, the absence of markets has meant that not even housing and real estate have been available as stores of value.

References

Commander, S. (ed.) (1991). *Managing Inflation in Socialist Economies in Transition* (Washington, The World Bank, 1991).

Edwards, J. and Fischer, K. (1991). 'An overview of the German financial system' (mimeograph, Cambridge University, 1991).

Fry, M., and Nuti, M. (1991). 'Monetary and exchange-rate policies during Eastern Europe's transition: some lessons from further east' (University of Birmingham Discussion Paper, September 1991).

Gelb, A. and Gray, C. (1991). 'The transformation of economies in Central and Eastern Europe', World Bank Policy and Research Series, No. 17 (Washington DC, June 1991).

Hinds, M. (1991). 'Issues in the introduction of market forces in Eastern European socialist economies in transition' in S. Commander (op. cit.).

Kornai, J. (1990). *The Road to a Free Economy, Shifting from a Socialist System: The Case of Hungary* (New York, Norton, 1990).

Mayer, C. (1991). 'Financial reform in Eastern Europe: progress with the wrong model', CEPR Discussion Paper No. 603 (London, September 1991).

Nevin, E. (1961). *Capital Funds in Underdeveloped Countries* (London and New York, Macmillan, 1961).

Nuti, M. (1991). 'Stabilization and sequencing in the reform of socialist economies', in S. Commander (op. cit.).

de Rezenda Rocha, R. (1991). 'Inflation and stabilization in socialist countries: some lessons from Yugoslav experience', in S. Commander (op. cit.).

Roe, A. R. (1992). *Financial Sector Reform in Transitional Socialist Economies*, World Bank Economic Development Institute Seminar, Report No. 29, (Washington, The World Bank, 1992).

VI POLITICAL ECONOMY

13
European integration: a political and institutional process

MICHAEL WATSON

1. Introduction

To begin with, I wish to dispel two important misconceptions about European integration which are especially prevalent in Britain, before going on to look in more detail at the political and historical reality of the process. While political and social forces provide the principal key to understanding the long-run dynamics of European integration, this is not, on the whole, in the adversarial sense of a collectivist versus a free-market conception of Europe. Such a dualistic approach to the question requires some 'deconstruction', in the context of recent developments, given its attraction to people on the left and right of the politico-economic spectrum. For them, integration is understood as directed either at establishing an interventionist European government or, in complete opposition to that, at creating first and foremost a single, unregulated European market, involving only a weak inter-governmental central structure. These 'projections' are seen, of course, as mutually exclusive and integration is judged as 'good' or 'bad' accordingly. If such contradictory conceptions were taken seriously by enough major political actors in the European Community (EC),[1] there could be the danger of a real 'deconstruction' of European integration by the growth of divergence and deadlock within the process.

2. Free-market versus collectivist views of integration

From a free-market point of view, the single-market idea sums up what integration is all about. The EC single market is interpreted 'as a pure exercise in deregulation' and seen as representing 'the triumph of free-trading, pro-market forces in the Community' (Price 1988, 12). Any possible connection with the development of a European federation is considered non-existent and the Single European Act (SEA) of 1987 treated simply as a means for implementing the single market. What this historically abstracted view overlooks, however, is that the single market and the SEA both arise out of, and are further steps in, what is an ongoing integration process; one, moreover, which from the beginning has had a political objective, whether described in terms of 'union', 'unification', or 'federation', for its prime movers and leading participants (as I shall explore later).

In the implementation of the single market, the free-market view is that the crucial task of eliminating non-tariff barriers can be left to market forces. There is little or no need for the development of EC policies to accompany the operation of the single market. Once national standards and regulations are no longer applicable to goods and services from the rest of the EC under the device of 'mutual regulation' (i.e. 'my regulations are as good as yours'), then they will be put under great competitive pressure to be minimized, allowing consumers to decide for themselves what standards they want. Mutual recognition is seen as giving rise to deregulation. However, as Lord Cockfield, the architect of the single market programme, has stated: 'It was made clear in the white paper that competition policy, transport, science and technology, regional and social policy, the environment and consumer protection were all closely related policies which needed to be developed in parallel with the [single] market programme' (Cockfield 1990, 7). A key reason he gives for this is a political one, crucial for the integration process even if its content in a particular stage is very largely economic. The reason is to achieve support for further integration amongst 'all member states and all sections of the Community'. This is a realistic recognition that the free market and free trade are not the overriding concerns, let alone fundamentalist-type philosophies, of many political organizations and other interests which form or influence European governments and EC institutions. Moreover, political pressures in the EC for higher quality standards cannot simply be ruled out of court, especially in matters affecting health, safety and the environment. It is evident that with the single market such standards can only be achieved by EC policy-making which transcends particular national or economic interests.

An understanding of the significance of the single market for integration is greatly enhanced, if it is recognized that a political market place operates alongside the economic market as an integral part of liberal democracy, with 'the political' going significantly wider than the state or government as such. Thus any conception of the liberal system in terms of the market or state – let alone market 'versus' state – is reductionist of a complex reality and leads only to truncated and partial assessments of the situation and associated problems. A *reductio ad absurdum* of this in free-market thinking is when the single market is seen as basically unrelated to the question of a European monetary system. Monetary stability is expected to result 'spontaneously' from competition between states producing convergence in relevant fiscal and monetary policies – meaning that no single currency is needed. However, the uncertainty inherent in the spontaneity of the market is implicitly recognized when it is also argued that ultimately there may well be a currency which emerges as 'the winner' from competition amongst national currencies.

It is the very uncertainty known to be associated with the spontaneity of the market which is a major factor in the importance of the political market-place and the recourse to political institutions. As Lord Cockfield notes, the single-market programme has acted as 'the catalyst and stimulus for progress elsewhere' (Cockfield 1990, 8) that is, in respect of policy competences. Or, as Jonathan Story has noted, 'the spirit of spill-over lives' (Story 1990, 49), referring to the neo-functionalist integration idea that Community reinforcement stems from second-order consequences of specific actions to meet new challenges to the Community's role and functioning (such as enlargement, Japanese economic ascendancy, or east European developments). He gives the example of the expectations aroused in European business and financial circles by the prospect of economic integration, which makes it difficult for governments to resist the momentum. Such expectations 'may not be deceived with impunity' (Story 1990, 49). (As Mrs Thatcher found – the concern her European back-pedalling produced in such circles playing some part in her downfall, as echoed by Sir Geoffrey Howe in his crucial House of Commons resignation speech in 1990.)

Similarly incomplete reasoning accompanies free-market advocacy of the opening up of public procurement to EC-wide competition in defence, a precondition for which, in practice, is a common security policy ('opening up' could otherwise make national-based defence dependent on external resourcing). But the main refusal to contemplate any policy integration is in respect of the 'social dimension'. EC social policy is seen as a superfluity, the need for which has been dreamt up by 'interventionists' to further their cause (as this has waned at national level). Regional policy is sweepingly condemned, viewed as equivalent to a (costly) attempt to turn back the tide, in trying to get industry to go where it does not spontaneously want to go. At bottom, there is fear that concern with 'social cohesion' at the EC level favours 'convergence and necessarily impl[ies] co-ordination at the centre' (Price 1988, 28), thereby threatening the vision of a free-market EC.

A real problem with the free-market view of the single market is the political nonchalance or naivety it can exhibit in respect of some of the effects. Thus an IEA study by Price explains: 'without the pain of restructuring there is no gain to be had from the single market' (Price 1988, 26). The basic point here is not simply that such social 'pain' powerfully stimulates political action, but that this can no longer be contained wholly in the national context with the shift in decision-making power and political life to the EC level, which the single market and the SEA themselves both reflect and promote. But probably a more crucial defect of the free-market approach for understanding the integration process is that it overlooks the commitment of leading players to the community aspect of what integration is about. This is because of the Manichean, state-versus-market perspective which makes it difficult for it to take seriously, for example, the conclusion of the European Commission report on the social dimension which combines what are seen as 'irreconcilable views (market and regulatory solutions), by suggesting a mixture of both, with a good dose of "social dialogue" added' (Price 1988, 31). Yet in practical, political terms, such a middle-way policy is perfectly viable, and in particular a surer path to follow in respect of the community commitment (whose importance in the integration process will be elucidated later).

To turn now to the collectivist understanding of integration, a basic belief has been expressed that, 'the essential choice is between a Europe dominated by a liberal market philosophy and one which incorporates liberal collectivist and socialist elements' (Cutler et al. 1989, 7). The EC is required to opt decisively for the latter and is to be judged accordingly. Thus as things are, for those favouring a major, interventionist state role, there remains a preference for the national context as still the best one to embody such a regime. In the EC as it is, liberal market philosophy is seen as dominant, notably in the single-market programme, even if it is recognized that EC policy cannot always be regarded 'as liberal economics in action'.

While the overriding motivation of integration is seen as political, it is generally held that the EC cannot achieve much to counter prevailing economic forces as opposed to facilitating them, since the Commission, as its executive arm, does not have sufficient political strength for that. Thus integration can only be furthered very largely on capitalist terms. Although the concept of 'social Europe' has something going for it, it has been watered down to 'sponsoring modest initiatives (by the Commission) in the areas of worker participation and health and safety' (Cutler *et al.* 1989, 149–50). It is seen as coming a poor second to the commitment to economic and monetary union, and able to function as a public alibi for making the poorer and weaker sections of society pay for further integration.

In respect of economic and monetary union (EMU), a collectivist view can be equally critical. It is recognized that the single market, and freedom of capital movement in particular, point irresistibly to such a union, 'which would have to be managed in some way by new supranational institutions' (Cutler *et al.* 1989, 144). The criticism is that the actual EMU plan vests such management in a technocratic European central bank, which would inevitably pursue a conservative monetary policy. Along with the freer rein given to market forces in the single market, this would produce higher unemployment in the economically weaker areas, and widen the gap between rich and poor. National governments would no longer have devaluation as a means of reviving a flagging economy. The logical conclusion thus seems to be that, 'as long as the instruments of national economic management can be used for progressive purposes, they should not be surrendered'. The minimum preconditions for substitute EC policy instruments are, in this perspective, 'expansionary EC monetary and fiscal policy at the macro level, plus some form of control over the location of industry' (Cutler *et al.* 1989, 163). This is tantamount to putting the cart before the horse; what is simply a policy position is treated as an end-state. This seems to be something which afflicts both free-market and collectivist approaches to integration. In liberal democratic practice, neither control over the location of industry nor refusal of the social dimension can be built in as permanent features of the European 'house' being constructed.

The term 'policy instruments' has a rather unfortunate ambiguity, so that what are policy measures tend to be given the status, or at least near-status, of institutions. In part this does reflect the fact that certain policies achieve a longevity which gives them that 'near-status'. However, it also arises from ideological commitment to particular policies. This leads to a misreading of the integration process. As an example, what are taken to be the exceptional benefits of free trade are regarded by some as overriding all other considerations shaping European union. Thus the single market can be seen as the culmination of a long historical process of economic consolidation in Europe. This simply overlooks the powerful motivations of peace and democracy that have guided the Community's development since the late 1940s (Noel 1988), and have pointed to ultimate political unification (or 'consolidation', if you like). In reality, these two aspects, economic and political (and others such as cultural roots; O'Connell 1990), are strongly intertwined.

The danger with giving policies precedence is that political institutions come to be viewed as instrumental to particular economic or social solutions and outcomes. If you do not get what you want in these respects, then there is the Procrustean temptation to mould the institutions to ensure that they deliver it. Hence, it is rather common to find amongst free-marketeers a tendency to denigrate representative, pluralist democracy (you do not know which pressures might win out in respect of policy or who might win the next election). Perhaps they are looking for certainty where they should not – and where, ultimately, it cannot be found. The same can be said to apply where collectivists are concerned, such as in the tendency to condemn the European Commission for its present strategy when this could change, as political pressures develop (it is by no means the autonomous body which its opponents tend to treat it as), or as integration leads to an eventual institutional outcome of political union open to the policies they advocate. Ultimately, free-marketeers and collectivists do not seem willing to put the same trust in the European democratic process as they do in an unregulated private capitalism or in a statist socialism.

Yet it needs to be recognized that it is not only on behalf of socialist solutions that, historically, the political market place has been curtailed or at least not valued very highly. Mrs Thatcher's basic objection to greater political integration was that European policies were quite likely to emerge of which she disapproved – so she sought to prevent this European political process from developing any further. Whereas classical liberals opposed universal suffrage and the majority vote, neoclassical ones seek to relegate pluralist politics to a subsidiary role, and the economic market is seen as largely self-sufficient in supplying people's wants. The integration process refutes this conception of liberalism, since it operates fully within the parameters of the hybrid that liberal democracy truly is. To see a single market as the self-contained fulfilment of European integration is to miss the political dynamics associated with it; even to interpret it on its own as the embodiment of free-market principles is rather misplaced.

3. Integration as institutional development

The EC has, from its inception, contained significant supranational policy-making elements in its institutional structure. The crucial battle, fought primarily by Britain, to establish simply an international free-trade association in western Europe was lost in the second half of the 1950s: the six founder members of the EEC, building on the success of the Coal and Steel Community, were altogether determined to extend the 'Community' approach into the economic field. Notwithstanding the brake applied in the mid-1960s by de Gaulle, there was further long-term reinforcement of the Community in the 1970s, notably by the introduction of direct elections to the European Parliament. In the mid-1980s, the launching of the single-market programme led directly to the Single European Act and then on to the 1991 Maastricht Treaty, both of which considerably strengthened the supranational character of the EC.

The SEA cannot be viewed as simply the means to ensure implementation of the single market, though it is that, providing for majority voting in the EC Council of Ministers on SM matters.

But, harking back to the 1983 Stuttgart Solemn Declaration on European Union by the European Council, it also incorporates a wide range of policy-making undertakings. Of great importance, especially in the light of the developments in central and eastern Europe, is the incorporation of the European political co-operation (EPC) procedure on foreign policy, which had developed in parallel with the Community since 1970. Article I of the SEA states that the EC and EPC 'shall have as objective to contribute together to making concrete progress to European unity'. Other areas singled out for the development of EC policy-making competence include to 'ensure convergence of economic and monetary policies' (Article 102A), social policy (Article 118A), the reduction of 'regional disparities and the backwardness of least-favoured regions' with a view to promoting the 'overall harmonious development of the EC' (Article 130A), research and technological development (Article 130F), and environmental policy (Article 130R). In the introductory heads of state declaration, the SEA's continuity with the original Community treaties is emphasized, the aim being 'to transform relations as a whole amongst [the member] states into a European Union'. The heads of state also committed the EC 'to improve the economic and social situation by extending common policies and pursuing new objectives' and 'to promote democracy on the basis of the fundamental rights recognized in member states' constitutions and laws, in the Convention for the Protection of Human Rights and Fundamental Freedoms, and in the European Social Charter', and in accordance with the basic values of 'freedom, equality and social justice'.

In the light of the SEA's content, Mrs Thatcher's subsequent stand in her Bruges speech seems somewhat strange, if ideologically comprehensible. Did it represent a waking up to a reality which had not previously been taken seriously, namely the development of common policy-making (in particular, given the strength of support for it in the social and regional policy areas)? What is clear is that it was by then too late to block the development of the EC as a political institution and market-place and not just an economic market and institution. While the SEA effectively recognizes and contributes to such development, it has been occurring gradually, if not altogether evenly, for many years. And a basic principle adhered to is that any new entrants into the Community have not only to accept the stage it has reached, but cannot be allowed to dilute that development, let alone obstruct it – hence the talk of a 'two-speed' Europe if the UK and perhaps Denmark did, in practice, seek to act obstructively.

In 1991 the Treaty of Maastricht signalled a further, significant reinforcement of integration. The EC member states agreed to institute a European union based essentially on EC institutions but including new spheres of inter-governmental co-operation, in particular associating the Western European Union as the EC's 'secular arm' (Article J4) of a common defence policy. Political co-operation on foreign policy is taken over by the EC's committee of permanent representatives (of member governments). Once the Council of Ministers has unanimously defined a foreign or defence-policy objective, measures to implement it can be taken by qualified majority. Title I of the treaty lays down that the 'unique institutional framework' of the EC, now formally including the European Council of Heads of State or Government, has the responsibility for ensuring 'the coherence and continuity of actions', including in the new policy areas. Economic and monetary union is to proceed by creating a European central bank and a monetary institute (by 1 January 1994), and a single currency for the EC (by 1 January 1999). New EC policy competences include education, industrial policy, culture (all requiring unanimous decisions), health, overseas development, consumer protection, and trans-European transport and telecommunications networks (these subject to qualified-majority decisions). A social cohesion fund is provided for, to finance environment and transport projects in less prosperous countries, and environmental and social-policy responsibilities are increased, including the use of the qualified-majority procedure. The UK refused to ratify the social-policy provisions, which were thus included in an annexed chapter.

A principal innovation is the creation of European citizenship, so that citizens of member states can stand for and vote in local and European parliamentary elections wherever they are resident in the EC. Other institutional initiatives are the establishment of a court of accounts for EC financial audit and control, of an ombudsman to investigate complaints about EC administration, and in particular the enhancement of the European Parliament's role (including choosing the ombudsman). A new co-decision procedure is introduced, with a conciliation committee between the Council of Ministers and the Parliament (similar to that existing

306 *European integration*

in some member states between upper and lower houses of parliament). If disagreement persists, the proposed law could be vetoed by an absolute majority in Parliament. Co-decision applies to single market measures, vocational training, free movement of workers, environment action programmes, consumer protection, R & D framework programmes, trans-European networks, the right of establishment, and the treatment of foreign nationals. Co-decision just on regulations applies to education, health and culture. The *avis conforme* procedure is extended in a number of respects, and committees of inquiry may be set up as Parliament determines. It is also to be closely associated with the appointment of the EC commissioners for five years following its own election, and may exercise a vote of confidence on the Commission as a whole. Altogether, Maastricht substantially strengthened the EC's institutional and political structure and increased its area of policy competence, notably encompassing political co-operation on foreign and security policy and incorporating the basic elements of EMU. There was undoubtedly some disappointment amongst both social and especially Christian democrats, that greater progress was not achieved in political integration, notably concerning the Parliament's powers and role.

4. The EC as an emergent polity

It remains true that the integration process involves, as Andrew Shonfield wrote, a 'journey towards an unknown destination' (Shonfield 1973), at least in relation to its political structure. Juliet Lodge (1989, 26) has emphasized the unique institutional nature of the EC, with its supranational and intergovernmental aspects. Although, of course, the intergovernmental element remains strong, there has been a progressive development of the supranational characteristics, to which the SEA and Maastricht are the latest contributions. The European Court of Justice, too, has played its part in significantly expanding European jurisdiction. The growth of policy competences itself points to this reinforcement. Most significantly, such growth is itself closely associated with the emergence of the EC as a significant political market-place − 'domestic' political life is no longer confined to the national arena. In particular, transnational political and social movements are active in the EC context, and find a specific embodiment in the cross-national party groups in the European Parliament. Brussels today is the focus of major lobbying activity, and by no means only in respect of agriculture (Mamou 1989, 4 – 6). Organized interests from individual states, including notably the USA and Japan, are substantially in evidence; but ones in western Europe have increasingly come together to co-ordinate their activities, probably most effectively on a sectoral basis (the motor manufacturers, the chemical industries, pharmaceuticals, etc.) as well as environmentalists and over-arching organizations like the Union of Industrial and Employers' Confederations, associating the CBI and its counterparts on the continent, and the European Trade Union Confederation. The large corporations generally have their own professional lobbyists in Brussels, and European multinationals have established a body – the Round Table – for mutual consultation on policy matters amongst their managing directors. (It has proved, according to Professor Story of INSEAD, a principal ally of the Commission on EMU; Story 1990, 46.) European regional and local authorities have also become major lobbyists and some, such as German Länder, have established Brussels offices.

Besides pressure directed at the European Parliament and the Commission, European interests also have formal representation in the policy process on the consultative Economic and Social Committee – a corporatist body of the sort so deplored by the free-marketeers, but which has been part of the system from the start and is seen as playing a part in the 'social dialogue' inherent in the integration process. Given the variety of pressures directed at the EC policy process from political, economic and social organizations, as well as those cross-pressures arising within the Council of Ministers, it is not surprising that in practice policy outcomes do not reflect a consistent ideological approach.

In the field of research and technological development, where the EC is particularly committed, Margaret Sharp has analysed the 'twin-track' nature of policy stemming from the SEA: there is the promotion of European competitiveness, both by a mercantilist approach bringing about cross-national industrial collaboration and concentration (public and private), and by a trade liberalization, deregulatory approach. While she recognizes the tension inherent in such a 'twin-track', she sees it as 'dialectically' creative, the two approaches being ultimately complementary. European industry needs R & D support, including in restructuring, organized through such programmes as RACE (for telecommunications) and ESPRIT, as the basis for competing openly with US and Japanese firms in the European and world markets. It may be said that the 'twin-track' approach evident in EC policy-making accords with John Pinder's interpretation of the integration process as deriving strength from 'reflect[ing] the best in European civilization', which in society's arrangements means that special blend of 'liberal individualism and social control' – what he calls 'walking on two legs' (Pinder 1978, 220). This might be translated, in institutional terms, into state *and* market, rather than the ideological opposition of state *or* market. Certainly, the integration process is sustained by drawing on Europe's main political traditions, which subscribe to democracy and internationalism, if not supranationalism. The political and social forces embodying these traditions are thus crucial for integration's progress over the long run. The emphasis that is often placed on contingent factors such as a particular conjuncture of events, while important, has to be set in this context.

5. Factors furthering integration in the 1980s and 1990s

In the 1980s various factors did occur, both inside and outside the EC, which undoubtedly favoured further integration. In these, strategic concerns loomed large, to do with western Europe's position and role in global politics and economics in the face of reinvigorated US leadership under Reagan in foreign and defence policy, of the economic and trading ascendancy of Japan, and the challenge of the newly industrializing countries (NICs). Negotiations and bargaining between the major economic and trading blocks were rapidly becoming the reality of the world economic order. As the superpowers' dialogue dominated security matters, so the US – Japan dialogue threatened to dominate trade and finance questions (Gilpin 1987). With the expansion of the Pacific Asian economy largely 'predicated on unequal access to OECD markets by mercantilist states and societies' (Story 1990, 39), the EC could readily be seen to require a more unified and organized approach to economic and trading-block relationships. Story notes that German corporations, particularly conscious of the Japanese threat, have, with the support of Dutch and French ones, 'prompted the Community to develop a more effective armoury of trade-policy instruments' (Story 1990, 60).

Some of these external factors encouraging further integration will certainly continue to operate in the 1990s, notably the tendency for international power rivalries to be transferred to the economic and technological spheres; what was formerly 'low' politics becoming 'high' politics (Hanrieder 1978). None of the European countries are individually strong enough in the global arena to ensure their interests are safeguarded. There is also, now, the challenge of central and eastern Europe with the collapse of communism. Political stability and economic development there are interrelated concerns, with which the EC is inextricably bound up; even if Germany is to be the main provider of capital, the effort needs to be shared and co-ordinated within the EC to ensure a predominant European stake in developments (also since Germany has not the political credentials in the East to go it alone). In addition, the question of further enlargement is posed, with such 'widening' sometimes set against, and with priority over, 'deepening' (the reinforcement of integration); however, the dominant view seems to be that these are not alternatives and indeed that 'widening' is only feasible *with* 'deepening'. This was certainly a factor that operated in the 1980s, the expansion to twelve EC members making the procedures introduced in the SEA, notably majority voting in the Council of Ministers (qualified according to country size), almost imperative, if EC decision-making at the highest level was not regularly to grind to a halt. Moreover, there is the question of the so-called 'democratic deficit' which has recently come to the fore, with reference particularly to the inadequacy of the European Parliament's role. The SEA did strengthen it somewhat, and Maastricht has carried the reform further; but as Juliet Lodge has pointed out (Lodge 1989, 26), with national parliaments' sovereignty, or simply power, being eroded, and not just by Brussels, the need for fully democratizing the EC institutions is becoming that much more urgent. The power of sectional interests in Brussels also adds to the case for a strong representative political structure which circumscribes and balances their policy 'input'.

Impetus to integration has also come since the 1980s from the commitment to it shown by the new entrants, and in particular Spain. This was encouraged by German support in the entry negotiations for more funds for the poorer regions, including increasing its own contribution to the EC budget from 40 to 50 per cent. Germany, indeed, began in the mid-1980s to assume a more leading role politically, to match its economic strength, in favour of moving to EC political union. However, the country that contributed most to the new momentum was France, because of its change of approach. Although the classical Gaullist stance had already been substantially left behind, a strong commitment to the integration process only emerged following the socialist government's economic difficulties in 1982–3. President Mitterrand made the decision to tie France's future to that of the Community, in the face of some significant pressures in his own party and government at the time to loosen the links and utilize national policy measures, including import controls, to the full. However, the commitment to integration was not to a purely economic and free-market embodiment of it. An attempt under Chirac (1986–8) to move to a more thoroughgoing neo-liberalism was short-lived. Similarly, the adoption of a Thatcher-style 'revolution' in Germany under the Christian Democrats after 1982 proved half-hearted; there was a 'considerable tension between emphasis on a Christian moral order and market individualism' and 'the concept of an organic society remain[ed] strong' (Grande 1989). John Major acknowledged in a visit to Bonn that 'we [the British Conservatives] owe less ... to the concept of 'solidarity' [than does the CDU]' (Major 1991).

The less than enthusiastic embrace of free-market philosophy by France, Germany and most continental countries of central and southern Europe can be understood in terms of the generally limited impact of classical liberalism there in the nineteenth century,[2] when in Britain it was carrying all before it. *Etatisme* and mercantilism can be said to have retained a relative strength in these other political cultures, with liberalism not having experienced, as in Britain, a long, uninterrupted and gradual development in which its economic and political aspects became inextricably associated. Thus, for them, liberalism could be seen as a self-contained matter of democratizing political (and other) institutions, with a mercantilist – even *dirigiste* – approach to the economy not necessarily considered incompatible with it, by the right and centre almost as much as by the left (e.g. Gaullism in the 1960s and 1970s). In so far as the nation-state came to be seen as an inadequate framework for the pursuit of economic and social goals, in which the role of the public authorities was largely accepted, then this was a major factor in both promoting and shaping a European level of policy-making.

6. Transnational social and political forces and integration.

On the continent there has been another ideological 'input' into the political culture which has come to fruition governmentally since 1945, and which has had a decisive impact on the development and nature of the integration process; this is Christian democracy, and the influence of social Catholicism which lies behind it to a significant extent. There is undoubtedly a religious impulse in the integration process, as the present Pope's interest in it demonstrates, as well as that of the increasingly important Conference of European Churches (CEC) bringing together Orthodox, Protestant and Anglican churches. The CEC, with the RC Council of European Bishops' Conferences, organized a European ecumenical assembly in May 1989 at Basel, which for the first time for nine hundred years, since the division between Orthodox east and Catholic west, brought together some 700 official representatives of all European churches and countries (except Albania). Its unanimously adopted final document (European Ecumenical Assembly 1989) called for a common security system in Europe, the extension and development of the process of European construction – the image of a 'common home' was adopted, while emphasizing that it should be an 'open house' – the recognition of minority rights, and for 'Christians and the leaders of the EC countries to ensure that implementation of the SEA will not lead to a levelling down of social provisions and ecological standards'. At the CEC's tenth assembly in 1992 there was a warning against a 'free market [without] strings on consumption of resources, without social guarantees and [without] a political structure controlling strong private monopolies' and against 'a fortress Europe creating new closed borders, greater differences between poor and affluent areas, increasingly non-sustainable economies ... and deficits of democracy' (Conference of European Churches 1992).

While the ecumenical church movement is an important social force in transnational development in Europe, Christian democracy represents a significantly greater direct influence as a political force. Since 1945, it has led the way in developing transnationally as a major political movement, regularly bringing together leading politicians and citizens from a very wide range of European countries.[3] The first organization, established in 1947, was the *Nouvelles Equipes Internationales* (NEI), associating representatives of Christian democratic parties from all the subsequent 'six' founder EC states as well as from Spain, Austria, Poland and Czechoslovakia. From the start, the NEI made European union a prime objective, with Franco-German reconciliation as the foundation stone. A model was developed for European unity different from either the USA or the Soviet Union, with 'community' seen as the key concept, involving a distinct identity and autonomy in world affairs (within the framework of the UN). There was a determination to overcome the nationalism, notably of the major states, which had ruined Europe and resulted in its division and subordination to external powers. The meetings and congresses of the NEI, and in particular the Geneva conversations between Christian democrat government leaders (notably Adenauer, de Gasperi and Schuman), prepared the way for the political enactment in the 1950s of the crucial steps on the integration ladder.

Monnet is often seen as the father of the EC, but the Christian democrat contribution has been central in terms of political ideas and action (Monnet himself excelled in the strategy of integration (Fontaine 1988)). In the formative stages, political forces to the left and right of it were divided or opposed to integration. Today M. Delors, though since the mid-1970s a French Socialist Party member, is clearly influenced by his origins in Christian democracy, shown notably in his strong support for 'subsidiarity' in the context of political integration. Subsidiarity, according to which it is 'a disturbance of right order for a larger and higher association to arrogate to itself functions which can be performed efficiently by smaller and lower societies', is a concept invented within catholicism.[4] Likewise, he emphasizes the importance of solidarity. For example, in a lecture to the Institute for Strategic Studies he said: 'Besides freedom and responsibility, solidarity is central to the Community both at home – between nations, regions and individuals – and abroad' (Delors 1991). This was part of an argument that security was a problem of society as well as of defence. Christian democratic political culture goes noticeably wider on the continent than the confines of the parties in the movement (including Community officials such as Emile Noël, Secretary General of the Commission 1957 – 87). The reinforcement of the integration process is also produced by the development of transnational political organization (Pridham and Pridham 1981). Following the somewhat unstructured NEI, the way was charted by the Christian Democratic European Union set up in 1965 and, within the EC, by the founding of the European People's Party in 1976 to fight European parliamentary elections. In the European Parliament (originally Assembly) Christian democrats were the first to establish an integrated, cross-national party group. Liberals, though a much smaller group, have long done likewise and today, with Labour's change of heart, the social democrats have become the largest single integrated group; only the conservatives and Gaullists, of major parties, remain distinct (a major bone of contention for conservatives is Christian democrat support for worker participation and a charter of employees' rights).[5] Christian democratic transnationalism has also operated, if for long in exile, through a CD Central European Union covering Czechoslovakia, Hungary, Poland, Yugoslavia, Lithuania and Estonia. Christian democracy played an important part in the downfall of the communist regimes there and is a major factor in those countries' moves to participate in the process of European union. This evidence of the transnational or interstate extension of political life is important in so far as the US case shows that this was decisive in establishing the Union, on the basis of what was, at the outset, a rather sparse constitutional framework;[6] the importance of constitutional engineering for integration should thus not be exaggerated (for example, the arguments over a federal blueprint). It is the development of political, social and cultural forces on a transnational European basis which is the real key to forging a European union beyond the single market – and the single market itself can only contribute to this development.

7. The 'community' view of integration as the primary motivation

Christian democracy is important not just for the strength it brings to the underlying integrationist current, but in giving a meaning to integration which rests on a philosophy which is neither exclu-

314 European integration

sively individualistic nor collectivist. This sort of dualism, which we examined earlier in the chapter, is alien to it. What it points to is an alternative conception of what is involved, reconciling state and market. There is more to this than John Pinder's formulation of a balanced combination of both, although in practical politics, mitigating the excesses of one by enhancing the other's role can be an acceptable strategy (as in a moderate market response to the 1970s statism). So 'economic Europe' has to be complemented by a 'social Europe', *but* both can only finally make sense in the context of a 'political Europe'. The over-arching principles are those of democracy and community, which provide the fundamental basis for peace and security (in its various guises). Subsidiarity is a key building block for realizing both principles within the EC, when applied in the sphere of socio-economic as well as political institutions and organization. The effort required is to create community at all levels, allying individual and social responsibility, with the EC as, in effect, a community of communities.

Rather than pitting market against state, or seeking only to balance one with the other, a third element or sphere of behaviour and organizations is brought equally into play – that of the autonomous intermediate structures and institutions of a pluralist society; both territorial and sectoral or functional bodies are included – companies, schools and colleges, local and regional authorities, churches, associations and trade unions, etc. The importance of the non-commercial aspect of their activities is emphasized, notably in developing community through the involvement of their members (or inhabitants), along with the strengthening of their democratic contribution to the wider polity and society, national and European. While the autonomy of institutions and organizations is guaranteed, they are set in a network of political and social relations which promote interdependence and solidarity. In this way both the forces of the market and the state's expansionist tendencies can be civilized and contained, and a distinctive and authentic European community – a 'European Europe' – constructed.

This project may be categorized as broadly 'federal', but clearly in a special sense. In the case of monetary union it is not a question of whether a European central bank is 'in control' or is under political control, but a matter of the political and monetary authorities being strongly interdependent; this would involve them in close mutual relations which, as in Sharpe's analysis (see above) of the R & D 'twin-track', are dialectical yet also inherently complementary (and integrative in policy-process terms). The concept of a European polity based on community, pluralism and subsidiarity, which is at the heart of Christian democracy's resolute commitment to integration, is increasingly shared by social democracy. It also accords with the resurgence of minority nationalism in Europe in the 1970s and 1980s (Watson 1990), given a further boost by developments in eastern Europe since 1989. Whether it is autonomy or independence that is demanded, there remains the need to be inserted in the wider European framework. Indeed, this has tended to become a major motivation for minority nationalism, to break free from the restrictions of the existing state system, the better to have a say in Brussels. Minority nationalist movements in western Europe have generally moved to a pro-Community, pro-integration stance and have also developed as a transnational political force (Watson and Jones 1992). Clearly they are not interested in a centralizing, homogenizing type of European polity — but neither are they in a purely market conception with, as they see it, its centripetal economic and social pressures from which their nations are likely to suffer. For them, as for Christian democracy, subsidiarity applies in relation to intermediate, pluralist structurescum-communities below the state level (even more so for them, and especially in a territorial sense, of course), and not just to the existing states as it seems to for the British Conservatives.

Two key factors thus emerge as determining the underlying dynamic and the prevailing direction of the integration process: (i) the development of a European level of political life, involving the transnational organization and activity of political and social forces; and (ii) the general ideological thrust of such activity spearheaded by the long-established Christian democrat commitment to political integration, which has increasingly been shared by other political and social forces (notably social democracy, regionalists, environmentalists, and the churches). Economic factors and considerations certainly play an important part in the integration process, in particular as catalysts for particular developments — and at times as restraints when national interests diverge too much in specific respects. In general, the disadvantages of economic nationalism and separatism, and of not participating in a process of economic integration, are perceived as too great. But in reality the political motivation and what sustains it, as we have seen, go well beyond this. In this respect, the view that the argument about European unity lies simply between either a collectivist or a liberal-market conception has been left well behind.

Notes

1. This might be so if the European Community were 'widened', notably to take in central and east European members, before its integration had been sufficiently 'deepened'.
2. Bismarck, after all, can lay claim to having taken the first steps in the development of the welfare state; and France likewise in respect of the 'mixed economy' – the role of public capital in economic enterprises.
3. The account of Christian democrat transnationalism in this paragraph is indebted to R. Papini, *L'Internationale Démocrate-Chrétienne* (Paris, Les Editions du Cerf, 1988).
4. The original statement of the principle by Pope Pius XI, in 1931, is reproduced (in part) in A. Adonis, 'Subsidiarity: theory of a new federalism?', Lothian Foundation paper, London, December 1990. See also K. Neunreither, 'Euphoria about subsidiarity?', Newsletter of the IPSA Research Committee on European Unification, No. 2, Spring 1991.
5. See the political programme of the European People's Party, reproduced in T. Stammen (1979), Appendix.
6. See C. Benwick, 'Giving life to the American constitution', Fifth Lothian Conference (London, Lothian Foundation, December 1990). He refers to the 1787 constitutional convention as having 'created a skeleton of a federal system' which 'needed a guiding nervous system and muscular network to complete it and give it life'.

References

Cockfield, F. A. (1990). 'The real significance of 1992', in C. Crouch and D. Marquand (eds.), *The Politics of 1992* (Oxford, Basil Blackwell, 1990).

Conference of European Churches (1992). 'Assembly X' (first draft document) (Geneva, CEC, 1992).

Crouch, C., and Marquand, D. (eds.) (1990). *The Politics of 1992* (Oxford, Basil Blackwell, 1990).

Cutler, T., Haslam, C., Williams, L. J. and K. (1989). *1992: The Struggle for Europe* (Oxford, Berg, 1989).
Delors, J. (1991). 'European integration and security', *European Access*, 3 (1991), June.
European Ecumenical Assembly (1989). 'Final Document' (Geneva, CEC, June 1989).
Fontaine, P. (1988). *Monnet L'Inspirateur* (Paris, Jacques Grancher, 1988).
Gilpin, R. (1987). *Political Economy of International Relations* (Princeton, New Jersey, Princeton University Press, 1987).
Grande, E. (1989). 'Neoconservatism without Neoconservatives? The renaissance and transformation of contemporary German conservatism', in B. Girvin (ed.) *Transformation of Contemporary Conservatism* (London, Sage, 1989).
Hanrieder, W. F. (1978). 'Dissolving international politics: reflections on the nation-state', *American Political Science Review*, 72 (1978), 1276–86.
Lodge, J. (1989). 'EC policy-making: institutional considerations', in J. Lodge (ed.), *The European Community and the Challenge of the Future* (London, Pinter, 1989).
Major, J. (1991). 'Evolution of Europe', Speech to the CDU, Bonn March 1991, *European Access*, No. 3 (June 1991).
Mamou, Y. (1989). 'Ces lobbies qui font l'Europe', *Le Monde (Affaires)*, 8 April 1989, 4–6.
Noel, E. (1988). *Peace and Democracy in Europe: Role of the European Communities* (London, Wyndham Place Trust, 1988).
O'Connell, J. (1990). 'The making of Europe: strengths, constraints and resolutions' (Paper presented to the Fifth Lothian Memorial Conference, Lothian Foundation, London, 1990).
Pinder, J. (1978). 'A federal community in an ungoverned world economy', in B. Burrows, G. Denton, G. Edwards (eds.), *Federal Solutions to European Issues* (London, Macmillan, 1978).
Price, V. C. (1988). '1992: Europe's last chance?' (London, Institute of Economic Affairs, Occasional Paper 81, December 1988).
Pridham, G. and P. (1981). *Transnational Party Cooperation and European Integration* (London, Allen & Unwin, 1981).
Shonfield, A. (1973). *Europe: Journey to an Unknown Destination* (London, Penguin, 1973).
Stammen, T. (1979). *Political Parties in Europe* (London, Martin, 1979)
Story, J. (1990). 'Europe's future: western union or common home?' in C. Crouch and D. Marquand, op. cit.
Watson, M. M. (ed.) (1990). *Contemporary Minority Nationalism* (London, Routledge, 1990).
Watson, M. M. and Jones, C. (1992). 'Minority nationalism and European integration' in A. Bosco (ed.). *The Federal Idea*, Vol. II (London, Lothian Foundation Press, 1992).

14
An American economist in Paris, 1919
CHARLES P. BLITCH

1. Introduction

The Treaty of Versailles, which changed the face of Europe and was a major factor in the resurgence of Germany as a fascist state, was composed in a few months in early 1919 in Paris. The victorious allied nations sent delegations, largely made up of legal and financial consultants, to participate in the peacemaking process. Although half of the treaty is comprised of economic provisions with literally hundreds of separate and distinct stipulations, only a few economists were in attendance at the Paris Peace Conference. Two of the principal economists of the day arrived with the British and the American contingents – J. M. Keynes and Allyn A. Young.

Keynes's activities and contributions during the conference and his opinion of its results are documented and well known. Young, who in a sense was Keynes's counterpart in the United States organization, also had an important role in the formulation of the treaty. He served as the American delegate and chairman of the subcommission on commercial treaties, served as alternate to the American representatives on the economic commission and was economic adviser to Bernard Baruch, Thomas W. Lamont and Vance McCormack, who were the United States members of the reparations commission. Nevertheless, Young's activities and contributions, as well as his views on the Treaty of Versailles, are virtually unknown. Young was one of the few participants at the peace conference who did not keep a diary, so the record of his work has to be derived from memoranda, diaries and books of contemporaries, letters and reports during the period. They reveal that he was intimately involved in two of the major issues at Paris – German reparations and the 'Italian crisis'.

2. 'The Inquiry'

In 1917, Allyn Young held a professorship in economics and finance at Cornell University. He had also been elected president of the American Statistical Association for the year. When the United States entered the First World War, he was called to Washington to direct statistical research for the War Trade Board. Early in November 1917 James Shotwell, professor of history at Columbia University, wrote Young a short letter. He and Shotwell were associated as the economics and history consultants to the textbook division of Houghton Mifflin Company of Boston. Shotwell's letter stated: 'I am trying to get light upon the handling of questions of economics in connection with the peace conference at the end of the war and will be needing both contributions and men to help in the work. This is highly confidential and I should very much appreciate a chance to talk things over with you.'[1] Young replied that he was very much interested and would be glad to talk with Shotwell at the latter's convenience.[2] The upshot of this contact was Young's appointment as economics specialist in a group of experts, drawn primarily from the nation's universities and colleges to study the problems and lay the groundwork for the peace negotiations. The organization was under the direction of President Woodrow Wilson's confidant, Colonel Edward M. House. It subsequently became known as 'The Inquiry'.

The members of the group along with Young and Shotwell were Charles H. Haskins, dean of the Harvard graduate school and specialist on northwest Europe; Charles Seymour, professor of history at Yale University and specialist on the Austrian empire; Isaiah Bowman, president of the American Geographical Society and specialist on Latin America; William E. Lunt, professor of English history at Cornell and specialist on Italy; Clive Day, professor of economic history at Yale and specialist on the Balkans; and Douglas W. Johnson, assistant professor of physiography at Columbia and specialist on boundary geography. The organization was headed by Sidney E. Mezes, president of the City College of New York, who was House's brother-in-law; the secretary was Walter Lippmann and the treasurer was David Hunter Miller, a prominent New York City lawyer who also served as a specialist on international law.[3]

The problems facing 'The Inquiry' were not only enormous in scope, but were new for the United States, which had never taken part in a general peace conference and, even though a world power, lacked a world view. The major problems of the organization such as delineating procedures and fields of work, recruiting competent personnel, and securing adequate funding were never fully overcome. The economics division exhibited in microcosm these limitations. In October 1918 the division was manned by just six persons – Young and five assistants. Out of a total budget of US $15,000 for September 1918, the economics division received about 10 per cent, or $1556.72. Young was forced to rely on outside agencies for much of the economic and statistical information. While some seven hundred documents and reports were prepared in advance of the peace conference, only forty-five, or about 6 per cent, originated from within the division. The external preparers were often uninformed of the purpose of their studies and only in a few cases received any remuneration. As a result, there was a wide variation in their usefulness, quality, and viewpoints. Young and his small staff attempted the impossible task of directing, co-ordinating and interpreting these reports.

A further and more important difficulty for the economists was the fact that 'The Inquiry' was organized along geographical lines. The continent of Europe was divided among specialists who prepared the historical, political, sociological and demographic analyses which were to provide the background for the group's recommendations regarding post-war national boundaries. Economic problems were regarded as common to all areas, and special reports on regional and national problems were to supplement the other information. This programme had the double disadvantage of both overburdening the economics staff, and focusing on national or regional problems to the exclusion of serious economic situations which involved wide areas, or which confronted Europe as a whole. Young recognized this deficiency and in a memorandum dated 25 February 1918 outlined a programme for economic studies:

> The economic information in these special regional studies relates, for the most part, to definitely circumscribed areas. Very little of it is shaped so as to show the *relations* between different areas. Nor is it sufficiently homogeneous to permit throwing it together in such a way as to show readily the economic significance of different possible boundary lines ... In short, there is no way

in which these regional studies can be pieced together to form a whole. What is needed is a general background of economic information, organized in a systematic and uniform way, covering those parts of the world in which the problem areas fall ... This information must be gathered by men or organizations working on subjects, rather than on areas.[4]

The problems to which the passage above particularly applied, in Young's mind, were those of the German reparations and the commercial relations between nations. Young's plea for comprehensive studies was to no avail, since the importance of economic matters in the forthcoming peace discussions and those associated with the distortions of war were not generally recognized outside the economics division. The latter problems in particular were spotlighted by the collapse of the central powers in October 1918 and the armistice on 11 November.

The members of 'The Inquiry' who were designated by an executive order to accompany President Wilson and the American delegation to Paris were Young, Shotwell, Bowman, Day, Haskins, Lunt, Johnson and Miller, along with Mezes. They were named as technical advisers to the American Commission to Negotiate Peace. Sailing with the president on the former North German Lloyd ship, *George Washington*, they witnessed the excitement of the presidential party's departure from New York and the tumultuous welcome for Wilson in Brest and Paris. President Wilson had only one conference with all his technical advisers aboard ship, at which he told them that peace must be based on justice – for example, in settling boundary disputes. On the German indemnity, he stated his strong opposition to any payments except for actual war damages done to civilians by the German armed forces. The president concluded the meeting by saying he hoped his advisers would given him a firm position to establish the justice or injustice of various claims. While he expected them normally to work according to the organizational plan of the conference, they should, in an emergency, not hesitate to bring to his attention directly any problem which was critical to peace with justice. His final words were: 'Tell me what's right and I'll fight for it. Give me a guaranteed position.'

Young himself met with Wilson once on the way over. They discussed the German reparations and the Italian territorial claims. Although Young kept no notes on the meeting he later wrote to his friend, F.W. Taussig, that he told the president that Germany's ability to pay indemnities even for civilian damages, was very limited and possibly would not measure up to her obligations. The president, he said, had not thought of that possibility and replied that he thought the first discussion should be on the basis of Germany's obligations.[5]

The Italian claims were based on a secret treaty, the Treaty of London, which was signed in 1915 as an inducement for Italy to enter the war on the allied side. Young sent the President a memorandum prepared by the specialist on Italy, W.E. Lunt. With respect to the port of Fiume, which was to be the centre of the dispute in the 'Italian crisis', the report said: 'It is assumed unnecessary to discuss in this memorandum any claim of the Italians to Fiume. If the Italians add that town to others which they claim, they will have in their hands the ports through which 98 per cent (in value) of the foreign trade of Austria-Hungary by sea has passed in recent years.' The memorandum also denied the Dalmatian coast to Italy and closed by saying: 'The acquisition by Italy of those areas would seem to violate the principles enunciated by President Wilson.'[6]

3. The German reparations

From the outset of the peace conference, Allyn Young was embroiled in the complex and emotion-ridden problem of the German reparations. Soon after his arrival in Paris he met with David H. Miller and Paul Cravath, legal and financial advisers to the American Commission, to discuss a memorandum on the German indemnity which Cravath had prepared. Cravath had shown the paper to Keynes in London before coming to Paris. Since he had to return to the United States, Cravath wrote to Keynes who was then in Paris:

> In view of my approaching departure to America ... I am turning over my data to Professor Allyn A. Young, head of the economic [sic] department of the American Peace Commission who is to be found at the Hotel Crillon. ... He knows all about you and your work and is very anxious to know you. I am sorry I will not be here to bring you together. (Miller 1928, II, 317–18)

Cravath sent a copy of this letter to Miller with a note asking him to introduce the two economists. This was the first meeting between Young and Keynes; however, they did not form a close relationship in Paris.

On 23 January 1919, the Council of Ten appointed a commission on the reparation of damage (CRD) with members representing each of the allied powers. The United States was represented by three persons: Vance C. McCormack, Bernard M. Baruch and Norman H. Davis, with Thomas W. Lamont as alternate and John Foster Dulles as legal adviser. Allyn Young was the economics consultant (Burnett 1940, I, 17 – 18). The CRD was charged with providing the answers to three questions: What damages was Germany to repair? What amount was Germany to pay? What was to be the manner of payment? It was not clearly understood in the CRD that the answers to these queries were all interrelated. Moreover, the economic effects of the reparations upon the paying and receiving countries was not considered.

Recalling his conference with President Wilson on the ship coming over, Allyn Young wrote a memorandum for the basis of the German reparations on 28 December 1918 and sent it to Colonel House, one of the American Peace Commissioners:

> To make it clear beyond question that an indemnity is *compensatory* rather than *punitive*, it is not sufficient that the amount of the indemnity should be limited by the amount of the injury actually done to civilians and their property. It is equally necessary – and this is the point of the present proposal – that the proceeds of the indemnity should be used for no other purpose than that of compensating for losses actually incurred. Thus interpreted, *restoration* involves payments to the French government, for example, not so much because the national economic fabric has been injured, as because the French government must serve as trustee for the French civilians who have suffered losses through the aggression of Germany. These losses are not merely the basis of the indemnity, they also define its *purpose*.[7]

A further complication arose with respect to the meaning of the term 'restoration'. Young sent an analysis of the word to Miller on 7 January 1919. He wrote that the French and Belgian claims for losses on account of damages to buildings were estimated on the basis of prewar values of pre-war costs of construction, multiplied by a factor expressing the rise in building costs since 1914. He argued that this method led to an exaggerated estimate of the actual cost of repair as it assumed reconstruction *de novo* was necessary, whereas in many cases excavations, foundations, walls and building materials remained. In some cases the reconstructed buildings would be located on different sites from that of the original. Young recommended that the materials remaining should be utilized and costs figured on repairs on the original site. This would simplify the problem. However, he cautioned that: 'Restoration, it must be assumed, is accomplished by replacing a damaged structure by one of equal utility and equal *value*, which need not necessarily be one of equal *cost*' (Miller, op. cit., III, 36 – 7).

The greatest controversy came over the amount that Germany should pay. The French initially demanded that Germany pay the entire cost of the war, estimated at two hundred billion dollars. Britain wanted one hundred and twenty billion. There was a naive notion circulating in Paris that there was a surplus of wealth inside Germany subject to direct appropriation, and which was easily transportable outside the country. Such wealth included Germany's gold, her merchant marine, railway rolling stock, output of mines, livestock, foreign securities, etc. It was Allyn Young and J. M. Keynes who provided careful and sober estimates of Germany's ability to pay reparations. Both reached independently an identical figure – ten billion dollars. Keynes's estimate was widely publicized in his book, *The Economic Consequences of the Peace* (Keynes 1919, 84 – 5), while Young's is buried in the records of the American Commission to Negotiate Peace.

Young discounted the seizure of Germany's gold reserves, as they were needed to stabilize financial conditions inside the nation as well as to redeem the large quantities of paper marks held in formerly occupied parts of France, Belgium and southeastern Europe (Young 1919a). He calculated the value of Germany's cash assets (ships, railway rolling stock, etc.) as approximately 6.4 billion dollars (Miller, op. cit., V, 110 – 19). He felt that if two years was allowed for liquidation of the assets under 'fire sale' conditions, they would not bring more than five billion dollars. Furthermore, more than half this sum would be needed to finance Germany's imports of food and raw materials during this period (Young, op. cit.). Other than seizing the German gold and the sale of her cash assets, Young said there were only two other ways in which Germany could make foreign payments. One was to borrow funds in foreign financial centres, and the other was to sell German goods and services in foreign markets. Since the former solution involved replacing one form of foreign debt with another, the latter offered the only practicable answer. It meant that Germany would have to run a surplus in her balance of trade with other nations, and there were serious obstacles here. First, Germany would not only have to regain her pre-war markets, but would have to expand them as she had run a small deficit in her best pre-war year of 1913. This would mean that the allied nations would have to be willing to give preference to German goods and services within their own borders and encourage German competition in neutral countries. All this seemed highly unlikely in the bitter aftermath of the war. Young believed that under the most favourable circumstances Germany could expect a trade surplus of only half a billion dollars (ibid.).

Young and Keynes pointed out that there were economic effects associated with the payment of reparations which must be considered. It gave rise to the 'transfer problem', that is, the problem of transferring the German marks raised by the German government into the foreign currencies in which the indemnity had to be paid. In the economic theory which was dominant at the time, the mechanism of transfer was not very complicated. Assuming an inconvertible paper currency and a freely floating exchange rate, the German government would, by continually purchasing foreign exchange, raise its price in terms of German marks. Assuming the internal value of the mark (purchasing power) lagged behind its external value, German exporters could make windfall profits by purchasing domestic goods cheaply and selling at world prices, and then sell the foreign currencies gained to the German government for relatively large quantities of marks. This premium would attract resources into export industries, so that not only would the volume of traditionally exported goods increase, but goods which previously had not been profitable to export would enter the trade. Foreign goods would become relatively expensive, so imports would decline and a trade surplus result. More importantly, Germany's capacity to export and to pay her debts would be increased (Taussig 1920).

While agreeing that this theory was based on sound principles, Young argued that its possibilities were greatly exaggerated. It ignored the fact that Germany's exports (aside from coal and potash) were made from imported raw materials whose prices in marks would rise as rapidly as the price of exports. The theory implicitly assumed that the differential between the internal and external value of the mark would remain stable. He said that since the domestic price level is tied to prices in the international market in innumerable ways, the domestic price level would eventually advance as fast as export prices thus leading, not to an export surplus, but to inflation. Moreover, the theory did not take into account the inelasticity of world demand for one country's goods and services. So an increased volume of German exports would lead to diminished proceeds in foreign currencies (Young 1927, 22 – 4).

Young and the Americans on the CRD urged that the German reparation be a fixed sum with a given payment period based on injuries to the civilian population and their property. Only in the case of Belgium were pensions sought for families whose civilian breadwinner had been lost through enemy action. Young's estimate of ten billion dollars as a minimum and fifteen billion as a maximum was accepted, and thirty years as the payment period. The French and British baulked at the fixed sum and pressed for the damage categories to be enlarged to cover military pensions and allowances. By the end of March 1919 the reparations debate had reached an impasse. Suddenly, in early April, President Wilson conceded all points to the French and British. The amount of the reparation was left open, to be determined by a reparations commission after the peace had been concluded. It would provide for military pensions and allowances, and no time limit for payment was set. Allyn Young blamed Colonel House for Wilson's concessions. In a letter to his friend, F. W. Taussig, he made his opinion clear:

> When it was suddenly decided to go at the matter on the basis of Germany's ability to pay, the problem was wisely put in the hands of Norman Davis. It soon appeared that Davis's estimates were so low as to be unwelcome to the French ... A few days later, it was announced that Lamont had been put on the reparations jobs where, for a time, he virtually supplanted Davis. I believe that Colonel House, with his strong tendency to compromise and to avoid a fight to the finish, was responsible for this. Lamont used my estimates, but doubled them in order to

take account of what he called the uncertainties of the situation, and in order to go as far as he could in meeting the desires of the French and the British. That is, a strong effort was made to get a general agreement upon some such capital sum as thirty billions of dollars, which was twice my maximum estimate and three times the estimate I preferred. Now I have always been immensely glad that this compromise was not effected. The treaty as it was, with its uncertain provisions, and with power given to the reparations commission, was vastly better than a definite agreement upon an impossible sum. That is why I have always defended the reparations provisions of the treaty ...

I have always thought that if at the beginning we had taken a courageous position and backed Norman Davis, a reasonable agreement might have been obtained. I have thought and I still think that Lloyd George could have been won over. I blame Colonel House and Lamont for making a mess of it.[8]

In the thirteen years during which Germany made reparations payments before the moratorium in 1932, there were thirty five international conferences on the matter. In the end Germany paid approximately five billion dollars, of which half a billion was loaned under the Dawes and Young (Owen D.) plans (Wheeler-Bennett 1933, 255).

4. The Italian crisis

Italy had entered the war on the allied side as a result of a secret treaty, the Treaty of London, signed in 1915 by Britain, France, Russia, and Italy. The treaty gave Italy large territorial concessions plus a share of the German indemnity at the war's end. Briefly, Italy would get the district of Trentino and the port of Trieste, both anciently Italian; a part of the south Austrian Tyrol in the Brenner Pass which had two hundred thousand Austrians in the area; and considerable territory on the Dalmatian coast of the eastern Adriatic Sea, where five hundred thousand Slavs constituted the majority of the population. Italy's support of the allies was the result of a deliberate bargain. Thus, she came to Paris with claims in fundamental conflict with Wilson's general principles of 'open covenants openly arrived at' and the right of 'self-determination' of people with respect to their government.

On 11 March 1919, Prime Minister Orlando of Italy gave a memorandum to the Council of Ten which greatly expanded the Italian demands under the Treaty of London. In particular it added the port of Fiume to their claims which, under the Treaty of London, had been awarded to the Austrian province of Croatia. Croatia was now part of the new nation of Jugo-Slavia (Yugoslavia). The American technical experts had prepared a report on the Italian boundaries on 21 January 1919 which denied the port of Fiume and Dalmatia to Italy and awarded both to Jugo-Slavia (Baker 1922, III, doc. 31, 256). On 16 March Sidney Mezes, the chief of the American experts, sent a letter to Colonel House recommending that the city of Fiume go to Italy, but that the harbour be declared a 'free port' and be supervised under the auspices of the League of Nations (Albrecht-Carrié 1938, doc. 26, 241). Five of the American technical advisers countered the Mezes letter with a communication of their own on 18 March to the American peace commissioners, which reaffirmed their position that Fiume and all of Dalmatia should go to Jugo-Slavia (Baker, op. cit., III, doc. 32, 263).

President Wilson summoned his geographic and economic advisers on 19 March and reviewed the situation using large relief models of the entire Adriatic coast. Each model had an accompanying map with detailed information on ethnic origin, historical and economic aspects of the region. As a result of the study, Wilson said to his experts: 'I am ready to fight for the line you gentlemen have given me, with one possible exception; it may seem best to make Fiume an independent port' (Ibid., II, 246). Alarmed by this statement, the five advisers who had prepared the 18 March report wrote a new one on 4 April and were joined by Allyn Young as a signatory. It asserted that 'it is unwise to make Fiume a free city', arguing that it was the only good port for the Slavs and that serious economic and political disadvantages would result. It said that the Slavs would be sensitive over an infringement of their sovereignty over their only major port. However, if the decision should be made to make Fiume a free port, the Jugo-Slavs should be guaranteed major economic rights (ibid., III, doc. 33, 266).

On 11 April Douglas Johnson, the Italian boundary expert, proposed an informal meeting with the Italians, the Slavs and some American technical advisers to discuss the problem. David H. Miller approved the idea, subject to Wilson's agreement which was secured. Johnson suggested himself, Miller and Young as the American party. Orlando vetoed Italian participation. On 14 April,

Wilson and Orlando met to discuss the situation. Wilson presented a memorandum in which he upheld his technical experts' position on Dalmatia, but proposed that Fiume be an international port. Orlando rejected this as unacceptable and Wilson promised to consult his advisers again on the matter. He turned the whole affair over to Colonel House for settlement.

Colonel House had Mezes draft a statement which would place Fiume under Italian sovereignty, but with administration by a commission of the League of Nations. Dalmatia would be administered under a similar arrangement with a plebiscite after ten years (ibid., II, 152 – 3). Mezes, without showing the statement to the group signing the 4 April memorandum, sent it to House on 17 April. Late that afternoon, Isaiah Bowman, one of the signers of the earlier declaration, accidentally found a carbon copy of Mezes's communication in the office of the technical advisers. It began with the words, 'Having consulted the experts', which suggested they had changed their position on Fiume and Dalmatia. Bowman hurriedly called the other five advisors together and they composed a letter to the president appealing that he should not accept the Mezes – House compromise. Not having direct access to Wilson, they agreed that General Tasker Bliss, a sympathetic American peace commissioner, should be contacted and given the letter. They found General Bliss in his room at the Hôtel Crillon and he read the appeal, dressed and drove to the residence of President Wilson who received him in his bedroom. Wilson took the letter and thanked him for coming (Armstrong 1971, 103 – 5).

In their appeal to Wilson the six experts reminded him of his direction on the ship that they should come directly to him if they perceived a great injustice to be in the offing, and repeated his words: 'Tell me what's right and I'll fight for it. Give me a guaranteed position.' They continued:

> Italy entered the war with a demand for loot. France and England surrendered to her demand. Of all the world's statesmen the president alone repudiated a war for spoils and proclaimed the just principles of an enduring peace ...
>
> If Italy gets even a nominal sovereignty over Fiume as the price of supporting the League of Nations, she has brought the League down to her level ... The world will see that a big power has profited by the old methods: secret treaties, shameless demands, selfish oppression.

Never in his career did the president have presented to him such a opportunity to strike a death blow to the discredited methods of the old world's diplomacy. ...To the president is given the rare privilege of going down in history as the statesman who destroyed, by a clear-cut decision against an infamous arrangement, the last vestige of the old order.

[They observed that] in our opinion there is *no* way – no political or economic device of a free port or otherwise – which can repair to Jugo-Slavia the injury done if any outside power prevents Fiume from being made an integral part of the Jugo-Slav organization. (Baker, op. cit., III, doc. 36, 275 – 6)

On the morning of 18 April Bowman found on his desk a note from President Wilson which read as follows:

I have received and read with the deepest feeling the letter which you, Mr Johnson, Mr Lunt, Mr Seymour, Mr Day, and Mr Young addressed to me under date of yesterday about the Italian claims on the Adriatic. I need not tell you that my own instinct responds to it, and I am deeply obliged to you all six for your reinforcement of judgement in a matter which, like yourselves, I regard as of the most critical importance.[9]

Unfortunately, in their haste to get to Wilson, the dissenters failed to notify Mezes or House, and when House brought the compromise position to Wilson as being representative of his technical experts' point of view, he was confronted with the letter from the six men. House and Mezes were both upset over the appeal and subsequently the signers were told that their responsibilities at the peace conference were complete and that they could return to the United States. Young and Bowman left Paris on 15 May 1919.

Wilson's stand on Fiume caused Orlando to withdraw from the peace conference as the matter had become a *cause célèbre* in Italy. The status of Fiume was not settled in Paris. In 1920, Italy and Jugo-Slavia signed a treaty which created a nominally independent Fiume and confirmed possession of strategic islands off Dalmatia by Italy. In 1924 Mussolini annexed Fiume.

5. The aftermath

Keynes's indictment of the Treaty of Versailles in his book, *The Economic Consequences of the Peace*, as a Carthaginian peace; his contention that the terms were set secretly by the Council of Four; and, in particular, his unflattering portrait of President Wilson as a Presbyterian elder 'bamboozled' by the clever Lloyd George and the sharp-witted Clemenceau, dismayed and disturbed Young and other former members of the American delegation. In his public utterances and writing, as well as in private, Young defended the Treaty of Versailles as the best possible under the circumstances existing in Paris. Keynes had sent him a presentation copy of his book, and Young reviewed it for *The New Republic*. In his review he wrote:

> It was not the adroitness of Lloyd George or the laconic single-mindedness of Clemenceau that balked the president. It was what he could see over their shoulders. Nothing less than unified and courageous leadership could have lifted public opinion in the allied countries (including the United States) up to a level of a peace that would have been an honest fulfilment of pre-armistice pledges. Public opinion – still reacting to war stimuli – was always there, in the meeting room of the Council of Four, in the guise of 'the domestic political situation'. It was Clemenceau's strength and Wilson's weakness. (Young 1919b)

Young agreed with Keynes on Germany's capacity to pay – ten billion dollars. With reference to Keynes's charge that Germany was forced to sign a 'blank cheque' which could be used to strangle its economic recovery, Young argued that the reparations commission would, as the passions of war receded, use its powers wisely because forcing Germany to pay enormous amounts would endanger the whole economic structure of Europe (ibid.). In a private letter to Keynes, Young explained his real concern about Keynes's portrayal of the president:

> What I have regretted is that your book has been used in this country as a weapon against the president, by men who are really very much further removed from your position than they are from the president's. There is no large and effective body of liberal opinion here, as far as the treaty and international relations in general are concerned, except that which supports the president. The president stands for the best we have and men like myself find our only possible course of action in supporting him. Just now there is only the choice between his policies, on the one hand, and provincial isolation and selfishness on the other ... The practical effect of anything

that weakens the prestige of the president just now strengthens reaction.[10]

Young was extremely disappointed by the failure of the United States senate to ratify the treaty, and its refusal to approve American membership in the League of Nations. He felt that the nation had a moral obligation to work towards a European settlement, whether or not the document was accepted. He expressed himself in an article written for *Foreign Affairs*: 'The treaty was framed on the assumption that the United States would accept it and would help administer it. It was on this premise that the other states represented at Paris agreed to its provisions. Our defection virtually revised the treaty for the worse' (Young 1923). Allyn Young resumed his duties at Cornell University in the autumn of 1919, and in 1920 accepted a professorship of economics at Harvard University. During the remainder of his life (he died in March 1929), Young sought to analyse and mediate the economic problems created by the war.

Acknowledgement

A portion of this essay was originally published in 'Allyn A. Young: a curious case of professional neglect', *History of Political Economy*, 15 No. 1 (1983), published by Duke University Press, Durham, N.C. and used here by kind permission of the publisher.

Notes
1. J. M. Shotwell to A. A. Young, 1 November 1917, general correspondence, A. A. Young folder, 'Inquiry' archives.
2. A. A. Young to J. M. Shotwell, 5 November 1917, ibid.
3. This and the following information, except where specifically noted, is drawn from chapters 2 to 10 of L. E. Gelfand, *The Inquiry* (New Haven, Yale University Press, 1963). Material used by permission. Copyright Yale University Press, 1963.
4. R. G. 256, box 19, 'Inquiry' archives.
5. A. A. Young to F. W. Taussig, 10 December 1921, general correspondence, S-W folder, A. A. Young papers.
6. Reel 385, Series 5B, 6, Woodrow Wilson papers.
7. General correspondence, W-Z folder, E. M. House papers.

8. A. A. Young to F. W. Taussig, 16 December 1921, general correspondence, S-W folder, A. A. Young papers.
9. W. Wilson to I. Bowman, 18 April 1919, general correspondence, A-C folder, A. A. Young papers.
10. A. A. Young to J. M. Keynes, 10 June 1920, J. M. Keynes folder, A. A. Young papers.

References

Manuscript collections

E. M. House Papers, Yale University Library
'The Inquiry' Archives, The National Archives, Washington DC.
Woodrow Wilson Papers, Library of Congress, Washington DC.
Allyn A. Young Papers, Widener Library Archives, Harvard University.

Published books and papers

Albrecht-Carrié, Réné (1938). *Italy at the Paris Peace Conference* (New York, Columbia University Press, 1938).
Armstrong, Hamilton F. (1971). *Peace and Counterpeace* (New York, Harper & Row, 1971).
Baker, R. S. (1922). *Woodrow Wilson and the World Settlement*, 3 vols. (New York, Doubleday, 1922).
Burnett, Philip M. (ed.) (1940). *Reparations at the Paris Peace Conference*, 2 vols. (New York, Columbia University Press, 1940).
Keynes, J. M. (1919). *The Economic Consequences of the Peace*, reprinted in vol. II of *The Collected Writings of John Maynard Keynes*, 30 vols. (London, Macmillan, 1971).
Miller, David H. (1928). *My Diary at the Peace Conference of Paris*, 21 vols. (Washington, privately printed, 1928).
Taussig, F. W. (1920). 'Germany's reparations payment', *American Economic Review*, 10 (Suplement) (1920), 33 – 49.
Wheeler-Bennett, John (1933). *The Wreck of the Reparations* (London, Allen & Unwin, 1933, reprinted 1972).
Young, Allyn A. (1919a). 'The practical basis of Germany's bill', *New York Times*, VII 6:1 (10 August 1919).
Young, Allyn A. (1919b). 'The economics of the treaty', *The New Republic*, 21 (1919), 388 – 9.
Young, Allyn A. (1923). 'The United States and reparations', *Foreign Affairs*, 1 No. 3 (1923), 35 – 47.
Young, Allyn A. (1927). 'War debts, external and internal', in Allyn A. Young, *Economic Problems Old and New* (Boston, Houghton Mifflin, 1927).

Publications by Professor Edward Nevin

Books

The Problem of the National Debt (Cardiff, University of Wales Press, 1954).

The Mechanism of Cheap Money (Cardiff, University of Wales Press, 1955).

Textbook of Economic Analysis (London, Macmillan, 1958; second edition, 1963; Irish edition, 1963; Tamil edition, 1965; third edition, 1967; overseas Papermac edition, 1967; second Irish edition, 1969; fourth edition, 1976; fifth edition, 1981).

Capital Funds in Underdeveloped Countries (London, Macmillan, 1961; Japanese edition, 1962; Spanish edition, 1963).

A Workbook of Economic Analysis (London, Macmillan, 1966).

The London Clearing Banks (with E. W. Davis), (London, Elek, 1970)

An Introduction to Microeconomics (London, Croom Helm, 1973).

The Economics of Devolution (ed.), (Cardiff, University of Wales Press, 1978),

The Economics of Europe (London, Macmillan, 1990).

Monographs and pamphlets

The Social Accounts of the Welsh Economy, 1948–52 (ed.), (Cardiff, University of Wales Press, 1956).

The Social Accounts of the Welsh Economy, 1948–56 (ed.), (Cardiff, University of Wales Press, 1957).

Wales and the Common Market (Carmarthen, Radical Publishers, 1960).

Wales in the 1960s (London, Liberal Publications Department, 1961).

'The ownership of personal property in Ireland', Economics Research Institute paper No. 1 (Dublin, October 1961).
'The Irish tariff and the EEC: a factual survey', Economic Research Institute paper No. 3. (Dublin, January 1962).
'The Irish price level: a comparative study', Economic Research Institute paper No. 9, (Dublin, October 1962).
'Public debt and the economic development', Economic Research Institute, paper No. 11, (Dublin, December 1962).
'An incomes policy for Ireland?' Irish Transport and General Workers' Union Liberty Study Group (September 1963).
'Wages in Ireland, 1946–62', Economic Research Institute paper No. 12 (Dublin, February 1963).
'The capital stock of Irish industry', Economic Research Institute paper No. 17 (Dublin, 1963).
'The cost structure of Irish industry, 1950–60', Economic Research Institute paper No. 22 (Dublin, 1964).
The Structure of the Welsh Economy (with A. R. Roe and J. I. Round), (Cardiff, University of Wales Press, 1966).
Economics: Waiting for Godot (Swansea, University College of Swansea, 1969).
Regional Policy and the Role of Banking (Federal Reserve Bank of Minneapolis, 1972).
The Pay of Policemen (London, Police Federation of England and Wales, 1975).
The Dilemma of Distribution Theory (Economics Association, 1977)

Articles and papers

1. 'Estimating departmental intervention', *Review of Economic Studies*, XX (1) No. 51 (1952–3), 49–61.
2. 'Monetary policy again – a contribution to a symposium', *Bulletin of the Oxford University Institute of Statistics*, 14 No. 8 (August 1952), 285–97.
3. 'The 30 per cent liquidity ratio – a rejoinder', *Bulletin of the Oxford University Institute of Statistics*, 15 No. 1 (January 1953), 31–4.
4. 'The origins of cheap money 1921–33', *Economica*, XX No. 77 (February 1953), 24–37.
5. 'The return of the just price', *Blackfriars* (April 1953),

178–87.
6. 'Social priorities and the flow of capital', *Three Banks Review*, No. 19 (September 1953), 27–43.
7. 'The instability of sterling commodity prices' (with C. D. Harbury), *Bulletin of the Oxford University Institute of Statistics*, 15 Nos. 10 and 11 (September 1953), 403–49.
8. 'A note on the valuation of British imports', *Bulletin of the Oxford University Institute of Statistics*, 16 No. 1 (January 1954), 23–7.
9. 'US capital in Europe', *Financial Times* (22 February 1954).
10. 'The German surplus in perspective' (with H. Lohmann), *The Banker*, CII No. 338 (March 1954), 151–6.
11. (with H. Lohmann) 'Das Problem des deutschen Zahlungsbilanzü berschusses', *Wirtschaftsdienst* (April 1954), 193–8.
12. 'Personal incomes in Wales', a series of three articles, *Western Mail* 30, 31 March and 1 April 1954).
13. 'The wandering Welshman', a series of four articles, *Western Mail*, 3, 4, 6 and 7 September 1954).
14. 'US foreign investment and dollar shortage', *Review of Economics and Statistics*, XXXVI (November 1954), 425–8.
15. 'My conscience hath a thousand tongues', *Financial Times* (17 November 1954).
16. 'Some facts about tap treasury bills', *The Banker*, CIV No. 348 (January 1955), 46–50.
17. 'The efficiency of Welsh industry', *Western Mail Commercial and Industrial Review* (31 January 1955).
18. 'Wages and salaries', *Western Mail Commercial and Industrial Review* (31 January 1955).
19. 'Professor Hansen and Keynesian interest theory', *Quarterly Journal of Economics*, LXIX (November 1955), 637–41.
20. 'The gross national product of Wales 1950', *Bulletin of the Oxford University Institute of Statistics*, 18 No. 1 (February 1956), 61–71.
21. 'The post-war British budget', *District Bank Review*, No. 117 (March 1956), 17–31.
22. 'Is there a Welsh economy?', *The Welsh Nation* (1 September 1956).
23. 'The economy of Wales is still dominated by coal and steel', *Western Mail Commercial and Industrial Review* (January 1957).

24. 'Window-dressing in a minor key', *The Banker*, CVII No. 272 (January 1957), 47–53.
25. 'Schizophrenia in Great George Street', BBC Third Programme and *The Listener*, LVII No. 1470 (May 1957), 863–5.
26. 'A comment', *Bulletin of the Oxford University Institute of Statistics*, 19 No. 3 (August 1957), 265–70.
27. 'Bankers and monetary policy', *The Bankers Magazine*, CLXXXIV (October 1957), 254–8.
28. 'The British National Debt' (with E. G. Jones), Part I, *Economica* (August 1957), 205–24; Part II, *Economica* (November 1957), 307–14.
29. 'The national debt', contribution to a symposium on the Radcliffe Committee, *Bulletin of the Oxford University Institute of Statistics*, 19 No. 4 (November 1957), 363–7.
30. 'The monetary aspects of independence', *Triban*, Cardiff, 11 No. 1 (April 1960), 3–19.
31. 'The problem of independence', *Triban*, Cardiff, 11 No. 3 (December 1961) 1–20.
32. 'Customs union in the West Indies?', *The Banker*, 414 (August 1960), 528–33.
33. 'The Welsh economy in 1960' (with A. Beacham), *London and Cambridge Economic Bulletin*, No. 36 (December 1960).
34. 'Some reflections on the New York new issue market', *Oxford Economic Papers*, 13 No. 1 (February 1961), 84–102.
35. 'Debt management – a general report', *Public Finance*, XVI No. 1 (June 1961), 9–26.
36. 'British debt management policy', *Public Finance*, XVI No. 1 (June 1961), 27–49.
37. 'The Irish economy in 1960', *Irish Banking Review* (September 1961), 12–26.
38. 'Ireland and the common market: some basic issues', *Studies* (Dublin), L No. 199 (October 1961), 271–82.
39. 'Wettbewerb kann heilsam sein', *Handelsblatt Deutsche Wirtschaftszeitung* (Düsseldorf), Supplement (22 October 1962).
40. 'The development of capital markets', *Development Research Digest*, 1 No. 2 (October 1962), 32–42.
41. 'Irish manufacturing industry: a comment', *Journal of the Statistical and Social Inquiry Society of Ireland*, XX Part V (1961–2), 247–50.

42. 'The economist and public policy', *Exchange* (University College, Dublin), 2 No. 1 (Hilary Term 1963), 17–18.
43. 'The factors which influence Ireland's economic growth', *Advertiser's Review* (World Press News), 70 No. 1797 (23 August 1963), 13–14.
44. 'El mercado de valores y el desarrollo económico', *Información Comercial Española* (Madrid), (August 1963), 23–7.
45. 'The life of capital assets: an empirical approach', *Oxford Economic Papers* (November 1963), 228–43.
46. 'Taxation for growth: a factor tax', *Westminster Bank Review* (November 1963), 13–25.
47. 'The cost structure of British manufacturing', *Economic Journal*, LXXIII No. 292 (December 1963), 642–64.
48. 'Wales – the neighbouring economy', *Irish Banking Review* (June 1964), 19–28.
49. 'The rural prospect in Wales', *Journal of the Society of Dairy Technology*, 17 No. 4 (June 1964), 185–9.
50. 'The second programme for economic expansion', *Studies* (Dublin), LIII No. 211 (Autumn 1964), 225–32.
51. 'Needed – nerve and luck', *Western Mail* (23 September 1964).
52. 'Welsh public finances', *Western Mail* (1 December 1964).
53. 'A new town for mid-Wales', *Journal of the Town Planning Institute*, VI No. 211 (March 1965), 104.
54. 'The real potential of mid-Wales', *Voice of Welsh Industry* (May 1965).
55. 'The problem areas of Wales', *Stock Exchange Gazette* (20 August 1965), 9–10.
56. 'The Irish budget', *Irish Times* (4–5 May 1964).
57. 'Stop again: the threat to Wales', *Western Mail* (18 July 1966).
58. 'The growth of the Welsh economy', *Transactions of the Honourable Society of Cymmrodorion* (1966), 134–48.
59. 'The case for regional policy', *Three Banks Review* (December 1966), 30–46.
60. 'The common market: a worthwhile gamble for Wales', *Voice of Welsh Industry* (December 1966), 10–11.
61. 'The plan for Wales that isn't', *Liverpool Daily Post* (14 July 1967).
62. 'We would like more than an apologia' (criticism of the white paper, 'The way ahead'), *Western Mail* (20 July 1967).

63. 'A strategy for regional planning?', *Social & Economic Administration* (November 1967), 20–2.
64. 'Slow recovery forecast for an ailing Wales', *Voice of Welsh Industry* (January 1968), 19–21.
65. 'Figures that damn government hopes', *Western Mail* (11 April 1968).
66. 'How much industry is there in the principality?', *Voice of Welsh Industry*, 9 No. 1 (January 1969).
67. 'Buchananville could be a threat to the true growth of Wales', *Western Mail* (18 June 1969).
68. 'The burden of the public debt: a survey', *Rivista Internazionale di Scienze Economiche e Commerciali*, XVI No. 11 (2 November 1969), 1074–91.
69. 'The economic future of south Wales', report of the proceedings of the town and country planning summer school, University College Swansea, 9–20 September 1970.
70. 'Keys to growth in the seventies', *Irish National Productivity Council* (Dublin, 1970).
71. 'The Welsh budget argument is political not economic', *Western Mail* (10 September 1971).
72. 'Joining the EEC will be an act of faith', *Western Mail* (23 June 1971).
73. 'Our chance to ditch empty regional policies', *Western Mail* (1 October 1971).
74. 'Miners' battle against destiny is one they cannot win', *Western Mail* (20 January 1972).
75. 'The price of coal could be your lost job', *Western Mail* (15 February 1972).
76. 'Breaking the fatal wage-price spiral', *Western Mail* (11 March 1972).
77. 'Reflation will not solve our basic economic problems', *Western Mail* (28 March 1972).
78. 'Wales and the European Community', Trades Union Committee for Europe, 1972.
79. 'How not to get a first', *The Economic Journal*, 82 No. 326 (3 June 1972), 658–73.
80. 'Europe and the Regions', *Three Banks Review* (June 1972), 3–27.
81. 'The same name, the same aim', *The Times* (2 March 1973).
82. 'The fatal flaw in new development boards', *Western Mail*

(29 March 1973).
83. 'Wales and the Celtic Sea', *Financial Times* conference on North Sea oil and gas, Houston, Texas, 14–15 November 1973.
84. 'The economics of tribology', *SSRC Newsletter* No. 23 (May 1974), 24–6.
85. 'Over the threshold and over to the slippery slope', *Western Mail* (25 June 1974).
86. 'The economics of corrosion and the car', Institute of Mechanical Engineers, November 1974.
87. 'Beyond the celtic mists', *Welsh Radio Times* (3–9 January 1976).
88. 'Does Denis make us squeal?', *Liverpool Daily Post* (30 March 1976).
89. 'Son of £6: a ray of hope in Britain's economic darkness', *Western Mail* (16 June 1976).
90. 'Go for growth: it's a good gamble', *Western Mail* (25 March 1977).
91. 'The greed factor', *Liverpool Daily Post* (16 February 1978).
92. 'Days of crisis', *Western Mail* (14 February 1979).
93. 'The way ahead is not so bleak', *Western Mail* (29 May 1980).
94. 'Regional policy', in A. M. El-Agraa (ed.), *The Economics of the Common Market* (London, Phillip Allan, 1980; revised edition, 1983).
95. 'The finance of university academic departments', *Applied Economics*, 17 No. 5 (1985), 761–79.
96. 'Inflation and the distribution of income in the UK, 1970 to 1986', *University of Wales Business and Economics Review* (Autumn 1988), 45–52.
97. 'VAT and the European budget', *Royal Bank of Scotland Review*, No. 157 (1988), 37–45.
98. Review of *The economics of European integration* by Willem Molle, *The Manchester School*, LIX No. 2 (June 1991), 208–9.

Unpublished paper

'The market in gilt-edged securities, September 1939 – December 1949' (Dissertation submitted for the degree of Master of Arts of the University of Wales, September 1950).

Index

African, Caribbean and Pacific (ACP) states 11
  EC capital assistance 245-65
  global loans via DFCs 251-62
agricultural policy
  and macroeconomics 9, 113-34, 210
  and Wales 10, 205-22
  as part of regional policy 218-21
  drawbacks of price support 218-19
  protectionism 126-31
  UK 213-14
  US 117-18
  see also Common Agricultural Policy; European Agricultural Guidance & Guarantee Fund
air policy 147-8

Beacham, Professor Arthur 2
Bretton Woods settlement 85, 267
Britain *see* United Kingdom
budget, EC
  effects of CAP 80, 98, 132, 205
  structural spending 195

capital controls, and interest rates 18, 21
capital funds
  constraints, and labour markets 172
  EC financial markets 33-4
  eastern Europe 267-94
  for developing countries 10-11, 245-65
  risk capital 250-1, 252
central banks
  EC, proposed 102, 103, 105, 301, 305
  RSEs 274-80
Chirac, Jacques 310
Christian democracy 311-13, 315
  Christian Democratic European Union 313
cohesion fund 153, 305

collectivism vs. free markets 297-303
commercial banks, and lending 34, 46, 275
  in developing countries 251, 263
  in RSEs 278-85
Common Agricultural Policy (CAP) 113-34, 137-8, 214
  and EC budget 80, 98, 131, 205
  effect on equity 98
  MacSharry reforms (1992) 127
  quotas 209, 216, 217
  reform, generally 98, 215-16, 218
  relationship with monetary mechanisms 119-25
Common Transport Policy (CTP) 9, 135-55
  air 147-8
  and the periphery 148-9, 150-3
  combined transport 143-4, 146
  development 135-9, 153-4
  environmental factors 144, 145, 146, 153-4
  infrastructure 139, 146, 149-50
  inland waterways 146-7
  maritime 148-9
  railways 144-6
  road transport 140-4
  safety 139
community support frameworks (CSFs) 200-1
competitiveness, and inflation 19-20
Conference of European Churches 311
consumer credit 8, 33-56
  EC provision 43-8
  effects on the economy 40-3, 49
  motives for using 38-40
  projected effects of harmonization 48-9
  statistics 50-6
  types of 36-8
core/periphery issues *see* periphery
counter-inflationary policy 15-32

344 Index

as objective of EMU 108

defence policy 300, 305
de Gaulle, Charles 303, 310
Delors, Jacques 312
  Delors II package 202
  plan for EMU (1989) 101, 104, 108
  reform package (1988) 79–80, 193–202
developing countries
  arguments for government intervention 268
  cf. eastern Europe 267–75
  EC capital assistance 10–11, 245–65
  financial intermediaries 285
  use of SAMs 77
development finance companies (DFCs) 251–62
  Interact group 259–61, 264
development areas 185–7
Development Board for Rural Wales 209, 215, 220
disinflation
  interest rates and 18–21
  other factors 21–6, 28–9

EC institutions, development 303–6
eastern European economies 11, 267–94
  and EC stability 309
  cf. developing countries 267–75
  constraints on reform 269–70
  financial institutions 274–90
  lower costs 152
  monetary and fiscal policy 270–4, 277–8
Economic and Social Committee 307
Edinburgh summit (1992) 202
employment issues see labour markets; unemployment
environmental issues
  agriculture 215, 216, 218, 220–1
  require EC-wide policies 298, 304, 305
  transportation 144, 145, 146, 153–4
equity, redistribution of income 5, 60
  corrective mechanisms 92–101
  EMU and 101–6
  principle of 75
  SAMs and 63–5, 75–82

theoretical effects of free trade 88, 91–2, 150
  trade/industry barriers 87–92
ESPRIT programme 308
European Agricultural Guidance & Guarantee Fund (AGGF) 96–8, 192
European Coal & Steel Community (ECSC) 136, 303
European Commission
  and agriculture 216
  and regional aid 187–90, 198–9, 200
  concentration on periphery 99–100
  lobbying 307
  redistribution policy 92–6
  social charter 96, 108, 304
  structural funds 96–8, 103–4, 192–203
European Court of Justice 306
  judgements under CTP 136–7, 142
European currency unit (ECU) 120
  'green' 124
European Economic Community (EEC)
  objectives 303
  period of stagnation 85
  UK entry 4, 186, 191, 202, 246
European integration 85–109, 297–317
  and regional economics 59–83
  as institutional development 303–6
  EC as polity 306–8
  economic aspects 8–9, 85–7, 297–303
  federalism 108, 314–15
  political economy aspects 11, 87, 308–11
  social/ideological aspects 311–13
  subsidiarity 312, 314, 315
  see also European monetary union; European political union; single market
European Investment Bank (EIB) 196, 198
  and ACP development 245–65
  constraints on lending 247–51
  EC activity 250
  global loans via DFCs 251–62
European Monetary System (EMS) 120, 162
  counter-inflationary policy and 15–32

Walters critique 8, 16–18, 26–8
see also exchange-rate mechanism
European monetary union (EMU) 87
  and regional policy 103–6, 202
  as means to equity 101–6
  as means to political union 106–8
  effects on labour markets 173–7
  objective 102, 103
  single market and 299, 301
European Parliament 303, 305–6, 307, 309, 313
European People's Party 313
  lobbying 307
European political union (EPU) 87, 107–8
  EMU as means to 106–8
  lack of defined objectives 102
European Regional Development Fund (ERDF) 96–8, 191–9, 245
European Social Fund (ESF) 96–8, 192, 197
European System of Integrated Economic Accounts (ESA) 60–2
  SAMs and 62–6
exchange-rate mechanism (ERM) 16, 17, 122–4, 202
  effect of Spanish excess credibility 26–7
  role of Germany 16, 18–21
  withdrawal of sterling 123, 217
exchange-rate theory
  agricultural perspectives 115–32
  and eastern Europe 273–4

federalism 108, 314–15
financial intermediaries 34–6
  developing countries 285
  innovating role 38
financial markets 33–4
financial services, eastern Europe 284, 288–9
First World War, *see* Versailles
food prices 121–2, 209, 214–15
  support policies, drawbacks 218–19
foreign policy 304, 305
France
  commitment to integration 310
  food prices 121
free markets/trade
  as producer of imbalance 92, 100
  as theoretical means to equity 88, 91–2, 150

vs. collectivism 297–303

GATT (General Agreement on Tariffs & Trade) 225, 226, 242
  Uruguay round issues 113, 127, 205, 219
general equilibrium models 62
  agriculture 127–31
  and VERs 227
Germany
  as model for monetary policy 105–6
  commitment to integration 309–10
  dominance in EC trade/industry 88–92, 100
  implications of reunification (1990) 67, 106, 284
  reparations (post-1919) 319, 322–8, 332
  role within ERM 16, 18–21
  transportation prices 142, 145
global loans 251–62
'green' money 121–2, 123–4
  devaluation of green pound 209, 217

income distribution/redistribution
  see equity
industrial development certificates (IDCs) 186, 187
inflation
  and labour-market flexibility 159
  impact of consumer credit 40–1
  see also counter-inflationary policy
infrastructure
  as object of EIB lending 247
  as object of structural funds 99, 100, 193
  cohesion fund 153, 305
  see also Common Transport Policy
inland waterways 146–7
integration *see* European integration
interest rates 17
  and inflation 18–26, 28
  capital controls and 18, 21
inter-government conferences (IGCs) 104, 107
International Bank for Reconstruction & Development (IBRD) 249, 250, 258, 262
investment incentives

EC 187−90
eastern Europe 288−9
UK 185−7, 191
Irish economy 2−3
'Italian crisis' (1919) 319, 322−3, 328−31

Jamaica 2, 267−8
Japan
and US, in world trade 308
EC lobbying 307
unemployment 160, 162
voluntary export restraints (VERs) 225−44

Keynes, J. M. 59, 319−33

labour markets/employment issues
agricultural, Wales 206−13, 218
capital and 172
effects of EC integration 173−7
hysteresis 169, 171−2
labour subsidies 186, 188−9
policies/implications 97, 102−3, 173−7
protectionism and 130−1
regional employment premium, UK 186, 190
trade unions 164−5, 169
trends (1960−90) 160−2
VERs and 234−5, 237
wage bargaining 164−5, 168−9, 171
see also unemployment
loan-rate scheme, US 117
Lomé Conventions 245−65
London, Treaty of (1915) 323, 328−9
Luxembourg, and transport infrastructure 149

Maastricht summit (1991) 108
Treaty (Union Treaty) 9, 150, 153, 202, 303, 305−6, 309
MacSharry reforms, CAP 127
Major, John 310
manufacturing industry, patterns 87−92
see also production structure
maritime policy 148−9
minority nationalism 315
Mitterand, François 310
monetary compensation amounts (MCAs) 121−5
monetary policy 15−32, 101−6

agricultural perspectives 115−32
and economic development 267
eastern Europe 270−4, 277−8
see also European monetary union
Monnet, Jean 312

Nevin, Professor Edward 1−5, 7, 12, 60, 135, 267
publications 335−41
non-tariff barriers (NTBs) 85−6, 298
Nouvelles Equipes Internationales 312

oil prices, economic effects of rises 160−2, 190
Orlando, Vittorio Emmanuele 328−31

periphery 9−10
CTP and 148, 149, 150−3
EMU and 103−6
emphasis on assisting 99−100
structural spending 195
transport costs 151, 153
unemployment levels 162
see also regional economics
Poland
exchange-rate pegging 273−4
potential securities market 288
political economy
and European integration 11, 87, 297−317
development of Treaty of Versailles 11−12, 319−35
price stability, as objective of EMU 102, 103, 105
price support, as agricultural policy 218−19
privatization, in reforming economies 272, 279, 286−7, 290−1
producer subsidy equivalents (PSEs) 215
production structure 60, 82
and accounting models 61−2
and SAMs 63
centralization of production 100
reform, eastern Europe 283, 287
protectionism
agricultural 126−31
equilibrium models 128−32
transportation 141−2
VERs 225−44
public procurement 299−300

Index 347

purchasing power parity (PPP) 116

quotas, generally 225
   under CAP 209, 216, 217

RACE programme 308
railways 144–6
redistribution of income *see* equity
reforming socialist economies (RSEs)
   see eastern European economies
regional development grants (RDGs)
   185–7, 190
regional economics 8–9, 59–83, 304
   and Wales 2–3, 5, 10, 59–60,
     185–204
   EC integrated accounts 66–75
   models 60–2
   regional accounting systems 8,
     59–83, 221
   regional assistance policies 187–90
   SAMs and the ESA 62–6
   trade/industry patterns 87–92
   see also labour markets; periphery
     structural funds
regional employment premium (REP)
   186, 190
regional selective assistance (RSA)
   186–7

road transport 140–4
Rome, Treaty of (1957) 136
   agricultural policy 137–8, 205
   and regional policy 150, 187
   transport policy 137–8
Russian Republic/Soviet Union,
   monetary reform 271–2, 274

Scandinavia
   labour-market characteristics 164,
     165–6
   unemployment 162, 176
sea transport *see* maritime policy
security markets, eastern Europe
   285–8
   external investment 289
services as products 138–9
single currency *see* European
   monetary union
Single European Act (1987) 86, 96,
   123, 150, 202, 298, 303–4, 309
single market ('1992') 60, 121
   and transfer costs 75, 142–3,
     149–50, 151
   as instrument for job creation
     102–3

   as means to unity 85–6, 101,
     297–300
   effects on EC accounting 66
   effects on labour markets 173–7
   implications for financial services
     49
   influence of 'green' ECU 124
   relationship with monetary union
     299, 301
social accounting matrices (SAMs) 8,
   59–83
   and income redistribution 63–5,
     75–82
   and the ESA 62–6
   and transfer costs 75
   depiction of bilateral interactions
     67–9
   EC integrated accounts 66–75
   in developing countries 77
social policies, generally 30, 301, 304,
   305, 311, 314
   cohesion fund 153, 305
   social charter 96, 108, 304
   see also European Social Fund
Soviet Union/Russian Republic,
   monetary reform 271–2, 274
Spain
   commitment to integration 309
   effect on ERM (1990–2) 26–7
special development areas (SDAs)
   185
STABEX funds 246
structural funds 96–8, 103–4,
   192–203
   features 195–6
   1988 reforms 79, 193–202
   1993 reforms 201–2
   principal objects 99, 195
   UK and 196–7, 199–203
Stuttgart Solemn Declaration (1983)
   304
subsidiarity 312, 314, 315
SYSMIN 246

Thatcher, Margaret 299, 303, 304
trade union 164, 169
trans-European networks (TENs) 150
transportation *see* Common
   Transport Policy

unemployment 96, 103, 159, 175–7
   benefit levels and 166–8
   duration 168, 169–71
   Japan 160, 162
   regional differences 162–73

Scandinavia 162, 176
single market and 174
skill mix and 172–3
UK 170–1
US 160, 162, 168, 174–5
see also labour markets
United Kingdom
  agricultural policies 213–14
  Agriculture Act (1947) 126, 205
  and structural fund reform 196–7, 199–203
  and Treaty of Versailles 319–33
  Channel Tunnel 144
  entry to EEC 4, 186, 191, 202, 246
  Finance Act (1984) 186
  intra-EC trade 89
  opposition to integration, under Thatcher 303, 304
  regional policies 185–92
  unemployment 170–1
  withdrawal from ERM 123
  workforce skills 175
United States
  and Japan, in world trade 308
  and Treaty of Versailles 319–33
  EC lobbying 307
  exchange-rate on agriculture 117 18, 119–20
  unemployment 160, 162, 168, 174–5

Unity Treaty see Maastricht

Versailles, Treaty of (1919) 11–12, 319–33
voluntary export restraints (VERs) 10, 225–44
  and economic unions 232–4
  costs/benefits to EC 234–42

wage bargaining 164–5, 168–9, 171
WALRAS model, OECD 129–30
Walters, Sir Alan, critique of EMS 8, 16–18, 26–8
Welsh economy 2–3, 5, 59–60
  agriculture 10, 205–22
  assistance to industry 185–7
  ERDF funds 192–3, 197, 200–2
  regional policies and 10, 185–204
Western European Union 305
Wilson, Woodrow 322–3, 327, 329–31
World Bank, see International Bank for Reconstruction and Development

Yaoundé Conventions 246
Young, Allyn A. 11–12, 319–33
youth training, as object of structural funds 99, 100
Yugoslavia, inflation 272